FORGOTTEN
FRONTIERS

FORGOTTEN FRONTIERS

DREISER AND THE LAND OF THE FREE

DOROTHY DUDLEY

AMS PRESS
NEW YORK

PS
3507
R55
Z6
1970

Reprinted from the edition of 1932, New York
First AMS EDITION published 1970
Manufactured in the United States of America

International Standard Book Number: 0-404-02188-3

Library of Congress Card Catalog Number: 77-119663

AMS PRESS, INC.
NEW YORK, N.Y. 10003

The Banks of the Wabash — Paul Dresser

It was wonderful to find America, but it would have been more wonderful to lose it.
      Mark Twain writing to a friend

423 years ago today Columbus discovered America. What made him do it. Except for Columbus I wouldn't have been born in Illinois or Kansas.
      Edgar Lee Masters talking to a friend

One is hounded by the thought that as with individuals so with nations; some are born fools, live fools, and die fools. And may not America perchance be one such?
One hopes not.
But —
      Theodore Dreiser: " Hey-Rub-A-Dub-Dub "

PREFACE

The more specific the detail the more accurate the immensity it projects.

In relation to the shifting parts of an undiscovered whole the one part constantly betrays meaning.

1

". . . and every thing shall live whither the river cometh." THE BOOK OF EZEKIEL

". . . I was punished like all who destroy the past for the sake of the future." SPOON RIVER ANTHOLOGY

The germ of this story had origin in a mood of love of country that would celebrate every American quickened by savagery. Lacking this, people make no monument of their country. They remain content with provinces. Somewhat lacking this, Americans have leaned toward being thin and shrill, since first they pushed away the Indians, and built their own safer homesteads. That is, until today, when, with influx of strangers, Jew and Negro, Mongolian, Syrian, Slovak, Lithuanian, and with pressure of machinery, we have arrived at a jungle of our own. If we succeed in meeting it and creating out of it a human order, or if it destroys us, depends, one might guess, on the measure of primitive force left in us.

In the midst of a ruling tameness, or at least of a tameness dictated by those ruling here toward the last third of the last century, Dreiser was one of those born outside the convention and living outside of it. His books, made in the face of tameness, are touched with wilderness — the way a sudden rain, an ice storm, April thunder shaking new small leaves in a city square, can strike a dingy nerve-worn city with waywardness. With reason people complain that not always words and syntax follow him. He has let loose shoals of words, they say, some of them to remain in the commonplace of 1880, 1890, 1910, 1920. Yet often detachments of them, and an electric wiring of the structure, have found their way with him into speech, which is drama. They create the shiver of wilderness, the holy ghost of the realist, the wind of reality, which like an aeroplane's whirr signals the nearness of its presence.

One could write of Poe, Whitman, Thoreau, Henry James, Herman Melville, Ambrose Bierce, Henry Adams; one could write of Stephen Crane, Sandburg, Masters, Frost, Carnevali, Carlos Williams, Charlie Chaplin; and of others named and nameless, if one knew them; wherever and whenever the grace of unaccustomed intellectual wildness, rare as radium in these States, has descended on them.

Then there is another thing — the enterprise of Dreiser. Enterprise of an engineer — no looking backwards, no regrets, except where like correctives they are to be used in the new plans. This is tonic. It makes a journey of inquiry for one more intimate with old worlds than new, for one less ready than the true modern is, to relinquish old loves until they have receded irrevocably into distance. The speech of the past, tonal through age, recalling ancient relations, elaborate and seasoned through age — these I used to want back, and not in museums, and libraries, but by some impossible alembic distilled and then fused into American life. I could not be on with the new for not knowing how to forget the old.

Discipline was futile. Years ago I tried to face the oncoming scheme; I tried saying to myself: " Food, not delectation! Canned food, ham sandwiches, hard-boiled eggs, soft drinks too sweet in drug stores, cup of coffee counter-slung! Food and ice-water! . . . Clothing, not elegance! Cloak and suit trade, ready-made novelties, smart fashions! Clothes, not impeccable fitting garments! . . . Publicity, not privacy! Electric-lighted sleeping porches, lawns, salvia, gladioli, roads and automobiles, no doors, no fences, just vistas forever from publicity into publicity! Not intrigue, not intimacy! . . . Radio, victrolas, not music! Extension, not intention! . . . Skyscrapers, never arcades! Men without women, women without anything! Segregation, not relations!

All this — new ways, new references — I wanted to accept them; I wanted to junk the old like any other native, to quit harking back. But the lists became lamentations. Even yet I find too little appetite for the new worlds we are making and remaking; except indeed as in quest of sunlight, we may at length be emerging from the diseases generated by Christianity. Yet with machinery we appear to be discarding a primitive color that the Catholics carried along with them from ancient times — a ritual that was sensual and first hand. So even this improvement might be another affliction.

Dreiser, on the contrary, has been one of the unafflicted: a modern without the doctrine of modernism. He has been one of those engrossed in the new voyage that science and machinery, enterprise and adventure, are taking us on. He has been swayed by the new uncharted seas, so swiftly charted and old; he has been lured by the new shores so heralded and perhaps never to be reached. Not exactly dealing in terms of time and place, he has dealt in the actual and recorded it and the lack of it, when and where immediately it surrounded him. Without doctrine, he is mineral and vegetable as well as human, and so has moved ensconced in the changes. This book attempts to follow him through to the new frontiers and to define them in relation to the old.

People deeply in love with tone find him difficult to read; he grates on them. Tone evolves out of intangible relations, gaged by a scrupulous ear and eye for detail, as the tonal message of a forest at a distance is concerned with detail of each pine needle, each leaf. Dreiser is without truth of language in relation to surface tone, exactly the way that our cities and our streets and our buildings are without it. Even today the modern skyscrapers have less intention of color, less accuracy of detail than the unchanging façade of a French *boucherie,* or the mud village of a Pueblo Indian. Dreiser is sometimes a sprawling, sometimes a soaring block of buildings, structural when seen as a whole; insensitive tonally when considered close up.

He is an American high water-mark, capable of waves that fall beyond. His story holds the story of Americans as they appear today — big waves washing up on the shores of history, in the years of their stupendous and childlike success. We have deep wells, we have freshets among writers, that have leapt higher with slenderer and more special jets. A few are impeccable mimics, terser poets. Artists concerned with intimacy; with the fibre of our language, the transmutation of it into their own. But Dreiser has been possessed by the circumference of our life, eager to imagine it all, leaving nothing out, even when there is only time for categories. His record more largely than others has the taste of American waters, by no means always agreeable — of that medium in which float buildings, railroads, banks, soda fountains, suicides, conquerors, murderers, joy-riders, evangelists, hypocrites — the he-men and the victims, the jokers and the fakers. To Dreiser these men and women are congenitally human, children of nature, while to the tamer writers who preceded him they are pious and impious puppets, and to the meaner writers, many of them his followers, they are toys of the satirist. Is it because where the idealist scarcely thinks at all, and the satirist thinks with his nerves, he is, and exotically so, one thinking organically —brain and other vitals not divorced?

The measure of his work is the measure of himself, as good as the best of him, as bad as the worst. His story reflects the story of Americans — big waves washing high on the shores of history, and washing away some of the old orchards and farms. The bulk of this life is in him, the uncouth rhythms of this flood, which carries in its wake the sea-weeds of other days, and is marked by human eager points and swift metallic counterpoints. He suggests our hugeness faceted with its many faces, mechanically intricate, humanly simpler. He is to this day a challenge to writers to sacrifice themselves as completely, and more intimately if they can, to our history. He is large more than intimate. Yet he has passages, too, of identity with the mood, moments of penetration, when he goes over from being the historian into being the poet. In him our disorderly order gleams with its mysteries. He says of himself, " The riddle remains. I have solved nothing."

More than a generation ago he started to excavate into American life, singly and without orders, after a while against orders. " All my life," he says, " some one, a critic, a publisher, a friend has always been telling me not to go so far, not to talk about this or that, to stay back, to keep still." Yet he has managed to get down to the floods underlying dirt and rock. They well up in his pages, and reflect lights. They create that medium in which fluctuate the structure and the wreckage known as America in this day of her enormous and childlike success.

2

> " *They brought me ambrotypes*
> *Of the old pioneers to enlarge* . . .
> *When giant hands from the womb of the*
>   *world*
> *Tore the republic.*
> *What was it in their eyes?* —
> *That mystical pathos of drooped eyelids,*
> *And the serene sorrow of their eyes?* "
> SPOON RIVER ANTHOLOGY: MASTERS

> "*. . . They lack the passions that make one enjoy life . . . Crystallization is made impossible in the United States. . . . I cherish far greater hopes for . . . South America.*"
> DE L'AMOUR: STENDHAL

A few people say Americans are cases of arrested development. Machinery has shot ahead of them. Most people are still content to say, " Americans are young, are adolescent, are children." Europeans say this indulgently — " Give them time." Chinese say it less indulgently. American Indians think it, though they have long since learned not to speak. Surprisingly one of them lately was heard to release this much of judgment, " The white man must learn to think with his heart."

Isn't it true that we have not learned to think with our hearts or with our loins; that we have not learned to think, and are not grown up? To conceive of grown-up people is to conceive of the shining reciprocal fact, sex, without which adults are still children. To think long of anything, it is necessary to speak of it, or to celebrate it by symbol or image. Else the thought perishes in you, becomes dead tissue, to be carried off if possible along with other waste, or to remain there to become infection later on in life.

At the birth of our nation, the parents, who were adult British fanatics, it is written, middle-aged people by temperament, determined to give birth to children who should remain as much as possible adolescent. That is, they should cross over into maturity not for their own sake but only to make more children. So the image became not the man, not the woman, but the child, the pure impossible child, undefiled by its own nature. And the men and women lost their heroic line and became just parents, uncles, aunts, servants for children. Then as the years went on, these young people ungratefully seemed to want to know more. They became aware of their human heritage, which of course had to do with adventures into articulation as distinguishing them from other animals. Having little speech among themselves, few songs or symbols or dances, they asked for books. And they were given books, mostly English and German books, a few Latin and Greek books. Deciphering these they tried diligently to find out about those distant peaks of civilization they suspected they had not reached. They were bright children, some of them, and with these books as models soon began writing a few adventurous pages of their own; though as yet they made almost no attempt to celebrate with paint or music. Immediately the teachers and governesses saw with sorrow that the children were in danger of growing up. So the records from Europe had to be expurgated or jailed, where only the least daring of the children were allowed to look, a few academicians and professors. The witches and wizards and dissenters were burned and hung for fear they might be ruthless artists, people of magic. And censorship set in, until at last completely the soul was separated from the body, color from line, taste from food, lust from love. And no one since has quite been able to bring these sundered parts together again. Of course very few have tried.

But the children had to have something to do. So they knew they were allowed to work, and they got to work. And they knew they were allowed to invent, and they fell to inventing. And they knew they were allowed to laugh, if their jokes were "clean enough for the kiddies," * as they came to be called; so they fell to joking. And they became delirious with work, and delirious with inventions, and loud with laughter, even laughed in clubs and smoking-cars at things they were not supposed to know about. "Get to work," "Get out a patent," "Stop me if you've heard this one," became part of the language. After a while these children invented objects much bigger than they were themselves — fantastic exciting objects, which the nurses and the teachers were too feeble to understand or to learn how to run. So finally the young people of America were left almost to themselves, became rude to anyone over thirty and even to each other, though still secretly fearful of European ghosts and phantoms. And they proceeded to put up, tear down, build higher, tumble over, shoot along giant mechanisms, mammoth electric toys, which have made the United States into one vast sublime Christmas toy department throughout the year.

Here then is the new world the artist has had before him to record, unless he preferred to be an exile or a mystic. As, for example, Mark Twain ran away into worlds of nonsense, Herman Melville to the sea, Poe to islands of his own, Henry James and Whistler, T. S. Eliot recently, to England and France, Gertrude Stein into a philosophy of grammar and syntax, Carl Sandburg to *The Potato Face Blind Man* saying, "Tomorrow will never catch up with yesterday because yesterday started sooner." And many shimmering artists escaped to circuses, comic strips, music halls, where they could be inviolate performers. So performance came to be honored above theme in this country. Only a few, a very few, have dared to be lonely enough to stay by their theme.

In the meantime while the young people worked and invented and joked, sometimes they would talk with the peddlers grown-up people turned away from the door. Children always find a way to talk with peddlers. So they had fun with Italians and Jews — wops and sheenies as

---

* As real an artist as Ring Lardner once used this phrase to describe to a producer the kind of show he would like to make for Broadway.

they learned to call them. And they showed them what they were making, and the Jews especially out of the dust of the many roads that had led them further and further from their ancient mountain said, " Nice, nice, lend us these things and we will sell them for you." So money set in as never before, and was deified. And finance became a ritual so intricate and tangled that many of the young workers and inventors themselves were unable to cope with it, and its secrets went into the hands of a few.

And sometimes the children talked with the servants — children may always do that — and among others they had fun with the Negroes. And the eyes of these dark people were dazzled by the shine and speed of the things the white children were making. And they said, " Give us some of this shine for our songs and dances, and we will teach you how to dance, and we will tell you our jokes." So entertainment began. And everything went wildly well — more money, more toys, more music, more money. Never was there so untrammeled a racket. And indeed it should continue to go as well, unless by chance, before ever these young people have time to grow up, they grow old and nervous trying to take care of this giant toy civilization — the United States of America — which today goes agreeably shrieking and blaring and reeling and plundering and killing for more, more, more!

If you say this is not true, is not still happening, read then as official evidence President Hoover and his committee of American business leaders in their report on Recent Economic Changes, published in May, 1929:

"The survey has proved conclusively . . . that wants are almost insatiable. . . . The conclusion is that economically we have a boundless field before us; that there are new wants which will make way endlessly for newer wants, as fast as they are satisfied."

So, completely the market gospel, speed and change, sales and produce, appears to spangle the banner, cash in place of the archaic stars. What chance yet for people who would think with their hearts and follow the wild deep wants of the heart? Just a ghost of a far-off chance, maybe, where the headlong committee slightly falters, qualifying " insatiable " with " almost " !

3

" Old prejudices must always fall, and life must always change." DREISER

Against this background of want and change, still clogged with European ghosts, in the early years of this race of the new away from the old, of the young away from the elders, of the raw away from the mellow, Dreiser was one of the new-born. In a youthful country as elsewhere there are strong and weak children, adrift in the argument of the few with the many as to which are weak and which are strong. And there are always, fixed in the tradition, the good and the bad — those who somewhat conform to, and those who nearly reject the ways of their parents. So it happens there are the good and the bad strong children, to be praised and denounced in accordance with the shifting conventions of the years.

There are the Rockefellers and the Garys and the Hearsts, some of them paying great fines of universities and libraries and good works to appease their Victorian parentage; some of them not even taking the trouble to do this. There is Henry Ford, who in his strength can junk millions of dollars of machinery in favor of abler machinery, and in his arrested virtue preaches the old-fashioned dances, and fills museums with the hoop skirts of presidents' wives and their attendant psychology. There is Thomas Edison in one and the same interview seeking to suggest the chemical physical nature of immortality and recommending *Evangeline* as his favorite poem. These are the daring, cautious, yes-you-can, no-you-can't Americans. These are the virtuous children, who have opened doors on extravagant playgrounds, where already grandchildren and their hoodlum friends have forgotten that this country ever had a complacent

Yankee past, and have scarcely heard of a Cavalier Virginian past. Yet they have been careful always to observe the signs put up by their elders in each new playground, " These are new playgrounds, but you are Americans, and you must be true to the past. You must not have any fun here. No fun allowed here." And some of the young bandits have been vicariously careful, too; they have paid their fines in support of the churches and the various prohibitions — no wine, no lust, no beauty, no fun.

Dreiser, one of these pioneers, was born to fit neither the good nor the bad tradition. He was born nearly unconditioned by the past. If conditioned at all, it was more by the decrees of the moment, by the American scene. And if today conditioned, what prejudices have grown into him, what unconscious native color has stained his intellect? The story of this is the psychic story of recent years. A man as highly conscious as Dreiser, and at the same time as interlocked with the world about him, becomes a cylinder, a record not only of himself but of the world about him. Yet, too, untouched by influences, he has sometimes made his way into solitudes. It is this nearly unconditioned quality of mind, which is live intellect, and rare the world over, which is Dreiser's pioneering gift to this country.

He saw the signs put up by the guardians in the new playgrounds. He could read them. But he saw also that the children were practicing fun in spite of them, and were almost forgetting the penalty — hell-fire. They were at any rate lying, stealing, fornicating, and making money; shrieking, laughing and destroying, which is fun for children. And, he wondered, why not, if they knew how, or if they didn't, if they were even awkward about it, if they had to go to prison for it, or even be executed for it? Why not if their new lawlessness was stronger than the old law? Then it became fact. Then it was interesting. Then it became law. Watch everything in this shifting, changing United States, listen to everything; make out what you can, what you have time for; you won't make out much in the hurry. Forget the parents and aunts and uncles, unless they still live and won't die in the new child, unless perhaps they are younger than their own time, or possibly timeless — small chance of that! Forget these people as such; keep the old photographs, give them a tear or a smile or even a caress, put them away in a drawer or in storage. But don't confuse them with the new, with the moment as you see it, which is sure to be different, to be old tomorrow. Put things and people down as you see them, hear them, feel them. Remember the new teachers science and change, science that made machinery, change that makes hurry. That way you will pass with high marks.

So this German-Slav from Terre Haute was to be one to live through this period of transition from the States into America, from British puritanism into material paganism; to live through it and remain part of it. He is at best both playwright and play; at worst, at least the play, that is, American. If we take it from Barbereau, a philosopher cited by Baudelaire as of his own mind: "The great poets, the philosophers, the prophets, are beings, who by the free and pure exercise of the will, arrive at a state where they are at the same time cause and effect, subject and object, magnetizer and somnambulist." At times Dreiser fills the order. He is then both native and stranger. He said one day, " Sometimes I see myself as a hoop in an arc reaching over from one phase of existence into another. What seemed unthinkable when I was young is a commonplace now."

Who are some of the other hoops in this arc of articulate Americans? Where did they start?

4

*" To understand! It is — not to die!
You will be in the circle of joy forever."*
AUGUSTE RODIN

In 1871 Dreiser was born in the Middle West, in Indiana. In 1842 and 1857, Ambrose Bierce and Clarence Darrow in Ohio. In 1833 Robert Ingersoll and in 1843 Henry James in New York. In 1834 and 1830 and 1836 and 1838 Whistler, Emily Dickinson, Winslow Homer, and Henry Adams in New England. In 1835 Mark Twain in Missouri. Three years before Dreiser, Edwin Robinson in Maine; a year before, Frank Norris in Chicago; and in the same year Stephen Crane in New Jersey. A few years before, Edgar Lee Masters, and a few years after Carl Sandburg, Vachel Lindsay, Sherwood Anderson were born in the Middle West; Robert Frost in California; and Gertrude Stein in Pennsylvania. Out of an overlapping background not far behind, came Poe from Massachusetts, Lincoln from Kentucky in 1809, Thoreau from New York in 1817, and Melville and Whitman from New York and New England in 1819. These are some of the people who have taken something American through and over from a previous era into one that is not yet characterized; and, for all we know, what with wars to come, and free speech again suspect, may never be deeply characterized before the next change comes. A random list, you will say, and one to disturb some of those listed, so that if dead they might turn in their graves; if living, they might claim damage to find themselves in each other's company even for the space of a brief paragraph. It is true these names are not closely related to one another. Some of them scarcely touch each other in what they would ask to stand for. Some stand for rudeness more than refinement, some for document more than tone, some for drama more than analysis, some for behavior more than philosophy. And then besides, it is the American way, people bear relation to things and events more than they do to people. These, as I see it, bear relation to that flood of change in the United States, indeed in the Western World, that has carried us away from the prophet to the scientist; away from the hand to the machine; from goods to money, from quality to quantity, from the fixed to the shifting. They are cited here as bearing relation not to one another but to a century of terrific transition. Some of them have been causes or tools or symptoms of change, at the same time standing out against it to crystallize and arrest it in art. Others more simply have stood in the face of it as you might in a storm, not celebrating it or ignoring it. All have won because they have dealt in moments of their work with essential quality. They have been electric people. They are not old-fashioned people.

5

The widest of our valleys

The Prairie, the Middle West — if you go by in a train or in a car, and you have never lived there, you might say in winter, " Bleak monotonous country! I don't care how many millions it is said to feed," or in summer, " Too flat, too green, too dusty, and certainly trivial! Why don't they go through in the night? " But if you have lived there, that is, known people you have loved there, it is disturbing as you jog through on a train or glide through in a car. Then the checkered quilted plains, gold, black, indigo and green, each sow with litter of pigs, each cow, each running horse, each roost fluttering with white hens, the hedge rows and the windbreaks, the foolish little houses beside the wise red barns and concrete silos, the lilac bushes and wild grape vines — these few visible creatures breathing or inanimate, that play with and slightly break the flatness, bring to memory a series of detailed patterns that used to emerge from the flatness for you, and return into it. You remember in winter long walks you have taken even alone that seemed lonely and yet not lonely, over frozen roads between frozen fields, where there was peremptory and solemn order of the fields between the windbreaks, put away by dogged patient arms for the three months of ice and snow. And although you knew not a friend for miles to speak with, hardly a face even in a farm house window — the people seemed put away too — yet because of this peremptory and solemn order, a single man, a single dark figure, fringe of coat and trousers velvety with wear, going from his back door to the barnyard to feed the pigs, followed by his collie, appeared to move like a cipher of the race of men. And the sun, sharp sphere of fire in the west would challenge the eye, until looking into it and into that alone, you began to worship not sunlight but the disc itself, which changed to orange and then rose, as reaching the horizon it leaned for moments on the snow, and then leaving, chilled and desolated near and far. That is, single facts like these, the man, the sun, or a tree full of white leghorns were ecstatic strokes on a clean canvas. They had to count for you. You took them or nothing in a country where there was nothing else to take. And years afterwards a memory of force and of economy persisted. The prairie laid away for winter — the railroad tracks carrying people from dirty raw cities east or west to more elaborate landscape — the little towns with today the bank, the drug store, the ice-cream parlors and movie houses, with before the general store and saloons, the few factories along the rivers, the school house and the churches — not much else to show, and all too light to disturb the sleeping prairie.

Or memory is tapped back to April on the prairie, to summer months and to the hazy opulent and nearly putrid autumns, so much has grown to decay from lack of hands to harvest. And the triple patterns of these seasons have many planes both intersecting and never meeting, which except for the birds and the clouds almost secretly contradict the flatness — so close to earth they seem. Not much of it is human; it is from spring to fall a parade which human hands help to make, but not their hearts to celebrate. People are stage-hands here on the prairie, have been since first they got settled here. Sometimes they make a rhythmic part of the scenery — rhythm of plowing, harrowing, sowing, cultivating, mowing, picking, harvesting, feeding, loading, unloading in railway stations, once by hand and horse, now by hand and machine. But the big parts in the play are not taken by people. The parts are taken by frogs and leaves, puddles, moons, thunder in the first days of spring; and later by the storm of petals, magenta to white, that fruit trees throw around each triplicate of farm-house, barn, and silo; by the cobwebbed dew on lawns before breakfast time in May, by the feverish tearing of dandelions over pasture and lawn; by hollyhock, dahlias, trumpet-vine, pumpkins; and all the blights, that play the part of villains to prairie fruit and vegetables. These gardens dating back eighty years and more to the days of our wars, Mexican and Civil wars, make drama through the summers more than people do.

Then the fields, musical successions, theme on theme, chord on chord. Crescendo of waving surfaces, emanations of bronze and gold dust into white noon air, green festoons of corn rows palpably ascending from earth to blue air — the fields with eyes and flanks of goddesses, large, lazy, shining, served by the hands of farmers, to keep them forever fertile, ready, young. These are both actors and drama, these make the fabulous ballets of this land.

Or to put it this way: Those who can't live without play of life to look at, have to find it on the Prairie in classic drama of the fields, in romance of gardens; in chamber music of birds, satire and burlesque going on in insect worlds — tiny red bugs under hedges, spiders, locusts, fireflies, the few ethereal butterflies; or orgies in the world of reptiles and weeds — toads, garter snakes, mullen, burdock, milkweed.

Why should the people take parts, or except for a few of them be even hungry audience? The young, the daring young, are not going to stay here. The fathers are not going to have their help for long. They are going away to "get on." The mothers for years have been telling their favorite sons to study hard, and some day they will be something in the great world. They will succeed; they will "get on." The mothers feed the sons to the city. The daughters jealously follow.

Of course in the shelter of little woods, or lost between corn rows or up in the choir lofts of churches, or in some darkened back room when the rest of the folks have gone off for the day, there have been doings and plenty of them in the century of pioneer prairie life — adultery, incest, perversions, and occasional murder and dark disposal of the bodies. And when these are brought to light and rest perhaps for months in the undertaker's morgue, which is apt to be also the furniture store for davenports and iceboxes and baby carriages, then the village gathers itself into a little morbid knot of drama, and yields intensive long-faced chatter, a sympathetic suicide, another murder or two. But for the most, all vile and all delightful lechery rests beneath the surface. Even today when in summer months high-school lust fulfills itself, in closed sedans along the roads between the radio and ice-cream parlors, these pleasures are suppressed, don't get into village chronicles. Nothing goes into speech; nearly everything warped by silence is tolerated. Only when some young high-school teacher begins candidly to mention evolution, sex-hygiene, or comparative theology, does a cry escape the elders. Then the teacher must pack his trunk and look for another job.

Is it any wonder then that those born to speak out, brilliant with the minerals of this soil, must leave the small town? Only a genius for cryptograms and elusions could quell loneliness with fulfillment in these unrelated provinces. Carl Sandburg in Illinois has been doing this, changing open secrets over into poems. Robert Frost in the narrower valleys of New Hampshire has refined and subtilized a set of ciphers that have movements of watches to tell infinite time with. Emily Dickinson, a woman, in Amherst in the sixties, Edwin Arlington Robinson in New York, the greatest of our villages in the nineties, have used this gift to lodge the theme in word masks. Dreiser has none of this magic, has had to manage without it, has not the narrow gift of language. He is wilfully explicit; implicit, when he is, in spite of himself, and by virtue of bringing into life a world so actual that it in turn has implications of its own beyond his control.

6

*"Many good men come from Indiana;
the better they are the quicker they come."*
GEORGE ADE

Theodore Dreiser in 1871 was born in this luxurious inhuman cradle, The Middle West; in Terre Haute, Indiana, one of whose sons, as quoted above, makes a dogmatic but famous axiom about men and Hoosiers. Dreiser was born on the 27th of August at 8.30 in the morning, the eleventh of thirteen children. Terre Haute was well to the south in Indiana, and so was a birthplace tinged with the warmer, lazier, more indolent South of the United States. And this flavor of the South spreading north in Indiana, he says, never met the resistance that it met spreading north in other states. The settlers of Indiana, though they were many of them children of New England, were not like the settlers of northern Illinois, Michigan, Wisconsin — so often stubborn and complacent, genitally warped, intellectually calloused. Somehow the gentler people, he maintains, the dreamier more whimsical men and women stopped here. Perhaps they stopped in accordance with the grand old saying of pioneer life as it travelled from east to west, " The cowards never started and the weak ones fell by the way." Perhaps they were the weak. Dreiser has described them caressingly, with a moving almost tearful voice, which has affected me the way delicate greenish plants embodying life have affected me — those plants strong and yet leisurely to grow with long idle stems out of shadowy swamp: " Indiana is different among Western States, just as people will tell you Connecticut is different from other New England States. It is a State apart. Anything could happen there. The people are credulous, they like to believe anything, preposterous things. You can't call them tolerant, they don't think in terms of intolerance; they are just softer, dreamier people. . . . Like life in warm bottom lands, deposits of ancient rivers. Many of them failures, don't you know, the kind that make good mediums and fortune tellers. The successful people can't tell fortunes, they build walls around themselves in order to succeed. They haven't much imagination about the next man. . . . A criminal of the worst kind, or a charlatan can get away with it in Indiana. The more irrational the story, the easier to get these people to believe it. . . . There's something fertile, solacing in a way, about the place."

To bear him out were his own father and mother, who believed in signs and auguries. When he was born, they told him, an apparition of three graces attended her labors. A few evenings before her marriage she saw thirteen will-o'-the-wisps dancing over a bog before her house; they predicted the number of her children. After the birth of the third child, and her rebellious wish one night to be young and free again, three lights appearing in the meadow and abruptly vanishing signified that her wish would come true. Not long after the three children died. Then she prayed to God that if only he would grant her more babies, she would never be a rebel again; she would dedicate her life to them. This she did to five sons and five daughters. . . . Dreiser himself has carried away from this credulous land a leaning toward the regions of the occult. It deeply colors his realism. He is willing to believe nothing and ready to believe anything.

Other gifted Hoosiers, though none so vigorous and smouldering as Dreiser, none so eager to carry the burdens of the whole country by recording them, are in themselves testimony to this mood of Indiana. James Whitcomb Riley and Lew Wallace come logically from a cradle of superstition and dreamy romance. George Ade, Eugene Field, Booth Tarkington, Dreiser's own brother Paul Dresser, John T. McCutcheon, seem like men who would be at ease with fortune-tellers or story-tellers or magicians or vaudeville sopranos or lion-tamers — with any of those more irregular, informal, looser products of the race. They can hypnotize and seduce lightly, and believe in airy hypnotism and light seduction.

1
Inescapable cradles

The human embryo living the life of creation over from the moment of the first cell to the moment of the complete child, knows how to unfold without help from the outside. The American because of cleavage from the parent has been forced to unfold in this same way in going from the child to the man — without help from the outside. And the Westerner, the Middle Westerner, more than any other, has had to learn the lesson of civilization over step by step or not at all, almost without help from the outside. In doing this the embryo has the advantage, repeating always an innate lesson of the ages. Civilization is no such racial habit and still requires teachers. And we threw away the teachers as dangerous or exotic or out of key. So the American from the point of view of human subtleties has developed gropingly or sometimes with a rush, skipping essential steps. He has been like an embryo who might forget to emerge with eyelashes or with all five fingers on each hand, or with the sense of three dimensions. Yet, to compensate, he might have piercing eyesight, four grasping fingers and a linear drive beyond all ancient calculations. In any event he has been that United States fruit of heroism, the self-made man. To begin at the bottom and work up all in a brief lifetime — this together with a stifling set of inhibitions and taboos preserved from the past, has been the boasted inheritance of each American child. And the phrase, " Get on, get on, push on," is scratched deep, swift and sprawling in the various lingos of our language.

Dreiser is a giant of this form of growth, one of the self-made titans. Yet unlike many of them he appears to himself a seed out of fertile soil, rich sediment, dramatic with rocky deposit. He has faith in his beginning as in himself. Out of it, as he tells of it, might logically develop a fluid spirit shot with flame — a solitary temper, native and yet new to the United States. He is a massive fluid man, an intellect personifying the modern doctrine of nature: Nothing fixed, even the rocks, even iron and steel in a state of flux. He is possibly a prophecy of what may yet be the American compensation — the gift of being large and flexible evolving out of what was apparently formless and yauntingly untraditional.

Here I am taking his word for it, from what he has written and told of parents and childhood. His father was born in Mayen, Germany, a small Catholic walled town set among hills at the juncture of the Rhine and the Moselle. Though escaping into Alsace, and then to America, when a young man, in order to avoid being drafted into the Prussian army, which had seized this hamlet, only a few years before belonging to France, he retained always a mediaeval nature. His mind was like an ancient hamlet encircled by German Catholic walls and hills. There must be something of the protestant in every German as in every Anglo-Saxon. The Latin Catholic reconciles the drama of church with ancient delights. The confessional allows him to do this. The German Catholic asks for no other fire or excitement than that which may come out of Catholic lore and ritual. He is a violent protestant against outside delights. He is intensely, darkly Catholic and so is ready when he breaks away to be as intense a Lutheran, or as intense a free thinker. So Dreiser describes his father, who in no matter what small village of Indiana, or in Chicago in his last days, was a man filled with the lurid shapes of the German Catholic night. With the unreal world of saints and devils as the one reality he fought to surround his ten unwilling children. Only one of them entirely succumbed, Dreiser says, though for years each one lived in the shadow of this volcano — the Church. The destructive lava of it perhaps first printed in Dreiser his enormous sense of doom.

His mother was an opposite temperament — Pennsylvania-Dutch, that is Moravian, a Slavic race. Her people were Mennonites — a faith refusing oaths, civic offices, support of the State in war, and buttons and buttonholes, hooks and eyes — everything must be tied. Largeness of spirit, mobility might easily have been a gift from her. She was, according to Dreiser, large, mobile, fertile. She lives in his story of his childhood, *A Hoosier Holiday,* like an embodiment for him of the soil of Indiana, just as early people have imagined for themselves presiding spirits of the groves and fields and mountains where they lived, and have made shrines for these spirits. " An open, uneducated, wondering, dreamy mind," he describes her, " none of the customary conscious principles with which so many conventional souls are afflicted." " A pagan," " a poet," " great-hearted," who was " taken over into the Catholic Church at marriage, because she loved a Catholic and would follow love anywhere." She was imbued with " the trees and the flowers and the clouds and the sound of the wind "; with " fables and fairies and half believed in them, and once saw the Virgin Mary standing in our garden . . . blue robes, crown and all, and was sure it was she! "; she liked " the ne'er do well a little better than those staid favorites of society who keep laws," and would laugh and cry with them. . . .

One night I heard Dreiser speaking of his mother. It was a New York night on the East Side, cold as knives. Frost-pictures on the plate-glass window panes were fabulous etchings. Pine-clad precipices, deities above the clouds, armies in conflict, cities on fire, bridges crowded with people intoxicated for that night the passerby. Satin quilts, pink, gold, scarlet, peacock blue, hung under white store lights, to be bought, one knew, for the double beds of tenements beside elevated tracks. Every block or so men and boys were warming nervous hands at street bonfires, on to one of which a red-bearded Jew flung an old mattress carried from some room above with a laugh and a kind of cry, " Now will we have fire," and an invitation to us to come and get warm. Glass, satin, lights and the gestures of people sharpened senses and memory through Sicilian, Syrian, Judean, Chinese streets. The mind made distant analogies, skipped time and space to a variety of scenes and legends. Under the oblong spangles of Chinese chandeliers at the oblong table, it was easy to go sharply here and there — Greek poets, Egyptian gods, French women, Inca ornaments, and whatever one spoke of to seem to find details and their essence. He described Indiana, took it away from the map, put it into fable, spoke of his beginning, the poverty of it and the luxuries. He said of his mother a thing which, if parents could find its secret, would mean more to them than much of the learned advice that educators give at parents' meetings: " She made our house seem to us like fairyland. . . . We used to complain of her sometimes, and yet none of us, not even those who were grown-up, could stay away from her long. We were always coming back — she was potent and alive."

Real fairy stories don't lie as to the horror and coarseness of life. Only the faint and too sweet expurgated echoes of fairy stories for modern children suppress the truth in the optimist's ever-rising tone of voice. So I imagine this fairyland did not lie to him. This first home, changing from house to house, five different houses in Terre Haute, one in Sullivan, one in Evansville, two in Warsaw did not hide dark shapes from him. Surrounding him were dragons and giants and their victims. His family had to accept them. There was the Catholic Church and the father under the spell of it. There was failure after success for the father, and the dream of a woolen mill which should some day be his, gone up in flames. There were debts and not enough clothes, not enough food, and the father under the spell of this misery. The mother not subdued, but worn, tortured, by facing it, by working out in other people's houses or washing for them at home — work that countless women set out to do, but she was meant to shine, and did, according to his legend, shine in spite of it.

" Was she beautiful? " — " I don't know if she was beautiful," Dreiser said. " She was plump, not very tall. I remember one summer day in Terre Haute, I was playing in our yard and I saw her from a little distance. She was cooking in a kind of shed near the house, making jelly, I think. I thought, ' My mother is very beautiful! ' "

"Was she really so alive, so 'pagan,' as you call her? Was your father enough for her then, or did she find others?" — "She did if she wanted to, I'm certain of that. She had a way of doing what she wanted to do without disturbing the rest of us. But I was too young, I don't know about that." — "Well, maybe she did. Maybe your father was not your father. How do you know?" — "I don't know, but there is an access of gloom, a brooding in me over long periods, so like him that I feel a close relationship."

His answers to these questions, ready to explore regions that to most people are closed precincts, testify again to a detached intellect, that un-American gift. Even his recent portraits of women — *This Madness* — diabetically published in the Cosmopolitan Magazine, have something of this. They make romantic heroines of these three ladies, come nearer than anything he has written to what Rodin once called the cream-tart of the bourgeois — the ideal. Yet they give you, as he goes the rounds by way of a number of other girls and women less important to him, an unashamed picture of himself, lonely and scattered for having to know variety better than intimacy. Out of this trait may have grown the untiring scope of his work, and the long stretches we have to travel without meeting intensity. Then, suddenly, to refute this, come penetrating thrifty moments. Patience for variety, detail, volume, and impatience to illumine with lightning, combine his meaning.

8
Terre Haute: aura of houses and yards

Dreiser has made two records of Childhood, *A Hoosier Holiday*, 1916, and *Dawn*, 1931. The first, less literal than the second, has the advantage of being nearer to Indiana, nearer to his youth, and nearer to a work of art. *Dawn* has the advantage of appearing when, partly due to its author, prudery for the moment has been partially defeated. It packs away endless unremitting detail, some of it agreeably shocking to a reader with the patience to uncover it. It is a breeding place of innumerable novels, undesigned, inchoate. *A Hoosier Holiday* is an annealment of these years as they came back to him on a visit to Indiana in 1914. It is charged with eager questioning and an air of candor, if not with each shredded detail. To me it reveals more of Dreiser alive and entire than does the explicit confessional, *Dawn*, to which, notwithstanding, one is indebted for many revealing facts.

He tells how in addition to the spectre of poverty, they lived under a chimera of social disapproval. " We were poor in the main, and worse yet because of certain early errors of some of the children (how many have I committed since) . . . we considered we were socially discredited." After his father's failure in Terre Haute, several of his sisters ran away to escape the tyranny at home and had " gone to the bad," so the father said, and gossips agreed; though later this decision was reversed, whenever " the bad " turned into money or position. And the favorite son, Paul, the song writer, the prince of the family life, got into jail, " innocently," Dreiser thinks, for having forged his father's name, and then for a time was exiled by the father.

They lived under a cloud of poverty and disgrace. Yet to his later mind it was like bright sun. With a mother who made out of the home a fairyland, not to be respectable was to live in the open, and not in a stuffy room, of now Catholic, now Puritan, now Victorian taboos and decencies. Even at that time, life was opulent. It was a fertile beginning, crossed by a father who could not be pliant nor yet quite impotent, but streaked with a mother's laughter and love. She could laugh, he told me, at very rough, ribald stories; and, destitute as they were, people came to her with their troubles.

Not that Dreiser's point of view has no traces of early privation. From these times of hardship, often repeated in later life, might date a hardness of mind, barbaric in its indifference. Expect nothing. People owe you nothing; you owe them nothing. Give if you like, take if you like, there is no obligation. Vitality, strength alone counts. The very doctrine of American finance! Then again I have heard him say as coldly and without sentiment: " Only beauty counts." Evidently for him beauty came to be looked on as the ultimate cruelty, the oblivious force from which there was no appeal, more difficult than money, more difficult than fame! Hence his restless searching!

Again if he has sentimentality, it is when he idealizes the rich and worldly, as if from a distance he saw them shining. Very nearly at moments he accepts their standards as desirable. This he does conspicuously in the case of two heroes, Witla in *The 'Genius,'* and Cowperwood in *The Titan*. He is large and powerful in making them, but not quite cold enough toward them to attain always the ruthlessness of art. At other moments he divests them of externals, and they are naked enough, whether spirited or pitiful. If there is ecstasy, it is concerned then with the physical perfection of luxuries surrounding the rich. Sometimes, as purely as a Frenchman, he loves the *maquillage* of wealth; and with how much less chance in the United States, even in New York, to apprehend its elegance of line and surface! Compared to the European, compared to the Oriental, we have been importers or imitators. We have assembled the parts of luxury. Few of us, millionaires less than any, have touched them with our own experience.

What he saw in grown-up life, what fascinated him, his eyes began to pick out in early years. . . . When he went back to Terre Haute, where they lived until his eighth year, he went back to an old red brick house, corner of Eighth and Chestnut, where his mother had once tried keeping boarders:

"All I could recall of it . . . there once was a little girl in blue velvet, with yellow hair, the daughter of some woman (it is a guess) of means . . . stopping with us, who because of her blue velvet dress and her airs, seemed a creature out of the skies. I remember standing at the head of the stairs and looking into her room or her mother's, and seeing a dresser loaded with silver bits and marvelling at the excellence of such a life."

"Silver bits" on dressers run seductively in Dreiser's brain to this moment. They recur in *Dawn* as symbols of childhood glamour. Conversely another even younger memory of Terre Haute:

"A hot day and a house with closed shutters and drawn blinds, and in the center of a cool, still room, a woman sitting in a loose negligee, and at her feet the child playing with the loose worn slippers on her feet . . . — 'See poor Mama's shoes. Aren't you sorry for her? Think how hard she has to work.' — 'Yes, poor shoes, poor Mummy.' — 'When you grow up are you going to get work and buy poor mother a good pair?' — 'Yes, work. Yes, I get Mummy shoes.' — Suddenly something in the mother's voice is too moving. Some mystic thread binding the two operates to convey and enlarge a mood. The child bursts into tears over the old pattens. He is gathered up close, wet-eyed and the mother cries, too."

Again another memory to do with these contrasts and the principal hotel, when he spent the night there thirty-five years later:

"Here, . . . my brother Rome, at that time a seeking boy like any of those we now saw pouring up and down this well-lighted street . . . was in the habit of coming, and, as my father described it, in his best suit of clothes and his best shoes, a toothpick in his mouth, standing in the doorway . . . to give the impression he had just dined there. . . . 'Loafers! Idle good-for-nothings!' I can hear my father exclaiming even now. Yet he was not a loafer . . . just a hungry, thirsty, curious boy, all too eager for the little life his limited experience would buy."

Of the ten children he was the fourth eldest, one of the most interesting, Dreiser says, a railroad man, who finally died of drunkenness in a South Clark Street dive in Chicago, about 1905. Here is instance of inordinate faith in the high voltage of life, coupled with despair for those too warped to be instinct with it or to let others be. Anyone, no matter what they do or leave undone, who insists on living is heroic to this writer — Carrie, Cowperwood, Clyde Griffiths, his own sisters and brothers when they broke laws to escape suppression. Tolerance, not lazy but electric, he offers as endowment to his country.

To the hotel in Terre Haute also his mother once in her hardest days came to look for work and got it. And years later his brother Paul went to a banquet there in his honor, because of his song " On the Banks of the Wabash," adopted as the State song. On the night of his return, long after these three were dead, he writes, " I thought of my mother — and Rome outside on the corner and Paul at his sentimental banquet, and then I felt very ' sad-like,' as we would say in Indiana."

In this way he treasures his childhood and the houses belonging to it in " this lush Egyptian river country." And with them his father's village, Mayen, at the juncture of two rivers and two wines, Rhine and Moselle. To have to seek to go back, by whatever threads there are, to the roots of one's self is a patrician pastime. Communists would call it bourgeois; nationalists would call it distinguished; Dreiser concerns himself with it.

What he records as having happened may every bit of it have happened, or may have been selected to have happened by later years of growth. This more likely is the case; his two records of childhood for example are not identical. They appear to vary according to the separate moods of forty and of sixty years. But both stories tell the artist's heritage, a genius for experience. He remembers distantly of Terre Haute, a vital " seeking atmosphere." And distinctly he remembers cellars, one where he was not allowed to go or the " Catman " would get him, and even his dog was afraid to go down there; and a basement in another house with a swing in it, " where I used to swing all alone by the hour, enjoying my own moods even at that time." He remembers a watchman who whenever he passed the house had a present for him, candy, peanuts or apples; and one day being taken to see him, " where he was lying very still in a little cottage in a black box with nickels on his eyes " — and he wanted to take the nickels, too. He remembers " old scenes and miseries " — picking coal off the tracks with his brothers Ed and Al, because there was none at home; losing the last fifty cents in the house, which had been given him to go for a sack of cornmeal; carrying dinner in a pail to his father at a woolen mill, and his father explaining to him the functions of a carder, a blower, a spinning jenny; of being taken at five to St. Joseph's school (for which his father in prosperous days had donated the ground) : " A nun in a flaring white bonnet, black habit, rattling string of great beads pointed at a blackboard with a stick and asked what certain symbols stood for," and he had trouble in giving the sounds for the letters.

This perhaps persisted in him. His writings are acutely conscious of situation and image, and of the atmosphere surrounding them, but less apparently conscious of the words. Words appear to be chosen like letters on a typewriter under the touch system; incident, structure and phrasing to be intentional; words to be ordered by reflexes, if that be possible. Yet I remember an argument with Gertrude Stein who contended that real art was never conscious, that the artist in creative moments was in every sense unconscious. It may be I am attempting impossible analysis of this novelist's style, which sometimes is an express train in the night, sometimes freight cars shunting endlessly back and forth — both ways notable for being of their own essence.

There was a bell in the church tower attached to the school that would get turned over and wouldn't ring until some boy climbed up and turned it back; to be chosen to do this was wonderful. There was boating on boards on a muddy pool, and once in a rowboat on the yellow Wabash River with a brother who whipped him for screaming when the boat rocked. There was a summer rain storm at Twelfth and Walnut, and his mother undressing him and telling him to run out naked — an adventure which seemed " splendid and quite to my taste." His brothers Paul and Rome seemed to him like men when they were only boys, and his elder sisters, thirteen, fifteen, seventeen, were " like great strong women." The first band he ever heard marched up the streets in Warsaw, " red jackets, white straps, black Russian shakos "; he was frightened and cried.

Around these houses in Terre Haute is the memory like an aura of big yards with trees, fruit trees, bushes, gooseberries, currants and flowers. Near one of them a lumber-yard and the smell of it; and the climbing and hiding and jumping from pile to pile. Beyond, a train-yard, where he used to go when most adventurous, and once climbed into an engine and examined the machinery. He felt around him the voices and tang of firemen, brakemen, yardmen, engineers, the clangor of an outside world. These are the common riches, if they know how to remember, of children of the old small-town America — yards around the houses, yards beyond, leading children away out of the family, rather than more deeply into it. " Life," he says, " was a strange, colorful, kaleidoscopic welter then. It has remained so ever since."

Each of these incidents is recalled with the enterprise he gives to details of later life, or to the multiple incident of the other lives he has invented or recreated. Dreiser moves from minuteness to vastness, weaves and stitches back and forth from the point to its extensions in the infinite. A trait of style with him. His words follow back and forth, now swiftly, now stumbling and falling, to keep up with him. People complain, and yet go in and out of his books, moved and ravaged, sometimes suddenly ravished. The balance of power is with him.

9
Alluvial lusters

His first years in Terre Haute had given these few flecked threads of memory, vivid against a background of gloom — movings from house to cheaper house, sickness of one and another, quarrels between mother and father for lack of means. Then, in his eighth year, to save expenses, his mother had taken the three youngest, Ed, Tillie and himself, to Sullivan, twenty-five miles to the south of Terre Haute, in a wide valley between two rivers, the White and the Wabash. On the way they had stopped in Vincennes and visited a friend, Sue Tinby, a wild creature, he remembers her, a French woman, who in more prosperous days had sewed for the family, and was married to the chief fireman of the town. In the night once they had gone to a big fire, and seen " their host disappear into a red glow and come back alive." But this exciting visit in rooms over the firehouse had to be broken off when his mother discovered that the firemen's quarters were an improvised brothel approved by their hostess. This, he says, brought about " their sudden and moral departure." In spite of poverty her children were not to be exposed to this. They had stayed long enough however to give him a memory transcribed fifty years later in words a little like Renoir paint; " I myself, being a restless early-rising child, one morning saw one of these daughters of desire, a corn-haired blond, her pink face buried in a curled arm, and lying on a bed allotted to one of the firemen of the night shift."

So they took up their bundles and went further into this " steaming land of wheat, corn, timothy and melons," where towns, crossroads and streams were of French origin or name, where autumn lasted into January, and spring came early. Dreiser, driving back these years later, felt the magic that had cradled him, " delicate, poetic, generative." He wonders with his friend and host, Franklin Booth, if the French temper had not tinged life in these valleys. The women, he says, were plumper, the men more solid than in the North, birds increased in number and kind. He came again upon the " turtle doves in beech and ash and hickory groves, the martins circling in covies, the blue jay and scarlet tanager, wrens in the eaves of cottages, the humming bird in the purple clematis, buzzards, hawks, eagles high in air, and the blackbirds over the fields," and " could almost hear again the pea fowls calling for rain " on Mr. Beach's opulent farm near by. He is taken back to " three years of sensory dreams and delights " — infancy gone, adolescence with its " sharp inquiries " not yet entered on. Outside the house in Sullivan had been a field of clover impeccable to a boy's bare feet early summer mornings. He had the luck, unknown to children brought up according to prescribed régime, to get up when he liked in the first daylight, and spend long days almost as he liked, ending in " the after-supper grouping on the porch, the velvety dusk descending, the bats, mosquitoes, tales of Indians and battle chiefs, the stars, slumber. . . . I can feel my mother's hand as I lean against her knee and sleep." Clocks were not tyrants over him, nor have ever seemed to rule him; for which perhaps his writings lose precisions and gain sometimes in freedom.

His mother took in washing; he and his sister carried it back and forth. They slept at first on straw mattresses on the floor. In winter they were cold, dismissed from school for lack of shoes. With the money from the washing she bought enough furniture to progress to boarders and beds. The boarders were railroad hands, traveling peddlers, coal miners, one of whom was arrested for murder in their house before their eyes. Their neighbors he describes mostly as miserable people, the kind known in the West as squatters, who quarreled and cursed each other, or vegetated and died, often half demented by squalor and ignorance. Twice the children assisted at grim death beds and funerals; it was a country custom and their Samaritan mother's code to "help." Among them she was loved and honored, but his sisters were called "loose girls" and his brother Rome was wild and roving. As a family they were shunned; once he heard them called with the rest of their neighborhood "no good, just trash."

Yet over and over he speaks of the sting, the mystic luxury of life with his mother, brother and sister, and sometimes others of the family, in their frame house in Sullivan, painted white with roses, fruit trees, a truck garden; a dog to run with, an elm tree to climb, great branches to play under; a gate to swing on; and the Busseron, where he and his brother used to fish, " a shallow stream pooled in places, its banks sentinalled by tall trees . . . ornamented by arrogant weeds and bushes blooming violently."

Did his mother ever tell him what he was like in these years? Was he different from other boys? He remembers her saying he was always listening, could dream and listen by the hour. He remembers going a little beyond the borders of their place, to where he could see the railroad yards, a turntable and a hay press, and listen endlessly to the switching and loading and unloading, for the cadence of these noises. He remembers sitting by streams and mud holes in this same hypnotic dreamy way. He lived the life of alluvial things, felt their coming and going.

If one were to read certain passages of this memory of childhood, and knew nothing else of Dreiser, American chronicler of doom, one would think of him as a boy about to deepen into a poet, a sensualist; and one endowed to match sensation and mood with speech equally sensitive. One would hardly guess that finally he was to forget or seldom realize the artist's pursuit of the physical word, the ritual of language; in order to stalk like a scientist, and record like a scrupulous interne, the restless human story, the confusion of footsteps and voices, the wild welter of symptoms. In these young years, in a land where human beings were scarcely more than stage-hands, where animals, plants and minerals took the big parts, a child in love with living, he chose the lustier phases of it. If one extricates them from their explicit network, names identifying the land recur rhythmically in his records of childhood. They become images:

"Warm bottom lands — ancient rivers — warm sudden rains — quick heavy rains — green fog — round healthy trees — fat river land — smooth green grass — wonders and dreams — low alluvial soil — roundness of flesh and body — stillness of the woods — steely blue and gauze of wing — black and white silvery fish — dark wet silvery cat-fish lovely and lustrous as porcelain — distant low of cows — grunt of pigs; deep-bodied green painted wagons hauling melons — long hot yellow roads — boys and their hungry restless ways; fat sheep — dams and rams — astonishing hogs — sleek rolling animals; sting of life deliriously gay — tingle and response of a new body; bloom and fragrance of the clover — mystery of flying."

He was a child obsessed with the luster of earth, careless of men and women, unless like his mother or the French seamstress or the chief fireman, they too were lustrous. The blighted people and things, "crazy Bowles," an ex-army man who used to come to their well for water, dancing and muttering; Mrs. Hudson, a neighbor whom they thought of as a witch; the disheveled butcher, Spilky, "avid" to kill and sell, and his slaughter house not far away, with "its yard of whitening bones"; Tish Herndon, called a bad woman, who drank and was in love with her father; his own father who would come "brooding from Terre Haute," and talk of hell more than Heaven — these figures had not seemed to dominate him. They are remembered more as one would the under side of logs, degradations rather than the lighted facets. Other life transcended them in the shape of dogs he played with, birds he envied, a comet that appeared at this date in summer skies, lizards and gophers.
. . . Years later many human failures are to occupy him, and he relegates to an almost sinister background the physical world surrounding them. This he has done imperiously in *An American Tragedy,* where the gorgeous earth turns a sickening grimace on the mimes and actors.

A poem in *Spoon River* defines this change. A letter from Masters in 1915 tells him: " I have you picked in my Anthology as Theodore the Poet ":

"As a boy, Theodore, you sat for long hours
   On the shore of the turbid Spoon
   With deep-set eye staring at the door of the crawfish's
      burrow,
   Waiting for him to appear, pushing ahead,
   .   .   .   .

   But later your vision watched for men and women
   Hiding in burrows of fate amid great cities,
   Looking for the souls of them to come out,
   .   .   .   .

10

> "*She must, like the man, marry machinery.*"
> Henry Adams

Yet, if we believe Dreiser's picture of himself, it was not until long after he had left these villages at the age of sixteen, and, like so many other sons and daughters of farmers and mechanics, had begun to wander from city to city in search of money, which could alone mean power, that the human drama was to enter in as a wedge, and finally become the first obsession. Then, non-human nature, when kind, became scenery, when cruel, a destructive force, as it is for most Americans. That is, we have not made a marriage with our portion of earth in the United States, in the way that each European country, France above all, has reveled in making, even in the cities; in the way that the Indians before us succeeded in making, no matter how hostile their mountains or deserts or glacial lands. In this Dreiser became true to type, but with one innovation. Actively he has refused the religions, catholic, protestant, liberal, on the ground that they betray human nature, that is, sexual nature and the wholeness of living. He has refused too as insufficient the various compensations society offers and religion permits in their struggle to curtail the inheritance of nature. In this he has not been faithless to the teaching of his senses in Indiana childhood.

Compensation through money and power, for example, has been accepted as an American way of life. Money can do anything, power anything. By a kind of hypnotic magic, skyscrapers, giant dollar signs, numerous enough now for one to stand for at least each rich man, have become unintentional symbols of the American man — erections rigid in air, in emptiness, in contact with nothing fertile. And today almost consciously they cater to his sense of completion. So he may appear to disdain sex in human form, no need of men even, or of turning in upon himself, by this holding of himself like a high building forever potent, fixedly erect. If he gives way, if he yields, if he forgets this posture of sublimed rigidity — except on a Saturday night, or on occasional trips to Paris or Havana, " Oh boy! " — then all is up. He may as well consider himself done for, a failure, take his money off to Europe, where there are paid attendants to voluptuaries, or look around for the nearest home for the indigent. Or for the rare and more powerful few, there is, unintentionally yet actually, a transcendent symbol, the wheel, the turbine, the impeccable power plant, in contemplation of which the industrial giant feels himself identical with planetary force, with the physical solar concept of wholeness. Beyond these there is the fast train hurling from coast to coast, the perfected and lascivious elevator to the sixtieth story and down, the one-man airplane to cater vicariously to the sense of mastery.

And for women what has there been, what compensations, wrenched from and permitted by society and religion? Compensations less native, though possibly more seductive than those discovered by men. No arcades, few arches, to stand beside the indisputable towers as vicarious emblems of their nature; few canopies, few fringed or ruffled curtains in window or doorway; or if there were, almost unfrequented by men. Women long have sat together in the first cool, then cold shadow of their sex, becoming clubwomen or intimates or lonely women. Or they have compensated these three hundred years, when rich, with importations — imported clothes, imported houses, imported jewels, imported art, imported men. When poorer, with romantic magazines, soft drinks and candies. When very poor like Dreiser's family, they have remained uncounted, and like the unknown soldier have become, some of them, the unknown saviors.

If this grotesque picture of a house divided against nature and practicing every subterfuge to simulate union is not as true of the United States as it once was, Dreiser in his refusal to celebrate the substitute for the real, in his sense of people as primitive beings before they become social puppets, is one of the first natives to correct it. He is a liberating factor as far back as 1900, and perhaps almost as potent as the automobile, the beauty parlor, or bootlegging, which unconsciously have followed in his steps.

Two aspects interest Dreiser — grace which is bloom, and the falling away from grace, which is withering. As a child the first more than the second; as a grown man the second chiefly. Yet even then the fallen are not pictured as fallen until there is nothing else to say for them, and then without censure. The murderer, the thief, the drunkard, the glutton, the lecher, still denote the grace of life, still display what he calls their "high blood moods," until society in mask of religion has finally pulled them down and drained them to the last drop of sap; either jealously to confiscate it, or to use it to replenish their own reduced vitality. To victims like Hurstwood, Clyde Griffiths, Isadore in *The Hand of the Potter,* Dreiser is true; he never deserts them. Such loyalty brings tears to readers, and should bring compassion, which is sunlight.

11
Venus on the Ohio and Catholic Evansville

Houses, surroundings, individuals, ancestry, countries — what relation have any of these to the other? Much or little? Not knowing, we have to say much, or else not count values at all. Three difficult years in Sullivan, for all she could do, brought the mother near despair. And then one winter afternoon, the minstrel brother, the one so tenderly thought of by other Hoosiers for giving them their song of gleaming candle lights, the fatted prodigal son with the sweet almost untroubled face, laughter and beauty of features, came with money and put an end for a time to their hard days. He came out of a snowstorm in a fur coat and high silk hat, with three years of adventures to tell them since last they had seen him. Almost I think Dreiser invented him, but I hope not. Disowned by his father, for forgery and jail, a runaway from a Catholic school where they had hoped to make a priest of him, he had joined a traveling troupe which advertised Hamlin's Wizard Oil. Progressing from show to show he was now a favorite song writer and comedian in the West, working at the moment in Evansville, a town not far from Sullivan on the Kentucky border. He was end-man in a black-face minstrel company, and ran a comic column in the Evansville Argus.

He went away, sending back groceries and clothes, among them "a complete outfit" for Tillie, the youngest sister, to accomplish her marriage to Christ, the first communion. Paul was a good Catholic, without practice but without challenge. Soon after there came another visitor, his mistress, by the name of Annie Brace, the first worldly beauty these children had looked on. In Evansville she was Sallie Walker and kept a house of prostitution. But his mother, Dreiser thinks, never knew it, and was fond of her because she was beautiful with " clear incisive black eyes and exaggerated whiteness of face and hands," and appeared to really love her eldest son. By summer these two had rented and furnished a cottage for his mother, and under their auspices the family moved to Evansville.

So at length they could leave their makeshift home in Sullivan with its " seven or eight rooms, sparely and poorly furnished," Dreiser supposes, " and yet with the art there is in bareness and cleanliness." They went away with mingled feelings. There had not been many friends for these children to play with. For one thing, for which they were happy, they had had to leave the Catholic school, and they were not allowed to go to another. Then he remembers himself as put upon by other boys, commanded to fight and he was afraid to; so he kept away as much as he could. But to make up, there were his many older brothers and sisters, more vital than the people around them, coming back to visit, and the getting ready of a room each time and the ceremony of a vase of flowers placed in the guest room, and the tales they told of the world outside.

It is impressive, this insistence with no matter how little money on the making of a home, for just a year perhaps, or two or three; his mother's courage to settle, as it is called, as if forever, and then pull up stakes and settle again. For Dreiser this gift of hers appears to have provided him through years of want and change, before he resolved himself into the necessity of being a writer, with a sense of background. Sullivan made part of it; he left with a pang and yet elated too. Now they were going to something better under the wing of their rich brother.

Here for a while life brightened. The chosen cottage was in a " good neighborhood " in the center of a big, fenced-in yard, and the new furniture included a piano. There would be no washing now for others, and no boarders. His mother was at ease at last; they had a chance, she thought, to be respected. Here they lived for two years before again they packed their trunks and boxes and this time moved north. These are deep years for Dreiser. They made more cavernous his hatred of the

Roman Catholic Church, his last days directly under its influence — that Church which like a nightmare he denounces hysterically to this moment as often as he can. And they made deeper his passion for riches, riches of earth and riches of human relations.

Since a man is made in youth, and is merely maintained or destroyed by events that follow, these years are important in the analysis of an American fashioned out of our isolation and our force. Dreiser is called slow and plodding; yet he walked swiftly and a long way out of a remote background hostile to his intelligence, sweet sometimes to his emotions. He had back of him a father who once told him that " if a small bird were to come once every trillion years and rub its bill on a rock as big as the earth, the rock would be worn out before a man would see the end of hell once he was in it. And then he would not see the end of it, but merely the beginning." He remembers his father's angry contempt when he asked if God might not change his mind in all those years and let someone out.

The Catholic church and school in Evansville offered the same tyranny. He learned nothing from them, and was terrorized by the nuns and priests, and by the principal, who had " black hair, black eyebrows, black beard, and a dynamic stride sufficient to shake the earth." Here boys' palms were crossed with red welts, ears pulled until the victim cried, buttocks beaten with a short raw-hide whip. These cruelties, I think, were Northern and pioneer rather than Catholic. In fact, Dreiser's hatred of the Church testifies to its failure when torn away from Mediterranean sources and set down among Protestants in a Protestant milieu. Of what avail absolution in a society ostracizing people for their sins?

For books the school allowed only a Bible history and a geography, though *Diamond Dick* or its equivalent was read from under the desk. But he remembers finding somewhere the *Vicar of Wakefield,* Anderson's *Fairy Tales,* the *Life of St. Francis Assisi* and other secular books; and there was a woman' magazine of his mother's which, like so many children brought up far from the centers, he cherished for the pictures of what must be the great world. Then there was the school yard, a place of leap frog, snap-the-whip, fights, all of which he says he dreaded and had no prowess for. Once by mistake he laid out his opponent and was cheered. Usually he was the loser, and grew to be " shy and unpopular," and wondered why " life was so fierce."

Next to the school was the church which still blazes in his memory with gilt altars, candles, statues, stations of the cross, where wound the unending processions of song, incense, banners, brocade and lace, crimson, white and gold — work of master showmen whose road companies were nearly as splendid as those in the cities. Here a stern bishop, pale on a high throne in golden robes, he remembers him so, anointed him and received him into holy communion. The church was better than the school, yet it frightened him. He talks of it thirty years after with a shiver, as one would of evil things:

> " Think of the dull functioning of dogma age after age. How many millions have been led shunted along dogmatic runways from the dark into the dark again. I am not ranting against Catholicism alone. As much may be said of (other religions) . . . Here they come, endless billions, and at the gates, dogma, ignorance, vice, cruelty, seize them and clamp this or that band about their brains, or their feet. Then hobbled or hamstrung, they are turned loose, to think, to grow if possible. As well ask of a eunuch to procreate or of an ox to charge. The incentive to discover is gone."

Not strange that in 1929 a Catholic judge and jury in Boston condemned a book of Dreiser's. Not strange that Catholics can't enjoy this picture of a lonely child striking out from their exacting shore toward whatever wilder seas there are. His story repeats the figure of a man who must leave home for the sea, prefers the freedom of hopeless waves to the prudent lies of the shore. The myth of him would be that of a swimmer become almost a fish who can't breathe for long on customary land.

But Evansville had other phases that counteracted the gloom of Holy Church. Fun of boys surrounded him here, a gang of them, who liked his brother Ed and " at least tolerated him." Whir of industries, a chair factory, a pottery and a foundry, engaged him. He liked to watch and listen to what they were doing, through their windows or at close range if invited in. His brother Al worked in a chair factory and allowed him to help on Saturdays, lacquering gold leaf designs on kitchen chairs. He loved, too, the levee district of the Ohio River and the darkies trailing over from Kentucky with song and dreams and jokes.

In the midst of these initiations was one more mysterious than the rest, and more luminous. Sent once by his mother to deliver a basket of preserves at the door of Annie Brace, he was told that his brother would like to see him, and then was conducted by a colored maid through corridors to an apartment upstairs with big windows and striped awnings on the Ohio River. Such houses had a way of selecting, along with darkies, the cool river banks in small towns, while the good citizens fearing dampness, or was it beauty, dried to mummies in the grit of their superior boulevards. At his best as when he sets down tragedy, Dreiser describes his first glimpse of dalliance, in " this semi-southern world, hot and bright." Paul in light clothes, with him " his Annie in a pink and white heavily beflounced dressing gown, surveying me with an amused if not very much interested eye "; the rooms — wicker, linen, flowers, music, silver, mirrors, glass — to him a kind of fairyland:

> " But to reach this suite . . . that passage through the house . . . several open doors. . . . Things so strange and to me so exotically moving that I felt I must not acknowledge them even to myself. . . . Segments of beds . . . odd bits of furniture . . . tumbled bedding . . . garments strewn about . . . and in one case a yellow-haired siren half naked before her mirror. . . . In a flash, and without being told, a full appreciation of the utility of the male as such had come to me . . . I wished that I might stay and see more. . . . Yet I also knew . . . that such things were still in the dim distant future for me, if at all. But these pink-meated sirens, however vulgar . . . wonderful to me as forms . . ."

So his life in Evansville traced in him a triangle of his grown mental pattern. Hatred of dogma, love of enterprise, faith in lust, however elementary. Surrounding these last, not excluding them, the mysteries!

Paul apparently was unconcerned over this visit of an eleven year old boy; but it seemed best to the boy to keep what he had seen a secret, a door opened especially for him into surprising volume. He shared it with no one, but is sure that he valued it even at that age as news of some center of life. It was a center news of which in his first novel would be one of the shocks to jar the code of a nation.

So the months passed in this town so remote and protected in a giant elbow of the Ohio River moving on its way to a greater river, where always his own house and yard, the streets and the river life were as agreeable to him as the church and school were sinister. Then one day Paul went away to New York and Broadway fame. Without him his mother decided to try luck in Chicago where some of the older children had gone. In the North perhaps she would be allowed to give her three youngest a " sensible free-school, non-Catholic education " — a long-time dream of hers. It was their first entry into a big city, a favorite theme in Dreiser novels. For a summer they tried it, long enough to buy furniture on the instalment plan; long enough for Thee and Ed to learn to be newsboys, and jump on and off of West Side cars, a delicious early sport in the stories of many self-made Americans. But the city was too cold and big for their means, and the perpendicular noise of their neighbors up and down the air shafts seemed more vulgar to his father and mother than the wretchedness they had sometimes overheard in Sullivan. Forfeiting their furniture, they moved back to Indiana, but this time to Warsaw in the north. There she would be nearer her own relatives and nearer the few acres her father had left her when he disowned her for marrying a Catholic. In Warsaw they settled, and stayed there for the final years of childhood.

And Dreiser, whose early intensities might have been linked with the shiftless droning South, was definitely exposed now to the money-making speed of the North. As the years went on, he was to make his fight against its Protestant meagerness and callouses, and find his joys never entirely separate from its smug vulgarities. A few hundred miles from southern border nearly to northern would make this difference. At this age, twelve years, he joined forces with conquering America, and though often hated by it, and as often hating it, has never entirely deserted it.

12

Protestant Warsaw

"Warsaw was an idyllic town for a youth of my temperament." Dreiser's picture of it in *A Hoosier Holiday* is an idyll of a mid-Western town in the eighties. He is not sentimental over it as other Hoosiers, belonging to more acknowledged families, have been over their small town, not bitter as Masters is with his *Spoon River*. Life was pleasing to him, more than it appears to have been to the lonely implacable Masters in Illinois. He had loved the northwest corner of Center and Buffalo Streets, its bookstore, oyster counter, pool and billiard room, where met what he calls the free masonry of generations. Here and in the post office, in Peter's Shoe Repairing and Shine Parlor, in Moon's and Thompson's Grocery Store, these boys ranging from fourteen to seventeen exchanged " the little bit of money, wit, gayety and schooling they had," which wonderfully to him included secret talk of girls. Here he came, a hanger-on almost as soon as they were settled in Warsaw, almost the first night, in fact, and to his intense joy came finally to feel himself one of a group of youths, " if not of girls." He was " taken in." Here was Jud Morris, hunchback son of the proprietor of the bookshop, Frank Yaisley, brother of Dora, George Reed now a circuit judge, Mick McConnel who died of lockjaw, Harry Croxton, later a mining engineer who died in Mexico, George and John Shouf, sons of the local miller and grand-nephews of his mother, Rutger Miller, Orren Skiff. . . . Then in Dreiser's unbiased way, he adds, " there were still others of an older group who belonged to the best families and somehow seemed to exchange courtesies here ": transient evidence of how boys rebel against class hierarchy, for depriving them of the range of life. What boy " carefully " brought up has not envied the sidewalk gang, and pulled along by nurse or parent, has not strained back toward the dangers of it, before finally he gives in to the vague rule of class!

Then there were the girls of the town — Augusta Nueweiler, Maud Rutter, Ada Sanguiat who was killed in a railroad wreck, Loretta Brown, Bertha Stillmeyer, Dora Yaisley, so beautiful and rich and supercilious that he used to dream about her. Their fathers were owners of clothing, drug and drygoods stores; one was a lumber merchant. And there were the children of Harry Oram who owned the wagon works and of Mr. Epstein, whose Wool Hide and Tallow Exchange stood across from the bookstore. Between him and the girls was always a distance. He was too shy to know them well and besides not quite thought of as an equal by those he picked as beautiful. Yet the public school, which he said was gracious to one and all, " never binding or driving," did bring them together, whom snobbery even in this village preferred to separate. This is the first group of people in his life, changing from grammar school to high school.* Perhaps they are parents to the many others he has had vitality to make live in his books. With them he went to his first party, saw the girls in their best dresses, was face to face with the shiver of that naïve license permitted these children of this period — the kissing game. The morning after, a Saturday, he and his brother went off to a favorite grove of ash trees to try and tell each other how wonderful life had been. It is singularly Dreiser to remember this callow indulgence and give it its distinction of young lips and momentous blood; how soon to fade before less vital games! His genius is to see value stripped of conventional implications — value here of boys and girls about to cross over into maturity. That few ever really cross, or how stingily they cross before they die, makes his refrain, that deepens into lamentation.

He defines himself at this period as:

"a dreamer . . . somewhat cowardly, but still adventurous and willing to take a reasonable chance . . . enthusiastic about girls or beauty in the female form, and what was

* Named here as in *A Hoosier Holiday.*

more, about beauty in all forms, natural and otherwise. . . . I tell you, in those days wonderful amazing moods were generated in my blood. I felt and saw things which have never come true — glories, gaieties, perfections — I wanted, oh! I wanted all that nature can breed in her wealth of stars and universe — and I found — what have I found — ?"

The town had rivers, the Wabash and the Tippecanoe, and was on the main artery of the Pennsylvania railroad, and around it were five small lakes.

They lived in two different houses. First, the Grant house next to the school, where there was a swing and a hammock under a pine tree. There he read *Water Babies, Westward Ho, The Scarlet Letter, The House of the Seven Gables,* Irving and Goldsmith. This was a town of books, a town of the British classics, his first town with a bookstore. He was coming into a heritage of books which these Puritans allowed their children, as long as they would think of them as classics and read none of their own life into them. It was here in this hammock his father found him reading *The Alhambra,* and said, " What is all this trash, Dorsch? " He was old enough by then to give the jeer of child to parent. A few days later as if to prove himself a modern, too, the father bought the whole set of Irving for seven dollars from a traveling book-agent.

After a time they moved to the Thralls Mansion, red brick, one of the first in the county, set back in a grove of pines; and there were five chestnut trees and an orchard, and below them a saw-mill pond where they used to jump the logs and skate in winter. They made apple butter in the yard over a fire of pine cones in an iron caldron. One knows the kind of house, infrequent and haunting in the West, built in the early nineteenth century, spacious and romantic and melancholy, with windows like eyes, as if its years were numbered and it had seen dark family joys, and time were eating it away. " Life in this house," he said, " gave and promised me more than it ever did again." He talked once of a night he spent there, appointed to sit up with a sick sister, and give her medicine, and go at two in the morning to get the doctor: " I remember it was the night of my first reading *Macbeth.* To this day the eerie cadences of that play, mixed with the sighing of the wind in the pine grove and the barking of my dog are sounds stamped in my brain as in metal or hot wax."

Here too in Warsaw girls became important to him, and with them sex defined itself. It was in the air under the shady trees and on the verandahs. The boys whispered and giggled and spilled little rumors of sex. One of them had paid fifty cents to go to a lecture with stereoptican views of sex, and could diagram it for him. There were village girls every so often " going wrong," and that meant sex. The very night they arrived in Warsaw they had nearly taken a house next to a house of bad name; the women who kept it were friendly to them; and they were only saved by the timely advice of the hardware dealer. Sex beckoned to you and sex disgraced you. Girls possessed him now like a fever. He knew he wanted them and he knew that to fool with them might disgrace his family, almost free of scandal here. Besides, it seemed to him, the delirium of it might end him like lightning. Then one day coming home from school, the baker's daughter dared him to chase her, and, before he knew it, they were down in a backyard of big packing cases and she had initiated him into what stood in their young bodies for sex. But she was too bold and like an animal, different from the girls who ravished his senses; he never went back. Of the others there was one especially, pale and spiritual, he thought, whom he had to adore at a distance like an angel or a saint. He frightened her, made her faint, she told him; it was the same with him. An unearthly poetic love burned him for months. Strength of passion made a coward of him, he says, and kept him ineffectual until nearly twenty.

Toward the end of their stay in Warsaw he was further removed from these village beauties by the behavior of his own sisters, who came home to visit and began to keep loose company. One of them had to go away to give birth to a child. He and his brother and sister were not invited any more to the birthdays and hay rides and skating parties. Again they were under the old cloud for all his mother had tried to free them. So he tells of these beginnings, typical of our evasive, careless civilization — this half discovery of their own nature that children for generations have been forced to make alone; and then have kept like a secret the rest of their lives, to be spilled only to other children as they progressed to smoking rooms and petting parties.

Yet these were days of a new freedom; the public school was giving zest to life. There were books, a profusion of books — Macaulay, Taine, Guizot, Dickens, Scott, Thackeray, Fielding, DeFoe, Cooper, Lew Wallace, Dryden, Pope, Herrick. He would learn and study and find out about life; somebody would know, somebody must know, knowledge would be the solution. Here was the optimism of the nineteenth century; knowledge was there to solve everything; with industry it was yours. Who knows today after all the experiments, the progressive schools, the self-expression, if knowledge, proud knowledge, peddler of " tidbits," is not the surer solace? *

To this child it seemed like paradise to study free of Catholic spectres. He could ask questions about religion and science here. There were classes in natural history, botany and astronomy. He could ask about Robert Ingersoll, who was not, it seemed, a fiend who would roast in hell, as his enraged father and the priest used to say; but a philosopher, mistaken perhaps, but brilliant. To his amazement this school wanted to help him, not terrify him. He was in love with liberalism, as if it were a girl he had always wanted, met for the first time. One subject alone he knew instinctively was taboo. Sex was never mentioned except in relation to plant life, not to human beings. The priest might perhaps forgive his sister for her mortal sin, but that would not reestablish them with the best families of Protestant Warsaw who directed this school. That however had to do with equations yet beyond him, not to be counted against these generous teachers.

There was Mae Calvert in the grammar school, nineteen or twenty, " vigorous and blond, entrancing," who helped him and petted him, told him he read beautifully,

* Bertrand Russell, asked if he agreed with the induction of the moment that there is no knowledge, said, " No, not quite, I think there are always tidbits."

and not to mind if grammar was hard for him, it would come to him in time — in which she, like her day, was optimistic. Without mastery of grammar she passed him on to the next class; and from there into high school! Here was Miss Fielding, the rhetoric teacher, an old maid, with protruding teeth and no money to straighten them until it was too late. She told him not to mind about rhetoric either, that he would be someone, indeed that he would go further without rhetoric than most people went with it — an indulgence for which many a critic in the thirty years to come would not thank her. They gave him faith in himself, these two teachers, or strengthened a faith instinctive in him that somehow he was to be part of the panoply of earth. One day in the last term of high school, for a rhetoric test none of whose questions he could answer, he wrote a description of a stream near the town, pattern of sunlight and shade, discord of a Jewish peddler he and his brother had found dead on its banks face down. The principal asked for him, praised him, walked home with him, and gave him advice: His mind had not formed itself yet, but it would; he would be something. " Take your life seriously. Don't listen to people or rules. Read Macaulay's *History of England,* a history of the United States, Shakespeare, Keats."

Fascinated by the miracle of this advice, both as given and taken, I asked him how he had interpreted the idea of being someone. Had he thought the principal meant he would be a writer. No, he said, that had not occurred to him, books were written by foreigners or by great people in cities. He had once read in the Warsaw paper an anecdote about Nietzsche, and wondered at a living writer so great that he could be news in distant countries. He could never have fame like that. He had thought that he might become a superintendent of schools perhaps, the head of something.

To jar brutally with his picture of Warsaw is a remembrance of Dreiser in a review of *A Book About Myself* in Winder's Travel Magazine. First, complaining that he had written more about himself than any biographer had about George Washington, the reviewer says:

" We knew Dreiser — it was spelled Dresser then — in his high school days in Indiana. He was a gawk then; kept to himself, had no dealings with the other boys; went along the street with his head down as if afraid to look anyone in the eye. We boys thought he was ' queer,' and in the main were as ready to avoid him as he was to keep away from all companionship, yet he is the only one in all the town that has succeeded in getting his name before an admiring public — even though that public be of a perverted mind. One of the boys of those days became a great preacher; another a millionaire broker, others famous travellers and merchants, some got into the newspaper business, but they are all unknown to the world at large."

This jerks you back to the human element surrounding him, so nearly inhuman in its indifference. In this stalks the loneliness of a young extremist, a child thought of as " different " and called " queer " in the incalculable isolation of the Middle West. Lincoln in Illinois was " queer " too, and then like Dreiser forged through to an audience. Their kind of force required an audience and of their own people immediately surrounding them. What of the even " queerer " ones who could not be bent to this America? Perhaps they have lived and died in some tragic desert, some devastating storm of the mind, which when exciting enough as in the case of Poe finally brought fame. And some of them have gone to Europe. Dreiser walking with his head down as if afraid of being hurt, must early have made some rule for himself which forbade him to be injured, forbade him to be the under-dog. Today he says, " I was always lucky, I always got the breaks."

He left high school before it was over with the thought that he must earn money. And his family made their last move to Chicago, where several of the older ones still lived. He went first, alone, impatient for a job, and after a while the others followed. So he left the hammock and the lawn, the honeysuckle and dark trees, dimly resonant with village kisses and wail of song — " My Bonnie Lies over the Ocean," " The Spanish Cavalier " — and went definitely into a bigger world of preachers and brokers and newspapermen. Not many of them would be very different from those who as boys had thought of him as " queer." He went, he tells us, without saying goodbye to his brother and sister, only to his mother — a detail of a piece with genius, whose sudden, ruthless decisions amaze the rest of us. We never get used to them. He went with high hopes. Perhaps he remembered a prophecy of his Aunt Susan's. Like his mother, a Mennonite, she lived up on Silver Lake with her " vagrom " husband and children " in company with a few cows and pigs." Silver Lake was " set in high green hills," yellow-gold grain and black woods. When he and his brother went to visit there they slept with the others in one room, in tiers of beds in each corner, scarcely curtained; where married daughter and niece undressed, and they heard the muffled blandishments of the ungainly husbands. These relatives both shocked and fascinated him; the uncle a fiddler for the local dances and a drunkard; the talk in the house loose and coarse, trivial but wild compared to what he heard in his own reverent hard-working family. And it was all braided in with the noises and smells of barnyard and near fields, pigs and crickets, whirr of reapers, calls to horses — the bright dust and dew and night silence of a farm. So he describes the visit — one of the hypnotic passages in that book of too confiding title, *Dawn*.

" It was the time for taking in the grain; hot, clear August weather." His Aunt Susan, who always " appealed " to him, " soft-spoken, dreamy, wistful," was telling his fortune in coffee grounds in the trumpet-vine shade of the east porch:

"'Now let's see what it says about you in your cup. . . . Oh, I see cities, cities, cities, and great crowds, and bridges, and chimneys. You are going to travel a long way — all over the world perhaps. And there are girls in your cup! I see their faces!' (I thrilled at that) 'You won't stay here long. You will be going soon, out into the world.' . . . Her face was grave . . . wrinkled, distant. . . . I thought nothing of her at the time, only of myself. How beautiful would be that outside world! And I would be going to it soon! Walking up and down in it!"

13

Chicago: The Windy City: The Prairie Skunk: Independent as a hog on ice.

Chicago in 1887 was a mammoth village, whose emigrants were profusely Irish and German, and incipiently Italian, Jewish, Swedish, Negro, Chinese, whose ruling class, naïvely called "best families," was chiefly New England, tough, shrewd Yankees — young men who had once been told to go West, so they did, taking with them their virtuous wives. Here in Chicago they kept a British passion for class, or their wives did, and out of the raw lake winds, they caught a racy contempt for form of any kind. They loved to be respectable and they loved to be shambling, what they called "plain." They were complacent and brash; their wives were snobbish even way out there. They loved to have a European prince visit them, and equally they relished telling how his millionaire host, Long John Wentworth — they reveled in nicknames, they invented lingo — made him feel at home in his "palatial residence": "All right, Prince, when you've finished your drink, we'll go on upstairs and wash up for supper." As quick as they could they got to be millionaires and built "palatial residences." Often their wives were ashamed of them, but they didn't care, they were going to make Chicago the greatest city in the world, second to none. Already they called it "independent as a hog on ice!" *

I don't know how Chicago looked in 1887, but I am not far from being a witness. Miles and miles of homes, never a wall, sometimes picket fences, occasionally hedges, most often low stone beveled copings between yard and sidewalk; flowerbeds beginning in the front yard and running back past chickens and a cow perhaps, or hammocks and

* Recorded by Carl Sandburg in *The Windy City*.

a tennis court, to the back yard and sheds of the poorer houses, to the stables of the richer homes, and to the alleys which I used to think were especially for burglars to escape through and for dark deeds to happen in. Sometimes there were half blocks of white stone or brown stone houses, like New York, people said, which established meager form and color; but more often the lawn divided houses each different in shape, in color, in material. Miles and miles of toneless Eastlake fantasies, north, south and west, lived happily together with the older wooden shanties interspersed. These shanties were like cottages in German fairy tales with ornate Victorian detail around door and window and sometimes even balconies. Some of them were painted white, but most of them were painted grey or not painted at all, and grew to be with the cinders of the railroad a rich disturbing black. Some of them had no detail, were plain and dark and clapboarded as houses could be, as if witches lived in them.

All the houses had steps going up past the basement to the parlor floor, and usually a porch, where people sat summer afternoons. But in the evenings they sat — mother, father, grandparents, children, aunts, uncles, callers, on rugs and cushions on the steps, with two in chairs on the wide top step before the door. Here they watched the city growing in the night, smelled the stockyards, waited for a lake breeze, bought extras, and on the Fourth of July felt the shiver and flight of Chinese fireworks. Rich and poor seemed to improvise their summer evenings in this way. Behind them was forever the mystery of Lake Michigan, impeccable and vast, but that was given over to the birds and the railroads, the wastelands and the kitchens and stables, the hoboes and fishermen. They were afraid of the northeast winds in winter, these people, afraid of the storms and the shifting sands; afraid of mosquitoes and dampness in summer; they were afraid of beauty. It was cozier, it was wiser for their porches and their front steps and front yards to face the smug, leafy streets of their booming city.

Like a heart of these homes was what they called Downtown, later known as the Loop, because of the elevated roads. There was the Board of Trade, Marshall Field and Company, the Fair, the Palmer House, where old-timers from the Far West, cow-boys, Mormons, miners, and supercilious Easterners at least passed each other in the majestic, marble lobbies, or sat on the same red velvet divans; and where silver dollars intercepted the white flags of the floor of the barber shop. And there were innumerable stores and offices where hundreds of young men were doing well, and a few were boosting the city into being " the greatest commercial center the world has ever known, second to none." Wasn't this the corn market, the meat market, the railroad center, the lake port of a great continent? If you woke up at night you could hear the trains coming in from east, south, west, north, and going out again. You could hear the foghorns on the lakes and the whistles from the river. To a child, to a boy or girl, maybe even to older people this was wide, mournful, adventurous music — mingled whistles of trains and boats and foghorns. The Thomas Concerts, established about this time in the Armory on the lake front, with its European symphonies never gave the city wilder fugues than these trains of a continent and boats of the Great Lakes.

The river cut in from the lake between the South and North Side, and then turning divided again the South and the West Side which straggled far toward the prairie. Murky warehouses and wholesale houses were shadowed in its dirty waters, rose out of them, entered into them in a marriage of brick and smoke and river. The bridges and the rigging, the tugs and scows were vaguely animated at night by gas lamps and oil flames, and in the day by seagulls dipping, rising with their potent serrated wings, black and white like the city. To walk in those dim uncertain days of Chicago across the Rush Street bridge or the Kinzie bridge, was to walk through air that stabbed you with wings and lights and the loom of shapes. There was a pledge in the air; older people told us so, we believed them. A far off adventure was making itself, we were part of something being made. If they lied to us, if the promise has not yet come true, has even receded, they were not quite to blame; there *was* something in the air which the wet lake winds and the prairie winds wafted about the street corners and river ways along with the cinders and soot.

Out to the north on the Lake Shore Drive, looking like something to eat was the German Castle-on-the-Rhine of Mrs. Potter Palmer, the city's queen. And not far from it a replica of Desdemona's palace and some isolated French châteaux and Tudor mansions. To the south you found them, too, on Michigan Avenue and Prairie Avenue, correct in grey stone or shameless in green stone, or brown with turquoise trimmings and Eastlake ornaments, turrets, bay windows, cupolas. Often they looked like something to eat, cake or ice cream, or they had faces, they looked like the people. English butlers answered doors, two men sat on the box of broughams and victorias, tallyhos blew their way to the races in Washington Park, and pleasant people drove about in their buggies and phaetons. As often the sidewalks were of wood as of stone, and you had to go up and down wooden steps because of the fast rising levels of the streets.

In wide patches over the city, especially along the west branch of the river, a desolate seductive scenery was evolving out of factories and railroad yards — out of lonely wooden viaducts, drums of gas tanks, grain elevators, chimneys, furnaces, derricks, grim board fences, dredges and wagons, and always the scattered grey shanties and the corner saloons on the corners of nothing. To the southwest and northwest this giant village trailed the flat borders of its skirts. And they were trimmed with row on row of freight cars, empty lots, junk yards — from the first there was passion for junking. Here and there a goat rummaged, pigs wallowed in pools of mud; wooden sidewalks led past the sparse wooden huts and the infrequent street lamps. In winter marvelous tonality bathed these different districts. A stark gamut of blacks and whites, hulking mysteries penetrated like lust and love. It was aphrodisiac scenery. Near the center of the town Custom House Place blazed with more literal venereal meaning in the half-naked women of the red-light district. Their rouge and peroxide, their satin and spangled chemises, their frontier eyes, their assertive bodies tore the air for a few blocks. Flaunting inept Venuses, they challenged the smoke and purity.

In the summer the city grew in the dusty green light of cotton-wood trees and willows. In the winter perhaps nowhere has there been such haunting velvet of black shapes and white snow and drifting white vapor under the canopies of smoke, shot with flame whenever the sky darkened into daytime fog or into night. It is gone now, that first low-flung improvised Chicago, with not one painter out of it, shaken by its bleakness, to change it over into pigment. But it did, I think, communicate its unintentional magic to certain writers; to Frank Norris and to Dreiser, to Masters and Sherwood Anderson; the tissue of whose work at times, even when of other places, presents the mournful racy haphazard lineaments of this city of smoke and puddles; and directly to Carl Sandburg, who has made poems identical with Chicago.

14

Fresh water learning

Dreiser in story and biography has told over the mood of a boy or girl from the country entering a big city alone, as if acutely he remembered this coming to Chicago when he was sixteen. They went to live on the West Side, on the corner of Ogden Avenue and Robey Street, that West Side which before the fire was sanctioned as a place to live in, and then gradually came to give low visibility to the people who lived there. So, dangerous labor leaders and specious cult leaders and illicit lovers and self-effacing people went to live there. If to any of them life was unendurable without attention, they almost had to move far away to other cities. In Chicago the taint of the West Side would follow them; for all its frontier pretense the town was inflexible, inhuman as that. Unconsciously for this reason Dreiser may have left the place and not rested until finally he reached New York. Yet traits of Chicago remain with him.

He found a job as dishwasher in a dirty Greek restaurant. He was helper to a scene painter in love with his sister. And then he went to work in the shipping department of a big wholesale hardware house, Hibbard, Spencer, Bartlett and Company, that backed on the river and shipped goods from its docks into lake freight boats. He hoped to become rapidly a successful merchant. Mr. Hibbard is an item of this background known to me. We used to play with his grandchildren in the open yard of his enormous red brick house, which had a stone fountain always dry and nice to play in. He was a millionaire, and he and his wife were *so* good and pious we felt sorry for his grandchildren for fear they would have to be good and pious, too. They gave their money to the Episcopal Church and St. Luke's Hospital near by, situated in a block called "the patch," so dissolute we were told never to walk there. We used to go into their house for birthday parties or to get warm. Sometimes it smelled of baking, but usually it was big and silent, and nearly, but not quite — something was lacking, maybe greed — gave the shiver of riches. The drawing room was dressed in pale green and gold brocade, and there were marble statues and black teakwood cabinets; it was always dark. The dining room was baronial and had elk heads with branching antlers and mounted trout on the walls. There were dark oil paintings everywhere — fruit pieces, religious pieces, marshes, meadows and game; we rarely saw anyone downstairs. Mr. Hibbard had a short, white beard and no moustache which made him look especially good and kind. People said he was a man of sterling character; his middle name was Gold. His one incongruous passion was fast and thoroughbred horses. Though he and his partners, Mr. Bartlett and Mr. Spencer, belonged among the self-made merchants and club-men whom Dreiser later characterized skilfully in *The Titan* as respectable hypocrites, I think he was not a hypocrite. I think he never wanted to be, nor for his children or his grandchildren to be, anything but God-fearing and charitable and solid and prosperous; nor for his knives and scissors and fishing-tackle and guns and saucepans to be anything but solid and irreproachable. "O. V. B." — "Our Very Best."

To his store on the river his shipping clerks, the Warsaw boy among them, came at seven in the morning and worked till six at night, for $5 a week, unpacking and storing and packing in a crowded loft under an Irish boss, who quite rightly, Dreiser says, despised him. And he dejectedly despised the work, felt like a "pointless unimportant bond slave." The one stimulant was "an acquaintance there who exercised a great influence over me . . . a Dane, a drunkard and a lecher . . . but with marvelous brains I thought. . . . He laughed Christianity off the boards," and made fun of high society in Chicago, in fact in all of the United States. He gave him his first lesson in sophistication. He would borrow money and calmly not pay it back. " But I forgave him because he was so valuable to me." *

One day the young shipping clerk was told to go down to the office, someone wanted to see him. It was Miss Fielding, his teacher from Warsaw, the old maid with the upper false teeth and " a whimsical emotional smile." She was now a school principal in Chicago. " Theodore," she said, " work of this kind isn't meant for you, really. It will injure your spirit. I want you to let me help you go to school again." He protested that his father would never allow him to borrow money. He remembered how any debt was to keep them all in purgatory, as they died. She said she had kept track of him, that she had heard he was not well, would break down in the city, that she wanted to help him go to the State University in Bloomington, Indiana, had even spoken to the president, David Starr Jordan, about him. It was true, he said, that he was sick, his lungs and stomach had gone back on him, but there was no way for him to live in the country. She told him she had some savings and she would rather he would use them than use them herself; more would come of it. She said she would talk to Mr. Hibbard whom she seemed to know. As Dreiser told the incident, though his memory differs in *Dawn,* the merchant's advice was like hers: " You must listen to Miss Fielding and get an education. It is best for you," he added, " you will never make a business man." This seemed final. In a few weeks, with his mother's consent he was back in the warm hills of Indiana, entering his first and only year of college, and getting well again. Life outdoors and clean air saved him, he is sure, from perhaps a fatal illness. The hardware job would have been the end of him.

I like to believe the story as I heard it. A flash of how, by such distant and indirect ties, people are joined sometimes for a second out of their lives! The teacher and the hardware merchant by good works, the high-school boy and the teacher by some cry of the intellect, all three of them by a second in fate. It is amusing, if true, that this

* Recorded by Frank Harris, *Contemporary Portraits.*

churchman had a slight hand in saving for future years an enemy of the code he lived by — a writer of books that were to challenge a religion where chastity and honesty and prosperity and charity attempted to go lovingly arm in arm.

His version of his two semesters of college life is unsparing of himself. He went, he says, too unprepared for academic learning to know how to learn. He failed, he thinks, for lack of mathematics and grammar. What he got out of it was a sense of how bewildering knowledge stored in books could be, not much of the actual knowledge. The fact of so many branches of learning, and so many men and women living and dying at ease within them, awed him and confused him. Though he almost wanted to, it was not given him to make them intrinsic with his life. None of the professors happened chemically to communicate a sense of life through learning to him, as the Warsaw teachers had done a few years before. Yet he says they were able and brainy and some of them focally important to this fresh water culture — David Starr Jordan, Rufus L. Green, Jeremiah Jenks, Edward Howard Griggs, stark dissenters' names. . . . None of them apparently had for him the warmth of Miss Fielding, "her heavenly, irradiating smile" urging him to go to college: "You may never learn anything directly there, Theodore, but something will come to you indirectly. You will see what education means, what its aim is and that will be worth a great deal."

What education did mean to him was just this — it challenged him, made him jealous, perhaps as his father had been when he bought the set of Irving for seven dollars. In the midst of it he was not willing to admit he was hopeless. "There must be some avenue of approach," he said, "to the intellectual life for me, too." He made several friends, one of them a serious scholar, a mental compass like Miss Fielding.

Another thing cheered him — he roomed by chance with the most popular boy in his class, a football star. They liked each other, shared the same bed, which appeared natural to him — he had often slept with a brother at home. Their room was filled with college life, and although he never made a fraternity nor was thought of as "popular," he "got on" well enough with the typical athlete and card player, and that pleased him. They even included him in their parties with girls, but here as in the studies he felt awkward, ill at ease. Two types again emerged as in Warsaw, the one who scared him by pursuit and the one too rare to be pursued. They made him miserable, he was a failure. He would never know what life was, and he alone was to blame. Another friend, "a kind of fox or wolf in his way," a card shark and a gambler, took him on a holiday to Louisville with two girls, one of whom was to be his. They took separate double rooms for an afternoon and evening at a hotel, but he was too shy or too self-conscious to make the expected use of his, and said bitterly to himself when it was over: "No girl will ever look at me. I am a fool, a dunce, homely, pathetic, inadequate." And though technically he somehow passed in his studies and could have gone back the next year, he left in June not to return, "unhappy, distrait, scarcely knowing which way to turn, but resolved to be something more than a cog in a commercial machine." He went away, bitter over "these youths and girls," the most of whom "had ignored him." And yet he said to himself, "They can all go to hell! I will get along and be somebody in spite of them."

Here in Bloomington must have become fixed two of the outside whips to Dreiser's life. He must succeed extravagantly. It was not success in the extreme to succeed commercially. Beyond glitter of money and things there were the keys to wisdom and sophistication. Without these you were on the outside, money could not get you in. Then he must have love, he must have beauty, he must have women or at least one of them. Without that, he was only half alive, he was beginning to be dead. Life told him this and there was no time to lose. What he had within him to meet these spurs was that intangible force, sometimes called genius, though it might as well be called appetite, curiosity, hard work, zest, concentration, endurance to an infinite degree. When a man has it, he is, for all his drawbacks, a mountain that people have to watch and talk about as it changes with the changing light of day. A country without such monuments, whether, according to the lay of the land, they are crude or subtle or both, is almost not a country. We could do with a greater number of them.

15

" They don't know me yet, but they will! "
AMERICAN FOLK TALE

When this college student of nineteen got back to Chicago he was careful to find outdoor jobs, out of a talent he had for hygiene, out of a terrific will to live. He drove a laundry wagon; looked up property for a real estate agent; collected for easy-payment instalment houses. In the first of these he tells in his account of his newspaper days, published in 1922, how he held out twenty-five dollars of the company's money to get a winter overcoat, and was caught unable to pay it back. He tells of his terror because of the difficulty of burying the disgrace and getting another job. It was his first and last offense of the kind, out of fear, he explained, more than out of remorse. It is typical of American criticism of even eight years ago that so many reviews of that book, especially those condemning him for lack of style, condemn him for shamelessness in recalling a theft. They call it bravado or egotism, rather than the wish of the scientist to present the facts even if they spoil the picture or bore the reader. To confuse the issue and so invalidate the criticism is still a favorite sport of ours — an Anglo-Saxon inheritance. Whatever his vices of style, Dreiser has among writers an enviable distinction which in itself makes style — the enterprise to keep the issue clear, and carry it to ultimates if he can, if not, into the unknown.

The job of collecting was not unpleasant, he says. His health was good; he worked and walked with such speed that his afternoons were free, and he had a fierce love of life in this raw lively city, said to be named by the Indians after the prairie skunk, or some say the wild onion. He loved the poor and rich districts, the scenery of manufacturing, the saloons, the churches, the wooden shanties, and the quick contrasts of one to the other. He collected payments for yellow plush albums and silk-shaded lamps from women whose husbands on the bleak fringes of the town were tanning hides. In the vice districts he was paid for shoddy rugs by " plump naked girls striding from bed to dresser to get a purse " and " offering certain favors for a dollar " to be deducted from the contract slip. " Black negresses leered at me from behind shuttered windows at noon; plump wives drew me into risqué situations; death-bereaved weepers mourned over their late loss, and postponed paying me. But I liked the life. I was crazy about it. Chicago was like a great orchestra in a tumult of noble harmonies. I was like a guest at a feast eating and drinking in a delirium of ecstasy." He was crazy about it, and not because often he accepted the adventures proffered — they were yet too strange — but because he loved the display of life. He is, I think, a man of an unrivalled appetite for display, which is expression.

In this extravagance of living at nineteen and twenty, this drunkenness at just the spectacle of life, he conceived the idea that intoxicating to the senses as were these rambles of a collector, he was meant for something more related to the show. Always he was improvising his impressions, humming them over to himself as he walked and collected. He decided he would write them down, he would write about life. Eugene Field wrote about life; he was a newspaper man. He must do and be the same. Once on a newspaper you climbed to " the top of fame and wealth." So he began writing and in " a fever of self advancement " sent a bundle of rhapsodies to the lank, savage Eugene, a Hoosier of the vintage before. When nothing came of that, undaunted he answered an ad in the Chicago Tribune which read, " Wanted — a number of bright young men to assist in the business department Christmas holidays. Promotion possible." But though he got the job of doling out cheap toys for ten days to the poor " who had hoped for food and clothing," promotion proved as intangible. Returning after Christmas he was told there were no vacancies.

In the meantime for prestige with a girl, a friend of

his sister's, who had come to visit them on this Christmas eve, he had called himself a newspaper man. There was but one thing to do, if he was ever to succeed, become a newspaper man. Besides in this year his mother had died, she who alone seemed to understand his moods and ambitions. At birth, a child displays his special quality to a mother like his. She had surely seen and felt it. And now she was gone. Now the home was falling to pieces in endless bickerings for lack of her presence, which had made of it " a thing as sweet as dreams." He must, he felt, strike out on his own, make a life outside for himself.

He had begun already to apprehend the culture evolving in Chicago — the Art Institute, the Thomas Concerts, the Ethical Societies. He went on Sundays to hear Gunsaulus and Jenkin Lloyd Jones, and sometimes to see visiting actors, Booth, Modjeska, Fanny Davenport, Mary Anderson, Jefferson. He wanted to be part of it, felt already he was " a man with a future " who belonged among sophistications. He was too young to know how imported, how little native, most of this culture was, and therefore how foreign to him, whose force consisted in part of being artlessly native; in other part of being elemental. Also the world outside of Chicago began to dawn on him, the fact of " five related and unrelated hemispheres." He read Emerson, Carlyle, Froude, John Stuart Mill, and he had heard of Nietzsche, Darwin, Spencer, Wallace and Tyndall, and intended to explore them. And at this age, he says, already the meaning behind Washington, Jefferson, Jackson, Lincoln, and behind the Civil War, was apparent to him, and " the drift of the nation to monopoly and so to oligarchy." This is hard to believe, and yet who knows? A man is made in his first years; a man who was to have a giant's eye with which to get a view of the world must have had that eye at twenty, and may have made this use of it.

In any event he lunged toward the newspapers, feeling that they by their nature encompassed the world.

16

"A mighty good Sausage Stuffer was Spoiled when the Man became a Poet. He would Look well Standing under a Descending Pile-driver." EUGENE FIELD

There was in Chicago at this time an incipient reflection of London and Paris sophistication, nearer than the newspapers to the air of culture this Indiana boy was eager for. There was beginning to be a timid echo of various English art circles centered by Rossetti, William Morris, Oscar Wilde, Meredith, Whistler, George Moore, Yeats and others, and of French circles created by Verlaine, Mallarmé, Rimbaud, Manet, Monet, Degas, Renoir, Courbet, Rodin. These various intersecting spheres abroad made but one faint exotic band in the Windy City. Yet it had a distinct personnel of aesthetes — book-binders, jewellers, polite pederasts, spinsters, professors' wives with jonquils in their bosoms. And, to give reality, there were even a few hard-headed poets, satirists and artists, who were indulged by their prosperous conservative families and friends, and were said to be making culture hum in this virgin city. Out of its stir and friendliness came Hamlin Garland with his *Main Travelled Roads,* William Vaughan Moody with rebellious verse, Robert Herrick with what were called sex-novels, John Dewey with his new program of education, Sullivan and Frank Lloyd Wright with a native architecture; and more coldly authentic and ironic than any of the others, Henry Fuller with tenuous intricate realism. At about this time Altgeld and Henry Lloyd (whose father-in-law was part owner and editor of the Chicago Tribune) and the young Clarence Darrow were making a stand for freedom of political thought. The city had creative life, and with it a shy naïve faith that they would catch up in art and in intellect as well as in commerce.

It was an odd circle of aesthetes on this strip between lake and prairie, joining hands more out of isolation than out of personal coherence. They had their clubs, The Whitechapel and The Little Room; they edited art magazines. Eugene Klapp, later an engineer of importance, started The House Beautiful at about this time, the first American magazine to deal specifically with decoration as an art. Herbert Stone and Harrison Rhodes edited for a few years a journal called The Chap Book, which published Bliss Carman, Charles Lummis, Yone Noguchi, George Ade, Eugene Field, Stephen Crane, Le Gallienne, Clyde Fitch, Henry James and other Americans who looked promising; and imported Henley, William Sharp, Edmund Gosse, Zangwill, H. G. Wells, Hardy, Max Beerbohm, Stevenson, Barrie, Mallarmé, Verlaine, Rimbaud. Chicagoans were vaccinated in their own town with these many names that stood for art or near art in the nineties. But sadly enough Fitch, Le Gallienne, Stevenson and Barrie took better than the livelier names in a frontier land doomed already to breed a race of men which was to be shrewd about business and sentimental about everything else. Though wistfully these devotees stained their walls a Morris brown or painted them a Whistler grey, and made mission furniture and green pottery, the intimacy of the life they read about, in the fragile speech of Mallarmé, in the fantastic satires of Max Beerbohm, never came to play within their houses. Culture, they came one by one to face it, was something that could not be imported ready-made, or filtered in from the top down. After this false dawn of the Nineties, which broke into something nearer reality twenty years later in the Poetry Magazine, in the Little Theatre and the Arts Club perhaps, the movement died of malnutrition. Its creative members broke away to the East or the Far West for a breath of life before they died. Two survivors, Carl Sandburg and Frank Lloyd Wright, are scarcely natives; fame reached them from abroad, not from Chicago. The real rebels today are the gunmen, the gangsters and politicians. Art, another word for expression, if ever it comes to Chicago, will have to come through them among other elements; through the people, high, low and mediocre, and because their life is stained with it and requires it; will have to come its own slow way up out of the dirt into the air. Norris, Dreiser, Masters, Anderson, Darrow and Sandburg are prophets to this.

To Dreiser at twenty these doors of Chicago aesthetes were not known. Had he been aware of them, it is not likely they would have opened to him. He was green and uncouth; he was a native, just what they were hoping to escape from. A right instinct took him to the newspapers in his search for a living and a training. The conquering American, the genius for enterprise rather than art, was helping to make Chicago through the daily press. Joseph Medill of the Tribune, Victor F. Lawson of the Daily News, Melville E. Stone, of the Associated Press, were forecasting the Chicago of today. Theodore Dreiser, " a dreamy cub of twenty-one," he describes himself, "long, spindling, a pair of gold-framed spectacles on his nose, his hair combed à la pompadour," having decided to be a newspaper man, made straight for their various offices.

It was April, 1892; "in a new spring suit," he says, . . . " light check trousers, bright blue coat and vest, brown fedora hat, new yellow shoes," he started out to force his way. He went the rounds, to be told each time by the city editor that there was nothing. Finally he decided that a small struggling paper might receive him. He picked the Daily Globe. He planned to sit in the outer office of that paper until someone noticed him. In this, too, instinct was with him. In Chicago in those days it was useful to be insistent like the Grand Canyon or Niagara Falls. Bold initiative in boys, in the face of rough repulses from their elders, was a virtue held high above others in this job-hunting, career-mad country. Stories of how the poor boy broke in and made good are favorite folk tales. It is told of a boy who later became a great financier, how, starting in one of the big packers' offices and tired of obscurity, he wore a purple and yellow striped sweater to business, until he was noticed and scolded and promoted. Dreiser used patience to break in. From twelve to two he sat in the outer office of the Daily Globe, waiting for the city editor to go to lunch, sometimes accosting him to hear the same words, " Nothing today, not a thing in sight." Finally, the copy reader, John Maxwell, with " hard, cynical and yet warm, grey eyes " got curious about him. What was he there for? How did he know he could write? Why did he pick the Globe, it was the poorest paper in town? Yes, that was why he had picked it. This got a laugh; he was told to stay around, the Democratic convention was coming soon, they might be able to use him. But it was a hell of a business to be wanting to get into.

So he entered that most American school of writing — the newspaper world. And Maxwell, because for some reason he liked him, took the trouble to be his first teacher, and his first cynic, being really in that day our one accredited native brand of cynic, the newspaper man. He cut and hacked to pieces his efforts with apparent glee, and yet, as he explained, to be good to him. " News is information," he would say, " people want it quick, sharp, clear, do you hear?" Or, " This is awful stuff, might be good for a book or something, but it's not news. You're a reporter, not an editor, don't forget it. . . . Who — What — How — When — Where — that's what they want!" Or he would grumble, " Life's a god-damned stinking treacherous game and ninety-nine men out of every hundred are bastards. I don't know why I do this for you . . . I don't expect to get anything back. . . . Nobody home when I'm knocking. But I'm such a god-damned fool that I like to do it. . . ." At this the wistful student would feel sad and uneasy, and yet tried with all courage to adjust himself to this life of his choice. " If I had a real chance," he told him, " I would soon show you."

The hazard came with the Democratic convention of 1892, and he slid through into a kind of success, an acknowledged newspaper man at $15 a week. Wandering " wretchedly " about the lobby of the Auditorium Hotel, loafing at the bar, looking for news, by chance he happened to flatter a senator from South Carolina into taking a fancy to him, into handing him a tip by which he made a scoop for his paper — the name of Cleveland, to be nominated for president. " In a day," he says, " by this small piece of news my stock had risen so that I was looked upon as an extraordinarily bright boy sure to carve out a future for himself, one to be made friends with and helped." And the senator had added to his sense of well-being by inviting him to drink a cocktail with him at a small table on the balcony of the hotel, grandly surveying the lake and the Michigan Avenue crowds. The convention itself thrilled him, a " vortex of national politics," and he was part of it, sitting in among famous reporters, George Ade, Peter Dunne, Charlie Seymour, Charles d'Almy. And soon he would be the equal of any of them, might even surpass them, now that he had gotten this far, why not?

17

> "*Here we have a Knife. It looks like a Saw, but it is a knife. . . . It belongs to an Editor. . . . There is Blood on the Blade of the Knife, but the Editor will Calmly Lick it off, and then the Blade will be as clean and Bright as ever.*"
>
> Eugene Field

In *A Book About Myself* and in *Twelve Men*, Dreiser has made portraits of the friends and encounters of his newspaper years, first in Chicago, then in St. Louis, Toledo, Cleveland, Pittsburgh and New York. Freed from the text they would place him as a skilled cartoonist, quite as his memories of childhood suggest the poet in him. They make his third series of groups since Warsaw and college days, more shifting than the others, but marked too by distinctive traits. These men had the tang of newspaper ink. They made a kind of brotherhood in the United States, with the same passwords, the same stories, the same code, the same pessimism; lovers of the low-down, the dirt, printers of what the public wants, what is fit to print; men leading double mental lives; men laughing, jeering inwardly at what outwardly they gave, and most often anonymously, to a world of breakfast eaters, and a world of families getting through the long dull evenings by drug of the afternoon papers.

A brotherhood and a double life, being marked with the same mark of duplicate ink, as cowboys were marked by life away from women, as labor leaders have been marked by a look of exalted failure, and quite as men in the trenches of the Great War feel the kinship of days when they were ordered over the top and never knew exactly why. These men were ordered out daily to get their story at any cost, every cost sometimes, and over the tears and frantic prayers of ravaged souls; ordered to pry, detect, bribe, go to any length to get their story before the other paper got it. Then when breathless they brought it in, they were ordered to make it over into what was fit to print; which in the case of the respectable papers was to tame it or at least to twist it, so the nice people might be still the heroes, and the rebels and profligates might be still the villains; or in the case of the yellow papers, to inflate it so that everyone might be equally sensational. In either case it was surely to confuse or deaden the issue so that the world might go along about as it had gone before, or anyway without detecting change, according to the politics, religion or commerce of the capital behind the paper.

So the hunters brought in their bags of warm lively stories, still breathing, wriggling, bodies not yet cold; saw them skinned and quartered and served up to the public as stews, the flavor cooked away under stereotype sauce No. 1 or No. 2. Yet they were privileged — indeed how prevent it — to save the blood and guts for themselves — who else wanted it? This, then, could be their visceral diet in hours off. Give so much as a morsel of it to the public, and they risked losing their jobs. They were cooks, these newspaper men, serving the public with tasteless meals, too watery, too sweet, too dry, too soggy; and yet what the readers liked; while they lived off the raw of what was left, no time to cook it, no time to make a ceremony of these vital bits.

Some of them unable to stomach a life of double nourishment, took to drink or dope, almost stopped eating. Others came around to finding the public fare easier to digest, cooked and served as it was after a fashion; and they succeeded in becoming managing editors, or publishers perhaps. Some spent spare hours with the heart, the kidneys, the nerves, the penis of these revelations of their daily work, trying to become poets or satirists of a high order. But there were snags. Forced to fool their readers, it was hard to keep the magnet needle of judgment and not to fool themselves. Then forced to speed things up, to deliver bleeding, to cut and hack, or cover up; no time to ripen impression or expression, they gained in speed, and lost in quality. At that, in the Nineties the newspapers beat the magazines for daring; adventurous brains went into the making of them. But for lack of time too much passed through them unresolved, putrefactive. Possessed of the facts of life more than others, they were yet prey to a miasma of class and mass opinion that veiled the facts. It was seldom that the clichés of the press did not block in their brains as definitely as they did in the printing room, defeating tough flexible intellect. They were men of irregular hours, irregular habits, belonging not to them but to the city editors. They lived and thought apart from others; more perceptive and more shocking. They were vagabonds, nearly shunned by others.

For one thing there was in each of these Western cities a vague quantity already known as society, with its society editors (the one woman on the staff except for an old maid or two who supplied a few dead words on literature and art). People struggled to be part of this vague myth, society, yet always furtively. The desire to enter, if revealed, would disqualify them, and the society editor was the alternate victim of insults and favors. So it was a joke among the irreverent reporters, this " soc-ed-stuff," as they called it. They jeered at it and yet it teased them too. It rankled. Who were these people to put on airs? The women dull beyond the dullest chorus girl, the men big stiffs! And yet they had something too; they had power, if nothing more than the right to be dull, the power to be mean, maybe even meaner than they themselves knew how to be. Christ! A good reporter could get in anywhere, into a hanging, a police court, an accident, a death chamber, a president's private office, an opera diva's dressing room; yet he couldn't get in here, often not even on business! He had the brains, the experience; he knew about life. What did these people have, so inane, so ignorant, really? Money, of course, but it was not only money. It was some divine right imported from the East. When you came down to it, it was cheek, nothing but cheek, the one thing these parents taught their children that seemed sweet and enticing. And it worked, they got away with it.

As they came in contact with this miracle, the newspaper men, crusaders of the Fact, were first puzzled, then irritated, then outwardly bored. What of it anyhow? Yet toward it they remained always slightly curious and resentful. Like education, like art, like the theatre, like men and women in these new cities, the mirage of " high society " by some puritan ineptness was doomed to segregation and suspicion, and the newspaper men developed a defensive mask toward it at the outset. They intensified rudeness, bad manners, feet on the desk, spitting, chewing, usually gum, going unshaven, wearing dirty clothes, and not first because they had to, but because they liked to. They gloried in it. Hell, it was a challenge to the whole god-damn stinking hypocritical disorder of society, with the nice pretty people at the top distilling the poison of cleanliness, respectability, down through the rest of it.

Some of them got to be radicals, famous radicals; some of them deepened into bums, tramps, hoboes, from city to city, paper to paper, no town worth devotion, suicide the best bet. There were those who had hobbies of books, pornography or the classics — a sporting editor in Chicago collected and read avidly the more obscene and obscure of the classics in Greek and Latin. But if any gentle scholar of the town thought that might make a bond between them, he could get to hell out of it with his nice English tepid ways. The same John Maxwell who initiated Dreiser into journalism became a student of the alleged Shakespeare ciphers. Years later he had completed a learned treatise about them, for which Dreiser, out of gratitude or out of interest, tried to help him find a publisher.

Yet others traveled in the wake of whatever war there was to far countries, and came back to their city editor, the brighter for unprintable exotic stories, and yet in slant and lingo unchanged. Some of them capitulated, and with their picturesque background as a lure " made good " with fashionable short stories and fashionable novels, to please the very world which in their newspaper days they loved to spit on. They graduated to that classier sphere, the magazine world, and got rich and fashionable themselves — a long list of them — the Irwins,

Irvin Cobb, Ray Stannard Baker, David Graham Phillips, are samples. Others, graduated through delicate native invention into the feature columns, the condiments of news — Eugene Field, George Ade, Peter Dunne, John McCutcheon, R. H. Little, Percy Hammond, among them. A few, a very few, have come all the way out into real letters, have gone into our speech, so bent they were on mulling over the heart, the nerves, the kidneys, the liver, the spawn of their storied days. One might say O. Henry has done this, and that Sinclair Lewis has done this. Above others and for years to come, I would say that Ring Lardner, Stephen Crane and Carl Sandburg have done this; one with an ear for human speech which is near to poetry; the other two with an ear for the elemental, with the springs of language at the source of their work.

Dreiser with an imperfect ear, imperfect sense of touch, with a marvelous eye, and a patient impatience has done this, come out into the world of letters, where not the story but the passion counts. There are those who say that he has not really left off chronicling, that he is in fact a "super-journalist," but one who has had to make and be his own newspaper in every department. This is stretching the simile; he never was quite one of them, his newspaper days amounting to but four years of his life. In that time he outstripped them in distrust of conventional morals; and none of their violent prejudices clung to him — their bashful scorn of art and learning as high-brow, and of fashionable society as the bunk. In a most un-American way he has not been ashamed of an interest in the fact of either realm, and has done his utmost to fit them as they changed into the changing puzzle of life. Perhaps he failed finally as a newspaper man just for a lack of these bitter prejudices; or else in order not to be hurried or directed; or because he was told to be funny or cheerful or diplomatic, when he wanted, or had to be, faithful. None the less he has traits of this Mid-West schooling, not in its love of brevity, but just in the way of a tang it gives of American newspaper ink.

Journalism had meaning a generation ago, and not

a trivial one: more than any other class its workmen stimulated opposite tendencies in this country. On the one hand they sidetracked readers to provincial sidings of thought, encouraged them to be backward and sentimental. On the other they kept alive among themselves the legendry of these states, low-down, dirty, sneering, lighted with the masculine horse-laugh — poetry stripped of sweetness, the meat and salt. It was a wild ferment of song and story out of prisons, whore houses, political rallies, salesmen's conferences, lonely ranches, lumber camps, mining towns, sporting events. And this loose Iliad, coarse in purpose, though often delicate in manner, was extravagant beyond the invention of other countries, because outstripping them in the need to compensate for repressions. It has been the undercurrent of comment, racing beneath the respectable crust, thrust slyly above in burlesque and vaudeville. It has kept the people alive. But for this elixir of ribaldry passing from one to another, I imagine that husbands and wives and business partners as well, dreaming apart, yet chained together, would long since have destroyed each other. Today a mild hint of it appears in the daily papers and in the books of the hour. When the last prude is dead, when it is time for another birth of giants to remind us of pioneers nearly gone, someone will piece these legends together and we will have our own archaic epic. It will not be a romance of the rose. It will be funny for dealing with a vast hypocrisy; it will be tragic for carving out chasms more lonely and immense than the canyon of the Colorado. Already Dreiser has approached it on the side of the horror involved, and Mark Twain on the side of the absurdity, but Mark Twain with the help of many more asterisks and blanks. Dreiser was the first, the publishers will tell you, to force them into the open.*

* A member of the firm of Harpers offered this as a fact: " Dreiser has historical meaning. He is the one man to have first created an audience for daring books."

18

The Chicago Globe: Maxwell, McEnnis, and Alice.

He had not been long on the Globe before he began to think of some quicker path to fame than that of reporter. He had found himself a room on the West Side in Ogden Place overlooking Union Square. His walk from there to the office took him through a district cheerfully known as slums. It occurred to him that these neglected patches might be as novel from the point of view of news as any foreign land where a star reporter might be sent for stories. He submitted articles, and they were run as Sunday specials under his name, with Theodore changed to Carl — a disappointment to him, but it was Maxwell's nickname for him.

" You know, Carl," at length Maxwell was praising him, " you have your faults, but you do know how to observe. . . . Maybe you're cut out to be a writer after all. . . . I think you're nutty, but I believe you're a writer." Then discussing further the aspects of the slums of different cities: " Jesus Christ, a hell of a fine novel is going to be written about these things one of these days." After that, Dreiser said, " he treated me with equality, and I thought I must indeed be a very remarkable man." While they talked, Stephen Crane, in New York, might have been writing *Maggie A Girl of The Streets,* and Frank Norris, in San Francisco, *McTeague,* both hell enough — young men of about Dreiser's age, but destined to shorter journeys, which today have more of value than of fame.

Carl Dreiser's Sunday specials featuring the Chicago slums were prophetic of Theodore Dreiser's volumes. They carried one of his burdens:

"Chicago's wretchedness," he explains, "was never utterly tame . . . or hang-dog . . . rather it was savage, bitter and at times larkish and impish. . . . Saloon lights and smells and lamps gleaming smokily from behind broken lattices and from below wooden sidewalk levels, gave it a shameless and dangerous color. Accordions, harmonicas, jew's harps, clattering tin-pan pianos and stringy violins were forever going; paintless rotting shacks resounded with a noisy blasphemous life between twelve and four; oaths, foul phrases. . . . In the face of such a scene, my mind, reared on dogmatic religious and moral theory, invariably paused in a question. . . . Why did nature, when left to itself, devise such astounding . . . human muck-heaps? . . . What had brought that about so soon in a new rich healthy forceful land? God or devil or both working together toward a common end? . . . I could not solve it. This matter of being with its differences . . ."

The query that perhaps this was not nature left to herself doing all this, but nature under the influence of St. Paul, Luther, Calvin, favoring passionless people, he makes at other moments, but not here.

In his second month of work on the Globe, he came under the influence of John T. McEnnis, managing editor: ". . . truly your Bret Harte gold-miner type, sloven, red-eyed at times, reminding me not a little of my brother Rome in his best hours . . . a man of great sweetness and sympathy . . . his nose and cheeks tinted a fiery red by much drinking . . . thought of as one of the most brilliant newspaper editors in St. Louis . . . whose wife, homely and pathetic, suffered anything to be allowed to live with him." A story that Dreiser made of a girl who had been kidnaped or had run away from the dreariest home he had yet seen was too romantic for Maxwell: "This will never do, Carl; read Schopenhauer, my boy, read Schopenhauer." But McEnnis praised it: ". . . I don't go much on this sort of thing . . . for a daily paper, but the way you have handled it is fine. . . . If you just keep yourself well in hand you have a future."

After that he was given more important assignments — among them, the showing up of a chain of fake auction shops — a political move, though he didn't know it, on behalf of the Irish politician and horse-racer back of the Globe. He describes himself as " open-mouthed " in these joints before the conspiracies of the auctioneers and their accomplices, thieves, policemen and detectives. To be for long periods an " open-mouthed " spectator, almost humble, and then suddenly to have to hit on some scheme that would bring him into the action — this appears to have made the repeated pattern of his history. In the handling of this campaign he became a small hero, he says, " the center of a hubbub of reform." He seemed to himself to be " swimming in a delicious sea of life." Already at twenty-one he could write; he would be famous.

The days of bickering with his father and sisters and brothers had been pushed behind him. Sometimes he went back to see them, but not often. Sometimes he remembered his father's words the night he had broken with the family home: " You're going, are you? I'm sorry, Dorsch. I done the best I could . . . I try, but it don't seem to do any good. I've prayed these last few days . . . I hope you don't ever feel sorry." The tone of the old German's voice, broken and with a kind of charm, haunted him, but not acutely then. In later years it must have recurred to him, when he was making the father of Jennie, the father of Aileen and the father of Isadore.

At this time he was engaged in the prime American pursuit, " getting on," and too in another quest, finding a girl to love, perhaps to marry. With us, rich or poor, distinguished or obscure, this creature a man finds for himself. Neither parents, nor priest, nor guardian will help him. Loveliness, then, is more often than not the test. With surprising care through many pages of *A Book About Myself,* Dreiser traces his first romance. It was not that by this time, that trivial deed so simple in fact, so direful in theory, that brief orgiastic moment for which or lack of which men and women have been made to pay with whole lives of ruin, had not already become fact to him. That small ingenuous delightful act was already among his memories. At fifteen, back in Warsaw with the insistent baker's daughter it had happened; and then afterwards in Bloomington and in Chicago with girls who made it easy for him. But he had not gone back to any of them, he had not " really cared for them." If asked, he answers carefully: " People might not believe it, and it *is* strange, considering the name I have when it comes to women; but I tell you, it's the truth, there always had to be some romance about it, or it meant nothing to me, some mental or chemic flare, something personal, spiritual you might say." — " And that is hard to find," I said. — " I have never really found it, nothing lasts, nothing is perfect."

At twenty-one he found romance in Alice, the girl of the Christmas Eve party of the year before. She lived with a foster father, a railroad watchman, in a second story flat in a small cottage on the southwest fringe of the city. He remembers the furnishings: red plush hangings in the folding doors between the two rooms, lace curtains and white shades at the windows, a piano, " a most soothing luxury for me to contemplate," a red velvet settee, a red plush rocker, and though not mentioned, it seems as if there must have been a vase of bright paper flowers on a painted stand — all out of the watchman's savings and her taste. Beside the green and brown corduroys and denims of the correct houses of the Nineties, lace, red plush and velvet, Latin bequeathals, however degenerated, still lived among the middle classes and in sporting houses — a faint perverted hint of Venus not prized in the United States.

In Alice's flat on South 47th Street, she used to play the piano for her Hoosier lover, and on the red velvet settee he held her and caressed her. Sometimes she danced for him " a running overstep clog, sidewise to and fro, her skirts lifted to her shoe tops." Or they met for dinner in the downtown crowds. Or Sundays they would go to a concert, or an Ethical Culture sermon, and later to Jackson Park, where she would plan what her wedding dress and slippers and veil were going to be, and he would half wonder whether they would ever be married. Once, he says, they threw some pillows on the floor and she begged him to love her recklessly, almost hoping perhaps that if a child came of it, that would bind him; but he thought it was wrong . . . " not quite fair." Twenty-five years later he troubles to reason this back and forth as if talking to himself. He supposes that had he been " desperately in love," he would have been " willing to starve her on twenty dollars a week." He never saw her, he says among these recollections of editors, politicians and reporters, " as anything but . . . a delicate almost perfect creature to love and cherish." It was not that he thought less of Alice, but more of himself. He was beginning to be fortunate. There was his victory of the fake auctioneer war. And there was another girl, of one of the " best " or anyway " better " families, he had met on his reporter's rounds — " A little blonde, very sleek and dreamy," not too snobbish to " go with him." She was less compelling than Alice, " too lymphatic and carefully reared," but she was " better dressed and better placed." She was a hint of a world he might sometime join if he kept himself unentangled — a world he had so often envied from the outside, as he passed its prosperous lawns and houses, its " strutting youth in English suits," its " high-headed girls in flouncy lacy dresses," at their croquet and tennis games. " To me, in my life-hungry, love-hungry state, this new rich prosperity with its ease, its pretty women and its efforts at refinement . . . set me to riotous dreaming and longing. . . ." To this extent the young man of *An American Tragedy* is Dreiser of the Nineties, just as, one imagines, Balzac remembers himself in the hero of *La Peau de Chagrin*.

Many reviewers of *A Book About Myself* have censored him for " shameless confession," or laughed at him for thinking that readers would be interested in a boy and girl of so long before in so drab a setting. In this they were ignoring his belief that there is no such thing as common place or common time or common people, if and when wired by drama. With the picture of Alice herself, one imagines, this type of reviewer had no quarrel. She is that forebearing, delicious, dependent creature that has made The Saturday Evening Post a king of magazines; and a great nation of he-men, young and old, hurries of a Thursday to the stands to get repeated news of her. She is, as are variations of her in other stories of his, very like the eternal nymph, whom movie favorites are yet registering for a public of tired business men. The shocking difference is that Dreiser himself was not the one-hundred-per-cent hero that would yield the happy ending for Alice, and create the ideal story for a candy-eating public.

19

Going, with the go-getters.

In November, five months after he had started his newspaper training, McEnnis advised him to leave the Globe. It was not a big enough field for him: "A great paper like the St. Louis Globe Democrat or the New York Sun starts a boy off right. I would like to see you go first to St. Louis and then to New York." So the story runs true to the fable of those picked for a race and a fight. He was never quite without someone who cared what happened to him. And, too, he worked fabulously. These five months read like a year or more in compressed achievement. McEnnis was true to his scheme. On a Tuesday a telegram arrived from St. Louis: "You may have reportorial position on this paper at twenty dollars a week, beginning next Monday. Wire reply."

What to do? There was Alice, there was Chicago now familiar and dear to him. He asked McEnnis, whose advice was: "Go? Of course go! . . . You will be working on one of the greatest papers and under one of the greatest editors that ever lived. . . . Hand in your resignation now. . . . And go Sunday. . . . I'll give you some letters that will help you."

They called themselves sons-of-guns, these self-made men. (The slogan was "Go"!) When they were young they went; when they were older they coached others to go. They were shot out to new jobs, new horizons, more pay, more life. Or they shot out to new countries, new victories, new deaths, like the last of these zealots, the doughboys in the Great War, and Lindbergh and his followers encircling the earth. Dreiser obeyed the contagion of the time. He went. He wondered what to do about Alice, left it till Saturday to say goodbye. Then after dinner with McEnnis, he hurried to her house; she was not there. The next morning speeding south toward St. Louis through the "wide flat yards adjacent to her home . . . a driving rain outside . . . I could see the very windows and steps by which we had so often sat." He thought he couldn't stand it. He would write to her and beg her to come, "to be his mistress perhaps, if not his wife." But he didn't write. Once in St. Louis, new problems annihilated loneliness.

"One gloomy December afternoon," he records, "in the reportorial room of the St. Louis Globe Democrat," a letter came from Alice asking for her letters back; he wouldn't want them now. Then, a postscript: "I stood by the window last night and looked out on the street. The moon was shining and those dead trees over the way were waving in the wind. I saw the moon on that little pool of water in the field. It looked like silver. Oh, Theo, I wish I were dead." Again, he says, he found himself on the two horns of his ever recurring dilemma. To think he could have left her. Of course she wished she were dead. But could he support her and himself too as he must now in his new position and with his new friends? Did he love her enough to make the sacrifice? He wasn't sure. And yet "this loss of honor and happiness!"

"I sat looking into the face of the tangle as one might into the gathering front of a storm. Words moved in my brain and then marshalled themselves into curious lines and rhythms. . . . Presently I saw that I was writing a poem but that it was rough. . . . I was in a great fever to change it . . . but more eager to go on with my idea, which was about this tangle of life." Could anyone describe better the drift and mood of Dreiser in relation to language? He would like it to be perfectly related to the thought, and yet is even more eager to be on with his ideas, which are forever about this baffling and irresistible tangle of life.

While he was writing, Bob Hazard, one of his new friends, looked over his shoulder: "What you doing, Dreiser, writing poetry? . . . There's no money in it. . . . You can't sell 'em. I've written tons of 'em, but it don't do any good. You'd better be putting your time on a book or a play." — "I know it isn't profitable," Dreiser persisted. "Still it might be if I wrote them well enough." Hazard smiled. Yet newspaper men did write poetry. Sullivan, the first managing editor on the Globe, had showed him poems of his in the "Whittier-Longfellow manner," and he had been sure he could do better and would some day. But now the thought of a novel or play, and for Hazard to suggest them as within his power, was tonic. In this creative mood he had nearly forgotten Alice. Finally he wrote her he still loved her and wanted to keep her letters, and if later he was "better placed financially," he would come back, but as he wrote the fear haunted him that he would not keep his word. Some months later a final letter came from Alice, saying she would be married the next day at noon, " unless — unless something happened." He let nothing happen. He knew, he writes, that "Alice in spite of my great sadness and affection for her was nothing more than a passing bit of beauty. . . . I was sad for her and for myself, saddest because of that chief characteristic of mine and of life which will not let anything endure permanently. . . . I was too restless, too changeful." So he was far from being the ideal hero and has as ruthlessly confessed it for himself as for other heroes of his stories. Ring Lardner, alone, has managed to circulate in the popular magazines as slippery a brand of hero, to disappoint and pique a hard-drink, soft-drink public. But Lardner's salesmen, prize fighters, base ball players and song writers, are less crucial, being less conscious of themselves than was this young reporter of *A Book About Myself*.

Dreiser, undoubtedly, would have it understood that he for one is a savage, tenderly reminiscent, but with the need to junk romance, or anyway to sacrifice one reality to another in pursuit of power, and sometimes of mere variety. Take it or leave it, this was his nature, and he felt that he was not alone in it; there had always been and always would be men and women of this necessity. For himself he appears to have appeased tenderness through tearful pity of the suffering around him and through little souvenirs, like Alice's postscript, of the quieter people he had felt forced to break with. His early scribbled poems he has since destroyed, but has twice preserved the memento of Alice standing by the window and wishing she were dead. It is quoted in *A Book About Myself* and before that it is used in *The 'Genius'* at the close of an incident in the life of Witla, similar in its beginning to Dreiser's life.

20

"St Louis: A diamond in a dirty shirt."
ROBERT INGERSOLL

The managing editor of the St. Louis Globe Democrat, John B. McCullagh, was for his new reporter all that McEnnis had said — " a real force, a great man." Through him he learned to feel the meaning of journalism for good or evil in the life of the nation. He had built up a paper in the easy-going indolent Southwest that had significance both here and abroad. He was " a kind of god " to his readers, natives of Texas, Iowa, Missouri, Arkansas, Southern Illinois, as he was to his own staff — a man to work for and up to. Dreiser makes a vivid portrait of him in his book of newspaper days, which revels in detail and moves like a novel:

> ". . . In that small office . . . waist-deep among his papers, his heavy head sunk on his pouter-like chest, his feet encased in white socks and low slipper-like shoes. . . . A solitary or eccentric . . . a few years later he leaped to his death from the second story window of his home . . . out of sheer weariness, I assume, tired of an inane world."

His paper was of necessity conventional — he liked to have it referred to as " the great religious daily " — and yet it had thrust and character. His own sentences " cracked like a whip; the paragraphs exploded at times, burst like a torpedo." He reads like one of those compensating tempers, who can make acceptable fairy stories, that yet convey the sense of life. Indeed if ever the human race struggles out into sunlight — no taboos, no superstitions — the loss will be in the old cleverness of ciphers, in the polite forms of whatever etiquette is in fashion to veil the truth. We may then be homesick for the masquerades of the past. Yet this editor was bored enough with them all to commit suicide. " Ursine rather than leonine," Dreiser describes him, " with keen grey eyes under bushy brows," and he had been a war correspondent with Farragut on the Mississippi, with Sherman in the Civil War.

Under his spell, which was the spell of American enterprise — the magic of new fantastic playgrounds of commerce — Dreiser "made good" for a time, and joined in the antics. At first, it was routine reporting, the covering of "a murder, a failure, a defalcation, a wedding, a banquet, a ball." Soon in addition he was given a column to write, "Heard in the Corridors." The work took him the rounds of the hotels and stations, gave him license to write more as he liked, to invent interviews with imaginary guests; and, too, it brought him in contact with a range of celebrities and charlatans. To each one, theosophists, spiritualists, mind readers, evangelists, " quack novelists," statesmen, scientists or musicians he would ask his favorite question — what did they think about life? Often he knew little of their import, but then Mitchell, the city editor, seemed to know less. With a " height of six feet, one and one-half inches," weighing only one hundred and thirty-seven pounds " with no particular blemish " except for " one eye turned slightly outward," and crowded upper teeth and " a general homeliness of feature "; his body " blazing with sex " and desire for " supremacy," Dreiser describes himself at twenty-one. This was the boy who made his way as best he could to audiences with Annie Besant, the Reverend Sam Jones, Eva Fay, John L. Sullivan, Hall Caine, Henry Watterson, Paderewski, Nikola Tesla, asking always the same question — what do you think about life?

What fixed his standing on the paper, and not long after he had come to it, was again as in Chicago a matter of luck. Though dealing so often with the tragedy of others, always he insists on his own good luck: " I always got the breaks." The breaks this time lay in the fact of a big wreck on the road near Alton, reported to him one morning before anyone else had come to the office: " If you people get up there right away you can get a big lead on this." With a note to the city editor and advice to send an artist after him, he went without waiting for orders. He " had never seen a big wreck, it must be wonderful." It did surpass all concepts of frightfulness. It engulfed him in horror and yet it was his big chance and he took it. McCullagh acknowledged the scoop with a raise of five dollars and a twenty-dollar bill and the words, "You have done a fine piece of work." He was a real newspaper man at last, his Napoleonic dreams might in fact come true. Soon after in the event of a vacancy he asked boldly to be made dramatic editor, and McCullagh said, "You're dramatic editor. Tell Mr. Mitchell (the city editor) to let you be it." More than any other chronicle of Dreiser's, this newspaper epic breathes the romance, nearly finished now, that went on for so many years in this country, between older and younger men, outstripping the romance that has gone on between men and women here, because more sanctioned and better understood.

In addition to being an apprentice in the business of learning about life through the ludicrous, cruel, and yet immediate method of journalism, he became too for the first time an apprentice in Bohemia, or in such would-be Bohemia as St. Louis afforded. This paper, unlike the Chicago Globe, had an art department. The mere word "art" had always beguiled him. The men here seemed to him distinctive and unconventional, two of them especially — Dick Wood, with wrist watch, cabalistic scarf pin, boutonnière of violets; and P. B. McCord, the "Peter" of *Twelve Men,* cordial and virile, with "tramp-like hair and whiskers." They had a studio together in an old quarter of the town into which exclusive aura they admitted Dreiser, Wood indulgently, McCord at once on equal terms. Their friendship, he says, lasted for years until Peter's death and to him he owes " some of his sanest views of life."

With these two and their circle of wayward souls, admitted because they burned with some fever of living disreputably or creatively, he felt that he had entered on a plane above poverty or wealth. They chattered till morning about art and artists, read their manuscripts to each other, strolled about the dark quarters of the town with mandolin, banjo and flute, or frequented the dives of Chinatown and the underworld. Wood delighted in their lingo and color, and was gathering notes to be made into tales that would recreate the lilt of life among such outlaws as thieves, pimps, dope fiends, murderers, and immigrants from the Orient. He had an eerie gift for making friends with these strangers and could retell whole passages out of their lives. With more stability Dreiser thinks he might have succeeded. I would almost say in a different land he might have succeeded. In a land where any race of another color becomes associated with " evil " and " filth," as it is called, what chance is there to give strangeness and dissolution their separate values? However silly and abortive Wood was, Dreiser records that he owed to him " poignant moods " that revealed " the beauty and romance of many strange places."

Then there were others on the paper, Jock Bellairs, posted at the Four Courts with other reporters to give first news of crime or accident — a bottle of whiskey in his pocket, a game of cards going on; a girl or two of one or the other reporters. And Rodenberger, whom Dreiser virtuously saved one day from suicide by dope, after alcohol, and was not thanked for it.

And then Bob Hazard, who with another man had already completed a novel which " could never be published in the United States " — " a direct outcome of Zola and Balzac, the scene laid in France even," since " such things as interested these two occurred only in France . . . or if done here were never spoken of." Dreiser calls this first novel he ever read in manuscript " the opening wedge for him into the realm of realism." It went deep in him, both because of the freshness of these boys who " burned to present life as they saw it," and because of their certainty that it was useless in 1892 to send the story to an American publisher. That struck him as curious at the time, but as the years went on he was to remember it as a tragic American fact. The book was never published. Ten years later the gay irresistible Hazard blew his brains out, leaving a brilliant newspaper job and a wife and child in Washington. " The other man," a friend writes him years later, " was killed in an opium joint (his baby died the same night)." So Dreiser's pages gleam with fateful rockets.

His own desire to write something real, he says, was fixed from this hour. He decided on a play as a form that seemed easier to him (" and still did after thirty years ") than a novel. His work as dramatic critic encouraged him in this; also his ever increasing desire for riches and luxury, every trace of which he envied as he went on his rounds and compared the grandeur of hotels and clubs and mansions and commercial offices to the squalor of districts where " the unsuccessful " lived. The plays that came to St. Louis, the best of them from Jones, Pinero, Augustus Thomas, were most of them saccharine and unreal, filled with the cruel rich, honest working men, betrayed daughters, splendid reforms, happy moral endings. But for him he confesses they had glamour — love made insidiously romantic by boudoirs and drawing rooms and expensively beautiful actresses. And he felt too that none of this was to be had in St. Louis; the home of it was New York or Paris or London. With McCord and Wood he discussed his dreams. Comic opera was probably the quickest and most gaudy path to success. He mapped out a scenario — a cranky Indiana farmer by magic transported back among the Aztecs of Mexico, and becoming a despot there. He wrote a rough draft of it, Peter made designs for scenes and costumes, and acted out some of the comedy for the other two. Dreiser was delirious with imagined success. And yet too the thing seemed not quite real to him. Others arrived by fantastic easy roads, but more than likely nothing so sweet was meant for him.

21

Last years of apprenticeship: new alliances.

The days passed now in bigger responsibilities — the covering of an important murder trial, a flood, a train robbery, and then the hurrying to his duties as dramatic editor. McCullagh liked him and still fascinated him. He was being sent out of town now, and might in time, he believes, have become a star correspondent, once, he had thought, a pinnacle of achievement. But newspaper work began to seem insufficient. For one thing, what did it have to do with art or with the kind of life he hoped some time to lead? Take the mere matter of dramatic criticism. McCullagh had small interest in it or he would not have trusted it to a young reporter, and coupled it with other work at that. Here Dreiser was the non-conformist; few Americans would have put criticism ahead of news in importance. It seemed to him, too, that Mitchell, the city editor, resented him and purposely gave him assignments that made the theatre work nearly impossible. One night in April, sent out of town to cover a hold-up, he had taken a chance and written notices beforehand of three plays scheduled to open in St. Louis that night. But because of washouts on the road none of them had arrived. The morning Globe printed his profuse praise of nothing, and the afternoon papers delighted in laughing at their eminent competitor.

The new dramatic critic, ashamed to face anyone, left a note on McCullagh's desk of gratitude and regret, trying to explain how it had happened, but taking the blame, he says; and then fled jobless to his rooms rather than wait to be fired. Disgraced in St. Louis, he must, he supposed, try his luck in another city, but first he had to make enough money to go. This need landed him a job on the Republic at eighteen dollars a week under another forceful editor, H. B. Wandell, without the greatness of McCullagh, but with a mania for the story, especially when it involved horror or scandal. Zola first and Balzac and then Loti were his models. Hugo and Dickens were invoked at times. No commonplace rendering was permitted. The paper must throb with human interest or with "cold hard pictures." He exhorted his reporters to read Zola and make "the drab and the gross and the horrible" drip with life. It is interesting that Dreiser, who is often alleged to have derived from Zola, says here that he never read him, not until after his own first novel, *Sister Carrie*. But in Wandell's presence he dared not admit it. He believes the Republic was a better place for him than the Globe Democrat. It gave him more scope for writing, in fact taught him how to write. On this paper he became important; Wandell often asked his advice as to engaging new men, and would take him away from work just to eat and drink and gossip about great literature, for which he had "the strangest, fussiest, bossiest love."

In these days he obeyed orders. He was told to write comedy for a summer charity drive which involved a fat-lean baseball series — he, who had never written anything funny in his life, nor even cared to make people laugh. He managed to get away with it; for five weeks or more he was a comic hit in the minds of Republic readers. His stock rose to the point of his being sent to Chicago as the paper's correspondent, with a party of school teachers selected by a state voting contest to visit the World's Fair of 1893 at the Republic's expense.

For all his subversive power, Dreiser has not been fatally disturbed by the flatulence of American methods of money making — to which fact undoubtedly he owes his chance of survival within it. Sensitive to its hypocrisy and banality, but not quite to the vulgarity of it, even in his proudest later days, he has not been a complete exile. Often he has joined in, and for that knows our commercial life from the inside more fairly than those who have been defeated by it. He went off with the school teachers in a holiday spirit, a trifle dampened by the Methodist look of the agent who was to direct the party, but rather fancying the superintendent of schools, acting as chaperon, who had " big soft ruddy hands decorated with several rings," and helped to put him at his ease among the girls. Before they were far out in their special Pullman, alive with " young buxom Missouri school teachers . . . as attractive as their profession would permit," he had lost shyness and was captivated by so many prize winners. " Look where I would I seemed to find a new type of prettiness confronting me." And why not? Here they were, sacrificed to making more inane and more popular the columns of the Republic; and yet how young, how blooming, not a wrinkle, giggling, blushing, exuberant in their prettiest clothes on a paid-for vacation — and he the one young man among them. A Greek goatherd never wrote of satyric dreams more lustfully than Dreiser remembers his school teachers in their plush and polished Pullman. A leading man caught archly among chorus girls is not his equal in zest. You may say his memory is gawky and ingenuous, but it has a touch of Stravinsky's *Sacré du Printemps,* before the dancers turn their black garments of grief to the audience.

Out of the bouquet he picked five or six incidentally, and two especially, Miss Ginnity and Miss W. to see the Fair with by turns — again the reckless brunette and the more aloof blonde, this time red-headed. Out of these, the blonde remained with him through years of excitation and then of marriage. She was his second romance, more skilful and less forbearing than Alice. If in the end she never turned the black coat of tragedy on him, it was a grey drab mantle anyway that amounted to gloom — a thing to escape from. Yet it was not really this dainty creature with " stark red braids " to crown " a flowerlike face and almond eyes," whom in later years he came to resent; it was what she stood for with rigid strength — monotony, conformity, routine — when he had imagined she stood only for something above him, more fragile and exquisite than he was, and entirely personal. In the Wooded Island of the exotic World's Fair, in the light of fireworks around the Court of Honor, which created, it is said, the splendor and elegance of older places than Chicago, the young man dallied with his school teachers, one so ardent and primitive, the other entangling and difficult to reach. Being difficult enhanced her value; he must reach her, even marry her if possible. Then, too, there was her sister Rose, who came to join them, more lively than Sarah. She might suit him better. Certainly he must not lose track of these two.

The weight of deciphering, however, was not yet heavy on him. Back in St. Louis he entered the race again — getting ahead of the other reporter when he could, desolate when he couldn't,* ferreting out secrets of lives even to the ruin of them, when the news exacted it. And he grew in prestige. In these days once out of the office he wore, he says, to please romance, a long military coat, a Stetson hat, gloves, a cane, soft pleated shirts; and would go thus to court Sarah of the World's Fair, when she came to visit her aunt from the place where she taught in the country. He says of her:

> "There was something of the wood or water nymph about her, a seeking in her eyes, a breath of wild winds in her hair, a scarlet glory to her mouth. . . . St. Louis took on a glamor which it had never before possessed. . . . If only this love affair could have gone on to a swift fruition it would have been perfect, blinding. . . . But love as it is in most places was a slow process. . . . There must be many visits before I could even place an arm on her. . . . Well, I reached the place where I could hold her hand, put my arms about her, kiss her, but never could I induce her to sit in my lap."

Instead she fanned in him an idolatrous passion, and like a staunch servant of society held him off, secured with the ring he had bought her. Over long months she held him thus, straining toward an income sufficient to pay for the hour when lust and love might be legally one.

In these days too there came to St. Louis other visitors, his brothers E. and A. as he calls them, because he thought that they should by now graduate from driving laundry wagons and working in shoe stores. With his new prestige he would find jobs for them in St. Louis. But they came and had to go back to Chicago without jobs, tired, as they said, of St. Louis, a "hell of a place, a third rate city."

* Chapter 64 of *A Book About Myself* and a *Story of Stories* in *Free and Other Stories* repeat one climax of this.

And there came also his favorite brother Paul, the ballad maker, "stout, gross, sensual," and yet a fountain of delicacy; the one member of his family who, not understanding him, yet caught the drift of his aims. He saw his face one day on a billboard, starring in a clap-trap melodrama, *The Danger Signal.* Now after years of absence he loved him anew not because he had to, not because Paul knew more of life than he did — in fact he decided rather less — but because " he reminded me a great deal of my mother," like her, " wonderful and tender." Speaking of him Dreiser reveals a novel basis of values: ". . . he was full of simple middle class tenderness, and middle class grossness — all of which I am free to say I admire. . . . *After all, we cannot all be artists, statesmen, generals, thieves or financiers."*

It was a delight to have this brother to show off to Wood, McCord, Hazard, and the others, and he took his fiancée to meet him. Paul gave him a box for the show, in which he was a comic switchman, and sang one of his own songs, *The Bowery,* for which unquestionably he was famous. He came back with the party to the younger brother's rooms for supper, by now as much a center of life as McCord's and Wood's. The week ended in what he hoped would be a " glorious dinner at Faust's," in honor of Paul, to which he had invited not only his more Bohemian friends, but the executives of his office, Wandell, Williams, indeed everyone he liked. He was bitterly disappointed when these diverse elements, dear to him, refused to blend; "it was all such a fizzle that I could have wept," he remembers. That one's picked friends should not be friends is one of the dreary discords on the way up the ladder of sophistication.

During a week of breakfasts with the comedian, he was to hear constantly of New York, the place for him to go if he was to compete with equals. Chicago would never do. Journalists from the East had told him the same thing, but he like a true mid-Westerner had been loyal to Chicago. Now his brother was weaving the spell of New York. He began to believe. But what of his fiancée? What did Paul think of her? " Well, she is charming, but if I were in your place I wouldn't marry anyone yet." At this time John Maxwell came from Chicago looking for a job, and gave him rougher advice. Looking at her picture he said: " ' Have you any idea how old she is? ' — ' Oh, about my age.' — ' Oh hell, she's older than that. . . . Along with this, she's one of these mid-Western girls, all right for life out here, but no good for the newspaper game or you. I've been through that myself. . . . She belongs to some church, I suppose? ' — ' Methodist,' I replied ruefully — ' I knew it! But I'm not knocking her; I'm not saying she isn't pretty and virtuous, but . . . she's older and narrower. . . . In three or four years you will have children, and you'll get a worried, irritated point of view. Take my advice. Run with girls if you want to, but don't marry. . . .' " Dreiser for a second almost believed this rude tutor, and " yet the delirious meetings went on and on." And the days went on, crying to him the need of hurry, if he was to count.

Marriage or not, he must make more money. With all his progress he was getting only twenty-three dollars a week and The Republic seemed in no mood to give more. And then somehow he must be on to New York. At this point there came a proposal from a young man for whom he had little respect, to start with him a country weekly in his town, Grand Rapids, Ohio; there would be money in it. Without confidence in the scheme, at least it would be an escape for him. He would look the ground over, and if there was nothing to it, push on from there, not back to St. Louis. He gave up his position on the Republic, finally to be offered a raise. But it was too late, he was booked for a change. In a farewell meeting with Miss W. he gave desperate pledges, that as soon as he could he would live with her the life she dreamed of, " in a modest home with children and money enough for a few needs . . . eventually to die and to be buried respectably." And yet at that moment a voice said to him that his destiny would be different from that — not so sad maybe; and " that any beautiful woman would satisfy " him. With a letter of endorsement from Wandell which, however, in the next years of wandering, quixotically he never used — he was afraid he could not live up to it — he packed his bags and said goodbye to what he thinks of now as his years of apprenticeship.

He discusses their influence. When he came to St. Louis already he was " not an ethically correct and moral youth." Perhaps he would not have lied, at least in big matters, or have stolen after his one experience in Chicago, and would not today " under ordinary circumstances do this." But already he felt that there was and could be no strict justice as between men and women. He had noticed that the women often did not want it, and that the world of youths at least was busy with " libertinage." They boasted of it and got away with it. He had no thought yet that he might be punished for it or even censored; others were not. And yet from his bringing up he was still " swashing around among the idealistic maxims of Christ and . . . the religionists generally, and contrasting them hourly . . . with the selfish materialism of the day as [he] saw it." He watched the poor and he watched the rich, and couldn't help indicting society for the fierce differences between them, and wishing he could " flail " the strong and comfort the weak with the Beatitudes and the Sermon on the Mount. He calls himself at twenty-one " a poetic melancholic crossed with a vivid materialistic lust for life." When he left St. Louis a year and three months later, hardened by a more factual philosophy, he was beginning to think that there was a law of life which was never to agree with the beautiful and " helpless " poetry of Christ. The realism out of his newspaper schooling was returning him this verdict, at variance with Christian dogma, which had divided the world into enemy groups, and had nicknamed them idealists and cynics, ignoring the original Greek meaning of these terms. Dreiser became accurately neither one nor the other, but rather a believer in what his eyes dictated — belief in the irrepressible spring of life, which by moments lifted some people and broke others.

22

The outside world: walking up and down in it.

A few days in the wintry triviality of an Ohio village cured him of running a country paper. He was not fitted for it. They told him that these small towns were soon going to be lively manufacturing centers. Many people would come, and they would get rich there. He knew enough of the trend of industry to believe it; America was on its way to " material triumphs." But then as always the thought was like lead to him. What use in these riches unless they could be translated into the splendors of art and the wisdom of artists, as a way of life? That might happen in New York, his brother had said it was happening, but perhaps never in Ohio. Besides, they told him, " We are a religious and hard working people — any newspaper here has got to take that into account." He was not the one to do it.

Here by " a charming river," he says, " I paused for a few days, and took stock of my life." His youth was behind him, and he could think of nothing ahead of him more definite than the same vague poignant ambitions that had always driven him. He then took his " first, free and unaided flight into the unknown," which landed him in Toledo. Strolling about this city, again he was stung by the contrast between rich and poor districts — " The spacious lawns, the shuttered and laced windows! The wonder of evening fires in winter! The open cool and shadowed doors in summer! Swings and hammocks . . . ! "

Children brought up in the smugness of such houses with their shameless yards open to the world, with their cruel plate-glass windows, their flaccid family life, or at least those sensitive enough to curse these dwellings as if they were prisons, will find it hard to understand the part they had in the dreams of a boy shut out from it all. He sings poems over the polish of the brass, the cleanliness of the lace, the accuracy of each monstrous cream-colored window shade pulled half way down, the fragrance of sidewalks and stone steps hosed by gardeners in June. He is the reminiscent poet of the " residences " of the Nineties.

But it is not to laugh. They are lyrics that half tell the story of the failure of our country to delight the soul, psyche of the five senses. The rich achieved these prosperous shells. The poor, permitted nothing except a few parks, where they had to keep off the grass, and saloons for men and " bad women," too tough to give a sense of ease, worked and slaved and schemed for what? For these very mausoleums, brass, lace, glass, bushes, grass, molasses-oaken doors and all, which they knew from the outside alone. And if they had gotten in, there was nothing more mysterious to know except further evidences of prosperity. From that day to this, when a president was hailed into office on the shoulders of that one word, Prosperity; exteriority of ever more shining surfaces has been the Grail. Dreiser with his usual candor admits the lure it had for him. Indeed, it was not until he had traveled to Europe at forty and had seen for himself the scheme of life in France and Italy, that he could be a colder critic of our code. Then he noticed the open voids almost obscenely public beyond these exclusive doors.*

In Latin countries a beguiling program motivated all grades of living, half mystic, half sensual, deriving from the Virgin and Venus, tempered in France by a spirit wrung from the revolution — every one Monsieur, Madame, Mademoiselle. And it varied not so much in design, chiefly in price. In houses humble and rich the same form of dinner, accompanied by wine, from soup to black

---

* " ' Ma! Ma! Have you got an undershirt in there for me? ' — I looked out to see . . . a man of sixty . . . intelligent and forceful looking, a real American business chief. ' Yes,' came the answer, ' wait a minute. I think there's one in Ida's satchel. Is Harry up yet ' — ' Yes, he's gone out.' This was six A.M. Here stood the American in the pretentious hall, suspenders down, meekly importuning his wife through the closed door." From a chapter called An American Summer Resort in *A Hoosier Holiday*.

coffee and liqueur, was understood. Restaurants and cafés served the different classes with nearly equal form and mystery. This was balm to mind and body. There was an order out of it animated by wit. But in the United States we were forced to get prosperous or be damned. Ease and enjoyment have been their virtues; ambition and activity have had to be ours.

Dreiser, the native, instinctively knew them as required virtues, and felt the dark bleak passageways where the shuttle of ambition worked ceaselessly back and forth. I think one can't understand the racial drift of his writings, without realizing how these " exclusive " districts have affected the excluded. Nor understand intolerants like Poe and Ambrose Bierce, without being faced with these facts of cleavage of the high from the low, and emptiness above. Now one hears it like a hymn of praise — native radio, automobile, movie, frigidaire, clothes, bungalows and apartments open at all prices to all classes! But as in Toledo, Ohio, in 1894, isn't it the same Divinity dictating this; and not Sex, not Art,* not Learning, as the young wanderer from St. Louis was hoping; not primarily Speed or Daring, as for a while it promised to be; but more and more firmly Respectability measured by Money, ruling through Comfort? The whir of life has not yet come to inhabit the " ideal home " furnished with these products. It remains back in the offices, and factories and power plants that produce them, and will remain there until Americans frayed and jaded turn from relations of people to things, to cultivate relations with one another. *An American Tragedy* is a summary of this.

Yet in these years Dreiser was still hopeful of a society held together by pleasures of body and mind. And in Toledo, applying for a job on the leading morning paper, he found in the city editor who engaged him, one of the " intellectual experiences " of his life — Arthur Henry: " A small cherubic individual, with a complexion of milk and cream, light brown hair and a serene blue eye." At once they gossiped about Chicago of the White-

---

* Except as in native music, women's underwear, and machinery, especially automobiles; hastily sex begins to rule in the first two, and art in machinery.

chapel Club Days, where one had known and the other known of Eugene Field, Peter Dunne, Ben King. They were at the moment linked spiritually, would have married, Dreiser says, if Henry had been a girl. Their friendship lasted for years "through storm and disillusionment." Arthur Henry was the spur to his first short story, and then to his first novel, *Sister Carrie*. Today Henry remembers their first meeting as vividly as he is remembered:

"I am vague as to dates — but I was city editor of the Toledo Blade when I first met Dreiser. I looked up from my desk one hectic day and saw him beside me. He was lank and tall. Nothing satirical in his eyes then — just a burning eagerness. We were in the midst of violent street car strikes. I had just received word that the company was about to start a strike-breaking car over the route and I had no one to send at the moment for so dangerous a consignment. The young man — gaunt, rugged, a little dishevelled and dusty from his travels, was asking for a job and I dispatched him five minutes after his entrance. He rode with the car and returned with a story. I read it, rushed it to the composing room, hovered over it and read the proof myself so that no loyal proof-reader could carry it to the Owners of the paper and have it killed or changed. It was a great story and nearly lost me my job. Dreiser and I were about the same age — both young — all enquiring and fearless. What did the loss of a job amount to compared to the birth of a great story and the finding of a perfect friend?"

For a while, after long lunches and dinners together, they were forced to separate, since there was no permanent place to be had on the paper. Dreiser went on to Cleveland, where again he was struck by the residences of the rich — "wide lawns and iron or stone statues of stags and dogs and deer." Here these were the homes of multimillionaires, John D. Rockefeller, Tom Johnson, Henry M. Flagler. He got work on the Cleveland Leader doing Sunday stories, about a new style of grain boat, turtleback, about a model chicken farm near the city. But at three dollars a column this was inadequate. So on again, this time to Buffalo, to find nothing to that except a trip to Niagara. James Oppenheim tells in one of his poems how he and Dreiser were looking one evening at an amazing sunset over the Hudson River, and Oppenheim said,

"Could you describe that, Dreiser?" The answer was, "Yes, that or anything." Niagara here comes in for a slight sketch, one paragraph, and it has with all his pictures a quality of discovery, of news about it — a trait of style with him.

After these weeks of wandering, finally Pittsburgh became a home again for six months. The town excited him. Set among mountains, which he saw for the first time, threaded by three rivers of beautiful names, the Monongahela, the Allegheny and the Ohio, under a mantle of fiery smoke and cinders, it was the setting for a drama going on between multimillionaire and wage earner, between success and failure — a theme he must have mulled over from then on until he had to write *The Financier* and *The Titan*, in which he decides upon the conqueror as hero. The picture he makes of Pittsburgh in *A Book About Myself* is among his best canvases — its steel works, its hovels of anaemic laborers' families, its rolling mills and power plants, and again its millionaires' houses. It was likewise the setting for a drama that took place in his own mind.

Pittsburgh in 1894 had come through two years of bloody strikes. Carnegie and Phipps were still protecting their properties with live-wire fences and an army of Pinkerton detectives. It was a war to combine Carnegie and Amalgamated Steel, to break the power of the single laborer, to fix prices so that multimillionaires should go over into the billionaire class. It was the first era of mammoth fortune-making in the United States, to be repeated on the heels of the Great War. "Like huge ribbons of fire these and other names of powerful steel men — the Olivers, Thaws, Fricks, Thompsons — seemed to rise and band the city." The least protest on the part of the people, like the March of "General" Coxey's hobo army on Washington, was played up by the press as a menace to the nation, just as in 1930 similar disturbances in New York have been treated. But nothing of the gigantic schemes of the magnates to pervert democracy into plutocracy, to take the country from the people without their knowing it, was allowed to appear in the two Pittsburgh papers — only the weddings and amusements of these families. What the Dispatch, where Dreiser had found a job at twenty-five dollars a week, valued most, aside from ordinary reporting, were leisurely idle stories, the lighter the better, nonsense if possible; since the real news was too subversive to print. These he found he could write to the satisfaction of the editor — his first actual " excursion into creative work." He became an accredited feature man, taken up as an original by the editors of the paper; and the fashionable son of the publisher told him he " wished he could write like that," and asked him to dine at his house. But he never went, though it was one of the very houses he had so often envied from the outside. Perhaps the difference in their clothes and manners made him shy. He speaks of him as back from Europe in " fine clothes."

Through this success he came to be an out of town correspondent. His work was easy, gave him time to wander about these precipitous terraces, to watch the city at all times of day and night, from all angles, dominated always by its furnaces and their " enormous group of stacks with red tongues waving in the wind." With a labor agitator, a reporter on the paper, as friend, he went among the families of the working men getting from $1.65 to at most $4.00 a day. In Allegheny, across the river, where he lived high up in a kind of cabin from which the rivers and the lights of Pittsburgh were inspiration, he used to read in the Carnegie library, paid for by the sweat and blood of the steel workers. He read Flaubert's *Madame Bovary* and Thomas Hardy. And especially he read Balzac, one novel after another, until he came to confusing Pittsburgh and Paris, seemed really to be living in the French city among the people of the Human Comedy. And he thought, why shouldn't he learn to make novels out of Pittsburgh as compelling and involved as Balzac's? Surely life ran high among these rivers and cliffs, veiled in cinders. And yet there was always New York. Perhaps that was the real city for him. His brother Paul had told him so, had recently written him to come for a visit, that their sister E. who had a house in Fifteenth Street would be delighted if he came. In July he induced the Dispatch to give him a vacation and planned to see for himself. First, however, he felt that he must go back to his fiancée waiting for him in Missouri.

He went just as Eugene Witla, the "Genius," goes back to his mid-Western sweetheart, and found her more inflaming than ever, among the cool shadows, and wild roses and crickets' chatter of her father's spacious farm. His memory of this visit recalls the house, " old French windows to the grass, graceful long rooms, verandahs before it, so Southern in quality"; and the other old houses, scarcely a village "in a sea of corn"; the distinction of the father and mother and brothers, all of them living within American ideals. He felt there "the spirit of rural America," the sentiment that made our songs — *Old Kentucky Home, Swanee River* — and that had made " the passion of a Brown, the patience and sadness of a Lincoln, the dreams and courage of a Lee or a Jackson." And yet he had seen the ferment in Pittsburgh of Poles and Lithuanians struggling to be Americans too against odds, and " had seen the girls of that city walking the streets at night." This gracious family with " their profound faith in God . . . in marriage . . . in no wise squared with the craft, the cruelty, the brutality, the envy . . . everywhere else."

They seemed to him like people asleep. He longed to wake their daughter up out of this, to seize her then and there. She was delicious, they were both in a torment of desire identified with the odors and noises of the fecund fields around them; but they let the hour go by without making it theirs. He went away, he says, the romance ended. Though three years later he married her, desire was gone; back in Missouri they had cheated life by holding it off. When he left on the train the world was already greyer. This experience is enough to account for his lifelong exhortations to men and women to drink deep, and instantly, not to wait and sip. All then would be better? Perhaps and perhaps not. But he would like people to try living that way. If he and his girl had at that moment struck fire together, he believes an annealment of temper between them would have taken place, and made a more enduring bond.

23

"New York is a city of many cats. Some say New York is Babylon. There is a rose and gold mist New York."
                                  CARL SANDBURG

New York in 1894: I know the things it did not have. Not automobiles, but broughams, victorias, hansoms and tallyhos; not electric lights, but gas and oil flames. No skyscrapers, unless the Tower Building, technically so because of steel construction. And it was still an island as approached from Pittsburgh. Travelers got out at Jersey City in a glass train-shed of a station, an achievement of Victorian America, more truly aesthetic, according to one difficult New York architect, John Oakman, than any modern skyscraper. And then by shambling ferry-boats they arrived in New York. It had no radios, no speakeasies, no jazz, no lighted billboards. But it had the social climate out of which the creation which is to-day New York and the decadence which is today New York were to emanate. It had achieved in the Nineties one phase of its exciting originality.

And these are the things it had that made this siren atmosphere — the sea and boats drawn to it as by a magnet. The rivers and estuaries, the sea lagoons, have made among three rocky islands an irresistible harbor through which have come the importations of the human world. Fabulous works of art, silks, foods, furs, laces, linens and jewels, unexcelled, and the toys of the peasants of the earth have docked through New York. And before they have spread to blunted cities and country places, and their flavor has vanished in houses half afraid of their sharpness, and they have got lost in a seasick nightmare of imported ineptitude — house decoration, exotic food and clothes — these products, as they were taken off the ships and stored in wholesale houses for a time, or displayed in stores, at least as they passed through the city, gave it an aroma that no other city has had. New York is the port that has had to take care of a country making few luxuries of its own. Then, too, strange people came with these things, to sell or manufacture them — Jews and Syrians, Italians and Armenians, Chinese, Spaniards, and Portuguese who were not forced to become native at once. They settled in the southeast portions of the city, in neglected streets or along the waterways, and scarcely changed their customs or language. Their life was like music or perfume or love to Westerners after the sanitary and conforming Middle West. In spite of smells, fleas and garbage heaps, these quarters have intoxicated susceptible Americans until today, when now the immigrants begin to cater to the rule of cleanliness and coldness, which is a matter of pride with New Yorkers.

Jean Cocteau was once quoted as citing in talk an advantage that France had over more antiseptic countries: " *C'est encore un fumier* " (a dunghill). New York in the Nineties, and for years after machinery ruled it, had quarters that fertilized the rest of the city. They were segregated districts; no proper person crossed into them except a few " damn-fool " or would-be " damn-fool artists." Yet a flavor of Eastern, Latin and Balkan races hung over the city, however assimilated. Today, tempered by British-Dutch precedent, it triumphs in Guggenheims, Lewisohns, Kahns, Roxys, Koblers, Ziegfelds, Zukors, Liverights, if I may be allowed to pluralize these names, now traditional. Some came from cultivated but unloved families in Europe, some will tell you how it is just " seventeen years from push-cart to Park avenue."

And then beyond the fact that in Avenue A large-bodied and coarse-pored Jewesses with rich undulated chevelures (who have produced a generation or more of acceptable chorus girls and light-weight champions and song-writers), have made street-counters of fresh eggs look by contrast more fragile than French glassware, and have made platters of exotic fish and pickles as inviting as Korean ornaments; and beyond the fact that already Sicilians and Florentines and Bolognese had hung their long sausages in pink, green, cobalt and lemon-yellow tinsel in the windows of condiment shops, and had placed their impeccable sugar tanagras on fête days in the windows of their cake shops; and beyond the fact that already in 1894 samovars and seven-branched candlesticks had undoubtedly given brass and copper orgasms to Murray Hill old maids and bachelors — beyond all this, illumined by the threadlike oil flames of innumerable pushcarts, beyond and slightly flavored by it, was New York the gawdy respectable descendant of British-Dutch merchants and trappers. It had like no other American town a background of luxury. Engravings of the streets of 1800 are as elegant as London streets of the same period with painted coaches and rearing horses and silver-trimmed harnesses. It was a town meant for extravagance.

In 1894 under a corrupt political rule Dreiser describes it as badly cleaned and lighted compared to Western cities, and then as bewildering to him in the sense of social splendor. Already his brother had given him a hint of this; and journals like Town Topics and The Standard, a pornographic theatre weekly; and the Pittsburgh papers themselves, who catered to their steel colony in its effort to connect with the Four Hundred and with the peerage of Europe. The names of Astor, Goelet, McAllister, Vanderbilt, Gould — at least Dreiser remembers these as names, though a classicist might say Astor, Stuyvesant, Lorillard, Spencer, Harriman, Wilson — these appeared to him to be those of men and women who held the city in their laps.

This German-Slavic Hoosier of twenty-three is like one who in a dream has concentrically climbed a mountain, on his way from city to city; and always at one point on each plane finds this spot of gilt and glitter with its antithesis of darkness and misery. Finally, at the top of the table-land there is New York, where splendor is beyond calculation, and squalor, too. " Nowhere before had I seen such a lavish show of wealth and such bitter poverty." It is said to be true by those who were part of it, that New York in the nineties had reached, through Yankee shrewdness and British snobbery, to a shallow social brilliance not since equaled. For a few years it maintained this equation. People talked of the menace of the nouveaux-riches from the West, of the dangers of the great melting-pot, of the submerged tenth and the army of the unwashed, but they were not frightened yet. They had managed a brittle aristocracy that extended to Philadelphia, Baltimore and Washington, and slightly to Boston, and met at Newport in summer. Edith Wharton was their novelist, Stanford White their architect.

Yet Mrs. Wharton never apprehended them from the inside as acutely as does Dreiser briefly from the outside. For one thing she is Puritan, indicting them for the loosening of their standards that came with power. In her books the reader is not so much dazzled by the display or effrontery of the Nineties, as irritated by a coldness and cruelty this novelist is unable to analyze. One does not meet there the Texan dandy from the East who, naked, puts on his silk hat on New Year's day and steps into a cab to make his rounds of the houses of pleasure, and maybe ends life in one. One meets there the bewildered lost lady, declassed and unloved, no one quite knows why, on her way down to being governess in the very homes where once she was a favorite. I supposed what happened to this society was that cautious rather than adventurous historians were integral to it. Mrs. Wharton (and later Mrs. Atherton and Willa Cather) too often reads like high-class society editors or feature writers for women. And when geniuses were born within it they divorced themselves as quick as they could and lent it none of their strength. That is, although this class grew away from Europe materially, intellectually it never grew at all; it remained Colonial. Mrs. John Jacob Astor, queen of it, was displeased with her son-in-law for dining with Mark Twain, and is quoted as saying that to have friends among artists and writers must be very unpleasant.* Ideas were noxious to them as a class, and the people who had them were shabby, untidy, impossible. The period died of the Colonial germ. When Jews, cultivated or merely emigrant, when unpedigreed " poor whites " came out of the melting-pot with their quick fortunes, the aristocrats had

* Thomas Beer: *Stephen Crane*.

nothing to fight them with that money could not buy, except brief right of birth. With no program of the spirit to justify this prerogative, it fell before the promiscuous billionaire. Today the story called The Four Hundred is a dead romance, never recorded by a master.

In 1894 Dreiser saw a corner of its entertainment world under the chaperonage of Paul Dresser. He tells how his brother met him at seven in the morning in Jersey City, and they made their way by ferry to Christopher Street, and past houses which seemed to him of " an aged and contemptible appearance," but Paul told him to wait, that the charm of New York was its mingling of new and old. In a narrow brown-stone house in Fifteenth Street, they found his sister waiting. Once she had been the bad heroine of the family, having eloped many years before with a Chicago business man, who had left wife and children and a good position to go with her. She was matronly now, no longer " trim and beautiful," and the husband somewhat fallen in fortune, but she welcomed him with " much talking and laughing," and the breakfast of steak, brown gravy and " creamy " biscuit was all that breakfast should be to a member of this family. As he sat with them, wondering if New York was going to be glamorous after all, or only huge and cold, he heard " strange moanings and blowings," and asked what they were: " Boats, tugs, and vessels in the harbor. There's a fog on." — " How far away are they? " — " Anywhere from one to ten miles." Then he says, " Suddenly the full majesty of the sea sweeping about this island at this point caught me. . . . Its great buildings and streets were all washed about by that sea-green salty food. . . . And beyond [was] the silence . . . the deadly earnestness of the sea." Did they ever think, he asked them, how wonderful it was to have the sea so close? No, his sister and husband said, they couldn't say that they did. It seemed to him now that he would like to live in New York. Paul agreed, " It's wonderful, my boy, . . . Great subject, the sea. . . . Didn't I tell you they all fall for it! Now it's the ocean vessels that get him. You take my advice . . . and move down here. The quicker the better. . . ."

Then they went out to see the city. First his brother

took him to his office in Twentieth Street and Fifth Avenue, Howley Haviland and Company — a song-publishing house, which through Paul's prestige, and the shrewdness of the two partners (one a hunchback, a luck-sign in Indiana) was to make a small fortune for him and a year or so later to give an opening to Theodore as an editor. Then in a hansom cab he pointed out the stores, Lord and Taylor, Altman's at Eighteenth, Tiffany's at Fifteenth and Broadway, Brentano's in Union Square; and very lovingly the theatres, The Old Star, once Lester Wallack's, and further uptown, Palmer's, Augustin Daly's, The Manhattan, The Casino, and Koster and Bial's Music Hall, managed by Oscar Hammerstein and patronized by the arrived originals of the town. His brother went back to twenty years before, when the great theatres were down below Union Square, Niblo's and The London on The Bowery, and sighed for the talent of a day gone by. Dreiser listened impatiently: " What had been had been. . . . I was new and strange and wished to see only what was new and wonderful."

So the brothers ambled and talked, slightly at odds, one the future author of *My Gal Sal,* the other of *Sister Carrie,* Paul gossiping about the big hotels, just which kind of people went to this or that, and explaining that the Waldorf and Delmonico's were " the last word for the rich or fashionable." At Forty-second Street the limit of the Rialto, they stopped, Paul saying, " Well here's the end," and went into the Metropole for a drink. Here, he says, his brother was at his best; everyone seemed to know him — prize-fighters, thespians, vaudeville upstarts, retired miners, and ranchmen. Both here and on their way back along Broadway, there was much slapping of backs, plucking of lapels, exchange of scandals and side-splitting stories. That evening it was the same, when the brothers met again, at the end of an afternoon in which Theodore had explored the upper fifties and sixties, agog as always before the " residences of the great." At a rendezvous for players and singers, the Hotel Aulic, in a " world of glittering spinning flies . . . in showy clothes . . . laughing, jesting, expectorating," his brother was a favorite. One can see these men and women — enormous sleeves that made their throats seem small and fragile, moulded bosoms, tiny waists, spreading skirts and petticoats that diminished feet and ankles. One can see the ruffles, flowers, plumes, curls and transformations; and then the pompous side-burns of the generation before, waistcoats, gold watch chains; and the cutaways, slender canes, striped and checkered trousers, derbies and long curling moustaches of the younger dandies.

He basked in the sense it gave him of being actually related for the moment to New York, through this magnet, who was not a power in the town, and yet was so endearing and successful a play-boy.

Paul was thoughtful too of his younger brother; and that first morning on their way from Union Square to Forty-second Street, pointed out the Century Company, and suggested that some day he might be connected with it. He guessed that " Thee " was destined for an intellectual field, without having to know what intellect is. Like Maxwell and the newspaper men he inculcated a germ: " Sometime you ought to write about these things, Thee. They're the limit for extravagance and show. The people out West don't know yet what's going on, but the rich are getting control. They'll own the country pretty soon. A writer like you could make 'em see that." Not experienced in literature, which along with all art was to be called " high-brow " by the run of readers for years to come, he could say this naïve thing, that his brother ought to write about these extremes and that the Century Company — might print and sell the work. Had he read Scribner's, Century, Harper's and The Atlantic Monthly for the year 1894, he might have known better.

24

" Change ' breech-clout.' It's a word that you love and I abominate. I would take that and ' offal' out of the language." — *" You are steadily weakening the English tongue, Livy."* From a Dialogue between Mark Twain and His Wife

" Frankness is a jewel; only the young can afford it." Mark Twain

Howells was the arbiter, also from the Middle West, Ohio, but out of New England parents. From the point of view of endurance and of nicety to native fact — or was it incident? — I suppose Howells was a writer. I am a reader who will never know. Try as I will, I can't read him, neither his Easy Chair for Harper's Magazine, nor his endless novels. He wrote for the gentry of his times, and must have put to sleep the more restless members, such as made the financial panics of the day and conceived the trusts and railroads, or died disreputably, or gave their fathers' money for European titles or to the Prince of Monaco. He and his associates derived from Hawthorne, Emerson, Lowell, Longfellow, Holmes, Whittier and Bryant. They never had taken much into account the unlimited Americans, Poe, or Melville, Whitman, or even Thoreau, except as he belonged to the Concord school. Emerson, a philosophic architect with a lucid brain, at eighty confided to a friend that " pink ribbons " were of greater importance than he had ever known how to make them. That is, he hankered after something he had been ashamed to take. And beyond that, though he is praised as a champion of Walt Whitman, he wrote a letter to Carlyle, in which he tells him he is sending him poems of a crazy protégé of his; possibly they will interest him; if not he can use them " to light his pipe with." His lucid brain was blocked with puritanism, and so blocked the softening American critics immediately to follow him. Hawthorne was a New England gentleman, too, with neurotic fears. When Melville sought him out in Liverpool after years of intimacy and then of separation, they walked together along the strand in Southport. Melville told him he could not believe in Christianity; that " there was no place for him in America, his best and deepest work . . . was lightly tossed aside [there]; . . . [he] would not commit suicide; that was a weak way out; but he might withdraw." * To this confession of loneliness, and outcry for understanding, Mumford records that Hawthorne had nothing to say. Already he had written into Ethan Brand a portrait of Melville where he endowed him with intellect and no heart, thus like a Christian dividing the two.

These sedate New Yorkers of the Nineties, William Dean Howells, George William Curtis, Brander Matthews, Robert Underwood Johnson, and their Boston confrères, Barrett Wendell, George Woodberry, Thomas Bailey Aldrich — a lyricist, nearly a poet — Charles Dudley Warner, Charles Eliot Norton, were surely sons of the New England legend where tameness triumphed over origin and etiquette over meaning and three names over two. Although the critical reviews of this decade made references to foreign art — to Zola, Flaubert, Turgenieff, Tolstoi, Hardy, Meredith; the issues they stood for are evaded as French or Russian, peasant or perverse, never faced as universal. And one looks in vain in these polite literary columns for news of the more fragile prodigies of that day — Yeats, Beerbohm, Rimbaud, Mallarmé, Verlaine, Adam, Baudelaire. And Anatole France, the modern youth of them, was unknown to Americans. It was a genteel record of life and letters, less fiercely ascetic and therefore less dramatic than with its Concord parents, but never quarreling with them; and in no way squaring with the new greedy material splendor New York was building for the country. Henry James alone apprehended its advent; and he took it off to England to extract its

* Lewis Mumford: *Herman Melville*.

fangs, as far as he was concerned, by exposing it to European worldliness.

At the same moment there was as compensation and as panderer, Mark Twain, lively as the human race, indisputable as the Mississippi. To read him gives unmitigated joy to one prepared for cold laughter and almost never for tears. Toward the end he says to a friend, "At last the luxury of writing for myself," and wrote *The Mysterious Stranger,* not to be published until after his death; in which he gives himself the luxury of sweeping away the human race, as if too unreal and ephemeral to conserve itself — a thing of pain and defeat. Mark Twain, the great nihilist! And yet impotent to annihilate either his wife or Howells as arbiters of what he should commit to writing! * Secretly and anonymously he at one time printed a conversation between Queen Elizabeth, Raleigh, Shakespeare, and others of an era he must have coveted, where much is made of "f--ks" and "f--ts." † It reads as if to Mark Twain, as to any good Christian, sex was dirt, not that excrement was a perverse mystery. It is probable that he never showed it to his wife or to Howells.

There were others in his wake as in the wake of Howells — Cable, Stockton, Kate Douglas Wiggin, Joel Chandler Harris, who filled the magazines with very charming stories of humor and adventure and local color, as influenced by Twain. They were lightly seductive stories, bringing gentle tears, and in no sense confronting their readers with fierce storms, or grey eternities or fatal ecstasies. Yet Twain himself never wrote for humor or color, but irresistibly for the meaning that was in him, which was crossed by but one foreign element — diplomacy.

Although already Dreiser planned to be a writer, apparently he asked little about the writers of the day.

* "Mrs. Clemens was the making of Mr. Clemens. He really had a very vulgar streak. She went over everything he wrote and took out everything he would not like to see published. He relied absolutely on her judgement." Related to me by a friend of Mrs. Clemens, a lady of the Nineties, type of the American dowager, now extinct.

† American wholesale distributors as late as 1931 still require the head in the sand for a number of such words.

It was not that aspect of the place that occupied him; it was the spectacle of living in New York, which meant to him American life at its highest voltage. And even if his guide had taken him among writers and painters rather than players and spendthrifts, he might have been disappointed, puzzled by the way that life was Balzacian and literature was moral. Even suppose he had had the luck to talk with the masterly Mark Twain, perhaps he would have met the mysterious stranger in a less generous mood than when he disillusioned the two boys in the forest. Or had he happened to fall among the rebels of his own age at Allaire's in Seventeenth Street, at Koster and Bial's, or the Lantern Club, or Mouquin's, where tradition says they met in the Nineties, it might possibly have been that he and Stephen Crane would have sparked as against tameness. But more likely Crane, with less patience than Dreiser and more prejudices, and with a head-start in awareness, was already tired of trying to " make out " in a raw and moral country, and was turned away from natives and toward England, where, he said, " You can have an idea without being sent to court for it." . . . At least in the company of Paul and his Rialto friends the young pilgrim had the fun of jokes and comments as ribald as Twain's Elizabethan dialogue, and more up-to-date. Unselfconscious, not critical, life was and has been Dreiser's chief medium of experience.

New York, he said to himself, was not beautiful, but it had " the magnetism of large bodies over small ones, . . . " a quality of zest and security and ease, cheek by jowl with poverty and longing and sacrifice, which gives to life everywhere its keenest most pathetic edge. . . . It had the feeling of gross and blissful and parading self-indulgence." He looked at the surfaces of everything, and tried to guess the meanings. He crossed the Brooklyn Bridge, walked in the Wall Street districts and through the areas between them and Union Square, less haunted by their miseries than a few months later when he came back to stay — alone. The city had worked its enchantment. But he needed money to enter. He would go back to Pittsburgh and see if he could save enough dollars to dare force an entrance.

25

Huxley, Tyndall, Spencer, Balzac, and Pulitzer.

Four months more on the Pittsburgh Dispatch, and Dreiser had managed to save two hundred and forty dollars, but only by living on so little that he believes his health suffered, and handicapped him when he did get back to the "great city." In these four months he embarked on another drama of the mind. He came upon Huxley, Tyndall and Spencer, read *First Principles, Science and Hebrew Tradition, Science and Christian Tradition,* and they "blew me intellectually to bits." Now " the last lingering filaments of Catholicism " were gone. And more than that with them he says went his personal attitude toward life, his "blazing ambition to get on." And he cut with old anchors completely like a disillusioned Catholic; not like his British teachers, who transferred divinity to themselves and inaugurated the era of the progressive individual, the age of the substantive: " I am the master of my fate, I am the captain of my soul."

Suddenly for this Catholic boy if man were but an infinitesimal speck in the solar system, and that in turn but a speck in the infinite universe, really there was no place to go. " One lived and had his being because he had to, and . . . it was of no importance." He ceased thinking of himself as a creature who must push up and on and at the top of the ladder would receive rewards. Out of this nightmare of magnitude and littleness that the scientists gave him, perhaps Dreiser has never entirely awakened. It colors him with nineteenth century radicalism, as science forced thought away from the intimate miracles of Jesus and Mary; and if it retained a shade of Biblical teaching, it was in harmony with the bleakness of the Old Testament — " Vanity of vanities; all is vanity."

Moreover, to measure by extensions in time and space was native to him; his dream of success had been measured this way. A more sensuous artist, a less American soul, would have been held within the seduction of inner relations; haunted by quality to the ignoring of quantity; infatuated with material for the particular crisis he could bring out of it; and would feel more kinship with the unhopeful inquirers of today than with these mastodons of the last century. By the echo of recent science — concerned with intricate arrangement — Dreiser, always courting the scientists, is not yet beguiled. In the Forum, November, 1930, he chants the aeons and the vastnesses of the universe, and the insignificance of the human being, to whom no answer at all is given.

Yet the change in thought that is called the present has seeds in the change of thought which is called the immediate past. And the giant of one mode of thought is related more actually to giants of another, than he is to the smaller people of his own mode. Labels are lost as intensity increases. Dreiser has reached through his years of achievement into a class where labels are indicative and yet contradictory. The metaphysician in him, still seeking a complete answer, presents a sea of data out of which relations take form. And the artist in him in pursuit of crisis recreates the data.

Alone in Pittsburgh at the age of twenty-three he was however for the time being that new thing — an infinitesimal atom, and so was everyone else. What to do about it? Nothing, except to live the patient life of an atom according to its properties. And what were his gifts as atom? To observe and record, he hoped, as Balzac in France observed and recorded and in ant fashion built a monument. Yet his old dreams of individual splendor still begged not to be forgotten. It might be, in fact now he was certain of it, that New York would be the city where he could enter into a combination more proper to him as atom. In November he resigned from the Dispatch, and with his two hundred and forty dollars proceeded to his sister's house in Fifteenth Street.

Again as four years before in Chicago, he went the rounds of the great papers of the town, first the World, then the Sun, then the Herald, and again met the answer just as if he had entered into a new planet, " No vacancies." Only here in this more elaborate city a company of office boys, " supercilious, scoffing and ribald," protecting the city editor, would fling the news at *him*, " He says to say no vacancies." If he asked to see him anyway, " No, he don't want to see anybody, no vacancies." At the end of the second day, he says, he looked at the cold buildings fronting on City Hall Park and at the loafers and bums and tramps on the benches chilled by December weather, and then walking up Broadway to Union Square past the Christmas throng at Tiffany's, comparing the excluded and the excluders, the idea of Hurstwood was born — that oblong triumph of the portrait of a failure in *Sister Carrie*.

The next day he determined to break in past the boys, and did, " brushed them off like flies," opened the " much-guarded door " and stepped into the editorial room of The New York World. Even then, he thinks he might have been thrown out, had it not been for a quick young man whom evidently curiosity led to ask what it was he wanted. " I want a job." — " Where do you come from ? " — " The West." It was, as if in a modern fable, Arthur Brisbane, inviting him to wait, stepping over to the city editor, pointing to him and saying, " This young man wants a job. I wish you would give him one." So these two, not much associated afterwards, were joined for a second in fate, undoubtedly by their fantastic native force, Brisbane recognizing this much of himself in Dreiser.

He got the job on the World under Joseph Pulitzer, " the Magyar Jew, a disease-demonized soul . . ." he labels him, " who had taken the championship of journalism away from Dana and Bennett, as Hearst was later to take it from him." Though on his yacht or in Europe or Bar Harbor at the time, not often in New York these days, Dreiser says the air " sizzled with the ionic rays of this black star." His road to success lay through attacking everything, social, political, financial, that he could control. He had submitted to horse-whipping once by a citizen he had libeled, and then had rushed to his paper to use it as news for an extra. A managing editor, without arrest or punishment, had shot and killed a man come to his office to protest against exposure. Five secretaries and seven managing editors maintained a spy system, one against the other and over all their subordinates, and carried the news to Pulitzer. Everyone, Dreiser came to think, had a " nervous, resentful terror in their eyes, as have animals when they are tortured." * To him, the air of the place was vibrant as generated by a man who had the unbridled ambition of his own dreams, and was terrifying as if disaster hung in it. One wonders as one reads if the cruel vitality of this atmosphere arose out of something native to Manhattan, or if the Pulitzer policy has not actually helped to lend these qualities to the town, since then become native to it. Many Westerners, like this reporter, have been stabbed by what they call the heartlessness of New York, and what Europeans call its frigidity. Anglo Saxons suffer from it; Latins deride it; the Irish enjoy it; Jews thrive on it.

To Dreiser it meant failure for a time — his first since he left the hardware business. He was given only minor assignments and what was worse never permitted to write them up. He was told he " couldn't write " — a thing said to him by New Yorkers ever since. There were men from St. Louis and their friends, reporters on the World — " completely disillusioned," with whom he used to sit about and talk. They came all of them to the same conclusion: " New York was difficult and revolting," and yet challenging too. He would not go back to the West, a failure — " not yet." He puzzles over his defeat: Perhaps he was too green, callow, to be of use in so " ruthless " and " subtle " a town: perhaps he was too much in awe of the social brilliance of the place. Once by chance a story of his appeared as he wrote it on the first page, and the city editor had noticed it enough to trust him with more important work. But unhappily the assignment involved interviewing " a well-known youth of great wealth," probably a scion of that so formidable

* From *A Book About Myself.*

"four hundred." His courage failed him, though if he had been sent among thieves and cutthroats, he would have gone and come back with a story. After that there were no more favors. Yet he was only five years, he reasons, from writing *Sister Carrie;* he should have been worth something to these editors. But more and more he came to feel their sense of his unimportance. One day complaining of neglect, he resigned, and the city editor said it was just as well, that he had not been of much use to them. He had better try the Sun.

26

The cleavage from ancestry: Fuller, Garland, Crane, Norris.

So ended his newspaper days in a swamp of depression, out of which he says has come much of his understanding of lonely destitute people. He tried halfheartedly to get a job on another paper but no one wanted him. By this time he had left his sister's house, unable to pay for so good a room. He took a hall bedroom on Fourth Street east of the Bowery at $1.50 a week in what was called a bed house. The landlady was good to him, gave him the room, he thought, as a screen against the police. He ate at Childs' restaurants. For the rest, he decided that though he had failed as a journalist, now was the time to succeed as a fiction writer. Reports of how Rudyard Kipling, R. H. Davis, David Graham Phillips, Stephen Crane, like him starting on newspapers, were now brilliant writers of fiction, embittered and spurred him. His money was not gone, he was not done for yet. He stalked the town to find stories to write about, and was diligent in reading the important magazines to see what kind of fiction sold best, or at all. He studied Munsey's, Harper's, Century, Atlantic Monthly, discouraged by the fact that " all their stories had the puritan complex; the hero and heroine were always saved, they ended just right in peace and sweetness." Yet back in St. Louis days he had read Henry B. Fuller's *With the Procession* and had felt in him a man seriously doing what he would like to do — write about life as he saw it. And he had read Hamlin Garland's *Main Travelled Roads,* clumsier than Fuller and yet true to the Middle West. The scene-painter he worked for in Chicago had told him that Whitman's *Leaves of Grass* tallied with his own talk and was great writing. The book was hard to find, he was still looking for it. Now apparently none of these men he had faith in were to be read in the journals out of which a writer might make a living. True, Crane's *The Red Badge of Courage* had been bought by Irving Bacheller's syndicate in 1894, and sold serially to the Philadelphia Press. But he felt that the book succeeded not as realism but as a sensational story about war. Had it been about everyday America, he questioned if its tragedy would have suited the journals of that year.

In 1928 in an introduction to Frank Norris's *McTeague* he dismisses Crane after this fashion:

" I find . . . H. G. Wells speaking of Crane as not only the pioneer but the most brilliant of all of the early realists of this generation. Stuff and nonsense! Crane was not the pioneer nor even the equal in any sense of the man who led the van of realism in America. That honor . . . goes to Henry B. Fuller of Chicago, who as early as 1886 published *With the Procession*,* as sound and agreeable a piece of realism as that decade or any since produced. And in 1891 he wrote . . . *The Cliff Dwellers* which preceded by three years Crane's *The Red Badge of Courage* . . . as did *Main Travelled Roads,* by Hamlin Garland. . . ."

Crane has meant as little to him as that; something rankled. Perhaps it was jealousy dating from that lonely day, when he was an outcast from the World, and Crane was known as a favorite of Howells and Garland, and was being sent here and there on exciting assignments.

Yet that poet reads like the one man in New York at that time with whom the potential author of *The Girl in the Coffin, In the Dark, The Hand of the Potter,* might logically have felt kinship. His struggle was fierce too, and swifter; it killed him. His first novel, *Maggie, A Girl of the Streets,* an attempt to record life as he saw it in the Bowery district, was for years only obscurely published. Though Howells admired it as " Crane's little tragedy," he could not sell it; Gilder disdained it; no one wanted it. He got less than one hundred dollars from Bacheller for *The Red Badge of Courage,* and when he published *Black Riders* in 1894, the critics, except for two of them, told the reading country Crane was mad, and that the poems were " obscene drivel." Like Dreiser he saw the

---

* A too zealous statement: 1895 is the date of its publication; and 1893 of *The Cliff Dwellers.*

world as a rudderless ship " going ridiculous voyages, making quaint progress, turning as with serious purpose before stupid winds "; marriage, he thought, was a base trick on women, and there was no such thing as sin except in Sunday schools. Little Lord Fauntleroy was a crime against children; Mrs. Humphrey Ward an idiot, and Stevenson insincere; sincerity was the first requisite of an artist.* In fact, aside from Ambrose Bierce, who does not figure to Dreiser at this time, and Dreiser not to Bierce at any time — "he was too much the pedant," Mencken says, "to like him " — Crane was the one published intellect resembling his in its ruthlessness, a thinker, one would say, after his own heart; and Crane thought more with his heart than Bierce.

This might be a trifling point to dwell on, were it not for the long loneliness of American artists, so that the maps of their histories have been those of scarcely intersecting roads. Yet since there are records of bitter enmities of man against man even in the wilderness in the face of a common danger, it is illogical to ask for understanding among the susceptible few in this wide land. Emily Dickinson in Amherst understood the need and the lack when she wrote, ". . . Just the miles of stare — That signalize a show's retreat — In North America." If, however, nature had decreed an alliance of great temperaments in North America, perhaps rotarians would not have had their undisputed way.

What kept Dreiser from valuing Crane might be a difference of temperament outside of intellect. Crane had a gift that led him hastily into sharp-shooting metaphors — " The sun was pasted on the sky like a red wafer " — into parabolic metaphors, joy-riding jokes and slang; and so away from what Dreiser would call the issue. And he had a gift for excitement that took him running into it as if on a spree — to New Mexico, Texas, Nevada, where a whole story could be made out of a hotel because it was painted a strange blue; took him back to New York to surround himself with what kindred

---

* As reported by Thomas Beer in his life of Crane, and proved by reading Crane.

people there were — the showman, Elbert Hubbard, the pioneer, Hamlin Garland, the charming Richard Harding Davis, the looser Huneker and Clyde Fitch, the deep Albert Ryder; and with others who jealously made him a victim, and tarred him with the name of dope-fiend, drunkard, sex-degenerate. Though he was none of this, it is agreed, New York had no use for a man with that legend; and he no use for New York, and he went to England, again as if on a spree; and it *was* a spree, what with Conrad, Henry James, Yeats, H. G. Wells, Harold Frederic, and many other live men and women in his house and he in theirs. In this spirit, it is said, as much as to verify *The Red Badge of Courage* he went to the Spanish-American War. He was a runaway, and Dreiser, though likewise a stranger to the code of the day, and likewise victimized through three times as many years, has remained a native.

Crane was a snob, too, slightly; delighted in talking of the peasantry of America to describe such a family as Dreiser came from. And Dreiser also is snobbish enough or else accurate enough for that to have prejudiced him, if he has heard of it. He, not Crane, is right — there are boobs, hicks, rubes and hayseeds as in no other country, but not a peasantry. Jefferson more than Lincoln has had his wish; socially, not politically, democracy has succeeded in the United States.

So this young poet among realists ran through twenty-nine years on a brilliant spree of life and work, and ended it just as the author of *Sister Carrie,* with more patience and no more resignation, was beginning that epochal novel. They are the two writers of that date, as I read intellect, least hampered by puritan prejudice, and most impregnated with life. Henry Fuller was less impetuous; Hamlin Garland was " corn-fed "; Frank Norris had a flaw that could give birth to romance for money; O. Henry reveled in the color of life but gave no thought to its structure; Jack London was a propagandist for the under-dog, and later a magazine prostitute. Out of this group Crane and Dreiser are the ruthless youth and the ruthless adult of the country. Crane's first product, *Maggie,* has the youthful trait of marching adjectives;

Sister Carrie was delivered mature without adolescent blemish. I think they are comparable, one to fireworks, the other to a powerful car, taking its time, and the whirr of the motor is low. What Dreiser accurately valued in Fuller and later in Norris was the measure and restraint not to explode, but to store their energy for a long journey and a long residence in a land that often seemed all too alien — a policy akin to his own.

And for the most part he was right in his survey of the fiction market. The magazines made a dull small mirror to look into, to find the reflection of a life which he knew was terrific and changing throughout the western world. There was a journal of the day by the inconsequent name of Mlle. New York, written mostly by James Huneker and Vance Thompson, which was flashing the same indictment. If he read it he found there his own verdict on nearly every page, in Thompson's fine critical editorials, forgotten today and yet more potent and shaftlike than the remembered Huneker:

> "I do not wish to rage against [Howells] as though he were the beast of the Apocalypse, but he and Gilder and that ilk are the chief defect of American literature. While Mr. Howells merits one's habitual indignation, Mr. Gilder is undoubtedly the worse of the two. I have never known a man so uniformly nul."
>
> And: "The painters, since they have begun to live like other folk and love their own wives to the neglect of their neighbors' wives, have given up all concern for art."
>
> And: "New York, this malignantly respectable city."
>
> And bitterly, but fairly then and perhaps even now: "The man who lives in America and pretends to be anything but a philistine is also ridiculous. We are all philistines. We may be incoherent philistines. That is the best we can be."

On the other hand Thompson was the older American, tired of being called the new raw child. He was less of a child, I should think, than whatever spirit guides a descendant of Mlle. New York — The New Yorker of today. He had known in Paris Verlaine, Mallarmé, Rimbaud, Paul Fort, Villiers de L'Isle Adam, La Forge, Charles Cros, Heredia — the last two, Negro poets — then an undreamed of luxury in New York. He had heard the music of the modern Russians, already established in

Europe, but "the impossible Damrosch" never gave it to New York. He had a theory that the incentive to modern art would come from America; in fact that already from Poe and Whitman had stemmed the two streams of new French poetry.* And yet this connoisseur in perfections strained toward France, more homesick for it than the Chicago aesthetes were for London with its reflections of Paris. It was time after all these years for Americans to be grown-up, and, I imagine, he despaired of its happening. He was impatient of the very men and women who were trying to make their country less respectable and more real in art: " Dull melancholiacs in the grey provinces, lean pessimists of Kansas and the West, neurotic criminals of the New England country side." He diagnosed the disease, but had no systemic cure for it, unless a European tonic beyond the capacity of the patient. Dreiser, had he read him, would have been alternately excited by his destructive disdain and disheartened by his flaunting of the superiority of European art. More visionary than satirist, though he has made labels and pronounced judgments on American life, they are loose and easy-going. Often he dismisses them with an " Or so it seems " or " Or nearly so." He appears to revel in uncertainty and therefore is at times purposely diffuse.

It is right here in the middle Nineties, from the end of which decade Dreiser was to take off as a writer compelling attention, that the cleavage between an art of British parentage and a native art might first have been apparent, had there been analysts to make note of it. It is here that a prediction made by John Quincy Adams, and an aesthetic-democratic dream of Thomas Jefferson began to come intellectually true, as for years it had been politically true. Adams felt that with Jackson's election in 1828 the country would go down grade from all the culture it had known, which meant imported European culture, and that barbarism would definitely set in. To

* I have lately heard Fernand Léger and Constantin Brancusi suggest the same debt: Out of the newness of the United States France has drawn new aesthetic life.

Jefferson on the other hand, up through the people out of the soil, the art of civilization would have to bloom in pioneer America, or not bloom at all. In a sense the change was imported from Europe and the Orient, though not in the way Adams craved, through their philosophy and their art, but more as Jefferson had pledged himself to welcome it through the "irresponsible" blood of emigrants streaming for more than a century into these states under democratic protection. Whitman had been the wedge among poets — the first poet on the reception committee for "the new people; the young strangers, coming, always coming." *
And now they had come. No use any more for the aesthetes of the Chap Book or Mlle. New York, or for any one of us in love with elaborate far-off backgrounds, to think they might, if we advertised them enough, become our own foregrounds. Mark Twain had popularly sneered Europe in *The Court of King Arthur* and *Innocents Abroad,* and had given confidence to "philistines."

The Yankees were getting their way in language, manners, buildings, clothes, food — every form of expression. And the real artist knew that he now had to vaccinate himself and his audience with this cleavage from ancestry, if he were to stay at home. The young Stephen Crane felt this; seduced by England, he kept there American slang and a native's sense of his country. He was according to Beer " vastly pleased by the startling McTeague of Frank Norris [though he] pronounced the book "too moral," at the distance he kept from the elders on the one hand and the money makers on the other of his United States, who were enough to make an evangelist out of a serious poet. He begged William Heineman to buy the next novel of Norris. That author at the time was planning a long work of vital interest, and it was morally to be about the people, for the people, " who caricatured and villified, are after all and in the main, the real seekers after truth." So, already fine intellects were beginning to sentimentalize over the importance of the common people as common, rather than as people.

* Carl Sandburg: *Broken-Face Gargoyles.*

This period of cleavage, the mid-years of the American Nineties corresponds culturally to one phase of the mid-years of the British nineteenth century. That is, excluding always individual rebels, and the definite and spontaneous popular arts — vaudeville, comic papers, horse-racing, minstrel shows, which in any one time are often ahead in freedom of the esoteric arts. But it corresponds to only one phase — since in England, though the genteel ruled in the person of Victoria, the libertine, antedating Cromwell, ruled out of older roots. Shakespeare, Elizabeth, Dryden, Pope, Charles I, Swift, Fielding, Blake, Hogarth, Keats, Shelley, Byron had not lived for nothing. Not all of the English peerage, not all of the rich compost of the lower classes could be turned away from extravagance into prudes and puritans. The middle classes alone succumbed completely to Protestant supremacy. In the United States, however, the middle classes inundating high and low, one psychology had by now prevailed — that of respectability. Any other code was looked upon as evil or foreign. And few could have seen that a hidden ferment was at work to turn the country away from its decorums toward unimagined excesses. It is like a platform, this mid-year of the Nineties, from which to look backward and forward. Looking back, we see a quilt pieced out of Puritanism, not without warmth and quality, strength and sensibility, which might be typified by a verse of Emerson's, commemorating James Russell Lowell, in the January number of Harper's, 1894: "Man of sorrow, man of mark — Virtue lodged in sinew stark . . ." and the word *noble* appears in the poem.

The imperishable artists of that early mark were not Emerson, not Hawthorne, not Lowell, but Lincoln, Thoreau and Emily Dickinson. As artists one cannot dispute them. Then looking forward through the native channels of Walt Whitman and Mark Twain, and the lesser more local channels of writers like James Whitcomb Riley and Bret Harte,* we come upon a lessening of stark-

* Twain, it is known, resented the linking of his name with Harte's as kindred writers. As new and limber a judge as Scott Fitzgerald disputes Harte as a native. "Pure Dickens," he says. But to me he reads like an old-timer, one of the homesteaders, who has turned countless others toward the staking of literary claims in these unsettled states.

ness and an increase of response to the immediate scene. And finally by the turn of the century there arrives that period marked by naturalness and curiosity rather than by antique background, for which many have made Theodore Dreiser sponsor.

27

> "*The school of literature to which Poe belongs . . . is one we thoroughly dislike. . . . It mercilessly exposes the secrets of the heart. . . . What we want is not darkness but light; not thorns in our path, but roses and everywhere dew and freshness. The literature which . . . does not make us happier and better is not true and good.*"
> R. H. STODDARD

At this date in the winter of 1895 in his twenty-fourth year this sponsoring giant cut a sorry figure, or so he says. His great schemes were checked for the moment — a long, fearful moment of walking the unwelcoming streets of Manhattan, money decreasing, hopes not rising. As I hear him tell his history, he seems to this date like a boy who, since his mother's death, has always been walking from city to city, west and east, to find another home. But these wanderings about New York in the winter of '95 sound like the loneliest he had yet known. Kicked out of the one profession he had learned — journalism, he wanted, if possible, to enter upon another — fiction. In a way he was glad to be forced out of the newspaper world, " since as I even then saw it, it was a boy's game, and I was slowly but surely passing out of the boy-stage."

Like Rousseau, who hoped to paint in the accepted way to suit the Paris Salon, and was too real to know how, he made his effort to suit the editors of the day, and failed. On his walks he passed plenty of stories to write, plenty of rude teeming life of slums and business districts, and cold enviable life of the rich streets. He should be able to take these and with them make a flying machine, and go up a space above the earth into mastery of it through understanding. Balzac did this, and went above the Paris streets and houses; why not he above Manhattan sidewalks. But try as he would he could not make his material fit into any of the several moulds of the stories accepted by the magazines. There were no " magazines to represent the realistic grip on life. Howells and Twain were the outermost outposts of a new era." As he studied the idylls of the sons of biblical starkness and marrow, he felt a weakening of the old fibre, and no new hardness in keeping with new orders of living. He wrote many stories in the hall bedroom, after the recipes he had studied. They must, he saw, be " all sweetness and gaiety and humor. We must discuss only our better selves and arrive at a happy ending. Marriage was a serene and delicate affair. Love was made in heaven and lasted forever. . . . If a man did an evil thing it was due to his lower nature, which really had nothing to do with his higher. . . ."

But these precepts were useless; life was not like that; he found it impossible to go so far afield. Always his stories came back to him — failures, he knew it himself, being neither insipid, charming romances, nor studies of the life he was miserably immersed in.* 150,000 people, as he tells it, were in the depths of poverty in New York that winter, many of them with no work at all, no place to sleep but over gratings or in doorways. They wandered in the Bowery and the streets off of it " in the depths of poverty " " a whorl of bums and failures," and he with them. More than ever he was haunted by the giant deductions of the scientists he had read in Pittsburgh: " Man was a mechanism, undevised and uncreated, and a badly and carelessly driven one at that. Then to embitter him there was always like an evil and enviable presence Ward McAllister and his gilded Four Hundred. " Life was

* In the field of verse sometimes, it seems, he was able to suit conventional taste. *Spanish-American War Songs* contains a poem signed Theodore Dreiser. The pathetic theme may well have been his, but the format betrays a need of acceptance: " Lo, no pain can thwart the holy — Nor yet fear retard the free; — Right makes giants of the lowly, . . . Losing fury to their plea. . . ." Occasional acceptable verse, however, was not enough to support him.

desolate, inexplicable, unbelievably accidental — luck or disaster." None the less, perhaps because of its desperate balance sheets, there was " zest " to the city, "something secret and thrilling." Four years later out of the ledger of these days came the setting and the figure of Hurstwood in *Sister Carrie,* going down out of prosperous glitter into the whorl of disaster and silence of suicide. And sketches now collected in *The Color of a Great City* — *The Bowery Mission, The Water Front, The Cradle of Tears* — were tapped from these memories. Often he has drawn on the mood that shrouded him then. It became part of him, a new base. In adversity his father was growing into him, superseding, undermining the " pagan " mother, so much adored. But at the time he never thought that melancholy could be changed over into words that readers would thank him for. Instead, he says, as the weeks went by offering nothing, " I got terribly depressed. My money was dwindling, I thought, my gosh, I would have to go back to newspaper work."

Today Dreiser is known and described as three different men contradicting one another. One is a brusque churlish fellow, who frightens people when he answers them on the telephone, and appears hard when accused of unfairness or indifference, who frequently is accused without troubling to defend himself. " The most disagreeable man I ever met, no manners at all ! " " Utterly unscrupulous, an S-of-a-B ! " they say of him and shudder. " A handsome dog, but the manners of a railway boarding house," Mencken writes him was the impression of a lady he had asked him to call on. Then there is the man people love to be with. They say that no one is better company than Dreiser to walk with, drink with, eat with, talk with (and there are women who have said to live with). His appetite is boundless for the human and the nonhuman, his five senses alert. Before joys and sorrows he is humble not arrogant. He tells fabulous stories and listens to them; laughs until he cries at funny things and preposterous things, and when the joke is on himself. He will go anywhere in talk, asking where he can't tell. He will go anywhere on walks; no limit placed on adventures, except time and the need to achieve. His books which are a weave of monotony shot with extravagance, offering immoderate and homely characters, and rare men and women as well, bear witness to the second man.

Then there is the solitary man, loose-jointed, wondering and wandering; eyes with worlds in them, aristocrat's nose, voluptuous mouth, and yet scornful, not snarling or jeering, but nearly ready to snarl or jeer if a heart full of tears and struggle would let him. This is the lonely intellect, the spontaneously conscious man, who over a period is spectator, and then suddenly is actor, good for the center of the stage. At times he has the look of a tough careless weed, burdock or mullen or of a giant radish — the Hoosier look magnified. Sometimes he has the magnitude of a river image, moulded out of clay, not yet in bronze, what with a potentate's hands, and a look of distances between the parts of him, as if it might be dogmatic, not leisurely enough, to bring them together into single purpose, unless that action were crucial — a birth out of headwaters, the descent over rapids, the fall over precipices, the wide delivery to the sea. Dreiser, the creator of disturbing chronicles and inquiries, is this man of the earth, mineral and vegetable as well as animal. He is a logical derivative out of the little boy who was looked on as " queer " in Warsaw. Today in New York, acknowledged and successful, in a crowd as at one of his own cocktail parties of editors, agents, celebrities and hangers-on, and their many preening girls, he has the look of ancient river-lands, of the clay and flow of rivers, remembering equally canyons and lowlands and cities, pine forests and weeds and tin cans. He looks solitary more than he does metropolitan.

I have met with no one but himself to describe him at this period, but I imagine Dreiser at twenty-four to have been solely this third man, the creative dreamer, luckless and puzzled as to how to get on. I imagine him to have been stained by the sea-voices and sea-odors of Manhattan and by the lurid extremes of life in that city, just as inoculated with beauty at birth by his mother, he had been drenched in the seduction of Indiana valleys up to the age of sixteen. I think he was not yet the wary ungracious Dreiser, nor for the moment the gregarious high-spirited Dreiser of five years before or even a year before, who alone but not lonely had found friends and patrons to be linked with — Maxwell, McEnnis, McCullagh, McCord, Hazard, Alice, Arthur Henry, his fiancée, Paul and others. I imagine that here in New York he was sharply alone, walking among these ghosts of the great city in a mournful luxury of contemplating them — phantoms of greed and failure.

Already he knew that when a man asked to succeed, the implicit questions were: " Are you a mixer, a good fellow? Are you a red-blooded he-man, rude and shrewd? Can you wear these clothes? No promotion for a man who can't wear American business clothes." And what was their purpose? To pander and to fight, to cheat and to pander, these business clothes were planned. To mix, to smirk, to join in with the right crowd — meet the wife, have another drink, send for a couple of floozies; and, of equal importance, to intimidate, to sneer, to snarl at the wrong crowd — to put something over, let someone out, give someone the merry ha-ha: these were the ways to come home with the goods. If a man knew how, the job was his; if not, he was the under-dog, the humble clerk or the derelict. Already he had learned this from the New York World, where he had been told he did not fit the clothes, which had to be smarter and slicker than what men wore with success in the Middle West. In a way he was glad; the artist in him disdained these juvenile uniforms. But now that he was nearing his last cent and getting nowhere, he would have to wake up and join in the fight; get in or go under; there was no middle way. To go under apparently was not to be his rôle. Mark Twain must have set himself the same problem — how to succeed in his own country. He solved it by posing as the respectable mixer, as least alien to his gift of genius; the merciless but ingratiating " king of humorists." Dreiser met it by wrapping himself, how consciously one can't know, in a kind of cave-man legend, cousin to the mammoth, as least alien to him, and became the fearful " realist." It may have been exactly in these months of lonely poverty that he began to evolve the formidable front of a conquering American, at variance with the poet in him, and yet well known now to those who stand in his way or try his patience or cut into his time.

Emily Dickinson wrote: " I took my power in my hand — And went against the world. . . . I aimed my pebble, but myself — was all the one that fell. . . ." Dreiser took his power in his hand too, but with it at this date, or another, he learned to couple some of the world's power. If he could help it, he would not be the only one to fall. For this undoubtedly he has allowed his texture to be loose. Having found the world's weapons useful to fight with, he has let the world into his weave of words too; takes from the outside where it suits him, yet without enough respect for it to acknowledge the debt; and without the agony that such help would cause a scrupulously intrinsic artist. The three men in him, competitor, companion, recluse, grow together and overlap in the artist. He is gold to be assayed and washed into purity by each new admirer, not found in sheer nuggets. He is an iron vein, not often tempered steel.

Like an iron prospect, he is impressive at twenty-four, immersed in a dream of realism, postponing the hour of expediency nearly to the moment of starving. A story he told me in another connection recreates these days. Once while planning this book, I had said that it would be one-sided unless it suggested the scope of his life with women. They were half of the legend surrounding him. To exclude them would make but another evasion, like most biographies. I wished he would catalogue them — the different blondes, brunettes, redheads, towheads, large ones and slim ones, susceptible and cold. . . . Their differences would help to paint his changing life. He said he didn't know; it was true there was no real story without them. He would have to think about it, perhaps he had told enough already. I would find them in *A Book About Myself*, in some of his short stories, *A Gallery of Women, This Madness, The ' Genius,'* which was not a portrait of himself but a composite picture, and yet he had drawn on his own life to make it. . . Then an idea occurred to me: Why not tell of the days and nights he had lived alone, and leave the rest to the indiscretion of the reader? That way my book would not grow too long. His answer was simple and serious: " But that would be only the first year in New York when I was thrown off the World. I was down and out. Sometimes I had hardly enough to eat. The rest of my life I have been pretty well taken care of. . . . And even then . . ."

He had pawned his watch, that last talisman of a man's distinction; the imprint of spirit on eyes, nose, mouth never having yet constituted a passport recognized by hotel clerks or policemen. It was a twenty-five-dollar watch, he had had ten dollars for it, and they were nearly gone. . . . He was walking in Carmine Street or Houston Street. A young Italian girl stopped him and asked him if he wouldn't come with her. He said he had no money. She insisted money made no difference, she liked him. She was the daughter of a restaurant keeper, who rented rooms above the restaurant. They went to hers. Afterwards she told him that her parents would like to give him a room for nothing next to hers; they liked him too. He imagined they hoped he would marry her. She was pretty and gracious and direct like a Latin of any class, though at the time he did not know how to account for her charm. But, he said, after he had left her, undecided whether to accept her offer and thus escape from misery and solitude: " I began thinking of that grand destiny of mine. Bad as things were, I could not get it out of my mind, and I never went back. For one thing these people were Catholics; already the Church had about done for me. I knew I must keep away from it. . . . Then they were too simple, too far from life." — " Too much out of the fight, you mean, too foreign? " I suggested. — " Well, perhaps."

As we talked I wondered how this story would have differed, had it been natural to him to apprentice himself to these frankly sensuous strangers, less simple, more highly seasoned probably than his fiancée's people in Missouri. Almost any Italian would understand better than a Methodist in Missouri the quest of a " grand destiny." But such an alliance was not for him. Always this writer has flirted with the exotic in himself: always curious, never for a moment scornful of it like Whitman and Twain and Sandburg, and even the melancholy Masters and the pliant Robert Frost. But for deepest penetration he has kept to the image of the native in himself, the Nordic American. What he knows of the universal, so often profoundly gauged, he knows first in native garb. What he has revealed of it is revealed because he has been tempted to strip it of its Butterick patterns, seduced first in spite of these patterns; and so has known the creature naked; and has attained to centers.

28

> "... I do count my syllables. But observe: my left hand lacks a finger — bitten off by a critic." "... Unfortunate man!" exclaimed the sympathetic monarch. "We must make your limitations and disabilities immaterial. You shall write for the magazines."
> — AMBROSE BIERCE

In May or June of this forlorn winter his brother Paul came back from the road. In the meantime he had been noticing on the stands a musical magazine published by Ditson, made up of popular songs, "semi-classical stories and pictures." At the same time he used to look at the foreign magazines — more "snappy," he thought, than any published in New York. The English Sketch, for instance, printed " really intelligent comments beneath the pictures." He told Paul that if Howley Haviland would let him edit a magazine, he could make an improvement on Ditson's. They agreed that he should try it at ten dollars a week to begin with, but not until autumn. He wonders now how he got through the summer, but October came and found him alive, ready to edit Every Month, ready to compete once more in the battle for food. So he went running like a fish from dark pools to pleasanter shallows, in search of a small living. He ran the paper for a year and a half, and made it a paying enterprise for new popular ideas. He remembers feature articles, suggested by his newspaper experience, about compositors, electrotypers and printers. He became at once an "idea-man." "Curiously enough," he says with pride, almost more than he shows at the vast response to his books: "I had numerous letters and contributions from all kinds of people." Then, gratefully: "I never made much money out of it, stayed on in my hall bedroom, but I got it through my skull what a magazine was."

One day it occurred to him that he was wasting his time " fixing up other fellows' articles." Why not market his own? He could see that magazine readers were asking for lively stories about real people and things. They would take him nearer to his heart's desire — to write about life as he saw it. Or at least it seemed to him that such articles would in a literal sense be true, while the fiction of the day must be false in every sense. He chose as his first subject American women harpists, of the sort eminent enough to play in Carnegie Hall. He interviewed them and made the article " a study in personalities." The editor of Munsey's bought it for $75 for the pictures and the idea; the writing, he was told, was worth nothing. His next article was a picture of New England society women, inspired by pictures he found of them at Sarony's, a fashionable New York photographer of the Nineties.

It is probable that they fascinated Dreiser. Though known as a literary roughneck, what is delicate and refined exercises fascination over him. Some of them were doubtless rational Unitarian matrons, proud to be " sensible," but others may have been quite exquisite flowers — sumptuous hair, billowy sleeves, suppressed bosoms, fragile waists, dainty hands; and all had an air of meticulous breeding, or else they would not have been listed as New England society women. One could know that their handkerchiefs were sheerest linen hemstitched with infinitesimal stitches, indeed that all their apparel was sewed with scrupulous stitches and faintly scented with lavender. When they traveled they wore at their waists silver chatelaines, which included little bottles of smelling salts. They were still such ladies, such yield of " virtue lodged in sinew stark," these leaders of New England propriety — one could not say fashion — since with them it was vulgar to be fashionable! The mystery of their refinement may have even gone like an arrow to the young journalist's sense of the exquisite and the unattainable. It was something of this he hoped he had found in his Missouri school teacher, and something of this he has cultivated in his way of living, which has a puritan order and precision, contradicting other phases of him.

He sold the article to the New York Sunday Journal at $125. The modern "idea-man" was developing in him. To various magazines he served articles about painters, sculptors, musicians, writers, financiers, inventors, always with photographs, etchings or drawings. Howells furnished him with material for a portrait, and liked it so well that he invited him to come and see him. After the visit he wrote a second article, calling him a "nobleman of literature." Today he says of him: "Yes, I know his books are pewky and damn-fool enough, but he did one fine piece of work, *Their Wedding Journey,* not a sentimental passage in it, quarrels from beginning to end, just the way it would be, don't you know, really beautiful and true." They drank tea together quietly this afternoon in 1897, a servant or so around, no one else. Howells was never to make much of him, nor invite him to a literary evening and read the poets to him, as he did for the more aesthetic "new people coming, coming." A boundless curiosity in the eyes of this boy coupled with a looseness of manner and ignorance of etiquette were doubtless alarming to the older Westerner, who cared so little for life and so much for New England deportment in the guise of letters. They talked agreeably without much in common. Dreiser remembers him as kindly.

These articles, between 1897 and 1901 covered ground, went out of New York, now and then out of the country. Musicians first, especially women, were served up, the step nearest to the musical Every Month. Then artists, financiers, inventors and statesmen — Anthony Hope, the real Zangwill, MacMonnies, Bayard Taylor, Nathaniel Hawthorne, William Dean Howells twice, Frank W. Gunsaulus, Paul Bartlett, Theodore Thomas, John Burroughs twice, Edmund Clarence Stedman, associate of Mark Twain, Alfred Stieglitz, Mrs. Kenyon Cox, Philip D. Armour, Marshall Field, Andrew Carnegie, Chauncey M. Depew, John H. Patterson, cash register magnate, Thomas Edison, Joseph Choate, Champ Clark, "so crooked," the wise-crack went, "he could not lie straight in bed "; and a quantity of painters and sculptors, now forgotten. Dreiser in picking essential names seems not to have made a mistake in the future eminence of a writer or financier, while today among painters and sculptors only Stieglitz and Paul Bartlett remain as names. His eye for the visual arts was more optimistic than it was educated. He lets his wish for them in American life stand for the deed. It is none the less a sign of a more eager world, that young and obscure artists could interest readers of Truth Magazine, Metropolitan, Cosmopolitan, Demorest's, The Family Magazine, Everybody's, Ainslee's, Pearson's. The American magazine was entering its last innocent decade, 1900 to 1910.

Further articles of his suggest the palate of that day: *The Museum of Natural History, The Packing Industry, Craze for a New Disease, Brandywine the Picturesque, The Making of Small Arms, Carrier Pigeons in War Time, Historic Tarrytown, Artistic Studios, The Making of Stained Glass Windows, The Home of William Cullen Bryant, Our Government and Our Food, Human Documents from Old Rome, New York's Underground Railroad, The Railroad and The People, The History of the Horse, The Trade of the Mississippi, The Apple Industry, The Rural Free Delivery, Plant Life Underground, Why the Indian Paints his Face.* Sightseeing for others was very soon for Dreiser profitable and unpalatable. In a year he had written some fifty articles at $100 to $150 a piece, and was not any more a dreaming pauper. But not one of them could be intensive or crucial. He could only skim the surfaces for magazine display. The deep reactions he got from these excursions he had to check for later use.

In the meantime he worked at terrific speed spurred on by new money, new friends, new prestige. There is a solemn fashion among critics to deplore worldly success for geniuses, to applaud them most when starved and persecuted. Van Wyck Brooks, for example, scolds Mark Twain incessantly through 267 pages, because he liked money and fame. He scolds him for his jokes even, about as Aunt Polly scolds Tom Sullivan, only in radical rather than Methodist language: " Can Mark Twain keep the golden thread in his hands long enough? . . . No, and the time is up. Circumstance steps in and cuts the golden thread, and all is lost." * And yet is it true that all was lost? Take a plunge into the wide promiscuous river, Mark Twain, and you will bathe in living language of which his virtuous critic is incapable. Sad of course that this giant of earlier days could not have coupled with his splendor the faith of Whitman, the purity of Poe or Jesus or Modigliani, but not quite so tearful as Mr. Brooks would have us think.

Dreiser too has been invoked as a paragon, and then assailed by earnest critics for lapses into money making which have lost him integrity of style, as they lost Twain integrity of theme. Yet those who blame him lack his talent for extremes — his appetite for glory, his compassion in the face of misery. To look at it quite simply, it is not in them to imagine the sheer delight of changing from a hall bedroom to a writer's " studio," of buying a whole meal and paying for it — the intoxication of being sought, not always seeking. Within a year these refreshments came to Dreiser and he had two years of comfort before again he forsook it for the unknown dangers of *Sister Carrie*.

His work for Every Month had already taken him among young people of his own interests, as in St. Louis, with the difference that here there were as many girls as men. Some of them had come away to escape the monotony of Western homes; some had already been to Paris and Munich, as much to learn how to live like artists, Dreiser noticed, as to be artists. Bohemian New York was in full swing. Once he had gone to solicit a double page center from a young painter later known for his Spanish-American war pictures, Louis Sontag, W. L. S. of *Twelve Men*. He was an inventor as well, made and played with models of war ships and railroad trains. His toy engine was " strong, heavy, silent running, with the fineness and grace of the perfect sewing machine," so Dreiser describes it. He devised a scheme that was a forerunner of moving pictures; was an expert

* *The Ordeal of Mark Twain:* A shrewd analysis of the great humorist, wherein it is forbidden to laugh.

fencer, bicyclist, trick-rider, photographer, and tenor. Dreiser who venerates skill and versatility in another became one of his friends and audience. He was equipped to do rapidly just what he himself in the old days had dreamed he must do — "succeed." Soon Sontag was illustrating Kipling! He reminded him of Kipling, facile and brilliant. And he had business sense; used to explain how he always put "a good stiff price on his drawings; it encouraged respect for them." Of course the studio, with Turkish corners, of so tense and volatile a creature was filled with friends. He "lived close" to them, Dreiser says, and "never neglected" them. One feels that this man was tonic to him, gave him a sense of aptitude and fitness he had not met before, that went almost for absolute values. Then one day he died of fever at Tampa; and left him with the feeling that he "had been looking at a beautiful lamp, lighted and warm . . . and then suddenly it had been puffed out before my eyes, as if a hundred bubbles of irridescent hues had been shattered by a breath. We toil so much, we dream so richly, we hasten so fast, and lo! the green door is opened. We are through it, and its grassy surface has sealed us forever from all which . . . we . . . crave — even as, breathlessly, we are still running." *

There were others too, who did not go through the green door — an alluring group to him, avid for a nascence of the arts and of the libertine ways of artists. He was in and out of their studios. They made a fourth group to bring later into his storied world. Some of them already were going through the swinging door of the saloon into disaster, and some of them through seductive doors of social prestige into worldliness. But they were young and hopeful then, and had before them the democratic ideal, the cream tart — Success. His acquaintance with Crowninshield, that American priest of the arts and of fashion, dates from this time. He admired him then and now, for talents important to the health and bloom of a city. Dreiser is the one American radical frankly obsessed with the need of social gaiety and luster. He loves New York for being Babylon, wishes it might

* *Twelve Men.*

be even more so; not for himself personally but for the splendor of the town. If unwittingly Emerson has helped to make and dessicate old Boston, Dreiser has helped to make and infect modern New York; by giving it his carnal blessing.

Three years now since his last delirious thwarted week with his fiancée. It was getting harder and harder to write to her. Her image was fading with time and distance. There were other intimacies. One of these, a beautiful creature with a voice and a career before her surprised him with the gift of a summer of romance in Virginia mountains. She was the first girl of distinction he had ever met, who unlike the Missouri school teacher, wanted to give and take freely; indeed who arranged it as one would a sumptuous party, and then withdrew to the pursuit of her career, explaining that they had known the best of each other, that the rest would be commonplace. She appears in *The " Genius,"* the image of a peony.

Another in this year 1897 to 1898 seemed so essential to him that he would have broken his engagement in Missouri, if only she had relinquished her ambition to be a writer. She came from a family of importance in Washington and was already engaged to be married, but felt that she belonged to Dreiser. Together as writers they would reach the promised land of fame. They needed each other, she told him. But he " couldn't see it that way." No household could succeed with more than one egotist in it. Perhaps he had learned to believe this from the Blue Ridge peony. Anyway again he thought of " his grand destiny " and again regretfully broke with proffered and accepted love.

Soon his means of earning a living became like sawdust to him. " There was nothing to it." If he had had an intellectual Aunt Polly to admonish him, he would have been quick to agree. The affluent magazine world, he felt, was " a closed door " to live work, to " art," which had been his unfound bride. " I did not want to fritter life away over magazine articles. The best a publicist could hope to become would be an Ida Tarbell, a Ray Stannard Baker, a Lincoln Steffens," he explains, looking back on that time; whereas he had pledged himself to intensive freedom of the mind. But how to live outside of magazines? How to use his own temperament and make it count?

Again he thought of his first ambition — a play. Today he says wistfully: "That form has always seemed most natural to me. Shakespeare was right, "the play's the thing." He wishes now he had kept to it. "A man is gloriously articulate in a great play; he is a voice; his words are no longer thoughts, they are acts, a challenge direct to an audience." I spoke of Frost's definition of poetry: "Words that have become deeds." "Yes," he said, " a poem *is* a play, it moves and speaks." He thinks it was chance, not preference that made a novelist of him.

Perhaps it was pioneer instinct that has kept him a novelist. Masters, Frost and Ring Lardner,* have likewise written plays and hoped for production. But what chance for any one of quick vision when Protestant code had for some centuries destroyed drama by prohibiting passion. We have had leading men and leading ladies and their able troupes all in the English tradition. But how could we have a vital theatre out of a people, the action of whose bodies had been locked by two centuries of protesting, until negation had been reached. Mitchio Ito, the Japanese dancer once said: "You will notice that your actors act with their faces; the Latin races act with face and body; the Japanese wear masks, they express the meaning with bodies only, like acrobats, like dancers, like soldiers."

If now we are about to become a dramatic people it will be as adopted children of the Negro music-hall and the Jewish theatre, set free by a lawlessness, which, following the law of change, will begin to seek a new order more in keeping with freedom of body and mind. The Nineties yielded a few stars and a nation of spectators and story-tellers; among them flawless mimics. There have always been clowns, and there begin to be dancers and athletes who might make actors for a playwright able

* Ring Lardner has appeared twice as playwright on Broadway but both times propped by collaborators alien to his genius.

to galvanize us into native speech. If ever this hero appears, I think it will not be fantastic to say that first Whitman, then Dreiser, then Masters among writers will have opened the way for him into the jungle of human passions.

29

" Arthur Henry blew in."

Toward the spring of 1897 there came to New York the chance which according to Dreiser made a novelist of him. He came as advance agent for Hermann, the magician, bent on a career of fiction and pleasure. Their friendship, begun in Toledo days, put to sea again. They complemented each other, the light and the heavy, ballast and sails. Henry was certain that they could write fiction, and that he himself could write it only in company with Dreiser. In the same room, at the same time, at the same table they were to work out their separate short stories, advising and encouraging each other. Henry had what he called " a doctrine of happiness," hypnotic to the heavier more sceptical realist: " Money? Pooh! It was for those who no longer had the capacity to enjoy life. Mind was the key to every secret and every delight." * He appears to have administered just the elixir necessary to start this gloomy uncertain young man on the road to being what is now called both in and out of the market " our foremost novelist." He was his second teacher in aesthetics; McCord the first one, to whose flute the black girls in the St. Louis *bagnio* used to " dance in some weird savage way that took one instanter to the wilds of Central Africa." † Henry taught him to trust himself and go the limit without thought of censor. And I imagine he awoke in him too a sense of style for the sake of style, most apparent in his early writings. He was a messenger from the gods to guarantee the way. Too bad that the lonely Melville found no friend like this; but only the morbid illustrious Hawthorne who grew to fear more than love the gist of Melville. A pity too that Clemens had no one to advise him more kindred than the

* *Rhona* in *A Gallery of Women*.   † *Peter* in *Twelve Men*.

eminent Howells, who was forever coaching him to be fit for the company of Emerson, Whittier, Holmes, etc., where he felt, he said, like a "bar-keeper in heaven." Whitman according to biography was luckier than these two, and like Dreiser, had a gift for friendships with men. When Emerson "saluted him on the threshold of a great career," and Whitman in modern style used the words to advertise his censured *Leaves of Grass,* Emerson was scandalized, and when they met, did his utmost to get him to suppress "offensive passages." But Walt with his sea-captains and bus-drivers, and intellectual cronies at Pfaff's on Bleeker Street, found it easy to do without famous patronage.* The ingredients of achievement defy analysis. But perhaps lucky friendships and fortunate love, when changed often enough, contribute to a hero's fidelity to theme.

Of Henry, Dreiser writes: "Because I liked him much . . . I was inclined to let him have his way. He was too delightful and interesting not to humor. . . . Everything he did and said and thought was right with me, even though I knew at times it was really quite wrong." And so, certain that no story of his could sell, he was swept into this literary partnership, which kept the two for a time inseparable. Then, he says, Henry became more sybarite than artist and gradually they drifted to their separate roads. Also, he complains, the sybarite had a "vaulting egotism" and "loved to direct and control as well as argue," which may have had more to do with the case. Knowing that Dreiser has a gift for estrangement nearly equal to the gift for engagement, I wondered what would be Henry's version of their friendship. Without it the history of the author of *Sister Carrie* was incomplete. I wrote him, saying that Dreiser had sanctioned the book I was making, indeed that he appeared to prefer pre-mortems to post-mortems, out of egotism some people said, but I thought more out of the wish of the scientist to establish facts; and that I hoped for his story. After some months in which he maintained a silence perhaps in Hollywood, perhaps in heaven — no one seemed to know — an answer came from Rhode Island, of which

* *Walt Whitman: Le Grand Flaneur,* by Cameron Rogers.

already I have quoted passages. It is so refreshing a tribute to a man as much defamed as he is exalted, that I give the rest of it here:

"Dreiser's chronicle of our association is correct. He is generous toward me but I who know him better than anyone know that he is the most generous — the least self interested of men. You are right as to his impelling desire of analysis and corresponding lack of egotism. . . . Unlike the scientist, however, his vision is obscured or rather colored by a profound tenderness which unfortunately he has learned to mistrust — by a compassion that torments him with a magnified idea of the misfortunes of others. He gives his coat to a beggar in rags, just as he seeks to clothe in virtue all the tattered characters of the world. I know no one more sensitive to beauty or . . . luxury and convenience, but he is at the same time more conscious than anyone I know, of the multitude who are deprived of these. He seems to feel responsible for all the misery of the world and for every unqualified wretch or abortive scoundrel born into it. . . .

"For many years I fished and hunted and played with Dreiser in a World of Thought and found him always a true sportsman. The ideas I caught seemed to him larger than his own. . . . If I inspired him it was because I insisted on his looking at and appreciating *His Own*. Dreiser will not have fulfilled his mission in the world until he sits down to a novel in the mood in which he composes a poem — and sustains that mood with all his people, rich and powerful and poor and weak, until he finishes it."

"When I cast off all restraints and went to New York with nothing but a pad and a pencil, I found Dreiser editor of a magazine. We lived and worked together — often finishing each other's articles. If I read them today I could not tell what was his or mine. Our stories were more our own. We talked them over together but wrote them with less collaboration. He helped me most with *The Unwritten Law* — picking me up when it had me down.

"Wonderful years — a forecast I hope of an eternal relationship in the spiritual life hereafter."

And finally the version of their separations, more delicate than Dreiser's; possibly less honest, as if being a negative matter, it were of small importance thirty years after, beside the reality of their life together:

"In answer to your question.
We drifted apart and drifted together again as the tide comes and goes. The moon controls such things — and must be held responsible."

At first reading, one would say that Henry remembered his friend only at his best, but the tribute contains two reservations — " His vision is colored by profound tenderness, *which unfortunately he has learned to mistrust."* And: " Dreiser will not have fulfilled his mission in the world until he sits down to a novel in the mood in which he composes a poem . . ." Perhaps more sensitive than creative, he hoped for his stronger partner to create *for* him according to his program, like a wife who is ambitious for her husband and alienates him that way.

Impossible to know the exact nature of the bond and the break between the two, only that success came to them together. The first story of Dreiser's to issue from their workroom he called *The Shining Slave Makers*. It is published now unchanged except for title, in *Free and Other Stories.** A man goes to sleep in the grass under a shady tree among ant-hills; he dreams of joining ant life in a time of famine and war between black and red ants. The irony of Dreiser's own struggle of the last ten years is in this allegory. The cruelty of enemy against enemy fighting for bread, fighting for life, blindly fighting, and the satirical tenderness of ally for ally aligned against an arbitrary enemy, is here — a full-fledged Dreiserian equation: A and B and C, which we know, equal X, the unknown. He seems to be thinking aloud, exposing what he had heard for many a year: Join the tribe, fight for the tribe, die for the tribe; that way alone lies safety. Death alone is safe.

Robert Frost, the most astute of our critics, though with him criticism is implicit in his poems or revealed in talk, once said in a lecture, that a man would strike his gait in poem or story or any other work of art in his early twenties, if he were ever to do it; that then there might be years of falling short of it, but once there in his youth, he had a chance to come back. I have read none of Dreiser's earlier writings, but I imagine that sometimes they held promise of this mature story written in his twenty-seventh year. It has in it the iron of his special temperament and little of the slag:

* *McEwen of the Shining Slave Makers.*

"McEwen, in a strange daze and lust of death seemed to think nothing of it. He was alone now — lost in a tossing sea of war, and terror seemed to have forsaken him. It was wonderful, he thought, mysterious —. . . Enemy after enemy assailed him, he fought as he best knew, an old method to him, apparently, and as they died, he wished them to die — broken, poisoned, sawed in two. He began to count and exult in the number he had slain. It was at last as though he were dreaming, and all around was a vain, dark, surging mass of enemies."

Their separate stories finished, he sent his to the Century Magazine. He had written the fable lightly enough, and he insists, chiefly because whenever he stopped, Henry stopped too, unable to go on. It is in keeping with his drama that with these first few pages, and unintentionally, he had then and there challenged the enemy he was destined to fight through so many years — Orthodoxy. The way a ring follows the pressing of a button, the emissary stepped out in the person of Robert Underwood Johnson, understudy to Howells, editor of the august Century, and resident then and now of Murray Hill.

30

"We like Boston. . . . Their hotels are bad. Their pumpkin pies are delicious. Their poetry is not so good. . . . Their Common is no common thing — and the duck pond might answer — if its answer could be heard for the frogs. . . . But with all these good qualities the Bostonians have no soul."   EDGAR ALLAN POE

To understand this emissary it is necessary to go back again a generation. When the young pilgrim, William Dean Howells (who appears to be one of the subordinate villains in this narrative of facts) came East in 1861 from his Ohio village to find the great world, he went first to Boston and Concord. There he talked in the Parker House over a bottle of Medoc with Holmes and Lowell, on the hillside with Hawthorne, in his garden with Thoreau, in their studies with Emerson and Longfellow. They welcomed him as a messenger out of the West, romantic to their cultivated nerves much as the United States has recently been to cerebral Europeans. They were disappointed to hear that he did not want to be a Lochinvar, that the West was cold and hostile to the Arts, that he had come to learn from them to be an Easterner. At the same time they were grateful for his faith in their culture made of their life's blood and juices. Truth was, with their sages' minds and spinsters' bodies, as the years piled up, secretly they began to be assailed by doubts. A tiny fear was creeping in that perhaps not they, but their victims, some of whom had asked to be their friends — the lost Melville, the erotic Margaret Fuller, " Poor Margaret " they called her, or even the drunken Poe, " that jingler " * — all successfully disposed

* Emerson to the young Howells in their first talk.

of, might return and be the heroes in their stead in the days to come. Whitman's " barbaric yawp " impervious and mocking had unsettled these gentle intellects, gossiping over the hedges between their yards around suppertime. The young Ohian's praise came as balm to them. Howells on his side venerated them as high priests dispensing culture with which he might help to civilize the rest of the country, perhaps even, given time, the Middle West. He pledged himself to follow in their ways. Then he journeyed on to mundane New York, whose literary figures, Artemus Ward and others, seemed rough and cynical compared to the exquisite New Englanders. According to his memoirs they drank too much, told " objectionable " stories, swore and laughed and were venal about literature. Really in these memoirs Howells indicts himself — academician and parson. He is ringleader, self-confessed, of henchmen, who dedicated themselves to the task of diluting native expression in the name of " ennobling " it. Without their set-back, verbal America, already vivid with Melville, Poe and Whitman, might have come into its own a generation sooner. And its products would have been richer, because less hampered, and more coherent with the tragedies and victories of the centuries.

Howells fancied himself a realist and a native, but beneath surfaces certainly he and his friends were agents of Royalist ghosts who still knew how to make Yankees feel inferior for having cut loose in the eighteenth century. They catered to a reactionary mood constant in us, and periodically ascendant. Our rhythm has been in recurring overlapping waves of independence and humility. Always we have been breaking with the old countries and always straining back toward them hoping for a kind word, which they never give. No people so brash and none so deprecating as we are! In 1861 Howells shuddered at our vulgarity. He had not left Ohio to brook so shallow an attitude toward the arts. He established himself in the Murray Hill district of New York which connected with Beacon Hill if not with Concord. He accepted a position on the Atlantic Monthly which took him in person to Boston; and later another as consul to Venice, which was quite as proper, since it was correct for these bachelors to " transfer " to Italy. He wanted the impossible to happen — he wanted experienced artists, living without experience. His code triumphed into the new century, and then when the intellectual revolution came, out of promiscuous America, drenched in all races, all classes, it was a good one, a brute for a time, like drinking after prohibition, like machine guns in an atrophied city.

And always the arch-enemies, hidden and outspoken, of this new culture were bred in the Howells-Harpers-Century-Murray Hill tradition. Though for money they often had to let the newly rich into their offices and drawing-rooms, the newly intellectual they vowed to fight to the last ditch, and much as if they *were* gangsters, for daring to trespass on their ground, that of the spirit. The sometimes awkward, sometimes crucial Dreiser was among the first to suffer. Repeatedly he has taken punishment at their gentlemanly hands, perhaps more than anyone else. Fighting his way to their sacred printing presses, it is now traditional that he cleared the passage for the rebels who were to follow. After a while they came to be welcomed. Today they are treated as equals; some of them like it. One of them receives the Nobel prize. In fact for the time being genteel America persists in little more than politics; and yet has been strong enough to give distinguished sanction to the murder of Sacco and Vanzetti and to the entombment of Mooney and Billings.

Robert Underwood Johnson was made in this dignified mould, and has been true to it, having later been appointed ambassador to Italy. . . . When in 1897 he had read the few pages of Dreiser's fable of war, faithfully he returned the manuscript to its author with a " personal " letter protesting its " despicable philosophy." If that was the way this young man thought about life, the less he said about it the better. The young man wrote back defending himself. Again the answer came that Mr. Johnson seriously argued the right to express such ideas in print; he could not agree with them.

So now with this encounter the lonely changing backgrounds in which Dreiser had been merged recede slightly, and he begins to loom. Soon they will disappear placenta-wise. And in various shifting foregrounds of the next thirty years the detached child, delivered now to the scene, will engage with its actors. Among them will be friends and champions, jealous followers, and enemies bitterly despising him. From time to time there will reappear the type of the editor of the Century to protest his philosophy. He will be the purveyor of one-hundred-per-cent-literature, the kind allowed presidents and school children. He comes in the guise of the Vigilantes at the time of the Great War. He reappears at this very moment along with the lengthening of skirts, the "Humanist" of 1929 to 1930. Always his attempt has been to be a detractor of the sun.

I wonder at this type of mind. What is it that frightens these people? Take for example this allegory: *The Shining Slave Makers*. It was not, I think, that the editor was disputing the truth of it, convinced that war is kind and kindness always disinterested. It must be that he and his sort deny the right to perceive outside of strict limits. And invariably they confuse the one perceiving with his perceptions. "Aha!" they say, "this writer tells us men are cruel and deceptive just as nature is. That proves he enjoys these qualities — the brute, the liar, traitor to the human race, social menace, dangerous citizen!" And they hound him for telling tales on them — and on himself, it may be, or it may not be. So all at once and suddenly Dreiser, who has a consuming passion for society, was yet lined up against it, for having shocked one of its timid ambassadors. Soon he will be forced to learn the role of enemy.

In the meantime, having sold his wicked fable for $125 to the unsophisticated Ainslee's, a ten-cent magazine already pleased with his wares, he wrote five or six new stories to Henry's five or six, and sold them to the popular magazines. Among them are *Nigger Jeff* and *The Butcher Rogaum and His Door,* now collected in *Free and Other Stories*. These perhaps were never exposed to the frown of any pillar of society, and if they had been, might have passed. Their only possible offense could have been an inborn interest in low life — a tenderness toward the mother of a negro lynched for assault, and toward a too Calvin-like German butcher who suffered tortures for locking the door on his wayward daughter one night. He was writing as if the characters were himself. He was writing about the life of men and women and boys and girls and babies, quite nonchalantly now, as one might write about the life of bees or ants or mosquitoes, if one knew it. He was recording the buzzing and the humming, now loud, now low, now joyful, now frantic, and then silenced, as he heard it. And he might have continued to write like this for some years, peacefully and reflectively, recording both detail and structure of life, and selling his wares to the less carping magazines — for to his surprise he *was* selling them, and even his feature articles could be more like himself now — except that again the effervescent Henry interfered.

They had written short stories and succeeded — some of them out in Ohio under the trees on the lawn of Henry's village home. They were both in a fever of creation from delight in the country and each other. Henry insisted, they must embark at once, each one of them, on a novel. Dreiser protested; the struggle for life was too fierce; he couldn't afford a novel yet; no novel of his would be accepted. But the sybarite prevailed. They were back in New York now. One day in October, 1899, Dreiser, according to legend, found himself writing two words on a clean sheet of paper out of a detached brain. Two words that have become a part of his history and ours: *Sister Carrie*. They rank in prevalence with *The Scarlet Letter, Moby Dick, The Raven, Leaves of Grass, Huckleberry Finn, Ethan Frome, Spoon River Anthology, Winesburg Ohio, Babbitt*, etc.

31

> *" Our civilization is still in a middle stage, scarcely beast, in that it is no longer wholly guided by instinct, scarcely human, in that it is not yet wholly guided by reason."*
> DREISER: SISTER CARRIE

I asked Dreiser if really it were true that the name came first and the characters and theme afterwards. " Yes, actually! My mind was a blank except for the name. I had no idea who or what she was to be. I have often thought there was something mystic about it, as if I were being used, like a medium." Curiously I remember hearing Masters speak of his *Spoon River* in the same way: " Sometimes I think I didn't write it. It passed through me, I was only the medium for it." So the two first imageries of the two Americans most native and subversive to their period were conceived mysteriously, out of the unknown, if we take their word for it. Though labeled realism, they bear in truth the footprints of the inevitable, the signature of Nature.

With Dreiser, the identity of Sister Carrie coming alone from her small country town to Chicago, to sink or swim in that " sea of life," and the identity of the other lives as they were linked with hers and unlinked — these, he said, followed as if out of a dream, whole and alive. He began at once to weave them into their story in October, 1899. He worked with ease until some time in December. Then something interfered, he doesn't know what, but he had to quit for a while. He and Henry were at work separately now, although they still advised and consulted.

Henry was writing a romance, *The Princess of Arcady*, and at the same time was engaged in Arcadian pursuits. A young woman whom Dreiser had found to copy their manuscripts, the owner of a successful typing office, had fallen in love with this blue-eyed, fair-skinned friend. She was ready to pay for his time by catering to every whim, chief of which was that the close partnership of these two men should not dissolve. She was generous and self-effacing to the proverbial fault. When summer came, she even rented an island near Nantucket and a sailboat, where they used to go luxuriously to play and work.* But none the less her entry broke the spell of friendship for Dreiser. Besides, so much romance and dalliance did not mix with his more desperate plans. Henry had provided the spark; he was beginning not to feed the flame.

A year before, another complication had entered in. He was called upon to face an almost forgotten bond — his engagement in Missouri. The note had come due, and must be paid now or never. If never, the flower-like face, the stark red braids, the passionate body not yet his, might not be alive to him or another. So he read in a letter from her sister, who feared for her health and perhaps for her life if this long waiting had to go on. The bond between them was tougher than with Alice of his first romance, or else the need for marriage was greater. And then, too, he loved the sister, he remembers in a kind of guilty after-thought. But what more natural? Sisters have often been loved in pairs, trios or even quartets. . . . On Christmas day the two daughters of the Missouri patriarch, bringing with them the fragrance of fields and hedges, met him in Washington. And Sarah White and Theodore Dreiser were joined in what she believed to be holy wedlock.

The book of newspaper days ends with an elegy and no song of praise to this event, which took place " after the first flare of love had thinned down to the pale flame of duty." Yet there are chapters in *The " Genius "* given over to the hero's early days of marriage, drawn from his own marriage, he says, which give a less dreary account of it. There are oblivious nights, followed by breakfasts which, besides making the mouth water, read like flawless erotic favors, hand-made and hand-served by his wife. Yet too there is a sense of

* *Rhona: A Gallery of Women.*

defeat, of being cheated, as if he were saying, "Is this all, wasn't there to be more?" Possibly this half-way exciting, half-way disappointing marriage interfered with the progress of *Sister Carrie*. Or it may have been the temporary loss of the magical Henry, by temperament a magician's advance-agent. Or else the enterprise itself was carrying him into problems yet beyond him — this lonely making of a novel without American precedent in theme or treatment.

Something blocked the way. He says of these months, December and January: "I had to quit, it seemed to me the thing was a failure, a total frost. . . . I think I experienced a defeat in the face of Hurstwood's defeat as to Carrie. I took it up again once or twice but had to quit. I tried writing stories; thought I had better go back to articles. . . . I had reached the place where Hurstwood robs the safe. I didn't know where I was going; I had lost the thread. . . . Then in February, Arthur Henry, off flirting with some girl, came back and read it. He thought there was nothing wrong with it, told me I must go on. . . . I managed to solve the problem and for a while it went pretty good, until I came to the question of Hurstwood's decline, which took me back to the World days. Then I had to stop again. Somehow I felt unworthy to write all that. It seemed too big, too baffling, don't you know? . . . But after a month I managed to get the thread, and finished it up in May. . . . Henry read it and said 'Don't change a word.' But I spent some weeks revising it; he helped me. In May or June 1900 I sent it to Harper's. I knew one of the editors. They refused it. Then I took it down to Doubleday's. In November it was out."

I quote this as he told it to me in July 1930, wishing I could get his tone of voice into the words, like loose earth, and into the memory like roots of trees, as if he were digging them up to transplant them. "I felt unworthy to write all that, you know," came like a surprise. I did not know. I think that I have not heard elsewhere such abject reverence in the face of misery as suddenly sounded in this man's voice. If genius is caring for human beings more than others know how to care, then Dreiser has genius. Or if it is true that the great Don Juans are also the greatly religious men, then Dreiser is proved to be a voluptuary.*

So in November 1900 *Sister Carrie* was out. Not easily or happily, though in a sense gloriously, a new birth in the history of our books, and a perilous delivery. The two friends believed they had stripped it to form by cuts amounting to about 40,000 words. Henry, the acknowledged stylist of the two, was sure that now there was nothing to be changed. There is a story that Mrs. Dreiser helped with the revision, in fact that with her schoolteacher's training he studied English under her, but this he denies emphatically: " Oh, no, all she ever wanted to do was to cut out what she called ' the bad parts,' and she hadn't a chance at that. If I learned anything about style from another at this time, I owe it to Henry." The legend is that he has learned nothing about style at this time or another, generated at the outset by the jeers of the country's critics, that followed like so many pebbles and rotten eggs on the heels of publication.

As usual, the critics were wrong. A man's style is a man's self. As much as he had learned about himself, he had learned about style. In reality, *Sister Carrie* is flexible prose suited to subtle and trenchant meanings, passing at charged moments over into poetry, in the manner of all prose designed to the pulse of life. More than that, the book has few of the archaic trimmings and no trace of the diffuseness which Dreiser seems to have wished to make part of his style in later years. In fact it was a skilful package, made in America with a key to the universal, that went to the house of Harpers asking to be published.

They sent it back without a word — no flattering protest, this time, no invitation to try again. Ten years later, after British approval, it was offered once more and they accepted it. Dreiser says they were ethically shocked. I think perhaps also they were verbally and syntactically scandalized. It was one thing, though tough, to accept the conscious lingo of Whitman, Crane, and certain famous humorists. But for gentlemen of the Harvard Club and

* *Don Juan:* Joseph Delteil.

Century Club to fall for the guileless vernacular in which *Sister Carrie* often progresses, was another thing. For their eyes to encounter, outside of any quotation marks, spiritual or actual, *nice, swell, palavering, vest, grip, valise, flashy, influential, showy, nobby, fancy, truly swell saloon, exclusive circles, lovely home atmosphere, elegant mansions, dress-suit affair,* laced in and out of the unceremonial speech of the Middle West and classes — this was hard on their eyes. Useless to have reminded them that Shakespeare did it and Chaucer and Villon, and Mistral would! They liked the pure welded speeches of those countries and those times better than they did polyglot American derived from many incongruous floating sources. But this author did not; he liked his own speech and country as well or well enough. He wrote apparently as he talked and thought. When the idiom he had always heard and used seemed too meager to convey his meaning, he trimmed it sometimes with grace-notes from high-school days: *lightsome, halcyon, prancing pair of bays, airy grace, fine feather.* These too were part of that Prairie language; the girls sang them to sweet tunes and people used them for special occasions, letters and speeches. Perhaps they seemed ultra-innocent to the innocent editors who first refused *Sister Carrie.* It is true, they make a curious blend with the text book language — *formative, affectional, actualities* — in which the story also moves, just as American talk moves in impersonalities, so as not to feel the accusation of neglected personal values.

But, as they must have read early in the book, if they read it at all: ". . . words are but the vague shadows of the volumes we mean. Little audible links . . . chaining together great inaudible feelings and purposes." Here Dreiser detects a secret of language. It must be that not the words but the current connecting them, dictated not by the theme even, but by something more intangible, is what counts. Whitman and his disciple Traubel used the same words and the same theme, and yet Whitman resembles Homer more than he does Traubel and Traubel Whittier more than he does Whitman. And so with *Sister Carrie.* With commonplace humdrum words and phrases, as well as choice ones, the life of the delicious Carrie and the lusterless death of Hurstwood, like two crossed sails in a boat, reared themselves out of the commonplace of middle-class Chicago and transient New York — a sudden creation, an event like April weather. That the Harper editors could not feel the rain in their faces was a pity for them. Probably Dreiser was right, the "shameless" theme, rendered electrically so that it shocked them, was too much for them, and the shameless diction gave them their alibi.

32
"He was a quivering personality."
HENRY LANIER OF FRANK NORRIS

Now the novel becomes a hinge on which hangs an incident like luck in an Homeric legend. In the publishing company of Doubleday, Page & Co. there worked as proof-reader and adviser, when he was not off bass-fishing with his blonde, the one man to whom *Sister Carrie* would be like sudden rain, like frogs in March, a matter for elation. The man was Frank Norris, a young San Franciscan, already heroic as a novelist. He came from a more sophisticated family than Dreiser's. He had been educated in the University of California, and then had gone to Harvard to study writing, and then back to the Golden Gate. There he had been one of the editors of The Wave, a magazine of strugglers for art in the Far West, akin to the Chicago Chap Book, but fanned by winds from both East and West, France, England, and the Orient too. Water is a carrier of atmosphere. Land stops it. Though three times as far from Japan to San Francisco as from Paris to New York, the flavor of the Far East reached that coast as actually as Europe ever reached New York. Perhaps the California Indians with their excessively bright feather-masked ceremonies helped to intensify their ancestral spirit wafted across the Pacific from an ancient home, and kept it doubly floating for the sons of gold-seekers and fruit-growers who had come upon them. And there were other riches out there — long summers, phosphorescent ocean, redwood forest and a background of Spain and Mexico to fertilize the spirit. However it happened, these Westerners were at this date more untrammeled and inventive than the other groups back East, preoccupied with making America real, that is, a land of the spirit. An eight year old child learns in a public school that Greece had something Phoenicia lacked. A halo attaches to Athens and an infamy of trade to Carthage in the child's mind, for all of Dido's beauty. And so why not to his own United States, unless heroes joined together to change all that? . . . That they failed in California, was surely not Frank Norris's fault, nor George Sterling's, nor the fault of Charles Lummis nor of Ambrose Bierce, nor of Edward Sills. They were a halcyon lot, witty and enraptured, worthy of the men and women who crossed Death Valley on foot to get there. They called themselves Bohemians, and they called San Francisco " the cool grey city of love." They made one more adventure with their various journals and festivals, perhaps the most resourceful one, to fall before the wheels of finance, as each adventure of the kind has fallen in the history of our culture, that is up to date — before the wheels of the Southern Pacific Railway in their case.

Out of it before its collapse, Norris went East. There used to be a saying, ideas travel West, stories travel East. Like Jack London, Norris was a great story-teller and traveled East. He went to meet ideas nearer their source with which to find his bearings. More than London, he looked on writing as an art, never as propaganda, and on the novel as a sacred obligation: " Each age speaks with its own peculiar organ. . . . Today is the day of the novel. . . . By no other vehicle is contemporaneous life so adequately expressed." To be vital, the novel must grow out of real life, and not out of the idea of realism. Howells was a realist, he said, Zola a romanticist, since life beneath surfaces, taken in all its phases, sordid, unlovely, abnormal, was romance. " Realism stultifies itself, it notes only the surfaces." * With this faith in his heart, he had written stories of San Francisco for The Wave, and one novel, *Moran of the Lady Letty,* and two unpublished novels, *Vandover and The Brute* and *McTeague.* He was twenty-seven years of age.

This was the story-teller who in 1898 joined the house of Doubleday, McClure as reader and literary adviser, invited by Samuel McClure, who saw journalistic virtue in the serial novel appearing in The Wave. It was dated

* " *Responsibilities of the Novelist,*" Frank Norris.

with a current event, the sinking of the Maine and the outbreak of the Spanish-American War. Doubleday published the novel, a fair success, and then the great *McTeague,* written three years before — a success of scandal at first and then ignored in our country until long after Norris's death in 1907. With *Moby Dick* and *An American Tragedy* it shares that quality most praised by moderns — sense of volume. Dreiser writes of it:

> "In the days of its first circulation there was considerable complaint as to *McTeague's* vulgarity, the ignorance and brutality of its principals and their associates. For that was the day of transcendental perfection (on paper) throughout America! . . . To me when I first read it in 1900, it brought the thrill of realism as related to America. And what a thrill! At that time I was but twenty-nine and had just concluded *Sister Carrie* . . . my own work about Chicago and New York. Who was this man? . . . I inquired of my literary friends and . . . learned it was a first book by a young man out in San Francisco."

Unknown then to Dreiser, Frank Norris was already in New York; and *Sister Carrie* fell to him as part of the day's work of manuscript reading. It made an instantaneous appeal, which Yeats has called the test of art. He talked of it to everyone: "It is the best novel I have read since I have been reading for the firm, and it pleases me as well as any novel I have ever read, published or otherwise." Morgan Robertson, a writer of sea-stories, told how one morning happening to call on Norris in his office, he was met with the news: "I have found a masterpiece. The man's name is Theodore Dreiser." When Robertson said he knew him, he said: "Tell him what I think of it. I am writing him to call. I hope the house publishes it. It's a wonder." With the notation that it *must* be published, he gave the manuscript over to Henry Lanier, the junior partner, born in Georgia, brought up in Baltimore (son of the poet Sidney Lanier and a friend as well as associate of Norris).

"It hit him hard," Mr. Lanier said, who graciously had consented to think back for me to this spring of 1900. I said: "Perhaps it hit him especially hard, because wasn't Norris going back on himself at this period — that is, on the quality you find in *McTeague?* Had they made him feel in New York the pressure of commerce, when he wrote *The Octopus* and *The Pit?*" — "No, I wouldn't say that," was the answer of the more temperate Mr. Lanier. "Of course he was disappointed by the reception given *McTeague;* I think he could hardly believe it. But I wouldn't say he compromised to money in his later works. As I recollect his feelings at that time he merely thought *McTeague* must be too lonely and aloof to be reasonable. He was the kind of man who had to be acknowledged, and then he believed in ' the people ' more than the rest of us do. I remember he came in one day full of his ' big idea,' a *Wheat Cycle* in three parts, of which he finished two before his death, *The Octopus* and *The Pit*. He was like a fanatic, ablaze with it. ' He would knock 'em cold this time,' I remember he said. . . . I don't think he was pandering, he was too much in earnest, but he got to intellectualizing over the situation, so that perhaps there is not the first-hand quality, if you like, that there is in *McTeague*. The later work approaches journalism, possibly . . . I don't know. They were all big books. . . . Of course he liked luxury, clothes, restaurants, wine, the bright lights you might say, though not in a greedy way. . . . Then he had to have his girl, and he got her, married her. . . ." — "Was she attractive?" I asked. — "Really I can't say . . . not to me especially, but then I am old-fashioned. *He* liked her, she was a blonde, rather a large woman. . . . He liked fishing, was crazy about bass-fishing. I found him a cabin up on Greenwood Lake near Greenwich where he used to stay a good deal of the time. If I'm not mistaken he read Dreiser's *Carrie* up there. Yes, I seem to remember his bringing it down from the country one morning terribly excited about it. . . . No, I don't think Norris ever thought of money in connection with writing. Of course he was under a good deal of pressure at this time, but he was too much the artist. . . . We all loved him. . . . He was a quivering personality."

So between a dynamic personality, Dreiser, and a quivering personality, Norris, there blazed for a minute the fire-brand truth, luxury, art, whatever you prefer to call it — that element from which over and over again people fly. Truth like love is a luxury. We don't want luxury.

Today we fly from it in an aeroplane. But this new fraction of it, *Sister Carrie,* got this time by luck a running start. " It must be published," Norris said. Lanier read it and hated it, and agreed that they must publish it. For him, he explains, a man loving old mellow things, it was hateful. " It had no background ": the characters were treated as of equal importance with the most cultivated delightful men and women: whereas " people are not of equal significance " in his opinion. Nevertheless it was powerful, unavoidable. Norris was right, it had to be published. Then Walter Hines Page read it, later ambassador to England, at this time partner of Frank Doubleday in the stead of S. S. McClure who had by now gravitated back to his magazine. He agreed with the younger men that it was a book to publish, " a natural," he called it. A contract was drawn up and signed by the author and these two gentlemen. *Sister Carrie* was on the way to the printing press.

33

Famous Women of literature: Mrs. Grundy, otherwise Mrs. Samuel Clemens, otherwise Mrs. Frank Doubleday.

The legend goes,* and Mr. Lanier partly corroborates it, that at this moment Mr. and Mrs. Frank Doubleday, who had been traveling in Europe, returned to New York; and Mr. Doubleday, the senior partner, arriving at his offices in 25th Street, among other matters was confronted with this initial novel of an unknown Hoosier. Since it was Saturday he took it to his home in Oyster Bay, a suburb of Murray Hill and Washington Square, to read it over the week-end. And then . . . and then, according to fable, again enters the villain, Propriety — this time, if you have not guessed it, in the refined and engaging dress of Mrs. Frank Doubleday. And here since no one can or will recollect this particular week-end, there is nothing to do but to imagine the scene. First, however, it is possible to identify the enemy — according to her friends, an almost perfect woman, wife, mother, church member, hostess, in this well-fed, well-bred apex of New York in 1900. Mr. Charles P. Everitt, who with his brother Sam worked also at Doubleday, Page & Co., gave me a dilated picture: " She was beautiful, she was a lovely woman, she was stately. In fact, not long before he died, I met Walter Hines Page on the street, and I said to him, ' Walter, I don't believe there ever was such a woman as Mrs. Frank Doubleday.' And he said to me with tears in his eyes: ' Charlie, I have never known the equal of Mrs. Frank Doubleday.' "

Wrapt in such an aura, I imagine her now entering the study where Mr. Frank Doubleday was busy reading and

---

* H. L. Mencken, *A Book of Prefaces;* Burton Rascoe, *Theodore Dreiser;* Frank Harris, *Contemporary Portraits.*

possibly enjoying *Sister Carrie*. This might have been what she read over her husband's shoulder, as he turned the pages and her virtuous eyes easily picked the " indecencies " after the first note of them:

"A dainty self-conscious swaying of the hips by a woman was to him as alluring as the glint of rare wine to the toper. He would thrill as a child with the unhindered passion that was in him. . . ."

"He appeared to great advantage behind the white napery and silver platters. . . . As he cut the meat his rings almost spoke. . . . He helped Carrie to a rousing plateful. . . . That little soldier of fortune took her good turn in an easy way. . . . Even then in her commonplace garb her figure was evidently not bad, and her eyes were large and gentle. Drouet looked at her and his thoughts reached home. . . . She felt that she liked him . . . there was something even richer than that running as a hidden strain in her mind. . . ."

"The jackets were the greatest attraction. When she entered the store she already had her heart fixed upon the peculiar little tan jacket with large mother-of-pearl buttons . . . all the rage that fall. . . ."

". . . ' I'll tell you what you do,' he said, ' you come with me and I'll take care of you. . . . Why don't you get yourself a nice little jacket. . . . I'll loan you the money. . . . Now why don't you let me get you a nice room? . . . I won't hurt you. . . . Aw, come Carrie. . . . What can you do alone?' . . ."

". . . She followed whither her craving led. She was as yet more drawn than she drew. . . . He would need to delight himself with Carrie as surely as he would need to eat his heavy breakfast. . . ."

". . . ' I wish I could get something to do,' she said. — ' You'll get that all right. . . . Get yourself fixed up, see the city. . . . I won't hurt you. . . . Got on the new shoes? . . . Stick 'em out. . . . George, they look fine. . . . Put on your jacket. . . . Say that fits like a T., don't it?' he remarked feeling the set of it at the waist and eyeing it from a few paces with real pleasure. . . . At Carson Pirie's he bought her a nice skirt and shirtwaist. . . . She was pretty, yes, indeed. . . . She caught her little red lip with her teeth and felt her first thrill of power. . . ."

In those days the more valiant New York matrons were occupied among their good works with purity leagues for the suppression of vice, for the lapsed and lost, for the social evil. Indeed at about this time they were making a pleasant sanitary prison where wayward girls too tender in years for the jail might be agreeably locked up — the Florence Crittendon Home. And here was Doubleday, Page about to publish a book about vulgar people, a Chicago drummer and a factory girl from the country, which apparently recommended prostitution as a way of life in little tan jackets with large pearl buttons. At least as she read Mrs. Doubleday could find no hint of condemnation. She looked into it again. Now there was a change of names, a new seducer, a saloon-manager if you please, and yet described as a handsome, well-dressed dependable citizen! It must have been she was mortified as she went from lewd facet to facet lighted by her orthodox mind:

> "He drew near this lily, which had sucked its waxen beauty from a depth of waters which he had never penetrated, and out of ooze and mould which he could not understand. He drew near because it was waxen and fresh. It lighted his feelings for him. It made the morning worth while."
>
> "Finally when the long flush of delight had subsided, he said: 'When is Charlie going away? . . . Come away and leave him. . . . I can't live without you. . . .' — . . . 'Well perhaps we can arrange to go somewhere.' — 'Suppose we didn't have time to get married here.' — 'If we got married as soon as we got to the other end of the journey it would be all right.' — 'I meant that,' he said. . . . She was extremely happy now. . . . As for him the marriage clause did not dwell in his mind."

Then if she read on she followed them to New York with the stolen money from the safe of the gorgeous saloon, and followed him satisfactorily enough to penury and suicide, but Carrie disgracefully to being a stage favorite and to heartless success. But I think she did not read so far without exclaiming: " But, Frank, this is immoral, disgusting! You mean to say that Mr. Page and that nice young Lanier are going to publish it? You must all be out of your minds! If you publish that book, I, for one shall be ashamed to face society. I would sooner go down on my knees and scrub floors than derive income from such filth." So slamming to the door of her mind, and locking it, what difference whether she read the rest of it or not. If she did, she read with eyes which never felt the fine distinctions and the cruel sorrows of these passages nor of others that could neither shock nor graze a literal mind: Did she, for example, get the adventure of the big first theme — the creeping out from a rural fringe of activity to a center of it, Chicago? Chicago of all places! That pork-packers' village, that no-man's land:

". . . To the child, the genius with imagination, or the wholly untravelled, the approach to a great city for the first time is a wonderful thing. Particularly if it be evening — that mystic period between the glare and gloom. . . . Ah, the promise of night! . . . What old illusion of hope is not here forever repeated! Though all humanity be still enclosed in the shops, the thrill runs abroad. It is in the air. The dullest feel something which they may not always express or describe. . . . It is the lifting of the burden of toil. . . ."

". . . The gleam of a thousand lights is often as effective as the light in a wooing and fascinating eye. Half the undoing of the . . . natural mind is accomplished by sources wholly inhuman."

Or, was she aware of the theme of winter, maintained as she was at an even temperature of 68?

". . . Not poets alone, nor artists, nor that superior order of mind which arrogates to itself all refinement, feel this, but dogs and all men. The sparrow upon the wire, the cat in the doorway, the dray-horse tugging his weary load, feel the long keen breaths of winter. It strikes to the heart of all life, animate and inanimate. . . ."

Or the melody of money, having never known the lack of it?

". . . Money: 'something everybody else has and I must get,' would have expressed [Carrie's] understanding of it thoroughly. Some of it she now held in her hand — two soft green ten dollar bills — and she felt that she was immensely better off for the having of them. . . ."

Did she see in the deathly drabness of Carrie's sister and brother-in-law in their West Side flat some of the seeds of American crime, now become so renowned? I think she called them virtuous lower middle-class people — the backbone of the nation. Nor could she have been expected to see in her own decorous mind other seeds of our crimes:

"Minnie was no companion for her sister — she was too old. Her thoughts were staid and solemnly adapted to a condition. . . ."

"When Hanson came home at seven o'clock he was inclined to be a little crusty. . . . This never showed in anything he said so much as in a certain solemnity of countenance and the silent manner in which he slopped about. He had a pair of yellow carpet slippers . . . he would immediately substitute for his solid pair of shoes. This and washing his face with the aid of common washing soap until it glowed a shiny red, would constitute his only preparation for the evening meal. He would then get his evening paper and read in silence. . . . For a young man this was rather a morbid turn of character and so affected Carrie. . . . She felt the drag of a lean and narrow life. . . ."

"He was as still as a deserted chamber. . . . Carrie on the other hand had the blood of youth."

Nor can you blame her that she could not see in the nonentity of Carrie the seeds of " that sympathetic and impressionable nature which, ever in its most developed form has been the glory of the drama "; nor gifts of allurement very like those of famous courtesans of history who likewise had been of humble origin, and yet never from Wisconsin! What right had this callow Hoosier to endow his trivial heroine with talents which certainly neither she nor any other Eastern woman of influence intended to permit in the country of their forefathers?

". . . Something delicate and lonely in her voice, but [Drouet] could not hear it. He had not the poetry in him that would seek a woman out under such circumstances and console her for the tragedy of life. Instead he struck a match and lighted the gas. . . ."

". . . How was it that in so little a while the narrow life of the country had fallen from her, and the city with all its mystery taken its place? . . ."

". . . Her little shoes now fitted her smartly and had high heels. She had learned much about laces and those little neck-pieces. . . ."

". . . She looked in the mirror and pursed up her lips . . . with a little toss of the head, as she had seen the railroad treasurer's daughter do from Evansville, Indiana. She caught up her skirts with an easy swing. . . . She used her feet less heavily. . . ."

". . . The mouth had the expression at times, in talking and in repose of one who might be upon the verge of tears. . . . The pronunciation of certain syllables gave to her lips this peculiarity of formation . . . as suggestive and moving as pathos itself. . . ."

And how could a Murray Hill matron, who was what she wanted to be, wife, mother, influential citizen, charming hostess, have felt with Carrie the sadness of her lot, equipped now, and yet for what?

". . . When she came to her own rooms, Carrie saw their comparative insignificance. . . . What after all was Drouet? What was she? At her window she thought it over, rocking to and fro and gazing out across the lamp-lit park. . . . Some old tunes crept to her lips, and as she sang them, her heart sank. . . . She was sad beyond measure, and yet uncertain, wishing, fancying. . . . Now for the old cottage room in Columbia City, now for the mansion upon the Shore Drive, now for the fine dress of some lady, now the elegance of some scene. . . . Finally it seemed as if all her state were one of loneliness and forsakenness. . . . She hummed and hummed, sitting in the shadow by the window, and was therein as happy, though she did not perceive it, as she ever would be."

Nor could an authority on manners and morals be asked to find interest in the emotions and pretensions of the "deep-feeling" saloon-manager or in his shallow family or equivocal "social prestige." Yet here they were brilliantly set down:

". . . He read the paper, which was heightened in interest by the shallowness of the themes discussed by his son and daughter. Between his wife and himself ran a river of indifference. . . ."

". . . True love she [Carrie] had never felt for him. . . . This was due to a lack of power on his part, a lack of that majesty of passion that sweeps the mind from its seat, fuses and melts all arguments and theories. . . ."

". . . These gentlemen Elks knew the standing of one another. They had regard for the ability which could amass a small fortune, own a nice home, keep a barouche or carriage, perhaps, wear fine clothes, and maintain a good mercantile position. . . . Hurstwood, who was a little above the order of mind who could accept this standard as perfect . . . was quite a figure. . . . Look at him any time within the half hour before the curtain was up, he was a member of . . . a rounded company of five or more whose stout figures, large white bosoms and shining pins, bespoke the character of their success. . . . The gentlemen who brought their wives called him out to shake hands with them. He was evidently a light among them. . . . It was greatness in a small way, small as it was. . . ."

The greatness of America today, small as it is, hated and satirized by Sinclair Lewis throughout a book, is noted impartially here in passing from one turn of the drama to another. But Dreiser making his way so easily among values apparently could not beguile the cultured wife of his publisher. Not even when he defined travel alluringly:

" Thus lovers are forgotten, sorrows laid aside, death hidden from view. There is a world of accumulated feeling back of the trite dramatic expression — 'I am going away.'"

Nor when with a single casual character, a young man met at a party, realms are revealed to Carrie before unsuspected, beyond those which money could buy: and never to be known to either of her lovers, drummer or saloon manager, nor to any of her stray friends. So he constructs the immensities of consciousness which the childlike mind gets glimpses of through holes in the roof, holes in the floor, cracks in the wall of her simple dwelling:

". . . 'He dosn't amount to much,' said Ames. . . . 'Nearly as bad as Dora Thorne.' . . . Carrie felt this as a personal reproof. She read Dora Thorne, or had a good deal in the past. . . . Now this clear-eyed, fine-headed youth made fun of it. . . . She looked down and for the first time felt the pain of not understanding. . . . [She] wondered what else was right, according to him. . . . 'Don't you think it rather fine to be an actor?" she asked once. — 'Yes I do . . . to be a good one.' . . . Just this little approval set Carrie's heart bounding. Ah, if she could only be an actress — a good one! . . . such men as he would approve of her. . . . She said good-bye with feigned indifference. . . . Still, the coach seemed lorn. . . . She did not know whether she would ever see this man any more. What difference could it make? What difference could it make? . . . Hurstwood had returned, and was already in bed. His clothes were scattered loosely about. Carrie came to the door and saw him, then retreated. . . . Back in the dining-room she sat in her chair and rocked. Her little hands were folded tightly as she thought. Through a fog of longing and conflicting desire she was beginning to see. . . . She was rocking and beginning to see."

Dreiser at twenty-nine could tell poignantly these chasms between the different strata of American society — bleak separations, almost peculiar to us, which are enough to account for our despair today. And too he knew that it was need of money that drove most people from one class into another. It was want, fear of cold and hunger, wedded to ambition that drove Carrie out of the humdrum classes into the special one of the theatre. And it was, I am afraid, the fact of these chasms that kept Mrs. Doubleday from crossing over into the lives of this book, either to follow Carrie toward the bright lights, or the " liberal opulent " Hurstwood into the dark velvet ways of poverty and death. The long slide downward, after he had taken the money, and his fine name, breath of life to him, had gone; the rich disintegration, punctuated by looking for jobs, then by ceasing to look for jobs, the days of sitting in hotel lobbies, then of rocking by the radiator to the reading of innumerable newspapers; the one pitiful climb up into activity, when as a scab he runs a car in a street-car strike; the metallic cruelty of jeers, stones, wounds, and the careering of the cable car under his ignorant touch over all humanity, that is, over all but the rich; then the final descent alone without Carrie, in this year when 80,000 men were out of work in New York City, into the ways of odd-job men, beggars, bums; and then nothing, not even a memory. . . . In a masterly way, the way of Nature, Dreiser weaves this descent into the design of the book, and as with Carrie's good fortune, into the changing sea of life in which the two of them floated for a while:

". . . Constant comparison between his old state and his new showed a balance for the worse. . . . The poisons generated by remorse inveigh against the system. . . . To these Hurstwood was subject. . . . In the course of time it told upon his temper. . . . His step was not as sharp and firm. . . . He was given to thinking, thinking. . . . The new friends he made were not celebrities. . . . He was left to brood. . . .

". . . If one thinks that such thoughts do not come to so common a type of mind . . . I would urge for their consideration that it is the higher mental development . . . which refuses to dwell upon such things. . . . The unintellectual miser sweats blood at the loss of a hundred dollars. . . . The Epictetus smiles when the last vestige of physical welfare is removed. . . ."

Step by step, little by little, until his brain, in solitude cold and hunger, is not the same brain. He dreams waking dreams of the old bright respectable days, and these blurred delusions are all the life left to him on park benches and in night lodgings. Then the final animate step:

"'Give me a little something, will you, Mister?' he said to the last one. 'For God's sake, do, I'm starving.' — 'Aw, get out,' said the man, who happened to be a common type himself. 'You're no good.' . . . Hurstwood put his hands red from cold, down in his pockets. Tears came into his eyes. 'That's right. . . . I'm no good now. I was all right. I had money. I'm going to quit this,' and with death in his heart he started down toward the Bowery. He remembered a lodging-house where there were little close rooms with gas jets in them, almost pre-arranged, he thought . . . which rented for fifteen cents . . . he had no fifteen cents. . . . On the way he met a comfortable looking gentleman . . . the gentleman looked him over and fished for a dime. Nothing but quarters were in his pockets. 'Here,' he said, handing him one to be rid of him. . . . With this the idea of death passed for a little out of his mind. . . ."

With a skilful suggestion of the wife and daughter and rich son-in-law of Chicago days, now like Carrie oblivious of him, who at the moment were whirling into New York in a fast Pullman on their way to Rome, through what will be Hurstwood's last blizzard, there follows the account of the final flop in a side street off the Bowery — a passage that may surprise critics who say that Dreiser is a writer who can't write:

"It was push and jam for a minute, with grim beast silence to prove its quality and then it melted inward, like logs floating, and disappeared. There were wet hats and wet shoulders, a cold, shrunken, disgruntled mass, pouring in between bleak walls. It was just six o'clock and there was supper in every pedestrian's face. . . . And yet no supper was provided here, nothing but beds. . . . His old wet cracked hat he laid softly upon the table. Then he pulled off his shoes and lay down. . . . It seemed as if he thought a while, for now he arose and turned the gas out, standing calmly in the blackness, hidden from view. After a few moments in which he reviewed nothing, but merely hesitated, he turned the gas on again, but applied no match. Even then he stood there, hidden wholly in that kindness which is night, while the uprising fumes filled the room. When the odor reached his nostrils, he quit his attitude and fumbled for the bed. . . . 'What's the use?' he said weakly, as he stretched himself to rest. . . ."

"Of Hurstwood's death she was not even aware. A slow black boat setting out from the pier at Twenty-seventh Street upon its weekly errand bore, with many others, his nameless body to the Potter's Field. . . ."

34
The début and burial of Sister Carrie.

So in this story everything is told just as it happened, with now the pathos of a bar-room ballad, now a ruthlessness of intellect. And why the editor's wife did not cry or even feel a pain around her heart to think that men are made for ends like this, is hard to know. Or why she did not feel that a precious record of the grim life on top of which she ate and slept and dressed and had her being, was in her hands, is hard to say. On Monday morning her husband took the proof sheets back to his office with instructions that the contract be broken. So do those without feeling and without much intelligence decree that life shall not be heightened or purified by understanding. Is it for fear that then it will leave them behind? At this particular period in this country of banks, Bibles and candy, the decree of such unofficial censors held singular sway.

There is an inclination, perhaps unconscious, among the men connected in that day with this publishing company to belittle the importance of Mrs. Doubleday in the suppression of a now historic book, which the firm itself can hardly repudiate. It is as if to protect her name from taint of prudery, now become unfashionable. The pellucid Mr. Lanier, for one, is not sure that she ever read the book: " It was Frank," he said, " who made the trouble. He hated it enough without other influence, called it ' indecent,' and begged us at once to break the contract. If we went ahead with it, although he couldn't stop us, he warned us he would do all in his power to ruin the sale." At the same time he volunteered that the publisher's wife was one of those deceptively beautiful characters who loved to dominate in the name of virtue. Mr. C. P.

Everitt, however, remembers the affair more in accordance with the legend.

He remembers a dinner at the house of Mrs. Doubleday, "A most distinguished gathering," where she had said: "Frank, I would rather get down and scrub floors than have you publish that book." But he added protectively: "Don't say I said she was referring to *Sister Carrie*. I got into trouble once telling that. As a matter of fact she may have been referring to Tom Dickson's *Leopard's Spots,* a libel on the Negro race. In fact I think she was. She felt just as strong against race prejudice as against the social evil — she was a woman of very high principles." . . . These high-principled American matrons! How naïvely ignorant they have been in their pursuit of good works! And how their men have deferred to them, hoping thereby to concoct some sort of social stability in a hit-or-miss land! What fine institutions they have gathered money to build up, to house the victims of their bloodless code! And what bright human hopes they have helped to tear down! . . . "But did they publish *Leopard's Spots?*" I ventured to ask — "Oh, yes, it went into the hundred thousand class: we made a pile of money out of it." — "And did she get down and scrub floors?" — "No." — "Then don't you think it must have been *Sister Carrie* she was speaking of?" — No, my reasoning was specious. He was not prepared to indict his glamorous hostess for a deed which since that time has become an embarrassment to the "fine and reputable house of Doubleday."

Yet I believe the myth has legs to stand on — a symbol of the way Americans have always entrusted to women the matter of art along with the matter of society, as unworthy of their important lives. It was the story told Dreiser in a letter from Frank Norris cursing the company for planning to withdraw the book: "In her absurd opinion it was 'vulgar and immoral.'" And some years later Thomas H. McKee, lawyer for Doubleday, gossiping over the affair with Dreiser, spoke of Mrs. Doubleday as the original censor, and wondered why with so good a cause against his publishers he had not brought suit: expecting it, he had at once prepared a defence. In 1903 William Heinemann too, the English publisher of *Sister Carrie,* had confided to him: " I fear my admiration for your book has cost me the friendship, not only of Mrs. Doubleday, but of Doubleday himself." At another dinner-party — Page and Norris were present — she had asked him how he could have published so " vulgar and disgraceful " a book: his answer had been that it was " a distinguished privilege " to have done so, which the husband had taken as insulting to his wife.

Whether husband or wife or both were to blame, the undisputed fact is that not long after the fatal week-end Dreiser had a letter from his publishers asking him to come in for a talk. Mr. Lanier remembers " acutely the unhappy fifteen minutes " spent in this talk. He and Page had felt that with Doubleday against it, publication would be unfair to Dreiser, that the book was too good to be smothered in that way. He was prepared, he said, to explain to the young writer how deeply he admired his novel, " a fine piece of work," and how he wanted to do all in his power to help him sell it successfully elsewhere. And he is quite sure he could have succeeded. He hoped to make him see how little it would mean to merely print and catalogue: how easy it was for a publisher to kill a book just by hinting to his salesmen not to push it, just by failing to advertise it. A heart-rending picture, but he was given no chance to paint it. He had calculated without the usually agreeable author of a first book. Dreiser, the terribly social savage after wistful years of neglect at the hands of society would not listen; had no use for Lanier's urbanities. He had been swimming against surf in the open sea long enough. This time he had his hands on the edge of the boat of acknowledgment. Whether they liked it or not he was going to climb in. " Crushed and tragically pathetic," Lanier remembers him, doggedly he repeated they had made a contract with him; they would have to go ahead; that was the end of the matter. And the tall, loose-jointed dreamer, less loose and dreamy than usual, gave his intense ultimatum and walked out of the office. That day the enemy in him must have taken a leap ahead, and have grown to almost full size, if not yet to full efficiency.

The office of Doubleday Page & Company was now hard put to it. How to placate young Hoosier and older Episcopalian, the rugged new artist and the shrewd middle-aged merchant, who was not going to promote a questionable book unless (like *The Leopard's Spots*) he was convinced it would sell a hundred thousand copies. Mr. Lanier with his civilized impartiality is quick to admit that then their business chief would have felt it his "artistic" duty to waive morals and promote *Sister Carrie*. But the literary partners could not honestly assure him of this degree of popularity. McKee, their lawyer, was called in; nothing to do but fulfill the contract, he told them; anything else might be disastrous to a new ambitious firm. So on November 8, 1900, *Sister Carrie* had her humble début — an edition of 1000 or so copies in what later reviewers agreed to call a "dull, cheap, red binding, with the name in small, dull, black lettering"; an assassin's edition in a country where books have to look expensive in order to be well thought of.

Then again the story of the disposition of these copies varies. It would be my instinct to believe the version repeated again and again in almost the same words in the reviews of the later Dodge and Harper editions, which must have been taken from these publishers' advertisements and from hearsay — that is, Dreiser's own version. According to him, and he had it from Frank Norris, the book was never marketed at all, but thrown into the cellar where anyone who felt like reading a "dirty book" helped himself. Norris, bitterly disappointed, salvaged as many copies as he could, and sent them to various book editors, and even after that continued dispensing them. Grant Richards, an English publisher, in a letter to Dreiser tells of Norris giving him a copy of *Sister Carrie* in 1901 with the hope that he would publish it in England. And then the legend divides again. Some say that after a while the remaining volumes of the disgraced *Carrie* were burned in the furnace of that cellar, and some that they merely lay there under the dust of years and that if one wrote enclosing a money-order for the amount, the book could be had. Mr. Lanier inclines toward the latter version, but probably a less dramatic account of the affair will in the end be held as fact.

In 1929 Mr. Vrest Orton published a bibliography of Dreiser's work, in which he gives a spirited account of his pains over several years to unearth the facts of this incident through the Doubleday office. At length Mr. S. A. Everitt answered that they had no records except the record of date, but that as he remembered, " the edition of from 1000 to 2000 copies was sold to the trade in the regular way, the same as any other novel published at the time. . . ." With this to encourage him he now wrote to Mr. Doubleday himself for a transcript of the sales-records, who doubted that they were " available," but would see what he could do; he did not believe that any copies had ever been " destroyed, burned, or remaindered." A day or so later a letter came from his secretary which for Mr. Orton contained " the whole story in a nutshell " as revealed by the analysis card: " The first edition consisted of 1008 copies, of which 129 were sent out for review, 465 were sold, and the balance of 423 copies was turned over to J. F. Taylor & Company," a remainder house now out of business. Yet an analysis card presented thirty years after the event is less convincing than a human memory recorded at the moment of it, and is as easy to fabricate. To support Dreiser's and Lanier's memory is the sensitive attitude today of the firm, as of people ridiculed beyond composure for a literary and commercial error. Two things are sure — their sense of propriety had its way for a time, and as certainly Dreiser has had his revenge, but it was to be a distant and expensive one.

35

"Not elevating mental food."
American press

"At last a master-piece out of America."
English press

The historic meaning of some men is aloofness, the virtue of hermits or of gods or stars. They shine impregnably from afar. Dreiser's meaning has in it the virtue of mingling, of engaging in spite of himself; in fact, of proving how the world is small. Here were the Doubledays introducing his obscure name into the circle of their sacrosanct dinner-parties. Here was Frank Norris, become a voice in the wilderness for this stranger, who, he felt, was writing according to his gospel. He loves him as a kind of miracle, an oriflamme in the windy dusty American skies. I. F. Marcosson writes to Dreiser in 1910: " Your name always brings to my mind the unforgettable picture of Frank Norris thrilled with admiration for *Sister Carrie*." Mr. Grant Richards, asked to describe Norris, said, " I don't know; what struck me forcibly about him was that apparently he was more eager for Dreiser's *Carrie* to be read than for his own novels." Then there were the critics to whom Norris sent the 129 salvaged copies. Their reviews, some thirty of them which Dreiser has kept, mirror naïvely our intelligentsia in 1900; so directly had he challenged their likes and dislikes, awaking pleasure in but two or three, and irritation or disdain in the rest. With few exceptions these scolding critics, even those who felt the power of the book, discuss it as a social or antisocial tract, not as a would-be work of art. The more sophisticated day of literary supplements and book guilds was not yet at hand. Quaint utilitarians still guarded the manners and morals of a hustling young people:

Life, New York, 1900: "Such girls, however, as imagine they can follow in [Carrie's] footsteps will probably end their days on the Island or in the gutter. . . ."

Advertiser and Union, New York, 1900: ". . . Not elevating mental food for all. . . . Peculiar and masterly written novel. . . ."

New York Tribune, 1900: "A realistic story of Chicago life might easily miss being a pleasant story. . . ."

Chicago Tribune, Feb. 25, 1901: "Needless to say the book is not a pleasant one to read if one is to maintain a cheerful optimism, but the author is right in assuming that America needs enlightenment rather than . . . flattery, if the present rate of advance is to be maintained. . . . In each case it is felt this fate is of the man's own making, that self discipline and well-grounded morals would have avoided every evil . . . that man is still the captain of his destiny, the master of his fate. . . . Not once does the name of the deity appear . . . except . . . as . . . profanity. *Sister Carrie* transgresses the literary morality of the average American novel to a point that is almost Zolaesque. . . ."

Newark Sunday News, Sept. 1, 1901: ". . . The reader longs for some relief from . . . these very real people. . . . There is no strong or noble nature in the book; neither is there any lady or gentleman. . . . This is the most serious criticism of the book, this and an utter lack . . . of a literary manner of diction. . . . The style is in many ways excellent, at times even nervous. . . . But one does not wish to have a writer express himself in the same way as do his somewhat uncultivated characters. . . . If only Carrie could be more like Trilby!"

Minneapolis Journal, 1901: "Carrie had a better fate than most pretty country girls who go to a large city, and become the mistresses of unprincipled men. . . . The story leaves a very unpleasant impression."

Louisville Times: "There is little sunshine . . . it is plain realism. . . . Mr. Dreiser can't expect success . . . but like Mr. Norris he is an artist. . . ."

Seattle Post Intelligencer: "You would never dream of recommending to another person to read it. . . . Yet it comes within sight of greatness. . . ."

The Book Buyer, March, 1901: "Mr. Dreiser . . . is the chronicler of materialism in its basest forms. . . . But the leaven of the higher life remains, nowhere stronger than with us. Of all this Mr. Dreiser betrays no cognizance. . . .

All too fairly, these excerpts reflect American mentality in 1900, or rather the lack of it. Almost there was none. Nearly three centuries of Europeans in North America had produced from time to time prize-intellects and ace-adventurers; and yet how few critics of thought and adventure, without which society drifts! The result had to be reviews like these. Reading them one wonders what had been the use of our original heroes — the bawdy Washington and Franklin, the aesthetic Jefferson, the savory Daniel Boone, Johnny Appleseed, John Audubon, Andrew Jackson, Abraham Lincoln, and all the others who had labored for hard glory more than easy money. What real use were independence and new inventions, and an exquisite democratic elegance as in Monticello and the University of Virginia; what use were new lands and apple trees and birds and native flowers, if they had established no traditions of enjoyment? Most of all, what use a house not divided against itself, if not to be divided meant that pious money-maniacs, the hands and stomach, were to rule the house in the stead of heart and brains and loins? And verbally speaking, what use Melville, Poe, Twain and Whitman, the first three become gift-books for children, the fourth jailed as lewd and mad, if these heroes had succeeded in establishing no standards of art by which to judge the prophets yet to come? It is not that the reviewers of *Sister Carrie* saw nothing in its author. They did in fact feebly praise him as their predecessors had feebly praised his predecessors. But it is the moribund nature of their refusals and acceptances as of men and women scarcely alive that is shocking. And especially it is shocking considered in relation to the boundless energy of the merchants and inventors who had hired these students to keep track of the intellectual growth of the nation. They seem like craven employees reclining on their jobs. And yet of course, had they not been, they would have lost their jobs.

It is interesting to analyse them in relation to this provocative book. Clearly for some hidden reason they are uneasy before some of the facts of life, and most uneasy of all before the agreeable fact of its pleasures. Even those who rather liked the book took refuge in admiring Hurstwood's tragedy, ignoring, if they felt it, that Dreiser's wisdom lay in a balanced awareness of bloom as coincident with decay. Some of them, to exonerate themselves, laughed indulgently at this upstart for imagining he could interest readers with " the plain unvarnished truth." A curious repellent psychology comes to light in these reviews, a fear of statement which Americans hide beneath a smirk. Dreiser, I think, more directly than any other writer had been born to challenge it. Unfailingly each one of his books inclusive of *An American Tragedy* (since that date perhaps he is less engaged) breathes its unequivocal statements for and against us, against which his opponents have felt coerced to make their one faltering statement, in brief this: Don't tell the truth, it doesn't pay. He has the distinction of having forced as best he could the issue, of having probed, perhaps even solved the mystery of a People Afraid of Statement.

In contrast to them two or three men had the force to speak out. They, like Dreiser, are remnants of a pioneer past. That is, they were attempting to carry greedy America, still recovering from civil war, and still inundated by the inchoate flood of immigrants, into the unexplored fields of the imagination and intellect. The axe had won, the railroads had won, the factories had won, the banking-houses had won, and, it seemed to them, the human spirit would have to win in commercial America, or these few would die of malnutrition of nerves and senses. There were at this time but five or six names for radicals to champion — Fuller, Garland, Norris, London, and then possibly Will Payne, Robert Herrick, Brand Whitlock, Hervey White, Vaughan Moody; and now there was Dreiser. Mark Twain had not yet published *The Mysterious Stranger* upsetting every bit of smug laughter he had generated. Stephen Crane was dead, and his friend Harold Frederic too, with his sardonic novel of Methodist insanity and class arrogance.* There was Robinson, a poet in New York, and Ambrose Bierce, a wit in San Francisco, too resentful toward their country to be the hope of anyone, who preserved the virtue of aloofness, and made a tiny dual aristocracy — two isolated drops of elegance of mind. Considering the outlook, it was not strange that the two or three live hopeful critics should

* *The Damnation of Theron Ware.*

have been almost evangelical in their praise of *Sister Carrie*. Their eagerness for creation to go on helps to compensate for the almost unendurably dull eyes and ears of the others. It is an eagerness, nearly gone from the Western World today, and seems to have lived over from the era of our discovery and to have carried forward the tradition we still cling to of a strong new race bound to create something to express, and to express itself.

One of these champions was William Marion Reedy, who for some years in St. Louis had edited a magazine of politics, science and art, as he and his friends knew them, designed to increase flavor and quality, and to counteract the cruel sentimentality of the times. If Norris was a voice in the wilderness, Reedy was an innkeeper in the desert to give hospitality to kindred wayfarers. He is remembered as a kind of tearful, laughing Rabelaisian, one of the last to fight for the integrity of individuals as opposed to brute industrial will. Mencken has called him a fool, but the more human and more original Middle Westerners, Dreiser, Masters and Sandburg, for example, separated now by bleak differences, would agree, I believe, to the end of time about " Bill Reedy," so much they loved him for himself and for the oasis he created out in God's country. He was a man's man, even to the point — or so I have heard it told with pride — of having taken for wife a man's woman, one-time mistress of a house of pleasure in St. Louis, that one approach to Bacchic priestess the country has known. Her money, it is said, made possible his *Mirror,* and her delectable table his enormous girth, noted as one of his charms. I have heard him described in words near to song; his appetite for food, drink, night-long talk, his ribaldry, his warmth, rare books and restless scholastic mind. Apparently one of the few men of his time who consciously wanted to bring the sundered parts of the Puritan soul together again. A recent newspaper jingle celebrates him: " O, the days of Diamond Brady, — Marion Reedy, Steevie Brody, — Great Teddy, Col. Cody, — and the rowdy rodeos! "

He writes Dreiser in December, 1900, at once, with almost a sob of pleasure over his novel: " It is damned good, I shall say as emphatically as this in The Mirror," which he does; and then in January writes again evidently in answer to a discouraged letter from Dreiser:

> "You say you have not much hope for *Sister Carrie*. I want to tell you that it is a tip-top novel. An elderly lady denounced it to me at dinner the other evening simply because she had seen just such drummers . . . doing just such things . . . on the trains running in and out of Chicago. . . . I am sure the thing will be a 'go.' " In another letter he names his rule of conduct: "My un-idealism in our little talk seems to have hit you hard. . . . Well, I have an ideal: it is to be cheerful and between you'n me it isn't always easy in the face of the facts. . . ."

George Horton too, a timid Chicago novelist, recommends the book to his readers, but its tragic rather than its idyllic passages. Perhaps only Reedy among Americans treats it as independent of plot. Horton writes for the Chicago Record Herald, January, 1901:

> "The characters are so genuine they produce that queer feeling . . . one sometimes gets from listening to a phonograph. You are certain that the human beings must lie just a little back of the talk. . . . Why a firm who can get hold of such literature must expend their resources in pushing . . . clap-trap . . . is a puzzle to everyone not in the publishing business."

And to Arthur Henry he writes virulently the kind of opinion which unluckily the critic, except for an infrequent Vance Thompson or H. L. Mencken, never dares to publish:

> "I had fancied something of the kind . . . Doubleday belongs to that species of long-eared animals which are not hares. Had he lived in Christ's time he might have attained to the supreme distinction of bringing the Saviour of the World into Jerusalem. That is the one crowning glory of the ass. Otherwise such fat-witted prigs as Doubleday have tried in all ages to pull down men of genius. . . ."

In addition there were a number of grateful letters, although most of them contained moral reservations: "I think there are a few objectionable features to the book, objectively speaking, though I know it is all true to life," one friend wrote. And another: "To sit fifteen minutes in a bar-room and hear the talk is interesting; but to spend a whole evening there might prove tiresome." So over the country little messages awoke on the wires of human thought and were flashed from the readers of the book back to its author. But they would have soon died on unpopular lips, had it not been for stimulation from the outside. Norris finally had his way, not at home but in England. William Heinemann, perhaps through Norris, perhaps through George Brett of the Macmillan Company, had seen a copy of *Sister Carrie*. In May, 1901, he published it, abridged for the sake of brevity not morals, in his *Dollar Library* of American novelists, which included Norris's *Octopus*, Payne's *Story of Eva*, Crane's *Monster*, James's *Sacred Fount*, Garland's *Rose of Dutcher's Coolly*. Without exception the English reviews of this edition are extravagant in praise. Their certainty is refreshing. Not one of them deplores the " dangerous morals " of the book, nor makes an issue of its diction.

The Daily Mail, London, 1901, exclaims: " At last a really strong novel has come from America, almost great because of its relentless purpose, its marvellous simplicity. . . . Mr. Dreiser has contrived a masterpiece."

The Daily Chronicle comparing *Sister Carrie* and *The Story of Eva,* both about village heroines adrift in Chicago, finds it interesting but hard to understand " that passion for social getting-on, which forms so often the mainspring of American lives," and the theme of Payne's novel. He concludes that though " more pleasant reading, its language always good," *The Story of Eva* is less " artistic, less relentlessly true to life," than *Sister Carrie*. . . . " Dreiser . . . draws no moral . . . simply a grimly grey story of life and life near the bone. In this lies the powerful attraction it holds, and it proves Mr. Dreiser an author to be reckoned with and never to be overlooked — a true artist."

The Academy is " impressed by the subtlety of description," is " startled into interest," has " never met such a description of an American heroine before," and then couples it with *The Octopus:* " The movement in them is large, racial; the vision poetic and comprehensive; the sentiment is never sentimentality. They exercise the highest function of the modern novel. . . . Mr. Dreiser is beyond question one of the most promising novelists writing in English."

Manchester Guardian, 1901: " Rarely even in modern work have we met with characters so little idealised, so patiently presented. They might seem to have something in common with the unchanging heroes of adventure. . . .

His work is faithful, accurate, unprejudiced, and it should belong to the veritable documents of American history. . . ."

The Athenaeum, London, September 7, 1901: "The sixth of the volumes . . . in Mr. Heinemann's *Dollar Library* and . . . the most important. . . . Between its covers no single note of unreality is struck. . . . It is untrammeled by any concession to convention or tradition, literary or social. . . . Throughout its pages one feels pulsing the sturdy restless energy of a young people, a nation busy upon the hither side of maturity. . . . It strikes a key-note and is typical, both in the faults of its manner and in the wealth and diversity of its matter, of the great country which gave it birth. Readers there are who will find permanent place for *Sister Carrie* on their shelves beside M. Zola's *Nana*. . . ."

Within these English and American reviews lies a paradox: The young Americans far from exhibiting " the sturdy restless energy of a young people " are like impotent dyspeptics as critics; that is, except for an occasional rebel who is too busy fighting for art to enjoy it. The adult Englishmen on the other hand exclaim with delight at the discovery of a new work of genius as a child is supposed to at a delectable surprise. Spontaneity associated with youth marks the older race; fearfulness, a trait of senility, the new. This faint-heartedness follows us today. Though an army of would-be sophisticates led by Wilson, Rosenfeld, Frank, Brooks and Krutch, considers itself embarked on definition and analysis, a residue of that same grudge and hatred against both artist and audience corrodes their enjoyment — a snob's uneasy seriousness in the face of basic immaturity.

The notion of the infallibility of the child, invented by Jesus Christ, supported by the disappointed Pilgrims, stylized by John Dewey out of his wealth of inexperience, having actually been put to practice in the United States, turns out to be a sentimental fallacy. The fiasco of American society is proof of this. Epidermically a child is indisputable; muscularly a child is promising; from every other point of view a child is an embryo and will soon become abortive, when not, as in the past, forcibly exposed to maturity. All the vitality in the world will only enable the child to cry unless this high voltage meets with narrower and inflicted exercise. It is the same racially.

Superficially — as from the point of view of surfaces now well outside the human being like buildings, airplanes and railroads — we have proved that a new race may be supreme. But intrinsically, as from the core outward to toes and finger tips, a new race is handicapped unless critically exposed to its own past, which takes it traveling back into other pasts and from them into other presents. Impossible to know the present except on a road that leads from the past. From a full-grown branch the ripe fruit falls, and the branch remains to bear again. What we think of as youth is a property of civilization wrested from the new-born by terribly patient and spirited elders. It is marked by ease and liberality.

These English journalists in 1901 displayed a young mind at the advent of Dreiser, just as previous Englishmen had been quick to recognize Melville and Whitman, and later critics would recognize Robert Frost before we did, and the French through Baudelaire would give their love and tears to Poe before we gave ours. It almost seems that with few exceptions we have waited for European sanction before daring to enjoy our own originals. Whitman could not admit this; it contradicted his delusion of our independence. By implication he threw the glory our way: " To have great poets, we must have great audiences." And yet in admiring him, Emerson and Burroughs solicited and welcomed British support. And, to go back of that, who but Carlyle had given Emerson his passport to security? Fight a revolution so that you won't have to live with your parents or pay them taxes, but you are not even then and never will be quite rid of them.

Dreiser, for all his rhapsodies a clear thinker, in which lies his strength, was frankly elated by English approval. It was refreshing to be praised because he had drawn no moral. Payne had made a moral issue of " social success," and had wed his Eva to the scion of an " old Chicago family," wealth rewarding beauty, position the spirit, to make a happy ending. Perhaps the reviewer felt too the way the vernacular of the one novel conveys the uneven shiftless rhythms of American life in that day; whereas Payne's quite sensitive English, for all its painstaking, never once flashes Chicago streets or smells or noises or shapes or tones to the reader. He was a Chicagoan, writing about Chicago, but in terms of some older city. Harold Frederic, writing about America in England, falls into the same falsely correct ways. Dreiser on the other hand walked with the gait and spoke with the voice of his own streets. He acted and reacted from surfaces to depths and depths to surfaces. The people of his book in their Chicago clothes were human animals of whatever place or time. The critics of the older city preferred him.

What was best of all, they were praising him for his consuming passion, more urgent even than the wish for luxury and grandeur — the necessity " to write about life as it is," just as Balzac, Hardy, Turgeniev, all of his favorites, had written about life as it is. Moreover, they spoke as if it were the thing to do, whereas in the United States even his friends decried it as the one thing not to do. To understand our unfortunate literary fortunes it is necessary to accept as an axiom this initial refusal of Fact among us. It was well for Dreiser that he had not the hypocrisy which pretends to scorn foreign patronage; he needed all that he could get. It was to be a long five years before *Sister Carrie* would emerge from the Doubleday cellar to be read as if just discovered by " the great country that gave it birth; " and ten years before Harper's decided to advertise it, with a word from Arnold Bennett, as " perhaps the great American novel." As slowly as that did ideas take hold in a land where industry galloped at breakneck speed.

36

Life near the bone:
" Life seemed an endless chain
Without meaning."   Dreiser

Through the winter and spring and summer of 1901 the new novelist lived on with his devoted wife in their small apartment near Riverside Drive. He began work on a second novel and together they watched the progress of the first. She felt that on the whole he was getting a good deal of notice in his own country, where every child was taught that repeated enterprise and long endurance in the teeth of neglect were necessary virtues; that to be noticed at all was risky and would spoil the child. Then of course they could share elation over the English reviews. There were kill-joys who pretended that these held but the irresponsible praise of grandparents. But that in itself was delightful, since evidently the reviewers looked on him as a legitimate American, whereas since early Warsaw days his native land looked upon him and his parents and sisters and brothers as not much more than immigrant waifs, scarcely to be tolerated, except that immigrants kept wages down. Sarah Osborne White a truly British great-grandchild whose parents had been pioneers in the obscure Southwest, at length was justified in having married beneath her. A clipping bureau sent them news of fame, which they pasted with the letters into a careful scrap-book. He praises her as a fine housekeeper; he had never been so comfortable before. She could cook, wash and iron, trim her hats, make over her clothes, mend his. . . If they were frugal and saved enough, some day her folded dream of family life might come true. She wanted love too, wanted to fulfil her dreams of youth. So do women, and men as well, pin their all to belief in a close partnership, when in reality the cracks of chasms greater than canyons are already there to separate them.

So she counted without real knowledge of her moody, cyclonic husband. Ancestry meant little to him, except to indicate what stuff he was made of. Class meant nothing to him, except as it meant to be on top commanding the scene, and not part of the dust to be swept up from the pavement. Adventure and supremacy meant everything to him — "Yes, pretty much from the first I thought I was a marked guy," was his answer as to whether he had always been conscious of his power. Perhaps for this the United States piqued him more than England; it had still to be conquered. "At times," he said, "I was afraid the English didn't know. Perhaps they were rather garrulous." Anyway he wanted his own people to acknowledge him. He was too thoroughly native to think of leaving them. Sometimes descendants of earliest settlers, English, French or Spanish have been throwbacks to the Old Country and forever homesick for it. But this child out of recent German-Slavic blood was one of the throw-forwards, one of the new Americans. Like them he had no nostalgia for the past, though unlike most of them he was endowed with a memory of it. An unseduced English protégé, by preference he remained at home to fight it out.

For some months it seemed that victory might come soon. His book was not selling, was scarcely on the market, but now surely with English publication, if Doubleday continued to suppress it, some other house would take it over. He was writing stories again and articles, and planning two novels, *The Rake* and *Jennie Gerhardt*. Since 1900 he had written thirty chapters of one and ten or twelve of the other. He wrote abundantly out of the momentum *Sister Carrie* had given him. Gradually, however, he began to notice a change in the attitude of publishers and editors. By the fall of 1901 he found it useless to present his wares. Almost as if because of foreign favor a stubborn resistance seemed to be growing against him — a manner of saying, "I guess we'll do our own thinking, without a lot of English snobs mixing in, who pick an upstart one generation from the steerage to represent our culture." Not that I have heard Dreiser analyse their attitude to that extent; in fact he appears never to give himself the indulgence of expressing resentment. But he recalls with a kind of relish phrases that escaped the editors in the next few difficult years, and that followed him even into success, which suggest such an interpretation. With the chapters and synopses of the two novels he approached McClure, Phillips & Co., and asked for an advance, to give him time to write them. They dismissed him, he remembers, in words that said: "If this is your slant on life, quit, get out, it's rotten." Successively Macmillan, Appleton's and Harper's coldly turned him down. Nor would anyone take over that "masterpiece" by an artist whom, according to the English press, "no one could afford to neglect."

Now it appeared that the very magazines which before had published him were refusing even stories and articles. He was banned, "a disgrace to America," one editor told him. Once coming out of Harper's he met William Dean Howells, who since the day of the interviews had been always friendly; but this time he passed him hurriedly with the words, "You know, I don't like *Sister Carrie.*" In the orthodox market he was shunned as if infected. Finally the commercial house of J. F. Taylor, the same that relieved Doubleday of the last traces of their unloved venture, consented to give him fifty dollars a month until he had finished one or both of the novels, and they made an advance of $300. This together with a few savings would last longer on a visit to his wife's parents in Missouri than it could in New York. An article about him in the St. Louis Post-Dispatch, January 26, 1902, gives this news item:

"Theodore Dreiser, a former St. Louisian, who has newly gained fame as a novelist, was in the city last week on his way to Montgomery City, Mo., to visit the relatives of his wife. . . . It is a first novel . . . which has brought him into prominence. The British literary reviews, in particular, give it high praise, ranking it with *The Octopus* by Frank Norris, at the top of a list of novels for the last year."

The reporter, perhaps impressed, lists and quotes from these reviews, after which I imagine Dreiser put them back in his pocket, where you could not blame him for keeping them as an amulet against "the great country that had given him birth," and so far little else. Then the reporter interviewed the new celebrity, just as ten years before for the same paper he had interviewed important visitors. If it was fun for the tables to be turned in the same city where with McCord and Wood he used to dream his grandest dreams of grandeur, he betrays no juvenile exhilaration, merely answers questions soberly as for one who really wanted to know:

" . . . 'I have not tried to gloss over any evil any more than I have stopped to dwell upon it. Life is too short; its phases are too numerous. What I desired to do was to show two little human beings, or more, playing in and out of the giant legs of circumstance. Personally I see nothing immoral in discussing with a clean purpose any phase of life. . . . If life is to be made better or more interesting its conditions must be understood.' . . . Mr. Dreiser is well remembered by St. Louis newspaper men and other citizens. He is still a young man."

I suppose, too, he spent an evening with the endearing Reedy to discuss hilariously "the sad vicissitudes of things," while perhaps their wives sat apart in the parlor finding less to say to each other. At least that was apt to be the way among the random wives of random geniuses in that decade. Then they were off to the Missouri village and to the dignified relatives, proud now of their son-in-law; to the good smells of animals and barns, to the winter fields, steaming under a Southwestern sun.

Alone with his wife among all but strangers to his new world of performance and audience, and again under the seduction of odorous, spacious days and nights on the distant prairie, this sojourn spelled a crisis for him — the realization that marriage after only three years already meant defeat. And was he to submit to it, to the "harsh compulsions of society and the State, which invariably seek to preserve themselves at the expense of the individual?" or somehow, some way, could he still be free to create and explore? Many of his stories, nearly all of them, are concerned with the muffled struggle that goes on between the people of intense desire for life and those content to be slowly put to death by custom. Carrie,

Cowperwood, Dreiser himself manage to come out with partial victory. Hurstwood, Jennie, Aileen, Witla, emerge defeated. So obsessed is Dreiser with this problem as it first victimised him, that he has made two stories out of it, attributed to other sets of characters; the sharpness of confessional is in them. One is an episode in *The "Genius"* which takes the depleted Witla back to visit his wife's relatives. There, "if it had not been for the lurking hope of some fresh exciting experience with a woman, he would have been unconsciously lonely . . . This thought . . . quite as the confirmed drunkard's thought of whiskey — buoyed him up." The essential tonic appears, a girl of eighteen in splendid bloom, out of these lowlands; and is denied him by his devoted wife and by society. Dreiser computes the disastrous pressure from either side, as if he remembered a moment of his own;

"The world said one life, one love. . . . Could any one woman satisfy him? Could Freida, if he had her? He did not know. He did not care to think about it. Only this walking in a garden of flowers — how delicious it was.

"No one here interested him save this girl . . . secretly he already cursed the day he had married. . . . That blossoming of life at eighteen . . . he could not be faithless to that. . . . It haunted him. . . . It remained clear and demanding. . . . He could not deny it . . . the beauty of youth . . . that was the standard, and the history of the world proved it."

The history of the world does not quite prove it, and yet it tells us that the famous haeteras have been those who prolonged into the years the despotism of youth, if finally by no more than emblem or spirit. In the sexually naïve United States, most of all in its distant provinces, he was right, there was no one to exert this magic except the young. Out of such simplicity have come the Ziegfeld Follies, and the schoolgirl complexion and schoolgirl mentality, for the tired business man. The native Dreiser answered to the rule of youth in company with the business men; but the foreigner in him rebelled against its early death decreed by custom. Again in *Rella,* a story written in 1923, told to him "one evening in Greenwich village by an American poet who has since died," he repeats an almost identical episode, " innately truthful and self-revealing " :

". . . the mere proximity of this girl was proving toxic. . . . A feeling of languor alternated with one of intense depression . . . a deadly drug could not have acted with greater power. . . . Married, married! The words were as a tolled bell. And yet, in truth, I was not interested (even in her case) in a long enduring marriage . . . darkly I speculated as to why love should necessarily pass into this more formalistic and irksome relationship, only later to end in death. . . .

. . . rows of corn whispered and chaffered of life. . . . The wood-perfumed air and wet grass under foot gave me a sense . . . of life dreamily and beautifully lived. A surging sense of the newness . . . of the world was upon me. . . . But . . . how much, if any, of this eternal newness for me?

The stark, merciless, unheeding nature of love was being brought home to me with a greater force than ever before."

Poisons like these invaded Dreiser. It was not exactly his wife, he says: " There was no compulsion there by that time. She was all right," except that she had no understanding of adventure and no need of it herself. It was the lambent earth on the one hand and the dullness of Missouri custom on the other that ate into him. He wanted new brilliance, he wanted variety, which Rodin has called passion. Melancholy like a blanket was covering him; his nerves beginning to falter, and then sleep and then digestion to give way. Now it was impossible for him to make progress with either novel, the very thing he was there for. He read over the thirty chapters of *The Rake,* and destroyed them. *Jennie Gerhardt* he kept but could not write it. So now he was living on a false advance. (Later when he could he paid it back to the publishers.) He thought perhaps if they traveled to the South he could write, but the white sands and the salt breezes of the Gulf did nothing for him. Again, as seven years before, money and hopes were dwindling. This time health was failing. There was nothing to do, it seemed, but for him to go to New York alone, untrammeled, and once more assail the market for any kind of a writing job. She returned to her parents to wait once more until he could support her. He lived in Brooklyn in a room not much better than the hall bedroom of other lean years, and tried to sell his stories and articles.

Those who remembered him still shunned him; the Atlantic Monthly wrote him that he was " morally bankrupt and could not publish there." No one had to tell him that soon he would be physically and financially bankrupt. Soon he would be too miserable to invite confidence when he went the rounds of job hunting. Soon the pawnshops would do their meager bit for him again. He contemplated suicide. It was that condition so glibly called a nervous breakdown. Asked to look back for the cause of it, he does not blame his wife, nor marriage, nor even the suppression of *Sister Carrie,* nor any outside agent. It was his own moodiness, he thinks, that got him. So he analyses it in talk:

" The book wasn't selling, there was no money coming in, but I got plenty of praise for it from people I cared about. I knew enough by this time not to want it from the general run of people; the country was too backward intellectually; I knew that. . . . Frank Norris liked it, Heinemann wanted it. . . . When he got here in 1903 he gave a lunch for me at Martin's restaurant, and asked some people, the editor of Harper's, the editor of Scribner's, some smart women — you know, the kind that counted. That gave me confidence. There was always something, someone to give me confidence — friends really after *Sister Carrie,* even before, who wanted me to write, made me feel that I was important. . . . I don't know, I think it was one of those periods when I got to meditating. It happened to me once before in 1894 in Pittsburgh, after reading Huxley, Spencer, Schopenhauer. . . . Here was this immense system about us, chaotic, meaningless as far as we could find out, even the best of us, and you personally, were nothing. Or, if you were, what were you? I got to thinking that there was no answer and that depressed me. It was the same thing now in 1902. The book was suppressed; I couldn't get accepted where I had been before. No one would touch my stuff. I was hard up, and I got to meditating — everything seemed futile, not so much myself but the whole field of effort. Life seemed an endless chain without meaning. I think it was that."

So he meditated — chaos, futility, suicide. From pride he shunned the friends who would have liked to surround him. It was best to see no one. And then quite by chance one day walking in the Broadway district he met his brother Paul. He had met him a few years before not long after he had left Every Month, and there had been a coolness between them for that reason. Paul was at the height of his success — gold-headed cane, silk shirt, smart suit, and a fine apartment in the Marlborough — out of royalties from many national successes — *The Letter That Never Came, I Believe It, For My Mother Told Me So, The Convict And The Bird, The Pardon Came Too Late, Just Tell Them That You Saw Me, The Blue And The Gray, The Bowery, On The Banks Of The Wabash.*

The last song had been his suggestion. Paul had said one summer Sunday morning at the Howley, Haviland office: " Why don't you give me an idea once in a while? " The younger brother's answer had been: " Me? . . . I can't write those things. Why don't you write something about a state or a river . . . something that suggests a part of America? People like that. Take Indiana . . . the Wabash river? It's as good as any other . . . and you were raised by it." — " Not a bad idea," Paul thought, but Thee must write the words. " Rather shame-facedly," he says, he did produce the first verse and chorus, almost as it was published; and not long after the coolness between them; his own fault, he thinks — " I was very difficult to deal with."

One night, " young, lonely, wistful," he heard a quartet of boys singing it, passing under his window — his words:

" Round my Indiana homestead wave the cornfields.
In the distance loom the woodlands clear and cool.
Often times my thoughts revert to scenes of childhood,
Where I first received my lessons, nature's school.
But one thing there is missing in the picture,
Without her face it seems so incomplete.
I long to see my mother in the doorway,
As she stood there years ago, her boy to greet!
Oh, the moonlight's fair tonight along the Wabash,
From the fields there comes the breath of new mown hay.
Thro' the sycamores the candle lights are gleaming,
On the Banks of the Wabash, far away."

Soon it was everywhere, in the papers, on the stage, on the hand-organs and whistled in the streets. And when they met he had felt a kind of unreasoning resentment against his brother over a success which he had scorned to be part of. " On the banks, I see," he had said. And Paul had answered, " On the banks. . . . You turned the trick for me, Thee, that time. Why don't you ever come and see me? I'm still your brother. . . . A part of that is really yours." — " Cut that, the words are nothing," and he had passed on brusquely. Now again they met after Thee's own success and failure. This time the ballad-maker would not let him go, he was shocked by his appearance, insisted on his address, horrified because the number in Brooklyn contained a thirteen. The next morning he was there with a cab to bear him off to the affluent Marlborough:

"I was so morose and despondent that I resented it, resented myself, my state, life. . . . 'I can't,' I said finally. . . . 'I don't need your help. You don't owe me anything' — 'Owe, Hell!' he retorted. 'Who's talking about owe. . . . For that matter I owe you half of *On The Banks*. . . . You can't go on living like this. . . . Why, Thee, you're a big man. Damn it — don't you see — don't make me' — and he took out his handkerchief and wiped his eyes. . . . 'Get your things . . . you've got to come, that's all. I won't go without you.' . . ."

He prevailed with " such tenderness and concern as [one pictures] existing between parents and children, but rarely between brothers — and he a man of years and some affairs, and I an irritable, distrait and peevish soul." So Dreiser tells it, remembering how he took him into the luxury of a good hotel, into new clothes, and then in a day or so in his car to a sanitarium kept by a friend of Paul's, an ex-wrestler, the famous Muldoon, whose fortunes were made by rich American wrecks seeking youth again. His portraits of his brother make him a cipher of that infectious American charm, belonging more to the men than to the women, which has kept us going. It is met in rich and poor, mechanics, salesmen, entertainers, even in bankers and lawyers. It pervades and persuades those who meet it, colors our songs and jokes and manners, and lack of manners, and is, so far, more specially than

Pullmans or bathrooms or office buildings, the spiritual flower of the United States — blend of the humor of many nations.

He was six weeks at Muldoon's in training under a ruder sample of American wizardry, whom he describes without sparing himself in *Culhane the Solid Man.** Then he returned to New York " fairly well restored in nerves if not in health." His brother's act of love and this strong Irishman's contempt of weakness seemed to have combined urgently with Dreiser. From this moment a new condition of mind and body appeared to direct his dreams and desires. He was on the way to the outside of them, and came to rule them more from the outside. He would not abandon them ever, but he would teach himself to fight for them and make them count — that is, sell the dreams and fulfil the desires. Not again would he permit meditations to let him down into something " lymphatic and flabby as oysters." He had seen too many magnates without their clothes at Muldoon's, and had heard that trainer's roar of scorn. Times would come when the fight would have equal savor for him with that of dreams and desires.

If he were really to regain strength, an indoor job would be fatal. He looked for something in the open air and through influence hired himself to the New York Central Railroad at twelve cents an hour and ten hours a day with a construction gang, and was glad to get even this. When he went to solicit the job he had left his lunch, a loaf of bread, on a window-sill outside the superintendent's office, and had come out to find that a neat porter had thrown it into a garbage bin — the end of food for him that day. His money was as low as that, and his decision to take no more from his brother as firm. For six months he worked as a day laborer, for a few days carrying and piling lumber. Then finding that too hard, under a wild Irish boss he ran errands, signing for shipments of bolts, sand, cement, putty, and carrying O.K. blanks to the main office for materials needed in the construction of concrete platforms, culverts, coal bins, sidewalks, bridge and building piers.†

* *Twelve Men.* † *The Mighty O'Rourke: Twelve Men.*

So passing from magnetic Irishman to Irishman, cured by fresh air, and by contact with the unintellectual world of day laborers and contractors, he went back into the market of books and journals, equipped to seek and find a job. He had been refreshed too by what was denied him on the Missouri farm — " a new exciting experience with a woman," or maybe with several of them. He is an example of a man who has catered to his necessities in spite of conventions, thereby suffering, if you like, a loss in sensibility, and yet exposing himself equally to a wilder and less habitual sea of the senses than most people swim in.

Rehabilitated he sought and finally received a position. He found it in a sheerly commercial publishing house, Street, Smith & Company. It was the fall of 1904; he was thirty-three years old. The head of the firm was nicknamed Million Dollar Ormond Smith, since he thought and talked only in terms of huge profits. " The worse the swill the better you can sell it," was his slogan. Dreiser calls his experience there " a riot, a scream." It was irresponsible editing, one of the first of the book rackets. He went in at fifteen dollars a week as editor of Fiction. His wife returned from Missouri to live with him and serve and save again. Soon he conceived the idea of starting a magazine, modeled on Munsey's, the most successful of the 10c to 15c variety. With a Scotch-Irishman, Charles Agnew McLean, whom he got to know and enjoy, and who was a great favorite with Ormond Smith, two new thrill-journals were evolved, Smith's and The Popular Magazine. Dreiser took charge of the first. In one year Smith's reached a circulation of 125,000.

In addition to these, he had a hand in Street & Smith's 5c libraries which had published for years such classics as *Diamond Dick, Luck and Pluck, Brave and Bold, Nick Carter,* to secretly regale the boys of the United States and the men whose minds could not grow up. They catered to that thirst for adventure and sheer marvels of which boys and men are never allowed to find enough around the corner or across the street, or next door, or in their own houses, or in their own selves. Perhaps there never could be enough of it for anyone this side of paradise, unless perchance for those born into gangland or among trappers, hunters, Mexicans or Indians. It was Dreiser's job to take whatever manuscripts of promise arrived, and bring them up to the standard of Street & Smith technique. This, he says, he usually accomplished by cutting them in two and tacking an end to the first half and a beginning to the second, thereby doubling the output for the firm.

In this carefree editorial atmosphere Dreiser progressed from $15 to $35 a week. At the same time he and McLean formed a project to make a publishing firm together, with an eye on his part to the re-publication of *Sister Carrie*. Doubleday, however, incredible as it seems, refused to give up the plates. McLean's advice was to go and buy them; he would help him. The publisher at length agreed to sell for $500, with which transaction his firm goes out of this story. In later years Mencken takes one last fling at them:

" For his high services to American letters, Walter H. Page had been made ambassador to England, where *Sister Carrie* is regarded . . . as 'The best story on the whole that has yet come out of America,' . . . another proof, perhaps of that cosmic imbecility upon which Dreiser himself is so fond of discoursing."

The plates were secured, but the publishing scheme fell through; Dreiser later paid the sum himself. McLean got jealous of his success as an editor. His fault it may have been, since as he confesses, " I was always difficult to deal with." Yet some such fact appears to have been accepted by the gossips. The Standard, New York, January 2nd, 1908, reviewing his career, says:

" So Dreiser came back, but this time with a purpose to climb to the seats of the mighty. . . . New York is not the most affectionate corner of the world to carry out ideas of this character. . . . He did break through in one spot where tons of printed matter are tobogganed to that class which revels in the . . . romantic, but before the news could reach the heads of the establishment that the house had acquired the asset of a brain, the lesser organs . . . combined to prevent the disruption of the nincompoops' union."

37

Further from the bone: Broadway Magazine; "The great American novel, perhaps."

Dreiser himself does not think of McLean as a nincompoop; he liked him, but he succeeded in forestalling him. He had heard that The Broadway Magazine, belonging to Ben Hampton, was looking for an editor. In the spring of 1905 he solicited the job and got it, and so could resign from the pulp-thrill factory to one of higher pretensions. He was by now in good trim for the battle called success, and not scornful of the ease it would give him. For this new position he needed to be "fit." Hampton, himself, like every other would-be live wire in New York, was a success fiend. The town teemed with young men mostly from the villages who intended no longer to be village nobodies.

It is formidable — this period of our development. Out of their high schools and fresh-water colleges what of the past were schoolboys remembering? Almost nothing it would seem, but the myth of Xerxes, Hannibal, Alexander, Caesar, Attila, Napoleon, who in their days and countries came singly and were paragons. But now in this land of machinery every boy was a potential conqueror, or he was a nobody. Why was it that the old maids and sad young men, who had to teach or starve, stressed so exclusively these mighty brutes of history to boys and girls eager to learn about the world outside of their provinces? Was it that in this way they satisfied their need of rape and violence? Certainly they taught that temper called Roman to American children, many of whom must have been born childlike enough — little new bushes in April, where birds chattered. They fast became Roman, and have made a two-faced empire, half puritan, half sybarite, and wholly material, even if less sophisticated than the Roman Empire. The school teachers have had their revenge.

But it is necessary to return to commencement day. Some of the pupils, slightly intrigued by intellectual prowess, were not quite ready to abandon it when they came out into the world face to face with the problem of "making good." These quite naturally veered toward newspapers or magazines with the vague hope that some day they could be writers or artists. Mr. Hampton, when he left Knox College, in Galesburg, Illinois, confesses to being one of them. S. S. McClure, John and Rob Findley, Brady, Phillips, had graduated not long before him and already shone in journalism in the East. He ran a paper in Galesburg for a while, and then with the money went on to New York in 1898 to make a fortune, preferably as a " serious " writer. But as S. S. McClure pointed out there was no money in it; " the highest price novelist we had, W. D. Howells, only made $4,000 a year." The magazine field looked more promising. He appraised it in terms of circulation and advertising. McClure's to be sure, had only a small circulation, 400,-000; Munsey's introducing half-tone illustrations, 600,-000 perhaps; Youth's Companion 800,000. Century, the best of the literary magazines, with a mere forty or fifty thousand, was not to be considered. But the Saturday Evening Post had reached already a million and a half and had swept up the country's advertising, such as it was. In connection with it Charles Austin Bates, a pioneer in advertising, had organized a ready-made ad-service. This gave Hampton an inspiration; national advertising was the gateway to the future. Literature and business could yet be married, or at any rate they could be made to lie down in the same bed together. So, always slightly leaning toward the arts, he bought the remnants of the Irving Batcheller Literary Syndicate, which, he said, was buying a mere name, though in the past it had handled some big literary merchandise. *The Red Badge of Courage* had been one of its minor purchases.

Into this obsolete business he introduced the modern pulmotor — an advertising service. Soon he was supplying R. & G. Corsets, Wesson's Oil, American Tobacco. With money from that he went on to his particular dream of a magazine. He bought the old Broadway, and in an office on 22nd Street, began pumping life into it to make it a vehicle of New York, as The Strand was of London. He employed, he says, about twenty-five artists and writers, paying as much as $18 to $25 a week for reporters and $100 for ad-writers, with the result that "newspaper men fairly beseiged his office." He lacked a good literary editor and advertised for one. Among those who applied was Dreiser. He remembers him well the day he came into his office, "a heavy-set, lunky fellow, obviously a newspaper man, singularly unattractive." It is certain neither caught the other's quality. They saw each other in terms of value, not of charm. "The minute I set eyes on him," Hampton said, "I figured the man was a genius. I said to myself, 'Jesus, here's a wow,' and hired him on the spot." He worked for $60 a week with a promise of $100 if the circulation went up to 75,000. It went fast to above a hundred thousand. The previously quoted New York Standard tells of his success:

> "Then he tackled the Broadway magazine, a publication of odorous memory, started by that celebrated adaptor of other people's ideas, Roland Burke Hennesy. Later on Broadway fell into the hands of the Hamptons, in class A as advertising experts, but nothing much on magazine editing. The job was an Augean one . . . for Dreiser. . . . He turned in a river of good literature and snappy special articles, changing the magazine completely, except in name. People began to sit up and take notice. . . . Instead of sneaking round the corner to read it they carried it in the sunlight and were proud of it. Circulation began to grow, and advertisers gave up real money for its pages. It was the prettiest piece of transformation work seen in New York for many a day. . . ."

So Dreiser made the magazines. He was on the inside now among the money makers. He could exclude as he had often been excluded. He was a procurer among the prostitutes of literature. He had left to one side the lonely realm of art, and behind him the vagabond newspaper men and fantastic song-writers and 5-cent thrill-makers, and was crossing over to that paradise of irridescent shaded lamps, perpetual palms and oriental rugs, shared by magazine and advertising agencies. Though all of journalism compromised to a lie, the newspaper lie ran nearer to the turf than the magazine lie. The offices of one as compared to the other had the look of stables as compared to parlors of the newly arrived. Newspapers disguised facts; magazines fabricated fiction. Their editors had the look of facial massages, and the sound of massaged manners. They never spat or swore, or put their feet on the desk like the newspaper men. They frightened elegantly, not gruffly. Sometimes their habit of polite pretence so emptied their faces of human expression that they began to look like dressed up animals — the great ones like foxes or cats or spiders; the smaller ones like weasels, ants and beavers, and beneath these were the chipmunks and mice.

Broadway Magazine was not properly in this grand powerful inane shiny-paper class. Under Mr. Hampton it was a compromise between the live and the static. Compared to the great whoring periodicals dominant today, it was not much more than a frontier *bagnio*. This was a period and a publisher still believing that vital news could be made to pay. He conceived the idea of increasing circulation by telling on the great and powerful. His success came partly through muck-raking. It was the day for it. The Interests already ruled constructively, but not yet defensively. Thomas Lawson could write and publish his American epic, *Frenzied Finance,* hoping thereby to change the course of the real Niagara, Big Business. Ida Tarbell had already slightly stirred the complacent nation, and stimulated the circulation of McClure's with her disclosures as to Standard Oil. Pearson's magazine, February 1914, prints a review of Hampton's progress, as Broadway came to be called — a story which appears in detail in Upton Sinclair's *Brass Check:*

> ". . . He never indulged in personal attacks and was painstakingly accurate; but it was every month a steady hammering at conditions as they really are. . . . There was not one great and powerful interest in America that he had not antagonised. . . . In four years the circulation increased from 12,000 to 440,000 — on the strength of the boldest muck-raking that had ever been done."

Initially also, according to Hampton and others, success was due to Dreiser's editorial talents. He slipped over every possible clever short story and article that came to him, like Hampton unwilling to believe that people preferred to be bored, much as their ideas differed as to what was boring. They were both right, it seemed; circulation soared. But Hampton was his own assassin; in the end advertising fell. In 1911, four years after Dreiser had left the paper, the game was up. The Interests had put an end to muck-raking, and on the best security Hampton found himself unable to get money at any bank. " Some of the banks," Pearson's says, " admitted that they had been instructed not to lend him anything." The magazine was stabbed, and died at the special hands of The New Haven Road, a Morgan property, and the object of Hampton's last exposure. Mr. Hampton retired to the position of advertising manager of American Tobacco, whose president of twenty years later has convinced the public that they will avoid laryngitis and won't get fat if they smoke Lucky Strikes. As fast as that did advertising travel beyond the dreams of men in 1905.

From the spring of 1905 to the autumn of 1907 in the last decade of rational magazines, and rational advertising Hampton and Dreiser worked together, one to build his paper into a great periodical, the other to secure his future, that sometime he might be a writer again. Mr. Hampton says of him, that he made a professional success; acquired a standing with other editors; that he had " a marvellous objective mind " but that above that was an even more remarkable " subjective mind," which drove him to the necessity of writing, and kept him from ever attaining the editorial speed of a Ray Long, for example. Such an editor, unhampered by the substantive " was an objective genius pure and simple." A very interesting distinction, unless the object in Mr. Hampton's mind could be boiled down to as pure and simple a thing as money. But I think there is more to it than that: an effort to define the impersonal conquering mind, unrelated to other people, or to oneself or to nature, related to things, to objects — the mind which at its best makes money; in distinction to the personal, reflective, creative

mind — the mind which at its best makes art. . . .
" Christ in Hell," he ended abruptly, and with intense admiration for his ex-editor, " Dreiser could no more keep from writing as he saw life than he could keep from breathing. Read him describing department stores or street railways and you know them to the life, physically, legally, socially." He himself had hated Comstockery, and was so moved by *Sister Carrie* that he would have liked to publish it for him.

Dreiser, on the other hand, perhaps unfairly, does not reciprocate. Almost, it would seem, an antagonism, which Hampton ignores, operated between them. In *De Maupassant Junior* he describes him with more bias than I have noticed elsewhere in his portraits:

" Our publisher and owner was a small, energetic, vibrant and colorful soul, all egotism and middle-class conviction as to the need of 'push,' ambition, 'closeness to life,' 'punch,' and what not else American to the core, . . . hourly as it were, demanding the ' hows ' and ' whyfores ' of the dream which the little group I was swiftly gathering about me was seeking to make real."

Since he was the publisher and owner one can't quite blame him for this demand, nor does Dreiser blame any other individual for being American to the core. He goes on to demolish him:

". . . While he wanted something new in fiction, something more virile and lifelike than that 'mush ' . . . to be found in the current magazines, still it must have a strong appeal for the general reader (!); and be very compelling in fact and *clean* — a solid little pair of millstones which would . . . end in mascerating everything vital out of any good story.

. . . He had a facile and specious method of arguing, a most gay and in some respects magnetic personality, far from stodgy or gross, which for a time attracted many to him. Very briskly then, he proceeded to make friends with all those with whom I had surrounded myself. . . . In addition to these there was a constantly swelling band of writers, artists, poets, critics, dreamers of social reform, who were now beginning to make our place a center; an amusing vivid strident world."

Again can you blame the publisher even if his editor had been a magnet for this circle, in wanting to be " artistic " too. Perhaps an antipathy grew between them because

Hampton had not the thick-skinned " objective mind " of the ideal editor; whereas Dreiser has found most intriguing those who don't know how to compromise. " Nothing by halves," is his preference. If a magnate, then be a ruthless one like Yerkes! If a hypocrite, a terrible one like Rockefeller! If a reformer, then a creator like Haywood or Lenin! If an artist, then one strong enough to stay lonely and isolated as he himself would soon find was his necessity. He held the artist's prejudice against an expedient reformer like Hampton — that is, one not coerced by anger. He besides was too much fascinated by the spectacle of unscrupulous finance to want to interfere with it, supposing that he could. He wanted to watch it and make people more, not less lustful, if he influenced them at all. For twenty-five years since that time he has watched it, until in 1930, he has denounced its greed as loudly as could any reformer, but too late. Better perhaps had he thrown some of his force of mind against it earlier. But, as in every other sphere of our life, different literary elements rarely mingled. Writers separated by so much as a slight prejudice kept away from each other. Dreiser, for example, never liked Jack London, because he called him and everyone " comrade."

He made two friendships important to him in these years on Broadway. One was a young man from the Southwest, Texas and Missouri, a writer after his own heart in the reckless line of descent of Poe and Stephen Crane — Harris Merton Lyon, whom he included on his staff and helped all that he could. He saw in him an uncompromising, scornful writer. But according to his portrait of him in *Twelve Men,** he lost him to luxury and dissipation and an early death, because of this publisher's influence over him, whom he represents as the villain of the story. I asked him if he had not been unfair to Hampton in the picture. His answer was: " Well, perhaps, in some of the details, but just the same I know he killed Lyon." — " How? " I said — " He made him put happy endings to his stories, I know he did." — " That curse of all American fiction, the necessarily happy ending! " It went hand in hand with " the uplift note " on Hamp-

* *De Maupassant Jr.*

ton's magazine, and he abhorred the liaison. He speaks of Lyon as a proud father or teacher might. Once after a long time of not seeing him, he came to dinner, " bringing of all things a great armful of red roses." An incongruous gift, it seemed, from the ex-railroad boy to the ex-Hoosier. Neither exactly knew how to give or receive it. The memory is none the less dear to Dreiser. And he likes to remember too that Lyon left when he died enough manuscript to make " two small volumes of short tales . . . in the clear, incisive, uncompromising vein . . . and with that passion for revelation which characterized him at first, that same unbiased and unfettered non-moral viewpoint." It was " wonderful and hopeful " that New York contained this new intellect in the midst of so much pretension, and monstrous that America should have killed it.

Also while with Broadway he met B. W. Dodge, " a most lovable alcoholic " and an editor with imagination. He was " crazy about him." Together they carried through the publishing scheme he had planned with McLean. Plots were thickening fast at this time. On May 18, 1907, B. W. Dodge & Co., that is, Dodge and Dreiser, republished *Sister Carrie*, though not before one more protest out of Chaos. The box containing the plates and sheets, for which five hundred hard earned dollars had been paid, went through a storage fire. Half of them, too charred to use, had to be made over again. But finally the book was really out in the light of the public, the first edition gone in less than two weeks.

38

The New Enemy, Sophistication

The reviewers, educated by British opinion, did better this time, with three times as many notices, almost all of them flattering either in anger or praise. In seven years the country had undergone a change of temper. Chiefly in those years there had come about a fever, an agony, among young people to force the United States to be habitable for men and women of imagination. Lone figures like Thompson and Reedy, and the several little magazines and theatres, and exiled professors in callow universities had sown seeds of envy. Young people were tired of vicarious romance. They must have experience themselves which is romance, and have it quick. There began that optimistic flowering, that nascence of the spirit, of which people ask today, is it over? Or swear today that it has just begun, or else that it is anomolous and can never be. *Sister Carrie* was welcomed on its merits — a strong plant out of our soil and despite our dust, the real thing. It satisfied many of the new Americans. Yet too, there would be those impatient of its crudities who could not stand it. They saw in it their own crudities, the flatness of American life, which at heart they knew would be the death of their aesthetic dreams. And yet how hard to admit defeat! There *must* be short cuts to quality by a process of transfusion, even in quantitative North America! They would make a forced growth of the art of living and the art of celebrating living, to enjoy the fruits before they died. Whistler and Henry James had done this by becoming European. They would do it at home. Such crusaders sometimes resented *Sister Carrie* as bitterly as did the moralists. A new enemy was entering the scene for the native Dreiser — the importer of more than fashion, the importer of sophistication.

The reviews of the book in 1907 are slides of American life in that year. You will find there the old style moralist to whom talk of sex was quite simply taboo; the new style moralist to whom talk of sex was entirely proper, if, and don't misunderstand them, sex brought unhappiness or taught an economic lesson. You will find there the old style high-brow, jealous of the English language, hugging Pater, Arnold, and possibly Swinburne; the new style intellectual, homesick for maturity in a senile juvenile land, and what difference the manner as long as the matter was a telegram out of reality? And then you will find already the new antagonist, the sophisticate, the fly in the ointment. This first novel of this first American Realist was a storm center:

> Boston Transcript: "A matter for regret that he should have deliberately chosen to devote his creative talent to a woman and two men who never quicken our nobler impulses. . . ."
> Ohio Journal: "Such books are to be shunned . . . there is so much in the world that is fresh and clean, elevating little stories . . . that are well worth telling. . . ."
> The Club Fellow: New York: "The modern writer should not make vice seem attractive. . . . But it is not immoral to describe the allurements that await the young girl in our over-crowded cities, so long as it shows that no breach of the moral law ever can result in happiness. . . . *Sister Carrie* shows bitterness and disillusion at the end of the path."
> Advance, Chicago: "No better sermon could be preached . . . on the necessity of leaving other people's money alone. . . ."
> New York Sun: "Mr. Dreiser should take a course in reading, Flaubert, Defoe, etc. . . . After such a course [his] gents will give up wearing pants, vests, Prince Alberts, and tuxedos of the slop shops. . . ."
> Philadelphia Ledger, Agnes Repplier: "[He] has the faculty of picturing his scenes so vividly in clear-cut English that they compel instant and abiding interest."
> Texas Post, Houston, Harris Merton Lyon: "I see in *Sister Carrie* one more evidence of a broader, American intellectual freedom. . . . Possibly the day will come when George Moore's *Memoirs of My Dead Life* will not have to be expurgated as if for children when . . . issued in the United States."

And then the opinion of the man of the world, deriving from Europe, the new enemy. Mr. Harrison Rhodes, a fashionable critic of that time, reflects the type. Writing for The Bookman, languorously he reminds his readers that Mr. Dreiser as realist and immoralist is like all good natives, somehow lacking. What had he told of lasciviousness, what really of gaiety?

> " The intelligent foreigner will find her amazingly typical of the chill in our . . . blood. No one need avoid *Sister Carrie* as an ' improper book.' When Miss Meeber yields to the blandishments of her drummer, there was unquestionably, from the point of view of the intelligent foreigner a ' scéne à faire.' That Mr. Dreiser avoids it is proof equally of his innate refinement and of the American sense that love involves many things besides physical passion. Indeed one is tempted . . . to the reflection that Miss Meeber considered that physical feature of life too unimportant to be worth even avoiding."

Here is the pessimist who despairs of celebrating life where there is so little to celebrate. Here is the self-exiled American with a small audience now to reinforce him. Perhaps, I am not sure, looking forward out of the struggle for authentic imagination in our country, from Poe and Whitman to the originals of the near past — perhaps we shall find, looking beyond them into the present, this type, the exile, self-deported to Europe spiritually or actually or both, to be the sole one among our artists enough nourished to survive. The intervening fifteen years, however, belong more to us than to Europe. They are years of vigor and revelation, years of artists, especially writers, who worked like tillers of the soil, or who worked like engineers, building bridges and viaducts and always roads.

Dreiser was one of them, unaware perhaps of the existence of an entering wedge of connoisseurs preoccupied with values alien to his foreground. He made no effort to cope with them. Instead seriously he answered the now familiar critics of his diction. He said to them: " To sit up and criticize me for saying ' vest ' instead of ' waistcoat '; to talk about my splitting the infinitive and using vulgar commonplaces here and there, when the tragedy of a man's life is being displayed, is silly. More, it is ridiculous. It makes me feel that American criticism is the joke that English authorities maintain it to be."

And to the moralists he took the trouble to say: " The

mere living of your daily life is drastic drama. Today there may be some disease lurking in your veins that will end your life tomorrow. . . . Life is a tragedy. . . . I simply want to tell about life as it is. Every human life is intensely interesting . . . even when there are no ideals, when there is only a personal desire to survive, the fight to win, the stretching out of the fingers to grasp — these are the things I want to write about — the facts as they exist, the game as it is played. . . . I said I was pointing out no moral. Well, I am not, unless this is a moral — that all humanity must stand together and war against and overcome the forces of nature. I think a time will come when personal gain will rarely be sought at the expense of someone else."

But with words and thoughts like these, he turned his back on the whole literary field, moralists, aesthetes and admirers, to enter with fellow natives into the fight against some of the forces of nature — hunger and destitution. At the same time his English champions, with nothing to gain and nothing to lose, were always being loyal to him — Frank Harris, William Locke, Arnold Bennett. The narrative must leave them, however, to follow the author of their favorite American novel into American commerce.

39

Life far from the bone: Butterick Patterns

In the same spring of 1907, John O'Hara Cosgrave came into the picture, an editorial friend, who under Ridgeway edited Munsey's which superseded Everybody's. Guessing that Hampton and Dreiser were destined to separate, he recommended him to George W. Wilder of the Butterick Publications. He had recently lost his combined editor and art-editor — " a young fellow," as Dreiser tells it, who killed himself over an affair with " some society girl," discovered and denied him by society. He was one of a number to enter into his meditations at this time as somehow related to him, men who came up and went under. A composite of them emerged later as his " Genius."

Impressed by his Broadway record Wilder offered Dreiser the position, at $7,000 a year and a bonus as the circulation mounted. So in the summer of 1907 he entered the Butterick Publishing Co., whose large factory building already stood at Spring and MacDougal Streets. He was at once managing editor of five fashion magazines, the Delineator, the Designer, the New Idea, the South American Delineator, and the German from which they imported material. Chief of this was the Delineator. He was a long way now from Indiana valleys, further than his brother Paul with his sentimental ballads which swept the country-lanes and parlors, and yet of course, he too was catering to the villages. New York was and is a vast explosion, made out of the dreams of villages, clasping in a distorted ecstasy the patterns of the older cities.

As five-fold Butterick editor and art editor, he came as near to big business as any periodical in that day could bring him. He had a staff of thirty-two people, whom he had selected each for his or her special value. He controlled the editorial policy of these journals — his condition so that Broadway difficulties might not be repeated. He was an " idea-man " and canvassed the country for men and women with ideas. Pretty soon, he says, " Any one who had any idea about the United States ran down to The Delineator." Forty-two thousand manuscripts came in to them in a year. He fulfilled a wish of his, an office painted green and bronze and hangings and furnishings to go with green and bronze; people came there Saturday afternoons for tea and talk; he held a kind of " salon." Circulation mounted, as it had in his previous ventures. In fact, this time, with stipulated freedom, he sent it soaring in four years from 400,000 to 1,200,000. Newspaperdom, October 24, 1927, writes about him:

> " Perhaps the most nervous man . . . I ever saw in an editorial chair is Theodore Dreiser . . . of that nervous, ever-active, never still nature; tall, but not broad-shouldered, generous of feature and alert . . . a typical Westerner, and there are few who would not pause on the street to look back at the tall man. . . .
>
> In the [six months] in which he has been editing *The Delineator* he has injected much new life . . . into it. [He] says: 'Get personality into your work. . . . I believe the average person likes best to read about people and their accomplishments and to know . . . something of the king-pin of the combination. . . .' "

Leaders interested him when he was editor of a woman's fashion magazine as acutely as at any other time. Luckily for him, he happened to be editor in the last decade of " personality." Soon it would be forbidden by Big Business, except as an empty slogan, along with alcohol and free speech.

The Butterick Publications (I tell it for those too young to remember life before the cloak and suit trade) like The Ladies' Home Journal had for years been providing dress patterns for virtuous women of moderate means, to make up at home spring and fall. The models originated in the clothes that Queen Victoria and her dowagers wore. Butterick subtracted some of the fullness but none of the goodness and diagrammed them for home use. Coming into New York in those days BUTTERICK in electric letters commanded the harbor. Butterick patterns were the grief of daughters who hoped to disobey their frugal mothers in the matter of dress. Advice was that they could be realized to good advantage in domestic materials, every thread by no means wool or silk or linen. And pitifully they were devoid of " sex-appeal," which at about this date was beginning to creep in. Here paradoxically was a flagrant libertine of American letters appointed to be purveyor of " safe fashions for home people." It is amusing to think that perhaps Whitman gave the first American impulse toward nudity, and Dreiser toward clothes. He was too innocent, however, and too politic to make any radical change away from domestic styles. That remained for more mundane importers to do with Vogue and Harper's Bazaar. He attacked from another angle. His friends laughed to think of him in this low-brow guise of fashion-dictator, but with characteristic seriousness and without shame he studied the problem — how to reach the ladies. He stimulated with ideas; ideas gave birth to longings, and longings to the need of new clothes. Women over the country felt that somehow a friend of theirs was breathing a tiny wind of danger into Butterick standards. New invitations appeared between the lines. Or if he did not calculate quite so nicely, anyway it was his policy to wake the women up. He would be the one to give them a " high-brow magazine," and they would like it.

When I asked Mr. William Lengel, at first secretary, and then editor under Dreiser, today assistant editor of Cosmopolitan, to tell me what he remembered of Delineator days, his exclamation was: " I hope you will do justice to Dreiser as editor; a book could be written about it." Too ignorant of American business to write this book, I can only submit what notes I took for it on my visit to Mr. Lengel, and to others who had worked on his staff. It was a hot July day in 1930 when I made the pilgrimage to the new Hearst temple of journalism at 59th Street and Eighth Avenue, which succeeds in being a distillation in concrete of all religious architecture, Greek, Gothic, Egyptian, Aztec, Assyrian, Christian Science.

Ascending in the aphrodisiac elevator, I reached the outer halls of the editorial offices where an impeccable Ziegfeld beauty nineteen years distant from Butterick patterns lisped telephone numbers and took down names. Mine was handed to a boy who could have adorned pages of Petronius. Soon with courtesy beyond belief for New York City or any city, I was told that Mr. Lengel was talking to England; if I could wait . . . ?

I waited, studying originals of International-Cosmopolitan illustrations and covers, which hung like treasures on the walls, and symptomized the various appeals — the mother appeal; the infant appeal, the virility appeal, the adventure appeal, the juvenile sex-appeal. Babies there were digging in sand piles, splashed with sunlight; Arabians descending on chargers over cliffs; American Indians glad that their friends the white men had come; bankers with tall glasses on golf-club verandahs; the American girl with translucent nostrils exquisitely equipped for the slightly pouting clean-jawed Young American. . . . I thought in these twenty years Mr. Lengel would have surely forgotten the amateur days on Spring and MacDougal Streets, but no! With scarcely a flash of the first manner of the magnate receiving no one, he recalled that the appointment related to Theodore Dreiser. Sitting across from me at his vast fumed-oak desk, imperial with bronze cigar and cigarette boxes, lighter and tray, blotter and paper holder, and the specially designed telephone instrument recently vibrant with London, he looked like a late Roman wish come true. In fine-striped lavender shirt and cool brown summer clothes he had been evolved, mouth, nose, eyes, hair and smile in crisp Dionysian curves. Yet in this interview he was an apprentice remembering his favorite master.

At twenty he was a drop in the stream that came from the Middle-West. Already having practiced law in a small Iowan town, he came wishing to be an actor in New York, or a writer. Knowing next to nothing about stenography, he said, but with " plenty of pep " and only twenty-five cents in his pocket, he had answered an advertisement which took him to the Butterick offices to apply for position as secretary to the editor in chief. He was told by the fiction editor, Mr. Charles Hanson Towne, that his boss would be the most disagreeable man in the world to work for; never praised anyone, found fault with everyone. . . . He had fired the last man because he had lost a book of clippings. . . . But somehow Lengel got on with him, not as secretary — he discharged him as that, but retained him as one of the sub-editors. He thinks Dreiser liked him because he was " brash," while most editorial minds were timid. One day he came upon *Sister Carrie* on a shelf in his chief's office. After a look at it he went out and bought it. It was Saturday; he read it in Central Park until nightfall, and the next day on the sands at Coney Island: " Dreiser was big, ungainly, homely, but after that I would have done anything he asked of me. . . ." In later days he *has* done all that he could for him, to the extent of recently publishing a Hearstian version of *This Madness* which even then, it is rumored, lost for the magazine all the advertising that articles by Mr. Coolidge gained.

I asked him exactly why he thought of Dreiser as a good editor: " He made people think. He had the biggest correspondence department of any periodical up to date. A lot of men got magazine training under him — Dr. Crane, Homer Croy, Charles Hanson Towne, Lee Harriman, George Creel, James E. West. They may not like to admit it but they learned a lot down there. That child-rescue campaign — West owed his position as secretary of the Boy Scouts to that. . . . He got up a rediscussion of spiritualism — *Are the dead alive?* — it made a lot of talk; some of the churches wanted to stop subscriptions. He made a strong virile magazine for women." — Here I interrupted: " I should think then commercially he must have failed. " No, it suited them all right. The trouble was, he put on so much circulation, the advertising couldn't equal it; I guess they're still trying to catch up. . . . The bigger the circulation, you know, the more expensive it is to publish. It's the advertising end that's got to pay for it." — " Then, the trouble was, he suited a large feminine audience, but not their husbands, the advertisers? " — " No, it wasn't that. The advertising department just didn't hustle around like he did to meet his circulation. It was the day for a lively publication; he knew it." — " And it's not the day now? " — " Perhaps not, psychology has changed." — " But didn't they think Dreiser was getting a little too interesting? " — " I don't know. There was a man came over from The Woman's Home Companion. He said, ' Make Delineator softer.' Dreiser said, ' Send a letter to all our readers, and ask them if they want a namby-pamby magazine.' He won out. He was a great editor."

Miss Katherine Leckie, another of his staff, a Chicago newspaper woman, the first, she thinks, to go as a reporter on a par with men, gave him almost the same testimonial: " The greatest editor I ever worked under! . . . A very fine mind! . . . And he always gave the woman the same chance as the man. . . . One of the few who considered women as workers, and that sex did not enter into the situation." Not long ago she met him by chance in a vegetarian restaurant on 56th Street, and they reminisced. She had said, " Those were great days." And his answer had been, " Yes, if they had lasted. They ought to have gone on for years. . . ."

Mary Field Parton, one of his contributors, was as zealous in praise. She describes Dreiser as seeming to her formidable in those days, and above all, sophisticated, already a man of the cities, but then as she says, she had come from Chicago and the Far West, and felt shy and young. She had come with a word of introduction from Clarence Darrow, whom he admired. She liked Dreiser enormously; he was always so ready to welcome a new idea, and so interested in writing for its own sake. She, too, attributes to him a disinterested intellect where women were concerned, which contradicts his legend. She remembers an article she made for him about Emma Goldman, *The Dynamiter,* whom he considered the most important American woman of that time because " she dared to stand alone." He told her how to write it to conform to Butterick standards. She was to make them think she was pointing a finger of scorn at the anarchist: " Emma Goldman dares to talk of free love; the true woman should never dream of freedom. . . . Emma

Goldman thinks human beings are good enough to govern themselves; ridiculous!" . . .

So here is a fourth group of people that came to surround this visionary who loved society so well that he was willing to fight it to be part of it — the magazine group. This time he figured as a nucleus. It took him among the arrived illustrators, litterateurs, musicians, and decorators of the city, to their parties in town and country, on to yachts and into expensive motors and houseparties. He never made the estuary that had now widened out of the original baffling Four Hundred, so much in his thoughts when he was young, but he met people rich and successful enough to skirt the banks of it, and he got a nearer sense of its place in the American scheme. What was more, he had the luxury now of requited love in more expensive dress than he had known it before. More than one woman, who seemed to him desirable, wanted him, and was willing to pay in money and grief if necessary. Women were part of these town and country excursions. He on his side was determined not to pay too much in any medium. Ambition carried him like a fast horse a good rider.

Wilder, the publisher, he says, got excited as he watched circulation soaring, and jumped his salary from seven to ten, and then to twelve thousand; and in 1908, four years from the time he was getting fifteen dollars a week, to fourteen thousand. This with the bonus mounted into money, $25,000 a year in the end, to be saved so that he could be free to write about life as he saw it. He and his wife lived now in a comfortable apartment on Morningside Drive, but even so, he says: "I was a very simple person with no money to spend on luxuries." They worked and saved. His will to choose the forces that would best serve him is in full action now. He began to write *Jennie Gerhardt* again, and completed twenty chapters of it, which in 1908 he sent on urgent request to the English publisher, Grant Richards. With a few reservations as to diction, hoping that he could perhaps reform him as to such words as *affectional,* and *pronunciamento,* Richards wrote him that it was "a very fine piece of work, a fit and worthy successor to *Sister Carrie*," and " would healthily depress everyone of its intelligent readers." He exhorts him to finish the book quickly, telling him he has " no right to hide his talent year after year," and hopes to be his publisher.

40
Breaking with unbroken traditions

In 1909 in accordance with this trait which forced selection and action, Dreiser and his wife separated, never to live together again. I have asked friends of his who knew them both what impelled the break. One of them, an illustrator of sensitive fibre, said: " I don't know, she would have irritated me. One night I went to see them up on Morningside Drive. There they were in the dining room. She was sprinkling clothes on the same table where he was correcting proof. I felt a lack of understanding in that. Perhaps Dreiser didn't mind. He, on the other hand, was subject to fits of terrible depression, impossible to live with, I should think." Another friend imagined that, though she tried, she could not stand his " varietism " as to women, and that he could not stand her melancholy over it. He had sympathy for both of them, for her tears and for his " wandering forth to others." Also he thought that she was jealous of Dreiser creatively, had always wanted to be a writer herself. Still another insists that it was because she rewrote at his request the first chapters of *Jennie Gerhardt,* and that he returned them to their original state, that they quarreled and separated. He himself cannot remember that it was any one thing. They separated because he had one code and she another too alien to maintain together. So Dreiser broke the American tradition that the artist should live like any other citizen with, for, and of the family and the home — that nucleus for radiator, telephone, refrigerator, kiddy-car, automobile, player piano, and radio to come. He departed from the wisdom of Howells and Mark Twain more flagrantly than other men of genius in the United States were known to do. Even the radical architect, Frank Lloyd Wright, married oftener and quicker than Dreiser. He was about to embark at this date on twenty years free of matrimony. No longer would the letters he received end with the invariable. " My wife and I join in the season's best wishes for you and yours."

In another year he made his second break with native custom. He broke with his last job under an employer other than himself. Erman J. Ridgeway, so successful with Munsey's, joined forces with Wilder. He was a strict Methodist and out of sympathy with the author of *Sister Carrie*. One rumor has it that Dreiser was tired of journalism and let himself out. Another that Ridgeway said, " Make the magazine as harmless as the Ladies' Home Journal or quit." Still another, that, contrary to Miss Leckie's belief, he did allow sex to enter ever so slightly into journalism with a young stenographer, in the beauty-correspondence department, and that Mr. Ridgeway was properly indignant and fired him. Dreiser himself says that these may have been contributing causes, but that no American publisher would let morals stand in the way of business. Circulation, he points out, was still mounting. He left of his own accord, not exactly that he was bored with editing but that he was no longer a free agent; and besides there was trouble about the bonus.

Back of personal causes, was the economic fact that the Interests had begun to fear the magazines. In May 1909 John Kenneth Turner in the American Magazine had gone too far, in articles sympathetic to Mexican radicals and to an uprising of slaves in Yucatan. President Taft at the bidding of Finance had had to " hotfoot it to the border to stage a love-fest with Diaz," in the words of Lemuel Parton, an ace newspaper man who thus dates the death-blow to a liberal press in the United States. In that year the American Magazine changed its policy, and soon after McClure's and Hampton's collapsed. Thomas Lawson and Ida Tarbell had been allowed to talk too ably. Just as once the Yankee religionists had persecuted the nonconforming children of their day, their successors, the financiers, were about to execute the new brand of wizards, the newswriters, who were leading their readers off to forbidden fields, away from the modern churches — Office, Factory and Store. From now on controlled syndicate news was to become the only orthodox news. The American press was about to divide into right and left wings. The right would grow fat and windy and prosperous. The left would grow lean, and self-righteous and unremunerative; would live on the sneers of rotarians and the money given by rotarians' wives; and would finally after two decades find itself narrowed to the Nation and the New Republic and a few art journals published in Paris.

I asked Dreiser if he thought he would have stayed on as editor of Butterick, if all had gone well, just for the chance of making a fortune. He couldn't say, but he thought not: " No man could stand it indefinitely; it would make a hack out of him. . . . Besides," he added, " I am a writer, not an editor." Even on the Delineator people featured him as a writer after the reappearance of *Sister Carrie*. He is sure that many contributions from important writers in England and America came to him as author of that novel. Letters he has kept bear him out — letters from Edgar Jepson, Albert Kinross, W. B. Trites, hoping to contribute to his journal and mentioning that friends of theirs, Zangwill, Frank Harris, Richard Middleton, Charles Flandrau admired the book. And letters from Gustavus Myers, Albert Bigelow Paine, Brand Whitlock, Fremont Rider, Edwin Markham, I. F. Marcosson, Adele Marie Shaw, Louise Closser Hale, Grace McGowan Cook, James Huneker, all pay homage to him as novelist. Usually they compare him to Zola, " even Balzac," sometimes to Flaubert, once to Strindberg, and quite wildly to de Goncourt and George Moore. One man, however, the Yankee John Kendrick Bangs balks at the idea of Butterick contamination. He writes:

> " What is the matter with you anyway? Do you really think that I could be such an ass as to submit those Nature Fakir stories to you as editor of the Delineator? . . . The tales were sent in response to your repeated requests to let you see something that might do for B. W. Dodge and Company. . . .
> " It will perhaps please you to hear that at least upon three occasions I was asked questions as to . . . the author of *Sister Carrie*. . . . I told the inquisitive Westerners that

you had served six terms in Sing Sing, were regarded as incorrigible and all the other nice things I happen to know about you, even going so far as to boom the Delineator."

In these years he had those who hated, as well as those who loved. He was a man among the men, a fox among the foxes, carving a destiny, making off with some of the spoils. He was at the same time in the strange position of being shepherd to the flock. It was in accordance with his three selves, the conqueror, the solitary, the good fellow, impeding and helping one another. What he had made in solitude followed him into the market. A woman on his staff writes to one of his associates, John Cosgrave:

". . . I am so thrilled because he told me Dreiser is the *Sister Carrie* Dreiser. I didn't like him a bit; he never is nice like you and says, 'That's bully.' I have been thinking of trying to get out of the Delineator, it was only business anyway. Now I feel just as loyal to him as I do to you.

I can't tell you how good work affects me. . . . I feel to Dreiser like one feels to a chief. . . . I don't care two cents about the money part now. . . . It's the one big serious true American novel with blood in it — not ink. . . ."

How long will it continue in the modern world — this personal need for mind, for intellect really, which human beings hold to, however vacant the outlook? On his side this hero remembers his trials, how for example, his fiction editor signed all acceptances with his own name and all refusals with Dreiser's, which in itself marked him as a very carping, formidable official.

41

> *" All the most valuable things are useless
> . . . to those who understand that life is
> not lived at all if not lived for contempla-
> tion or excitement . . . that we can do
> almost what we will if we do it gaily, and
> think that freedom is but a trifling with
> the world."* — W. B. YEATS

At length the days in the market were over. Dreiser had done, in a sense, the impossible, what so many would-be artists start out to do and abandon. He had gained independence through hiring himself out for a space of years — in his case six years. Friends write to him now as one might to a champion fighter, among them James Huneker: " I'm sorry for the Delineator's sake that you are leaving it and I hope you have something better. *But* — if you, Theodore Dreiser, could or would return to your old field, the gain for our literature would be something worthwhile. We have but one *Sister Carrie,* despite the army of imitators." As it happened Dreiser set about to fulfil this hope, since even more passionately it was his own desire, and at last he felt able and equipped.

He had enough money for a while and plenty of the honey of esteem. Sex received him variously. A various world was beginning to tell him he was important. Love and self-love were being fed; lust and vanity, the two forever intermingled insatiates, which when fed become relaxation and strength. He was thirty-nine years old after all these preparations, but now, he was convinced, not yet too old "to write about life as it was," as he saw it. And the restless way that he saw it, he was certain was not far from the way that it was. He set about completing *Jennie Gerhardt* in earnest.

He brought to it a brain and heart toughened by the parades he had witnessed and taken part in. He had watched finance like a dragon get possession of the minds and bodies of Americans. He had lived in the narrow rooms of wedlock and found their comforts irksome. Friends had gone in these years. He knew the agony of separations. One had been a love who had jilted him, his dream of all that he wanted. " Peter," the wonderful McCord,* cartoonist, writer, collector, was dead in a flash of pneumonia — he who had taught him to " love life's every facet," whether pollination or decay. With him he had traveled back to ancient ornaments and scripts, and equally he had given him a keener appetite for the modern world, no matter how vulgar or cruel — for anything, anyone that entered into crises. In these years too, his brother Paul, who meant to him his mother and Indiana and the lights and jokes of Broadway, had died of a broken spirit when his song business failed him, and with it his bright guests and friends. He was fifty-five: " With a slightly more rugged quality of mind he might have lasted till seventy," so the younger brother mourns him.

Frank Norris, his intellectual brother, was gone. O. Henry was dead, who after he had served in the penitentiary, he thinks, had come to know life and how to write about it. Jack London had compromised with reality, had confided to him once in a saloon on 23rd Street: " I'd like to write the real thing, but I can't sell 'em." And there were others, Harold Frederic, Hamlin Garland, Hervey White, Will Payne, Robert W. Chambers, who had started brilliantly with one or two first novels, and had not known how to endure. They were dead or they had given up. " They were too sensitive," he supposes, " to stand the face of reality; and fell by the way or leaned against the bar." In these years, it seemed to him as if a storm or a war had swept over the men of his age and interests, and knocked them all out, himself included. When it had cleared away the others were miss-

* *Twelve Men.*

ing; somehow, he doesn't know why, he was still there. He would try to tell the story of the storm in a novel. It would be called *The " Genius."*

At the same time new friends were coming in. In the first year with Butterick, he conceived and edited on the side a journal called The Bohemian, in company with some others, chief of whom was, " Billy Smith, a fascinating character, an architect, who built extravagant houses for Long Islanders." There were also Fritz Krog and Phil Goodman, a producer, who later liked to boast that Dreiser had fired him, and who is known today for having first put the side-splitting W. C. Fields into musical comedy. The houses of some people have many sides, one side opening on one of the finite or infinite sides of another house. If you walk around the conglomerate house where Dreiser has lived, you will find a side touching on a side of nearly all the houses of his period, which, like any one period, comprises an untold number of periods.

Into The Bohemian could go material too racy for the " highbrow " Delineator. As one of its contributors, so crucial a figure as H. L. Mencken drops casually into this biography. Willard Huntington Wright, who started as a novelist and excellent critic, and ended as the rich Van Dine of detective story fame; George Bronson Howard, a precocious writer of popular novels, who finally committed himself to morphine and suicide; André Tridon, acid pro-German translator of French and German novelties, who, later a war suspect, committed himself to the practice of psychoanalysis and died obscurely; George Jean Nathan, carefree critic and humorist, Mencken's future partner in journalism — these and other young men came to be friends of Dreiser's in these years through their admiration for *Sister Carrie* or through The Bohemian, or through Mencken's genius for bringing people together. They pooled some of the same sympathies about the need of a libertine life and a libertine art in America. " We used to take our girls to the same restaurants, and drink together — it was before prohibition — in other words we had a grand time! " is the way that Mencken remembers it with an exquisite lilt of reminiscence in his voice. It must have been that they made that slide of life known as "men about town" — that shifting, glancing, joking plane which, introduced into soberer living, lends courage to the gloomiest pessimist.

In 1908, one of Dreiser's English admirers, William J. Locke, whose *Beloved Vagabond* was a mad success in the United States, landed in New York with an appropriate number of reporters to get his advance impressions of the country. One of his first questions was: "And what is your Mr. Dreiser doing these days?" — "Dreiser?" they had not heard of him — "The author of *Sister Carrie!*" — They did not know it. "Americans do not know," he said, "that England looks on *Sister Carrie* as the finest American novel sent over in the last twenty years, and to Dreiser as the biggest American novelist who has sent us anything, and is waiting for Carrie's successor?" One of the interviewers hazarded the information: "A recent French critic characterized Mrs. Wharton's *House of Mirth* as the greatest American novel" — "Really? dear me! I would hardly consider that a just characterization . . . a charming writer, a poet, a fine novelist . . . but I should scarcely think she had as yet reached the stature of Hawthorne."

In the midst of these occurrences, dark and light, Dreiser gave himself to the completion of *Jennie Gerhardt*. In the spring of 1911 through the agency of Mae Holly, he sold it to Harper's, the firm which eleven years before had refused his first novel without a word. . . . In November they published it with the agreement that they would take over that book from the defunct house of B. W. Dodge. They agreed, too, to bring out the next novel, already more than half completed, *The Financier*, which appeared in 1912. And *Sister Carrie* in 1913. These three years make the keystone of his success.

At length after the long struggle, Dreiser had arrived in his own country, sanctioned by a leading firm, presented with a public. No longer a novice, he was heralded as a pioneer who had reached a difficult frontier. "The first American to force American publishers into the handling of mature literature without expurgating it," Mr. Wells of Harper's says today, in that manner of the parent who has accorded to the child the privilege to stay up till, say, twelve o'clock. " More than any one writer, the first to turn the current of public taste into new channels, so that there is small fear of censorship!" A militant modern, in fact, in the eyes of Mr. Wells, forcing the elders to get out of the old wagon and get into the new train! If you put the question to other students of our books, they agree, often regretfully, that, yes, they suppose " Dreiser deserved the title."

He was, in fact, the entering wedge. Whitman, though purer, had not accomplished this. He was too pure, or he came too early, to mingle in a conflict with the past. He was a dawn breaking in the busy afternoon of an elderly but not ancient day; a dawn breaking when the prudery of the *Scarlet Letter* seemed like a faint ray of sunlight to people who kept their blinds closed and had no way to know when it was morning noon or dusk in their airless best parlors. It was not Whitman, it was this diffuse realist who had finally forced the issue. It was a double triumph of newness — a step toward free thought and a step toward illiteracy, which this combative son of an immigrant, this nonentity, had wrenched from the genteel house of Harper.

Having gotten thus far, what did he say and think about it? He did not say in approved blasé style, " now that I have it, it isn't much." In fact, now that he had it, it was food and wine to him. He worked and played as never before, and seems not to have doubted his fought-for and paid-for right to take from the elders the reins of thought and conduct. To the attic or the graveyard with their puny colonial sophistication! It was time for immigrants to be natives, for the vulgarians to rule. For the parlors to know what the stables and kitchens and sheds and streets and saloons and offices and factories were doing and thinking. For all the American realities to step abroad and see the world, and be seen by the world. It was time for promiscuity to stalk in and through the parlors, since they held nothing strong enough to enforce awe.

" Old prejudices must always fall and life must always change," is an axiom he has made. He would be found among the changes, he would never be static. Recollecting this vantage point in his story, he pauses: " Well, that's about all. The rest was easy enough. I had risen against the wind."

Yet to most people, the fifteen years until the appearance of *An American Tragedy* would not be looked upon as easy enough. He had risen against the wind of custom up to where there were other conflicting wind currents that would bear him on and help him in the struggle. The opposing wind had chiefly been that of American morality, which, as a condition dictated a dead temperature of seventy, windows doors and cracks closed for the victims within, but which could blow up quite a cold gale for the nonconformists outside. Dreiser had long felt its hostility, and, though fortified now by other friendly winds, still had it to resist as best he could. He tells how Ben Dodge had taken him one day into Putnam's and Dutton's bookstore to introduce him to the manager, a friend of his. He had left him in the front of the store for a few minutes to ask this favor, but had come back alone, embarrassed: " Well, I know you'll be able to laugh it off, he doesn't want to meet you."

In the Harpers' office there was the same cold shoulder. Not on the part of Ripley Hitchcock or F. A. Duneka, the literary editors. Though they were Century Club gentlemen, they had acquired the letter paper and handwriting and indulgence of English liberals. It was Mr. Hitchcock who had first seen fit to publish Stephen Crane, expurgating him, however, for the Nineties. Nor did the managing editor, Major Leigh, a Virginian democrat, not especially of the first families, function as a cold shoulder. He was " wonderful, hospitable," Dreiser thought. In the old Knickerbocker bar he remembers the Major, " pretty well loaded," proclaiming him to one and all: " the only author I have ever loved! " He had said to him early in his connection with the Harpers: " I am going to back you for a long race, and I want you to meet Colonel Harvey." But the Colonel, one of the partners in the firm and later Ambassador to England, refused to meet him. Ambassadors, it seemed, were inevitably society meat and Dreiser poison. Another genteel editor, who in his luckless days had turned him down, now hailed him equivocally: " Well, for your sake I'm glad of your success. Times have changed, literary standards have lowered." So it went. He was in all these years until he made money from *An American Tragedy* to be looked upon as an outcast, almost an ogre. For one to speak of him in the presence of conventional people, at a dinner-party for instance, even if they were writers and supposedly interested in our literature, was received as improper; the subject was instantly changed.

In a sense it is possible to analyse the prejudice against him. Here was a giant who had carried since childhood scars of ostracism, for being first the child of a German Catholic, an always unpopular settler, and then for being one of an unforgivably poor family which had more than once outraged the Indiana code. Fortifying scars like these could not be becoming to anyone. A timid soul would get deprecating; a fearless sensitive temper would get ungracious, whenever exposed anew to the enemy. And then besides, why should these men like him, when without their manners and advantages, he did more exactly as he pleased than they did? They had wives they could not shake, they had jobs which kept them at their distinguished desks, slaves to clock and calender. They had homes in town and country which they had to report to, every evening, every night. He on the other hand, as he was, without office, servant or telephone, almost without address, " wallowed," so it came to be said, unpunished, in what? " In sex," of course! What else? Therein lay his frightful legend; though what women saw in him, homely, boorish, God only knew! He was irritating, that was all. The exhilarating ankles, disturbing knees, the arch of unfamiliar thighs, the eternal flicker and fire of these, they had to catch as best they could from the front rows of music halls; while these same delights, it was said, walked voluntarily into the lair of this uncouth realist. . . . More than he needed, more than he wanted, so grew the fable. You can't blame them for being jealous. You will have to blame the country where morals had been honored beyond love and art, and where strangeness was always suspect, and nature had become strange. The forces of nature were to be segregated in engines and power plants. Men were to be denatured. Genius, the digit of human nature, was to be dethroned.

42
New monuments for old

So Dreiser was a high powered car, which women nearly always like, forced into the paradox of running a race with the brakes on. If you ask him what he thinks of these handicaps, his answer is that he is glad of them: "A career needs hardship." But does it? And how much hardship does it need? *Sister Carrie* had weathered handicaps. What of its successor *Jennie Gerhardt?* The soil hostile to creation differed in the making of it. The first novel is a figment of the cold streets and highways, up and down which Dreiser had had to travel often alone and hungry. The second had its start in adversity but its completion in a more alien sediment, that of commercial success, at the end of the period of magazine editing. The drama came through with symmetry and bloom, but with a fractional loss of wildness. It is irrefutable in its first chapters, written before his prosperity, in its tragic moments, and in the theme of class over individual:

> "The world into which Jennie was thus duly thrust forth was that in which virtue has always vainly struggled since time immemorial; for virtue is the wishing well and doing well unto others. Virtue is that quality of generosity which offers itself willingly for another's service, and being this, it is held by society to be nearly worthless."

And yet in the face of all the expert praise this book has had, until it has become a near classic, I read it with the sense that Butterick has brushed its surfaces. They are slightly and unconsciously tamed as if to suit immature indoor eyes and judgments, parlors and offices. To have been excluded any longer from these precincts would have been for this novelist to die altogether. And yet to have been included had for the moment tempered his original quality. How to be that paradox, a primal successful artist in America? — Always the unanswered question!

Jennie, his favorite heroine, he has called her, is the flower of a family like his own, and seems to resemble his mother more than any of his sisters. Her father is to the last inflection the picture of his father, except as he is bigoted Lutheran instead of Catholic:

> "Father and grandfather before him were sturdy German artisans, who had never cheated anyone out of a dollar, and this honesty of intention came into his veins undiminished."

There is not in our writings a more flawless cinema of a poor family of foreigners set down in the midst of our freedom to get ahead a little if they can. Jennie not far removed from German soil, removed only to the cottages and sidewalks of immigrants fringing a strident industrial city, Columbus, Ohio, is as whole a creature as Hardy's Tess in her Devonshire. Successfully Dreiser moves her into relation with a United States senator, who lives in the principal hotel of the town, like a palace to Jennie. He gives her dignified presents and caresses, befriends her family, and then, one night when she has gone to ask his help to get her brother out of jail for stealing coal, the fairy story takes a quick realistic turn. His "senatorial quality" vanishes, her beauty and his pleasure make a bridge between low life and high life more rapid than those to be found in romances that travel to happy endings. Dreiser sees reality in this way — drabness shot with brilliants for one or another, and then drabness again. High life moving in the sky like a bright ball touches someone below with its fire and draws him or her up into ease and luxury, until this very realm close-up grows drab in turn. He is chronicler of the fierce differences in the scale of civilized society more than he is of the subtle conflicts between different temperaments.

The story develops with broad strokes not new to melodrama — the sudden death of the senator, the birth of the child, the anger and collapse of the religious father; Jennie and her more patient mother moving the family and baby to another city, Cleveland, to escape the talk of their neighbors, whom, just as it would be in the raw

West, they scarcely knew. The son of a rich carriage-manufacturer in Cincinnati, a guest in the house where Jennie works as maid, takes her out of her own class into no class, preferring her to the meager women of his world. " There was something about her which suggested the luxury of love." He installs her illicitly in Chicago, where he directs a branch of the family business. She on her side had been growing as she watched the people she served:

> " She began to get a faint suggestion of hierarchies and powers. They were not for her perhaps, but they were in the world, and if fortune were kind one might better one's state. . . . [Yet] Who would have her to wife knowing her history? . . . Her child, her child, the one transcendent gripping theme of joy and fear. If she could only do something for it — sometime, somehow! "

So far Dreiser's handling of this melodrama in major key changes melodrama into realism. The story unfolds in the actual glare of these fresh-water cities. Jennie is real. The carriage-prince is real, and their eventual idyllic home on the Chicago South Side with its lawn and flower-beds and shady trees, where after a while he allows the old father and Jennie's child to live with them. Especially to the life is this type of business man who makes anti-social laws for himself without losing commercial efficiency. Likewise his father, the solid conservative, and his brother, the hard bloodless executive, are precisely set down in relation to American business and to the awkward human event of unmarried love. The fate of Jennie, unAmerican in her devotion to the man she lives with, breaks with logic out of the conflicting wills of these three manufacturers, united in one aim, the carriage-industry. They embody the optimism and enterprise and starkness of the towns that were being whistled into shape on the shores of the Great Lakes in the Eighties and Nineties. Dreiser knew and remembered the ground, and had interviewed just such men for more than one of his special articles about business leaders.

But somewhere here the author falls short of his material. Whenever he takes these men into what stands for their social fabric, among their wives and children and would-be fashionable friends, he is inexperienced. He sets down his hero, Lester Kane as:

> "thirty-six years of age ... an essentially animal man, pleasantly veneered by education and environment ... like the hundreds of thousands of Irishmen who in his father's day had worked on the railroad track, dug in the mines, picked and shovelled in ditches, and carried up brick and mortar on the endless structures of a new land ... strong, hairy, axiomatic, and witty."

This is specific, but besides this the Kanes were " socially prominent "; Lester was " raised a member of the socially elect "; Mrs. Gerald, who takes him away from Jennie, is " the picturesque center of a group of admirers recruited from every capital of the civilized world." She captures him by telling him he is " too much of a social figure to drift," and he feels that she is too much of " a social opportunity " to refuse. The scope of the task Dreiser has set himself is remarkable, covering the gamut of the respectable midwestern world, as it reached toward New York and Europe. It covers the class he himself came from of hard-working artisans, brought into relation with the sphere of those great homes founded often by sons of that class — stags on the lawn, Duchess lace and Holland shades at the windows — which piqued him as he worked his way toward New York in the Nineties. His plans are good, but his high-life characters are imperfectly developed and even fall back on newspaper clichés for definition.

He is right in his major premise that this superstructure in the West, which he calls the " socially elect," did include the families of manufacturers of carriages, soap, harvesting machines, bathroom fixtures, sleeping cars, as well as dry goods merchants, wholesale grocers and fabulous butchers. This always happened whenever the self-made millionaire married into the Colonial tradition of aristocracy. His Eastern wife then dictated a formula more utterly refined and circumspect than perhaps has ever been put into practice in any other land or time. So fearful they were of being considered " typical Westerners " that they succeeded in creating a vacuum, which segregated them from the ungainly life that swirled around them. They became humorous, never serious, decorous, never decorative. Intimacy was vulgar; love and hate were unmentionable; crises were improper. Art was something to be endowed in museums or symphony concerts, never to be met with in the person of the artist. Beauty was melodramatic and belonged to the stage and opera. " Good taste " and " a sense of humor " were the requirements. A fear of life inconceivable to the greedy powerful Dreiser stalked among these socially elect, and terrified the lustier nouveau-riches who waited outside their doors, hoping some day to qualify. They held hideous sway over the growth of new red-blooded cities, these elect; they paralysed the senses and froze the spirit. But they existed. You could tell them, not by any fine web of relations they had woven; they scarcely touched each other physically or mentally. You could tell them by their *Things* — their embroidered linen, their antique furniture, their restrained dinner-parties, their quiet carriages, conservative clothes, and by the thin well-bred inflections of their voices into which almost no vulgarity and no fire ever entered. Go to the museum in Columbus, Ohio; you will find there the elaborate imported *Things* of these western aristocrats. Or read the lives of Mark Hanna or Nicholas Longworth. Sons and daughters too sensitive for their fathers, who reverted to human type and rebelled against this anemia of their mothers, escaped to Europe or lost their minds. Many of them, more than has been written, went crazy, got queer.

Apparently Dreiser did not know his material well enough to define the irony and drama inherent in it, as he did throughout *Sister Carrie*. His socially elect would have been despised from above almost as much as they despised the Gerhardts. The women tweak the men's ears, use cosmetics unheard of then in the West, are pert and familiar; and falsest of all, men and women lack facetiousness, what was called " a sense of humor " — that weapon of polite society with which to kill emotions, and ridicule a thing as vulgar as illicit love. They, like Jennie, would have been insecure in their relation to the " socially elect." Jennie's lonely end is real, but the Kanes' victory without her for their class is at moments conventionally designed. There are mortal agonies in the book when death makes separations for Jennie. Five times the bell is rung, twice fatally, when her child dies and then Lester, who calls her back to say goodbye. It is a novel presided over by funerals. But in the latter chapters of her defeat, where there is neither love, nor birth nor funeral, the hierarchy that rears itself above her lovely head is not as real and flexible as Dreiser wished to make it. Even, he had to resort to the society column to suggest it:

"There was a simple cottage where she lived in retirement. . . . Mr. and Mrs. Lester Kane when resident in Chicago were the occupants of a handsome mansion on the Lakeshore Drive, where parties, balls, receptions, dinners, were given in rapid and at times almost pyrotechnic succession."

43
Interlude: "Americans are infinitely repellant particles." EMERSON

The great novelists of modern times, Dostoevsky, Turgenieff, Victor Hugo, Balzac, Meredith, Proust, have not been content to create their monuments to human living without an effort to define the entire conflicting scale from low to high materially, from ordinary to rare spiritually. Was it Shakespeare who first gave them the idea? Dreiser, isolated in America, valiantly assumed the same problem, and tried first in *Jennie Gerhardt* to encompass it. More than that, he was, so far, the only big intellect except for Henry James and possibly Robinson in difficult narrative poems, to have attempted this synthesis. His guess at the whole scheme is in fact a proof of intellect. It is terribly significant that he failed in details, and that afterwards he never quite set out to define except by implication our uppermost classes, from the point of view of social values. And why was it that he had to fail, just as Edgar Lee Masters later was to try and fail? Because for some reason fashionable people in America have never had any curiosity about their artists as artists. Mrs. Astor is remembered for having scolded her son-in-law because he dined with so vulgar a fellow as Mark Twain. The tradition had not changed, in fact is scarcely changed today.

One wonders why. First, I suppose, the Colonists were afraid of creative minds, much as the old Jews were; they made images. And then as time went on American business men, I imagine, were afraid to let writer, painter, or musician into their houses, since dangerously they could come around in the afternoon or even in the morning, and amuse their wives. They on the other hand had to stay in their offices until six o'clock or more. It was, in contrast to Europe, a country where men and women never lunched together until recently, never met from breakfast till the dinner hour. Then there was another thing; a man with " ideas " was a menace to business. He might be a radical, he probably was. Somehow they trained their wives to fear an artist or poet as they would a beggar. One reason perhaps why writers from among them, Henry James, Henry Adams, for example, went to Europe. There could be no one to talk to in their own houses. And now that the floodgates were loosed, that the lower classes were getting into print, to admit a man of genius was all the more precarious. Probably they wouldn't wear clean collars or have good table manners. It was a thing not to be risked.

It was different of course, with foreign celebrities. It would be inhospitable to exclude them. They were accepted in Europe and were distinguished, and besides they wouldn't stay long. Even so, Europeans have had curious impressions of American hospitality. The composer Stravinsky, recently fêted at lunch, dinner and cocktail hour in Chicago, is said to have complained to a friend: " My trip has been a failure, I am not appreciated in America. I have met no one." She remonstrated with him: " How can you say that, no composer has ever been lionized as you have." — " Yes, among these nice people, *mais où sont les cervelles?* " And an English philosopher tells how, lecturing in a fashionable women's club in a Western city, he was given a dinner at the house of his hostess and one of the men at the dinner began a speech of welcome with the facetious threat that American business men had " quite as much sex-appeal as their distinguished guest, even if they were not pacifists! "

The chasms were deep in 1910 that separated " high society " from ideas, just as they were deep that divided business from art, and remain deep today except that now class mysteries are breaking down before the various rackets. A writer might make a fortune out of the movie rights of a book and become a pillar of society. A debutante might turn into a chorus girl, a billionaire's son into a song writer, and everyone into aviators or aviator's wives. The words "socially elect" perhaps are following "Mrs. Grundy" into antiquity.

But that is going far ahead of the story whose hero, unknown to fashion, was one of those innocently to effect the change. Prosperous editor though he was, his excursions to Long Island house parties could not have taken him among the Eastern equivalents of the people he wanted to set down in *Jennie Gerhardt*. Or, with his rapid eye, subtracting the arrogance of New York over the Middle West, he would have known how to define them, and his book would have gained in value. These comfortable people, for one thing, discovering themselves in the book, would have then found him authentic, and would have been less comfortable and more alive to realities. As it was, a spiral of estrangement instead of a spiral of understanding was working up through the various classes.

Possibly this has come near to being the defeat of both manners and art in America — the fact that the two have been insoluble, one in the other. An anecdote about Dreiser in 1911 illustrates the cleavage. It was Arnold Bennett's turn to visit the great United States. Curiously he is quoted as asking the same question asked by Locke a few years before: "And what is your Mr. Dreiser doing these days?" The scene was a banquet given him by distinguished publishers and authors, most of them socially experienced. The story was told me by Floyd Dell, then a young Chicago critic, who had been an instant admirer of Dreiser. Delighted that this English novelist shared his enthusiasm, he listened with all his ears. But no one seemed to know precisely what Dreiser was doing or appeared to care, and yet the company contained members of the firm of Harper, contracted at that moment to publish three of his books. But they were not proud of it, would not talk about him; in fact the subject was changed. In the face of their indifference Bennett was then said to have declared: "Dreiser is the most significant figure among your writers. Oddly enough, I spend most of my time asking people if they have read *Sister Carrie,* and find they haven't. I always say, ' Well, get it.'" There was a slight well-bred stir at such insistence and at such evident disparity of opinion between England and her lost Colony. Perhaps some of the guests went home and thought it over. Several newspaper articles of the time quote Bennett as always with the same obsession: " I can't read American authors in general, they write for money. . . . I like Theodore Dreiser best. . . . Then there is another, David Graham Phillips, but whenever I mention his name people shrug their shoulders and say: ' Yes, no, I don't know — well, anyway he is very crude.'"

The American Review dug up an article, *The Future of the American Novel* which Bennett had written for the Atlantic Monthly in 1903, but that journal had suppressed it as a piece of British perversity. It was printed now in 1912. There, he had prophesied that Norris and Dreiser would be the forerunners of a new literature, " big and romantic like American landscapes and fortunes." Balzac, he was sure, confronted with " Pittsburgh, the sixteen hour express between New York and Chicago, Wall Street, Mr. Pierpont Morgan, the wheat growing states . . . would have said, ' This country is steeped in romance; it lies about in heaps. Give me a pen quick, for Heaven's sake.'" At last there were native writers who realized this for themselves, was the burden of the article. But these words of hope had been withheld for nine years from whatever American Balzacs were languishing on the heaps of romance. And now that Mr. Bennett had come to see for himself, he found the number reduced to the one mysterious Dreiser, and possibly Phillips. And it seemed that they lived incognito. He must have learned, however, that Phillips had been shot and killed not long before by a madman who mistook him for another. And he managed to discover that Harper had had the enterprise to publish after ten years one more American canvas from his favorite candidate. He would get it at once, and really he would like to meet the man. On October 26, 1911, Major Leigh dictated a social gem to his secretary who mailed it to the socially unelected Hoosier:

" Dear Mr. Dreiser:
 Mr. Arnold Bennett leaves today for Boston to stay over there till next Monday. It has been in our minds to bring you two gentlemen together and next week we will try to fix it up as speedily as possible.
 Mr. Duneka and Mr. Wells have both had considerable conversation with him about you and *Jennie Gerhardt*, and of course we have given him a copy of the book. It is hoped that we may have whatever benefit there may be in having the book praised by Mr. Bennett. Mr. Bennett is so much in the public eye and ear at the present time, that I suppose we would all agree aside from all other considerations, that Mr. Bennett's good opinion of *Jennie Gerhardt* would be desirable.
 . . . I will immediately look up the *Kansas City Journal* and see what can be done with the fine send-off they gave *Jennie* that you told me about. . . ."

Very little, I suppose, could be done in the opinion of Major Leigh with praise from Kansas, and yet Dreiser always banked on the support of the whole United States, in which there must be exceptions like himself, hungry to read about life as it was. As for Arnold Bennett, he would like to know him of course, but he was shy about it under his publishers' auspices. It was evident from the letter that they were not to meet as equals for pleasure, but merely as a business concession. He managed to evade the invitation; he could be aloof and sensitive too on his side. Besides, perhaps people were right, he did not know exactly how to get in and out of a room. . . . Later in London, however, where he found himself fêted as an equal, Dreiser and Bennett met and enjoyed each other.

44

"... Then I asked again
Why Cato Braden died at fifty-one,
And Will said: 'Winston Prairie, Illinois
Killed Cato Braden.'" E. L. MASTERS

I stress these rifts because they appear to me to have made half of our difficulties, and to have been ignored by most of the experts who have attempted to analyse the temper of the country. While on the productive side business men and politicians and crooks were always cementing their common interests just as in other countries; on the side of enjoyment, which is the side of life, there was no trust, no loyalty, no cohesion between the different elements. Arnold Bennett's amazement at the one fact of Dreiser's obscurity in 1911, ten years after the publication of *Sister Carrie,* is a tiny etching of the whole scheme.

The scheme differed in Europe. In England, a civilization based on class arrogance, always there have been aristocrats who sought to enliven their lot with people of genius; if, that is, they could induce them to be guests. They were curious about them, needed their wits if they could capture them for occasions. Bennett himself, out of the "lower middle class," after his first success was forced into knowing everyone, was forced into being a writer, as he tells in a burlesque called *The Great Man.* Perhaps he was never completely at ease in the new circles where his talents were taking him, but at least he had witnessed the program of manners from peers to commoners, and knew them first hand. He knew also that personal distinction, genius if possible, was the element that welded into some kind of meaning the various parts of society.

Take another example, D. H. Lawrence, son of a coal

miner, as Dreiser was son of a foreman in a woollen mill, and Sandburg of a blacksmith, and Anderson of a house painter. In *Lady Chatterly's Lover* sex seems awkward, even inexperienced, but English manners are authentic enough to create the illusion of society. And why? Because Lawrence found himself dragged into drawing rooms, whether he liked it or not — a tribute to a new poet in their great tradition of poetry. It was the same with Hardy, and Meredith whose father was a tailor, and today with James Joyce wherever he writes openly enough to betray the tones of voice. Existing hierarchies are accurately implicit in their novels, so that each character has the special weave in the design ordained by the fabric.

This sophistication is even truer of French writers, the products of a long legend which has deified the intelligence as we have deified money. To the artist, whether originally peasant, vagabond, bourgeois or aristocrat, white, yellow or black, doors open in proportion to the degree of talent the critics allot to him. To a genius in fashion no important door is closed. He may exclude what he now calls bourgeois society or run away from it, but he is not excluded from its calculations as long as his day of glory lasts. It is no wonder then that we feel a cool ease of surface in the works of the French giants and in those of smaller writers. From Proust in deliberate detail, from Appollinaire involuntarily, to take two Jews, we get a sense of the subtleties, intricacies, distances, intimacies, which together create that suspended, miasmic, varied, welded state of mind — the city of Paris. Yet if these same men had lived in New York or Chicago, being Jews, they would have been excluded from all but Jewish society and would have had to guess at what went on in other leisure classes, which very possibly was almost nothing at all. There are countless examples. To select at random, among the projects of the sculptor Brancusi, runaway child of Roumanian farmers, a princess was originally a subject in company with a bird, a fish, a newborn child, a sorceress, a negress. Joseph Delteil, the son of a woodcutter and wine-maker in the Midi, knows the types of his country and of other countries as if by heart, no matter what the class. He serves them like tennis balls, hardly counting them — kings, heroes, peasants. Elegance, an aesthetic principle, permeates classes and races.

Art penetrates in Europe to the honor of artists. Comedians and music hall favorites are fêted officially. The negro singer, Paul Robeson, was given a lunch in the House of Parliament; Charlie Chaplin, a child of English slums, was guest of honor of Briand, Foreign Minister of France; while in our exciting democracy whom does official Washington select to invite to the White House for ice cream and tea? Explorers, inventors and boy scouts! A good start, but a meager sense of plot; we complicate nothing. In Europe in a measure dreams like Dreiser's have come true — art reflecting and deepening reality through the alembic of special temperament.

Contrastingly, " America's most powerful novelist," as the newspapers now call him, wrote his first and his second and his third novel, all of his works in fact, until after *An American Tragedy,* unknown to the ruling class in the city where he lived. It was the same in Chicago when that town produced a few years later a crop of modern men of letters. They were known far before they were known near. Edgar Lee Masters, much as he coveted " luxury and refinement," being after all the son of a country lawyer who was a friend of Lincoln and partner of Herndon, and for all that the heroic Harriet Monroe could do for him in Poetry, was never known among the " socially elect " of Chicago until he got into the papers for his cruel sonnets to his wife, and felt that he was ostracized. He moved to New York where he joined as many clubs as he could and became a recluse and a Victorian. Meanwhile, sophisticated people in London were praising his *Spoon River Anthology* as fifteen years before they had seized upon *Sister Carrie* as important. And the " great Carl Sandburg," as he has been called, Chicago's poet, who never has deserted the city, what of him? I think if any one of the " socially elect " had confessed to knowing him in the days of *Cornhuskers* and *Smoke and Steel,* they would have been suspected of leading a double life — that is, until his biography of Lincoln became a best seller, and he had a chance to be respectable, had it pleased him. He had, however, the reporter's scorn and the socialist's hatred of upper classes: (perhaps the poet's hatred) and assumed a kind of burglar's disguise, which made a formidable defence against what overtures Chicago might have offered him.

In old countries there are walls, everywhere walls, through which, however, beauty and genius sometimes penetrate like radium. To escape walls emigrants have come to these shores, only to meet barriers worse than walls — intangible chasms which insulated even that volatile element creative genius. What made the chasms? Stupid religions? Money? Machinery? Yet money and machinery were beautiful and new, not mouldy like old Europe; the poor and hungry came to enjoy them. Perhaps paradoxically it was democracy that made the chasms; that star they watched from the steerage as they crossed. It was hard to say, except that there were these barriers.

To go to the end of this decade, 1910–1920, there was the example of a young Italian, known only to a few, but who figured in this period of letters.* He is a symbol of the disillusioned emigrant, and of the many moderns who wanted to make America see how modern she is and failed. He came with the Latin faith that a poet would count in a new country, especially in Chicago; and succumbed to these chasms across which intelligence could not jump. He was tough, but not tough enough for this glacier, Western society, where in precise fact a poet was held in no more favor than a " kept woman," if as much. He screamed a challenge among the whistles and sirens which reads like revenge for its victims.† A poem to a young lady of the " socially elect " places a curse on them:

 . . . " I wrote insults,
  Called you a liar for saying:
  ' Sex and life are two different things.'

 * " Emanuel Carnevali, the black poet, the empty man, the New York which does not exist . . . I celebrate your arrival." Carlos Williams.
 " . . . one of the two contemporary poets in America whose work attained an international standard." Regis Michaud.
 " He seemed sometimes to be throwing himself at the sun." Carl Sandburg.
 † *The Hurried Man.*

... I said
'If God intervenes you will be a poet,'
But God never intervened."

He went away to Italy and wrote back:

... " I arrive in the land of wine —
Wine for the soul. . . .
... You are young and hurried; what threatens you
That you rush so, America?
... I have feared for you
The revenge of Love, O America!"

Dreiser all these years was a counterpart of his two heroines, patient like Jennie, adventurous like Carrie. He could not and would not run away from " that oblivion of hurry," America, or be oblivious to it. He knew there were doors closed to him, forbidden thresholds, for all his appetite to understand. He would have to measure life beyond them from the outside. Somehow he would manage to apprehend it. Perhaps even, unlike Jennie, in the end he would dictate to it. He was one of the older stronger natives ready to fight intangible chasms. Sandburg, Masters and Anderson were others. Now and then in company, but most often singly, they watched the crevices deepening between art and society, and between art and commerce, and watched the cracks filling up between society and commerce, that is, between manners and money. What they and others have made of American life, on their side of the great gap, launched its most productive period in the arts — the years between 1910 and 1925 or 1926. Almost, it seems, such writers may have been the antecedents of a new kind of American society. I think it is not too pompous to say that, although they wrote to create and not to reform, each of them in his separate way hoped fervently for change.

45
Jennie and her lovers

Jennie Gerhardt, published in October, 1911, and Gertrude Stein's *Three Lives,* published in 1909, head the list in these creative years. *Three Lives* would in the end effect a revolution in method. Dreiser's novel was at once producing a change of theme. It was an immediate success in modern red-blooded America. Considering it aside from its permanent value as language, the story had three merits as story. In newspaper lingo, the forsaken Jennie, unlike Carrie, was made to pay for her sins against society; that pleased everybody. Then the presentation was called " clean "; that is, her hours of flagrant delight with both senator and carriage-manufacturer are silent chapters. An advantage, since the men could imagine them anyway, and their virtuous wives, reading the book, would remain unenlightened. Above all, Jennie was an ideal woman for American business men, who had no time for romance and great need of comfort; she gave everything and asked nothing. It is colossal how Dreiser has written their poetry for them, not verses about their mothers and wives and children, but about their secret sweethearts — the little girls, the swell babies, news of whom was winked from one to another. And it must have gratified them too because he drew them and their girls with the dignity of vital organs, in true relation to the rest of the world of human beings. He never made fun of them. With tears in their words, the newspaper men, spokesmen for American manhood, cheated so long of the luxuries, proclaimed him their writer. I believe a railroad conductor or a brakeman, or a railroad president, had he read *Jennie Gerhardt,* would have said, " This guy [or this fellow] knows his stuff." But in 1912 these valiant animals rarely read. Returns had to come in from their understudies, the newspaper men. They came from many cities and states. New York, Brooklyn, Chicago, Detroit, St. Paul, Los Angeles, Utica, Hartford, Washington, Alabama, New Orleans, Oshkosh, Kansas, Boston, St. Louis, Pittsburgh, Cleveland, Kentucky, San Francisco, Indianapolis, Baltimore — these and more received the author of *Carrie* and *Jennie* (but Jennie chaperoned Carrie for them) with high praise or if by chance the reviewer was an old maid or oldfashioned, with traditional censure:

> Chicago Record Herald: " . . . Jennie was sinning against society . . . while she yet remained unspoiled in heart. . . . Not suitable for immature readers. . . . The story of a young woman gone wrong . . . European rather than American. — Almost as perfect as Balzac or Flaubert."
> Philadelphia Telegraph: " . . . Jennie is the type of woman really too unselfish to be virtuous. . . ."
> Evening Star, Washington: " In 10,000 years from now, Mr. Dreiser, when the animosities of sex, mayhap, are somewhat mollified should put out this book again. Then we shall see what can be done for the Jennie Gerhardts."
> New York Times: " . . . Panku chopped out the sun, the moon and the rest of the universe with a sledgehammer. . . . Both the Chinese author of the Universe and the author of Jennie went at their jobs with about an equal absence of false modesty, with an equal amount of courage."
> Philadelphia Inquirer: " . . . Not to be mentioned in the presence of Mrs. Grundy. We have gotten so far along that we no longer ignore real life in literature. . . ."
> Cleveland Town Topics: " Jennie Gerhardt in all except the one essential, seemed purity itself."
> Post, Covington, Kentucky: " If one were to guess the literary parentage of Theodore Dreiser, one would say . . . Dostoevsky. . . ."

And then the warier, more expedient reviews. The now dying moralists wrote:

> New York American: " Jennie is no model for any girl who sees life on all sides. Every girl should put a high price upon herself; the price of the woman is the man. . . . Is a woman ever justified in smirching her womanhood, in staining her virtue, in order to help her relatives — even to save them from starvation? This must be answered with an iron ' NO.' . . . There are misfortunes worse than starvation."

Morning Telegram, New York: "He ought to choose a bigger theme than the story of a kept woman."
San Francisco Chronicle: "The fact that she accepts money from both her lovers may be taken . . . as against the heroine, but . . . she should be credited with spending the coin on her poor relations."

These reviews are most of them naïve, in that they consider a novel as incident rather than as drama, or style. But historically they indicate how the critics have shifted ground since 1900. Many more in 1912 enjoy a story of life as it is, and because of the vulgarity they read into it; and those who denounce it already begin to sound antiquated. It is evident that an old system of morals is beginning to crumble, and that the iron of Dreiser's realism was like a drill heading into the decay.

Two writers especially loved the book for itself, both of them men who were to count in this most lively period of our letters. One was the young Chicago critic, Floyd Dell, who had taken the place of Francis Hackett on the Evening Post, that inventor of the " literary supplement." At about this time Floyd Dell had almost lost his job because someone had told the publisher there was a drawing of himself and his wife in the nude on the walls of their flat; and soon after he did lose it for a review which began, " Have a cocktail! No. . . ." But the No was negligible; in those days a family paper should not mention cocktails even to disparage them. *Jennie Gerhardt* was for him promise of a heaven of our own, not English, not French, not Russian. He was one of those who wanted to make the country a land of the free and brave in spite of graveyards and academies, and did do his share until recently, when life in capitalist America appears to have made him reactionary. In 1911 he wrote in his literary review:

"W. B. Yeats has put the case against professors and manuals of literature . . . in the current Forum: 'They come between a man and literature,' he says, ' substituting arguments and hesitations for the excitement at the first reading of the great poets which should be a sort of violent, imaginative puberty.' "

And of *Jennie Gerhardt,* he wrote:

" The melting mood . . . the sign of great art, is what this book continually evokes in the reader. . . . Dreiser writes of meetings and partings, festivities and funerals, as though no one had ever written of them before. The life of Lester and Jennie together is as familiar as a sunset, and as perpetually interesting. He sees everything eagerly, clearly, without prejudice."

The other is H. L. Mencken, German-American champion of a native speech, sophisticated and free. And yet for Mencken it must be authoritative speech: That is, free speech must be the orthodox ritual for a land of the free. For a number of years he was to be an advisor, almost a confessor to Dreiser, the most adventurous and authentic writer he could find to champion. He wrote what would make a small book in unreserved praise of *Jennie Gerhardt* publishing it in various journals and newspapers, The Smart Set, The Free Lance, The Baltimore Evening Sun, The Los Angeles Times. Here is an abridgment of it:

" If you miss reading *Jennie Gerhardt* . . . you will miss the best American novel that has reached the book counters in a dozen years. On second thought change ' a dozen ' into ' twenty-five.' On third thought, strike out everything after counters. On fourth thought, strike out everything after novel. . . . I am firmly convinced that *Jennie Gerhardt* is the best American novel I have ever read with the lonesome but Himalayan exception of *Huckleberry Finn* . . . [which is] not a boy's story, not a comic story, but a merciless picture of the decay and break-up of a civilization. . . . A canto in the epic of the Old South. . . .

". . . Once again Dreiser's heroine is a woman whose gentleness is her undoing. Once again he is in the midst of a tragedy whose moral it is that all the stock morals are untrue. Once again he sets forth like Conrad and Moore and the great Russians, the eternal meaninglessness of life. . . .

" The thing is done with superb assurance. . . . Not one eyelash is out of place. . . ."

This was a time, and Dreiser and Mencken prime factors in it, bent on a new discovery of America, the chance of intellectual exchange, the event of ideas circulating from one to another. In the preceding century, intellect was a provincial thing fermenting chiefly in New England. Or else, when rebellious, it was a terribly lonely thing, which doomed Poe to death, and Whitman and Thoreau, and Dickinson, to hermitages, and Melville to silence. Now rebellious thought was beginning to be a game and a pastime. It would have its censors, its umpires, its champions. Marriages of minds were giving birth to an intelligentsia. Mencken appointed himself one of its guardians in all three capacities, champion, umpire and censor. This story is incomplete without attempting his portrait.

46

*" The volume will be a slaughter house.
Positively no guilty man will escape . . .
I shall even denounce myself."*

H. L. MENCKEN

By temperament more than by immediate birth, Mencken was a child of the German stream that had flowed toward America to commit a Protestant paradox — enforce freedom. The country, initially settled by perhaps the worst of the English and the best of the Germans and Dutch, and always a sprinkling of master Swiss minds, had long ago pushed the Indians on to their reservations and pueblos, the French into New Orleans, Detroit and Canada, the Spaniards into Southwestern deserts too hot and strange for northern races. Into this initial mould had flowed and overflowed more English and Germans, and then Irish, Italians, Scandinavians, Jews, Balkans, Orientals. All of them were still trying to fight it out and become a race. Mencken was the first to assume the care of their common language, American.

Bill Nye distinguishes George Washington as the only one of our great men rich enough to support a French nurse in his youth. Mencken appears to be the one writer of his day with the luxury of a pedigree, which, however, being German, has not afforded him its proper prestige. His grandfather came to the United States in 1848 and settled in Baltimore. Back of him was a Saxon-Friesian family of merchants and scholars, some of whom delighted in agnosticism and music — faithfully traced by his biographer to the 16th century.* In the 17th century Otto Mencken, professor of ethics at Leipzig, founded the first learned German review, *Acta Eruditorum* with

---

* *The Man Mencken* by Isaac Goldberg.

which to attack the pedantry of the day. His son Johann was famous for a satire, *De Charlataneria Eruditorum,* an exposure of sham and fraud.* The portrait of Otto has the sceptical sensitive mouth of H. L. Mencken, and Johann wrote a phrase in his book characteristic of his American nephew of three centuries later: " So great, oh listeners, is the power of impudence, even in serious matters." Add to this inheritance an ancestral aunt who was the mother of Bismarck,* and you will find Mencken is an amazingly logical scion of his family, with his two contradictory passions, liberty and order, freedom and authority. Into the bargain he is a verbal buffoon, a genius for joke and paradox. The result has been our first scholastic statesman of masculine proportions, our first modern encyclopaedist, an American Diderot, though more cautious and less voluptuous than that 17th century Frenchman. Beginning with Mencken, American letters began to be noticed by men and to be feared by women's clubs and neuters. He brought literature into the field of action. In America that was to bring it shorn of some of its rightful subtleties.

To meet him professionally in the cause of letters was at first like meeting a busy politician with no time for frivolous exchange, his face a round mask, decorous, unrevealing, voice cold, manner formidable. But, which was engaging, at first flicker of something indiscreet, diverting or essential, his eyes, locked behind the mask, seemed to turn a kind of somersault, and were green and alive, and his voice took on timbre. Beneath the politician you saw then the buffoon and the crusader — buffoon for sake of enjoyment, but diplomat for the sake of a cause. His enemies are the well-known puritan and bourgeois, the last known now as Babbitt: " As you say yourself," he writes to Dreiser, " it is quite impossible to trust any American. Scratch him and you will find a puritan." And he calls them names enough, *moralists, uplifters, Pecksniffians, Comstockians, virtuosi of virtue, donkeys, vermin, degraded swine:* " Let them squeal. We can stand the noise if they can stand what's coming to them." But to satisfy his need of authority the enemy may be also the

* *The Man Mencken* by Isaac Goldberg.

extreme aesthete when he is free and rebellious. He distrusts anarchical poets; and beauty where it is dangerous to reason; he distrusts madness. " Poetry lies," he has written repeatedly. For beauty he resorts to classical music. Most of all, and paradoxically, he distrusts sex. Talking recently about Dreiser he called him opprobriously a " professional sexologist ": " The importance of sex is much over-rated. If all the women were shot at five today the men would go on just about the same." Yet there was a question mark in the statement which allowed me to suggest: " Well, perhaps, in a country where really there are no women, just wives and secretaries!" He had not thought of that. He had not, it seemed, thought of women or of artists to the extent of their powers. Was it that he was determined to function as critic in a society hostile to sex and art, and so for years had drawn arbitrary lines?

Perhaps his gift of writing would have gained in subtlety, had his grandfather never emigrated. To champion the cause he loved was to fight the moralists, loud and incessantly. His diatribes in spite of brilliance have caught from the enemy the moral voice of the scold and the elder. Yet sometimes, as in his great work *The American Language* it is modulated — a voice of learning and relish. And his letters to friends, to judge by those I have been privileged to read, unite judgment with ribaldry, and create speech enviable as a freshet. That Mencken's published writings have not the spontaneity and depth that belong to him, indicates our tragedy — a background of separations and irrelations disjointed almost beyond hope, even today. They have prohibited except in a few rare cases — Whitman and Dreiser sometimes are two of them — the artlessness without which art is pompous.

This American figure, a deliberate instrument of change for fifteen years, as it happened, became a close ally of Dreiser's, just as Arthur Henry had once been. Only where the more feminine Henry was concerned with the intimate task of his writing as art, Mencken proclaimed him to the public, and exhorted him to fight to be a public character. The spirit of the day was with him; publicity counted more than intimacy.

Isaac Goldberg prints in his Mencken biography Dreiser's earliest impression of him. In the summer of 1908 Mencken had come to the office of The Delineator about some articles on the care of children he had written with a Dr. Hirschberg of Baltimore:

"... a taut, ruddy, blue-eyed, snub-nosed youth ... yellow shoes and bright tie ... enormously intriguing and amusing ... reminding me of nothing so much as a rich brewer's son.... With the sang-froid of a Caesar or a Napoleon he made himself comfortable in an almost archepiscopal chair, designed ... to reduce the over confidence of the average beginner.... From that ... unintended vantage point he beamed on me with the confidence of a smirking fox about to devour a chicken. So I was the editor of the Butterick publications. 'He had been told about me.'"

What he had been told was especially the fact of *Sister Carrie*, which his friend, George Bronson Howard, had given him to read in Baltimore in 1902, when they were both in their early twenties. He had treasured it ever since, and laughed to find its author editor of The Delineator. Dreiser perhaps on the defensive laughed back: "'Well, well,' I said, 'if it isn't Anheuser's own brightest boy out to see the town.'" Having thus in true American fashion exchanged insults, they could proceed at once to being friends, forgetting the original purpose of the visit in a riotous exchange of ideas and prejudices. (Mark Twain describes these required preliminaries exquisitely in *Tom Sawyer;* Tom and a new village boy must first knock each other down before there can be friendship.) "From then on," Dreiser says, " I counted him among them whom I most prize ... he visited me in New York and I in turn, repaired to Baltimore. We multiplied noisy and roystering parties. . . ." Some months later he recommended him to Fred Splint, a new editor of Smart Set, previously one of his sub-editors, who had come to ask for advice as to policy and style. Dreiser suggested that "as intriguing as anything else would be a book department, with a really brilliant and illuminating reviewer "— in fact, Mencken. So in a sense was launched a critic who for many years would be dominant in forming American opinion.

Although Mencken likes to disown it, being today

estranged from Dreiser, at this period he worked like the trainer of a champion for him. *Jennie Gerhardt* had convinced him. Dreiser had sent it to him a month or two before it was published, as also he had sent it to other friends for their expert judgments, perhaps not wishing to run the risk again of suppression. He had had various advices. He sent it to his wife, who gave amusing advice: ". . . I also cut several dozen ' Jennie was charming,' and ' Lester was a big man in his way.' You won't mind if I laugh a little, will you? The book is so much bigger than these little things. . . ." A Delineator contributor, Vera Simohson, who gave illustrated lectures on Africa, "never knew that men made such sudden bold proposals to women." However she resigns herself: " I had rather the theme would have been a more pleasant one, but life of today breathes sex. We've got to accept the truth. . . ." C. B. Decamp wants him to dispense with the funeral scene; it is too " gloomy." James Huneker calls it "a big book eloquent in its humanity"; it made him " happy because it attempted to prove nothing." But his style is still too "literary"; his " fashionable women are not well realized "; and he begs him to cut out the epilogue that follows his " superb ending on what musicians would call a suspended harmony ": " I take off my hat to you, Theodore Dreiser! That funeral scene and the last few paragraphs . . . are those of a master. Don't spoil [it] for the sake of moralizing." This last advice Dreiser took. These and other varying advices are almost antiques, even the astute verdict of Huneker, in their leisure and seriousness. Today there is such haste to publish that I doubt if even the publisher, and rarely the writer, has time to read each word of the book before it is executed in print.

So these different friends had their reservations, but Mencken, except for noting a few technical errors, had none. He writes:

". . . it is probable that more than one reviewer will object to its length . . . detail . . . painstaking — but rest assured that Heinrich Ludwig von Mencken will not be in the gang. . . . I get a powerful effect of reality, stark and unashamed. It is drab and gloomy but so is the struggle for existence. It is without humor but so are the jests of that great comedian who shoots at our heels and makes us do our grotesque dancing.

. . . If anyone urges you to cut down the book bid that one be damned. And if anyone urges that it is over-gloomy call the police. . . . It is at once an accurate picture of life and a searching criticism of life . . . my definition of a good novel.

. . . David Phillips might have done such a good story, had he lived, but his best . . . *The Hungry Heart*, goes to pieces beside ' Jennie.' "

Mencken was right; Phillips never equaled Dreiser in calibre, nor perhaps could have. He was a hope because he talked candidly of sex, a virtue in itself twenty years ago to the impatient few like Mencken. But his romantic heroines, who had to be rewarded, blinded him to irony. When Sinclair Lewis appeared ten years later, he suffered from the same bias, though with him it was he, Lewis, for whom life must somehow be agreeable, if not in Minnesota, then in England perhaps or in Italy. The result, though not exactly romantic, is not irony in the grave sense of the word; it is sarcasm. What Mencken felt in Dreiser, underlying the unmoral tone, was what Cézanne has called the dark line — and Mencken, too, by coincidence * — the line of doom which can relate the merest lyric or brush mark, or can relate diffuseness like Dreiser's to inevitable equations. For Mencken he " stems directly . . . not from Zola, Flaubert . . . but from the Greeks. . . . A motto to his books . . . might be: ' Oh ye deathward going tribes of men, what do your lives mean except that they go to nothingness.' " In *Jennie Gerhardt* he finds " a primitive and touching poetry." In fact, perhaps he comes about as near to poetry as he permits himself to travel when he grazes this dark line in Dreiser, which, he says, reveals " the life of man, not as a simple theorem in Calvinism, but as a vast adventure, an enchantment, a mystery." This fellow German-American excited Mencken's emotions. For him as for Conrad and Nietzsche, he abandoned prudence. He suggested him in terms of his favorite ancestral art — music: " After the Fifth Symphony or any of

* *A Book of Prefaces:* H. L. Mencken.

the Nine . . . it is not easy to listen to a Chopin nocturne, and after Mr. Dreiser's story, by the same token, you will not find it easy to read the common novels of the month." So started an allegiance of one mind to another which it would take some years to defeat.

47

A Traveler at Forty:
*" I accept now no creeds. I do not know
what truth is, what beauty is, what love is,
what hope is."*   DREISER

"Dreiser is not a modern but a belated Victorian " was the idea of an English reviewer of 1911, thus varying the verdict of that day. " No doubt," he adds " this is due to his nationality . . . he is dealing with a society that is at least thirty years behind Europe." It happens that once I heard him say the same thing of himself throwing the emphasis differently, and in company with an idea startling enough to stay with me. It was late afternoon some time in 1918 on a walk along the Hudson. The sun was over-brimming the river with light as it might have done for the first Hollanders on the afternoon of their invasion. The Hudson had the look it knows how to wear of being a gateway to new amazing victories. Dreiser in the face of it said dryly: " This turn of the century — you know I believe it's the end of something not the beginning of anything."

It seemed to me perverse of him or old-fashioned. Wasn't it after all a period of ferment in our culture, a birth of new elements, a revival of old? For four years the war had thrown talented Europeans our way who preferred not to fight, or were sent on missions. New York shimmered with different and eager eyes. There was as yet no prohibition to flatten and dull our features beyond recognition. The war was a ghastly but exciting fact across the seas, in the face of which it was dangerous but daring to maintain an unbiased intellect. The daring counted. People cared. The war was a heartrending nightmare, but to one like myself not visited by personal deaths, it did not seem like a catastrophe that would mean unhealing wounds for years to come, it might be for the rest of any of our lives. Instead perhaps the war would be more like a storm, which when spent would bring brighter skies. The anemic Christian formula for one thing might be going out in death, leaving survivors with a degree of actinic life not acknowledged in ages. I said something of this to Dreiser, naming new American poets and new enterprises, live forms and live ideas of our own — a revival in which certainly he was a factor. And in France modern art played like a fountain, like fireworks for, the dead from the living — " Ancient pre-Christian principles and new shapes! " I said.

" Well, perhaps, but I don't see it that way " was his answer. " Whatever we have came out of the last century, and it's about over. We're the tag-end of it, the grand finale. Look at it any way you like, who are the new giants in art or science or philosophy? Rodin, Anatole France, Einstein, Freud — the end of a long line of giants, not the beginning. And who else? " — More glib in art than in science I gave a list, Matisse, Picasso, Cocteau, Stravinsky, Satie, Brancusi, Diaghileff, and a number of others were high-geared, and they were moderns. Life would be newer and more brilliant because of them. — " Well, if they're any good," was his rejoinder, " they belong to the past. What's more I believe the big radicals came too soon for their time. We're in for a reaction. A few more years and an idea outside of business won't get a show anywhere."

So much for this belated Victorian, who in 1911 went to Europe for the first time. Today the fact of his going brings to mind our conversation of five years later, and is evidence on his side of the argument. In 1911 for this self-made intellectual to go to Europe for the first time was as distinct an event in his life as for Columbus to sail to America or Lindbergh to fly to Paris. Today it might be an event for a European to cross to the United States to study for himself our contagious code of money-making as the sole index of power. Or an event for any philosopher to visit Soviet Russia and study its proposed tyranny of brotherly love. But it is not any more a like event for an American of like calibre to go to Europe. Twenty years have made that difference. An intellectual epoch has ended. It is doubtful that another has begun. Today an American writes or paints as a matter of course from Paris. Unknown to the French it is his aesthetic suburb, where he can live in what is left of the demoded modernism of the past. Twenty years ago Europe was the frontier and the background of thought, without knowledge of which a man remained the boob that an American was supposed to be and still may be for aught I know. Today the new epoch is dropping Europe from curriculums as the old dropped Latin and Greek.

Dreiser owed his adventure to an English friend and would-be publisher, Grant Richards. After Heinemann's success with *Sister Carrie* and Norris's praise he had sought him out in New York. "I knew no American whose friendship I enjoyed more . . . for the five years it lasted," Richards said. Perhaps it delighted him to know a prodigy from the people scorned by our polite society, which in turn used to be scorned by Englishmen as a mere imitation of their own. Anyway the English have never stopped discovering America, while we have chiefly discovered other things, not often ourselves. Dreiser wrote of Richards: "I have always liked him. . . . He wears a monocle in his right eye and I like him for that. . . ." One morning in the month of the début of *Jennie Gerhardt,* this personage appeared for breakfast, and proposed England, the Riviera, Rome and Paris, and a book of notes to be published on his return. Dreiser's answer was, "If it can be arranged." Richards arranged it with an advance on the travel book from the Century Company. With Mencken at home as it happened as a willing custodian to send him clippings and proclaim him to his public, with the urbane Richards to tell him what to wear, where to tip and what and whom to see, in November 1911 the author of *Carrie* and *Jennie* set sail for the headquarters of western imagination — Europe.

To Baldwin Macy, interviewing for the Chicago Evening Post, he gave his reasons for going. He wanted to know the cities where the Financier, the hero of his next novel, a trilogy, would be going. And then he had an idea about America as the coming world-power, and yet he had his doubts. He was going to see for himself "how we rank in our chances for the future among the rest of the nations." Here he was in truth at forty a belated titan, inquirer more than cynic, and a true American — world-power a personal dream. He writes of himself at this moment: "I accept now no creeds. I do not know what truth is, what beauty is, what love is, what hope is." And yet he sailed to observe and discover Europe. He sailed looking for creeds, truth, beauty, love and hope. He belonged with the giants of the past who were one after another arriving after long travail at the same impasse: in a hypothetical universe there can be no ultimate answer. But he had not joined with immediate posterity which was soon to say: " Then why bother to ask any questions?" He sailed to Europe looking for questions and answers.

And then besides he sailed for fun: ". . . a host of gulls — an air of delicious adventure . . . at the foot of Thirteenth Street. Did ever a boy thrill over a ship as I over this monster of the seas?" There were two actresses, friends of Richards, who gave them their perfumed time; one sang coon songs with him; there were the machinery and the stokers of the Mauretania portentous to him; and in the nocturnal " all's well " from the crow's nest " an echo of old journeys and old seas when life was not safe "; and when they landed in Fishguard, gulls again, " their little feet coral red, their beaks jade grey, their bodies snowy white or sober grey, wheeling and crying — ' My heart remembers how.' " He was a traveler at forty hard to define — a cold realist, a somber mystic, or at times as high-keyed as a nigger with a watermelon or a diamond or a bar of jazz.*

Grant Richards was in his way quite as belated. He liked to believe in genius as well as money. In an interview I asked him how he had come to take Dreiser to Europe: " I liked him, I suppose, and valued him. He was an American who would be remembered after his death. Why not give him a chance while he was living. I knew that friends of mine would be interested to meet

* *A Traveler at Forty.*

him." — " And you didn't think of him as socially crude or inexperienced the way New Yorkers did? " I was impelled to ask in pursuit of one of the themes this book was bringing me. — " Why should I? " he answered with logical surprise. " A man is interesting or he isn't. Dreiser was delightful, a great man, an original."

So here he was admitted, not excluded, for the first time, where he imagined he belonged, among people who valued social relations. Here from November until April he would be enjoying life, making notes with the lust peculiar to him, untroubled, perhaps stimulated, by the thought of the thousands who had been over the ground before him. Whether it was an English drawing room or village or prostitute, a painting by Degas or Picasso, a cathedral, the casino at Monte Carlo, a café, a castle, the pope, a cocotte, a new friend or ancient background, he sought to define it as he did Niagara Falls — a pristine experience. It is a time to leave him pondering the distinctions between European nations, and between all of Europe and America, to review the literary scene into which he had entered as a wedge signifying change.

48

"He proposed the religion of World's Fairs. The chaos of education approached a dream." HENRY ADAMS

What were some of the other symptoms of change and birth? Chief among them was the fact that education was coming to an exotic crisis, the germs of which dated back some years and figure in previous pages of this book. " Be native " was beginning to be written in people's minds, but " be native exotically " was a concurrent demand. Now that that fondling, parentage undefined, the American language, had surely drifted out of the streets and offices and railways and riverways and music halls into its own idiom, own cadences, diction and spelling; now that a number of writers from Whitman to Dreiser were lending the creature their names; and that Mencken and others would soon grow learned over it; this young language turned about impatiently. Used now to convey what culture we had, our speech grew suddenly conscious of our lack of literate and aesthetic experience. At last a real minority, more than a handful, became dissatisfied. We looked jealously toward Europe again, and Europe met us with exports, especially if we would pay for them.

But now the escape was no longer to England or Germany or Scandinavia. Matthew Arnold and Pater and Swinburne were scrapped. Opinion turned away from Ibsen; too moral and fog-bound. And away from Wagner; too heavy and Teutonic. Everything a-Nordic was coming into fashion, Gaelic, Iberian, Latin, Gallic, and Slavic. And French culture was forwarding applicants to the near and far East, Africa and South America, especially to the art of primitive peoples, even back to

American Redskins. What Kipling had called *heathen* was growing sacred now. So while the business man advanced creating our relentless destiny, the intelligentsia was undergoing a foreign transfusion. As many races contributed to our culture as to our population. People's minds got dressed in these importations. They wore them like charms and amulets as if to be cured forever of their past. A violent phase began of that difficulty from which we have suffered — our sense of inferiority contradicting our independence. Costumes kept arriving at our ports, causing countless costume parties. Were they ever grafted into our habits of living, and become more than mental trinkets? Henry Adams asked himself this question, when he visited the Chicago World's Fair of 1893: " Was it real or only apparent? One's personal universe hung on the answer . . . if the rupture was real and the new American world could take this sharp and conscious twist. . . ." But his friends who made the Fair, Hunt and Richardson, La Farge and St. Gaudens, Burnham, McKim and Stanford White " talked as though they worked only for themselves, as though art to the western people was a stage decoration; a diamond shirt-stud; a paper collar." Today it is as difficult to know if it is real; though easy to say, " Not yet perceptibly, but perhaps."

There would at least be one profit to this fever to be foreign — the country's treasures from all over the earth, stored in private and public collections. The industrial billionaire was doing his contradictory part to perpetuate the memory of civilizations he was busy destroying. Foreigners coming with their wares to a market not yet closed to them were lending us vitality. Natives were giving their strength in behalf of old splendors and of new ones soon to be old. What dividends have come of this, or will come, let other accountants compute.

Although it was as much his idea to define our own present and future as to travel elsewhere, one of the importers in this period was Henry Adams. The grandson of the president who died heart-broken to see Washington's paternal program fail, Adams was educated from childhood to feel the vague failure of New England as the cradle of a nation. Born in the shadow of the Boston

State House yet he never felt that he belonged there, but rather with his grandmother and her Louis Seize chairs and 18th century house in Quincy. Nor as the son of an ambassador to England, where he was for a time a 19th century European, did he feel that he belonged there. Always he was in search of polarization. Finally at sixty he made two books, a kind of hammock between "Thirteenth Century Unity" and "Twentieth Century Multiplicity." And it happened that these volumes printed privately in 1904 and 1905, radiated beyond the 100 friends to whom he sent them, and, before they were printed publicly, had turned a sensitive minority into being world-wise. They gave Americans, if they cared to take it, at last a related point of view:

"... as the unit by which to measure motion down to his own time, without assuming anything as true or untrue except relation ... [Adams] began a volume which he mentally knew as *Saint-Michel and Chartres*. ... From that point he proposed to fix a position for himself which he could label *The Education of Henry Adams*. ... With the help of these two points of relation he hoped to project his lines forward and backward indefinitely, subject to correction from anyone who should know better."

Had his readers followed him forward they would have found close predictions as to the war of 1914, the crash of 1929, and the "new social mind of today." But rather than an appetite for the future presided over by the machine, whose headquarters would be the United States, they caught from him a nostalgia for the past presided over by the Virgin, identified with Venus, whose headquarters were France. He gave the gist of Catholic Mediterranean Europe, whose centuries had perpetuated the gist of Pagan Antiquity in a threefold Latin Culture — the Virgin behind screen of chastity secretly inspiring the rites of ancient goddesses. And this he gave in terms of America, and America in terms of Europe.

Then there was another pagan yeast, likewise presided over by the Virgin. It came from the south of Ireland, brought by Yeats and Lady Gregory and the players of the Abbey Theatre. They assisted at a miracle of birth here. They gave an impulse to a choral of poets who combined like birds in the early morning to startle a people who thought that poetry had been dropped in favor of the machine forever. Celtic wit had long run in our blood and exploded in laughter; it made part of limber, racy, coarse American. But Gaelic music and imagery had been left behind or confiscated when the emigrant landed. Now spoken by Yeats and these players in 1911, if they did not enter our common speech, the germ of them operated esoterically in the birth of poetry about to occur. Yeats said that a poem was " passionate speech," not a literary ornament; poetry was idiom violent with emotion; " the muses love violence."

In this year 1911 the hopeful and somewhat fragile Harriet Monroe went unashamed from door to door of bankers and packers and public-utility magnates, paraphrasing the words of Yeats. Poetry, she told them, was as real and vital a force as industry; Chicago was as instinct with poets as any other city, if only there might be the money to buy their wares. Perhaps they did not believe her, though some of them wrote verse secretly. But flattered to see Chicago in this new light, flattered to be valued instead of sneered by a high-brow, they gave her a little of their money and then, I suppose, turned to their next deal, and then a highball and a blonde at the College Inn, perchance. *The Poetry Magazine* printed its first number in November 1912.

I think Miss Monroe was as brave as Joan of Arc and almost as successful. Poets sprang into action over night, natives, exiles and strangers. The Chicago post office became a station through which traveled the verse of many peoples. Hindoo and Chinese appeared translated in her pages, deepening the sense of Eastern forms which years before Lafcadio Hearn and Yoni Noguchi had proposed to us. The Iowan Ezra Pound, self-deported to London, was foreign editor, sending her paraphrases from the Chinese, old French and Italian, and with them much scornful advice as to how to wake Americans up from their long provincial sleep. When she sometimes returned them to him as insulting to the noble bankers who had listened to her prayer, he dissented, and from across the sea launched an independent aggressive campaign; as indignant a critic as Mencken and a hundred times more exacting. He did his best to ram up-to-date culture down domestic throats and even introduced modernism into England. Yeats admits to revising his poems, making them less "poetic" at Pound's suggestion. The great Bostonian, Amy Lowell, untiring prosodist, connoisseur and salesman, joined both camps and spread the propaganda of free verse and imagism on the French plan and the Japanese. Transfusion flourished in the art of verse. Under its sway two overlapping methods emerged, one free and native, informal and tough like American life; the other precious, even snobbish, bent on refining the technique of verse, however alien to our shiftless talk and manners. And true to native precedent new chasms appeared to separate these new poets.

There were other importers. Alfred Stieglitz, a Jew born in New Jersey, with the fervor of his race for religion and propaganda had a dream of converting New York, perhaps the whole country to Art. He believed apparently that if he could effect a mystic union between Art and the Camera, then Art would get a passport into the machine age. He brought to this faith a mastery of the camera and a flair for the work of the great moderns in Europe at a time when few other Americans had the eye to see them. In 1905 with Edward Steichen he established a gallery at 291 Fifth Avenue, *Photo-Secession,* and a journal called *Camera Work.* "291" came to be thought of as a temple, and Stieglitz a high priest, a god, just as later Georgia O'Keefe, his favorite painter, became a goddess, to some of the devotees. One of them, Waldo Frank, composed a rhapsody to 291 : *

"291 is a religious fact . . . an altar where . . . no lie or compromise could live. . . . New York was a lying and destroying storm; 291 was a candle that did not go out, since it alone was truth."

Frank believed too that 291 was a kind of high-class factory for painters, a group "more brilliant, self-conscious, hardy, radical than any on earth," he calls them.* An exaggeration of which two retrospective exhibitions, European and American, in the fall of 1930 were proof. But these same shows testified to the exotic

* *Our America:* Waldo Frank.

virus to which artists had succumbed in the last generation. And Stieglitz was one of those to administer it not only to his own small sect but to an uncounted clientele throughout the country. Perhaps the infection took more crucially among writers than painters. Carlos Williams, Carl Sandburg, Sherwood Anderson, I imagine, would pay their tribute to this brilliant teacher as having indirectly deepened their education. He was a voice in the wilderness preceding the famous Armory exhibition, of 1915, after which the United States was inculcated with modern art.

First Rodin back in 1905, then Cézanne, VanGogh, Gauguin, Matisse, Picasso, Bracques, Derain, Pascin, Brancusi, Modigliani, Léger, Duchamps, Picabia — all of the innovators, realists and surrealists — were preached by turns at 291. Their fame spread and with it the fame of some of the writers and musicians who in that most conscious of centers, Paris, were collaborators with the painters toward an art that would match the new age, and its fabulous discoveries in science and machinery. Appolinaire, Cocteau, Jacob, Cendras, Satie, Stravinsky, Milhaud, would as the years went on become vague terms in New York.

In 1909 Gertrude Stein, a Jewess born in Alleghany, Pennsylvania, brought up to the age of five in Paris and Vienna, and then in California, had published a volume of three stories, *Three Lives*, a sheerly original work in which one could detect no foreign influence. At Radcliffe she had been a favorite student of William James, with the wish to become a psychologist. Her excursions among states of mind carried her into incursions into language. *Three Lives*, the stories of three servant girls in terms of their hidden minds, initiated a method of writing as new and real as Dreiser's themes were real and startling. Later she became a part of the education of Sherwood Anderson and later still of Ernest Hemingway and of no one knows how many others. She went with this small volume literally into the language. Had she been content to stay there we might have had an essential novelist defining the conflicts of states of mind as revealed by American speech. But soon she followed the line of exiles to Paris, where under the influence of Picasso she came to use words disassociated from ideas as if they were paint. She set a style of writing exotic to letters, which sought to give the color and tone of thought rather than the thought itself. In this way she has produced some alluring poems, and perhaps has liberated her own soul. But I think that so far she has enslaved the minds of her many disciples in a blind attempt to emulate her, and has helped to stunt the growth of our articulate talent. In 1925 however, toward the end of this fruitful era of letters, she published *The Making of Americans,* in language open to all, an epic which ought to be required in courses of American literature.

In these years too translations from the Russian, Tchekov and Dosteovsky, for example, were set up like altars to an alien divinity: Tragedy.* " America has always taken tragedy lightly," according to Henry Adams. And Frost in his malicious way has scanned the thought " — How are we to write — The Russian novel in America — As long as life goes so unterribly? " Had he said, " is supposed to go," Dreiser could have told him it was next to impossible. Soon, as a bright accompaniment to sorrow, the Russian ballet, Pavlova, Nijinsky and the Moscow Art Theatre and Opera and the Habima Players would come and play their ultra violet rays upon us. And American drab greens and browns would try to get dyed, quite ineptly, with the spectrum of Southeastern Europe. People who had never danced or noticed tragedy would buy vermilion, tyrian and turquoise scarfs and flirt with flexibility and intensity. At this time too the mysticism of Maeterlinck, in the whole tone scale of Debussy, and the musical innovations of Satie, Stravinsky, Ravel, Milhaud and the other five of *Les Six* surprised the ears of the United states.

Then there was another seduction nearest home out of the Negroes by the Jews — ragtime, syncopation, and toward the end of the decade, jazz! The Castles were

---

* Macmillan published the translations of Constance Garnett: *The Brothers Karamazoff*, 1912, *Crime and Punishment*, 1914, *House of the Dead*, 1915, *The Idiot*, 1913, *Possessed*, 1914, *Raw Youth*, 1916, *White Nights*, 1918.

teaching the debutantes to dance as only the half world had danced before. French dressmakers were teaching the girls to dress as only their half world dressed in Paris. Cocktails were teaching them to talk and carry on far away from the sacred institution, Home. " Out " * was suddenly " wonderful " to all the young and some of the elders of this moral land. Here perhaps would be the one real fusion of exotic and native. An intimation of sex was finally claiming the young as its subjects. On this one frivolous plane, intricate technique, grew angular flowers, not deeply rooted, but rooted, in American soil — Sophistication of shoulders, wrists, ankles, buttocks, of piano and trombones and nasal song became a ritual of speed, to unconsciously celebrate fast trains, rapid building, fast workers, racing motors — the one ritual Europeans so far have imported from us.

So all these bright and distinguished packages kept arriving and spoke to us of life lived deeply elsewhere. Always in love with externals, each time we saved the wrappings and imitated them as best we could. Did we put our own essential content into them, or are they now empty wrappings? It is not easy to know. The most we can say is that these imports stimulated us and took us to a different plane; and that with individual artists a new culture occurred.

* *Adventures in a Perambulator:* John Carpenter.

49

*" I doubt whether the world is ever . . .
inclined to face its darker phases any more
than it is capable of . . . acknowledging
its most exquisite pleasures. . . . In the
main the vast majority are comparable to
spindling underbrush or grass. Here and
there in this jungle . . . are giant trees,
sequoias, banyans, and some lives are no
longer comparable to trees. They soar like
vast and lonely uplifts of rock, not only in
thought but in action."* DREISER

Into this changing America, Dreiser came back from Europe, not changed but immeasurably strengthened, he says. He had been, for a minute, part of liaisons not just between himself and one other man or woman as at home, but between a number of men and women who joined for the surprising purpose of personal exchange. He felt in the houses where Richards had taken him in London, and in the cafés on the continent, and from delightful people he met on his way, an intimation of liaisons between infinite numbers, intangible and valuable to life; not to be known to Americans yet or perhaps ever. And how can they be known to us when leaders among us appear to praise above all loneliness, and have made a cult of silences and solitudes — a perversion out of the " great open spaces "? So that perhaps exaltation increases, but wit as certainly decreases. In Europe Dreiser felt precisely the values which Henry James asked of his novels to define — the values of human relations. And now he knew for himself " the wine-like air, the net-like movements . . . the dancing lights . . . that indescribable tension . . . sense of life at the topmost level of nervous strength," which is Paris. He had felt the " great artistic impulse of Italy" which had made "perfect things," and the appetite for extremes which had made murderers like the Borgias into the patrons of "perfection." He felt Germany like a "forge or workshop" and "its blazing force or defiance"; and "in England the distinction of the fireside, the family heirloom"; London "more fatalistic and therefore less hopeful than New York" but at the same time "not so hard or foreign." Neither had his voracious sensibility missed in Holland "that delicate refinement of soul" which had allowed the Dutch painters canvasses in which "life is revealed static, quiescent, undisturbed, innocently gay, naïvely beautiful."

The book, *A Traveler at Forty*, is like the *Hoosier Holiday* a book of young rapture and old questioning — the two most lyric records Dreiser has made; in both cases as if a child with adult brain were entering the world for the first time. But toward the end of the trip there was something to kill joy: money gave out. In "Madame G's Bar" they talked it over, and their two tempers, one suave the other foreboding, clashed. Richards who had managed the finances had to admit the money was gone. "But," he said, "why not stay in England and write this summer and draw on your future." "No," was the realist's answer, "I've got to buckle down to work at once at anything that will make me ready money"; best "to drop the writing end . . . and return to the editorial desk." — "'Really,' [Richards] said with a grand air. 'You discourage me. . . . Here you are a man of forty. . . . Your work is all indicated and before you. Public faith such as my own should have some weight with you and yet after a tour of Europe, such as you would not reasonably have contemplated a year ago, you sink down supinely and talk of quitting. Truly it is too much. . . . You must cultivate some intellectual stability around which your emotions can center and settle to anchor.'" *

Much seemed to have happened in this Hoosier's mind while he sat with the Londoner in Madame G's Bar. For one thing he thought of New York — "The subway

* *A Traveler at Forty.*

like my library table — it is so much of an intimate. Broadway . . . the one idling show place. . . . The pull of the city overseas was on me — and that in the spring! I wanted to go *home*. . . . All in all the Atlantic metropolis [was] the first city in the world to me . . . richer and freer in its spirit than London or Paris, though so often more gauche, more tawdry, more shamblingly inexperienced. . . . It was definitely settled at this conference that . . . I was to take a boat sailing from Dover about the middle of April. . . . This agreed, we returned to our pleasures and spent three or four very delightful days together."

" When the day came to sail I was really glad to be going home, although on the way I had quarreled so much with my land for the things which it lacks and Europe apparently has.

Our boasted democracy has resulted in little more than the privilege every . . . American has of being rude and brutal to every other. Our early revolt against sham civility has, in so far as I can see, resulted in nothing save the abolition of all civility. . . . Life, I am sure, will shame us out of it eventually."

So the American went home where one had to be more gauche, more shamblingly inexperienced than in London or Paris, or be different. Though never shambling, he belonged there, perhaps, and not with Richards of the monocle. Now, in the way of genius of whatever birth, resenting criticism, he deserted the critic, and used the criticism. Once home, with an advance from Harper's of $1000 to get there, he did not go back to editing, but went to work to finish *The Financier*. But he compromised this much to " ready money." He let it go at the cost of style and brevity to please his publishers. Mr. Duneka writes him:

"I have just finished re-reading *The Financier*. I was really shaken by it. It does not seem possible for you to keep up the sense of power the book gives one. I am trembling for the rest of it. Not that I doubt you, but because of the greatness of it all. The book promises to be unhumanly big."

Then in the way of publishers he stopped trembling to say:

"We are very keen to publish *The Financier* in August if that is humanly possible. It would stand a much better chance to get a running start of the other fall books. This is important."

Dreiser got back in April; the book was published under pressure in October.

And he worked for money in other ways. He coached Harper's as to how to advertise, and they made use of his quite modern suggestions. He had not boosted circulation for Smith, Hampton, Butterick for nothing. The other concession to trade was to let the breach widen between himself and his European host. He too may not have been above reproach, but then we expect more of artist than of publisher in the way of delicate precision; the artist has come to be thought of as the natural martyr. Apparently Richards imagined that the English rights of his guest's four books belonged to him. Already he had taken over " a few copies " of *Sister Carrie* from the former publisher, Heinemann, whom evidently Dreiser was under no compulsion to see in spite of that luncheon at Martin's in 1903 which had given him so much courage. Heinemann writes with distant reproach as if some courtesy may have been dispensed with: "As one of the first admirers of *Sister Carrie* I shall be very sorry not to see you before you go." Certainly Dreiser had flirted with Richards; but now threw him down casually in favor of Harper's who told him they would not think of handling his books at home if another firm was to dispense them in England; " unless of course very substantial payment were made for the right." *A Traveler at Forty* dedicated to Barfleur, alias Richards, is the one book confided to the house of Richards. In December 1912 he writes to Dreiser from the Hotel Knickerbocker in New York:

"I make friends with too much reluctance to surrender them with anything but great unwillingness and regret, but your letter . . . left me no choice. With regard to your books I write not as a disappointed publisher . . . but as a wounded admirer [of your work] to whom you had made almost extravagant promises of association. . . .You speak of business reasons for our meeting. I cannot imagine what they are . . . but all the same . . . I will say that I shall be here, with intervals, from 2:30 till 3:45 when I go down to the boat."

They met for the last time " for just fifteen minutes "; and I imagine " Barfleur " went down to the boat in sadness, perhaps in anger. In 1914 however he had recovered himself enough to remind Dreiser, " though it goes very much against the grain," of a debt of £3, 17s, 6d. He " sees no reason why it should run on from year to year." Lately, when interviewed this urbane Londoner of the old school upset the delightful image of two friends on a spree in Europe, which Dreiser makes in his travel book. He said: " Theodore Dreiser, your distinguished novelist? But really I can't help you; I don't remember any voyage we took together. I never knew him." Dreiser on the other hand says wistfully: " I would give anything not to have quarreled with him, and over money too! I owe him so much; that trip to Europe! It was like a tonic that lasted me for years; it was new life to me. I shall never forget it."

The incident is slight and not important as gossip, but it is enough to stand as sign of the kind of temper which, with perhaps less remorse than the business man can take personally all that it wants and give nothing back, unless publicly in the integrity of art. Or put it this way; the man of affairs often makes no personal relations at all, only rotarian connections, while the artist excels in the personal. With few exceptions creative genius has been known to be blind to friendship, and at the same time to be more alive than others to the need of friends. Devotees of beauty think of genius as heroic; other men, including most psychologists, think of it as abnormal, mad, insane. One thing is sure, there can be no consistent pleasure in contemplating it unless we begin by accepting its cruelty as hand in hand with its tenderness — cruelty to the one left behind; tenderness to the one about to be embraced, as it travels its road to the happy ending, Fame. No synchronization except in the annealment of the moment of Art. There may be a current of giving too, as always in the case of Dreiser to unknown writers, uncommercial journals, friends in need; but these are gifts not for gain or duty but for luxury of giving. Genius chooses and rejects associates, and so the drama is maintained. Take for example a man at opposite poles in most ways from Dreiser, Edgar Allan Poe. Griswold writes of him:

> "There seemed to him no moral susceptibility; and what was more remarkable in a proud nature, little or nothing of the true point of honor. He had to a morbid excess, that desire to rise which is vulgarly called ambition, but no wish for the esteem or love of his species; only the hard wish to succeed — not shine, not serve, — succeed, that he might have the right to despise the world which galled his conceit."

And Poe says of himself:

> "I love fame — I dote on it — I idolize it — I would drink to the very dregs the glorious intoxication; I would have incense arise in my honor from every hill and hamlet, from every town and city on this earth; Fame! Glory! — they are life-giving breath, and living blood; no man lives, unless he is famous; how bitterly I belied my nature and my aspirations, when I said I did not desire fame and that I despised it!"

One might say that Dreiser was not this man wild to conquer, but merely the burned child, who would not again find himself reduced to a loaf of bread and a job at 15¢ an hour. But I don't think so. I believe that like Hurstwood it would have been quite possible for him to lie down in a flop and inhale the gas at 15¢ a night; *if*, and it is a mammoth *if*, he had not had some of that desire for fame that links him with other differing aesthetic geniuses, Whitman, Poe, Bierce, Mark Twain; and links them all with the business geniuses, Rockefeller, Yerkes, Hearst, Al Capone, on the one token of desire for power. Dreiser knew the link when he wrote: "After all we cannot all be artists, statesmen, generals, thieves or financiers." If you asked such a temperament, especially when bent on art or wisdom, "Do you think you are God?", and he were honest, he would say, "Yes, that's my business."

Despite the wide differences between the most word-wise and the least word-wise of our poets, there is, beside the wish to dominate, a more special likeness between Poe and Dreiser. An exquisite among critics, Jean Cocteau, asked the question: "What is it in America in the climate or in the soil that can have made Poe turn entirely toward horror and mystery? To find that out I would be curious to visit your country. It excites me." The Americans he questioned said: "You are wrong, there is nothing; Poe was an accident; the country is the most cheerful in the world, depressingly cheerful, and the most open, a literally ingenuous land." But Cocteau guessed right; there is something. Poe and Dreiser are two writers whose speech bear witness to an element of horror and mystery special to the United States. Melville, Hawthorne in his neurotic way, Bierce, and Masters are others. The humorist Ring Lardner is another. Back of each laugh in which he is as lucky and fantastic as a player with four aces, are hatred and frustration.

Poe expressed his sense of it by completely defying it. He painted it as the decay of beauty, the rule of evil; he made himself an exile with " the few who love me and whom I love . . . those who feel rather than those who think " in the valleys and islands of his spirit, never free however from the terror of the American world in which he knew he lived: " Of my country and of my family I have little to say. Ill usage and length of years have driven me from the one and estranged me from the other." And yet he said much about his country by inversion in each poem and story. He turned the horror about and made the victims not the victors shine. Baudelaire lucidly points out that Poe's flight was not from himself but from his country, " that barbarous land lighted by gas."

And Dreiser has felt the horror of our optimistic land and the mystery of it; but has expressed it by marrying with it and celebrating its enormity. He has made the conqueror shine. And what could it be that would triumph over these vast spaces; a wilderness much of it for years not even lighted by gas, but only by stars; which cast their spell of beauty and thereby complicated the question? What could these great children take with them across the country as they traveled in their covered wagons? Not love, not beauty, as civilizing forces to a land dedicated to " life, liberty and the pursuit of happiness." Their tolerant religions could not tolerate those twin lodestars.

They traveled in covered wagons with covered souls. But to bridge the chasms that remained chasms for neglect of old human principles, there could be other new power; executive, mechanical, numerical, mineral, and finally electrical — lucrative power pursued into excesses. It was and is as cold as it is brilliant, white to some, black to others according to their senses. It is never colored. Only conquerors from Tamburlaine to the American billionaire have known that certain rich coldness, black or white as you will. The American has heated it with speed, steam, electricity, money, booze and blondes; the moon, sun and stars and what they naturally brought being inadequate. That is, they have wandered far from nature which perhaps seemed too much of a vast problem to cope with. And yet before them the Indian and the Spaniard managed to make their bow to nature and make a living too.

Henry Adams puts it dryly:

"Even Commodore Vanderbilt and Jay Gould lacked social charm. Doubtless the country needed ornament and needed it badly — but it needed energy still more, and capital most of all. . . . To fit out an entire continent with roads and with the decencies of life would exhaust the credit of an entire planet. . . . Such an estimate seemed outrageous to a Texan member of Congress who loved the simplicity of nature's noblemen; but the mere suggestion that a sun existed above him would outrage the self-respect of a deep-sea fish that carried a lantern on the end of his nose. From the moment that the railroads were introduced, life took on extravagance."

"For a hundred years, between 1793 and 1893, the American people hesitated, vacillated, swayed forward and back, between two forces, one simply industrial, the other capitalistic, centralizing and mechanical. In 1893, the issue came on the single gold standard, and the majority declared itself, once and for all, in favor of the capitalistic system with all its necessary machinery. . . . The whole mechanical consolidation of force . . . ruthlessly stamped out the life into which Adams was born, but created monopolies capable of controlling the new energies that America adored. . . . After this vigorous impulse nothing remained for an historian to ask — but how long and how far!"

Nothing indeed, except that perhaps an historian might take a step further back to a basis of earlier days — in fact to the birth of the nation. He might perhaps see that an American became a " deep-sea fish," with a need of energy more than ornament, just because his religion forbade him to obey the sun and wear the ornaments of the sun. And perhaps it was not " the majority " that declared itself for the new order, but the craftier deep-sea fish who forced the new order, to outwit a religion that belonged to incongruous pastures, and had nothing to do with the giant waves of the sea of American life. Certain it is that Dreiser with no more censure than Adams plunged in among the deep-sea fish and planned an American Odyssey to be known as *A Trilogy of Desire,* where the burden of the action depends upon the conqueror more than upon the conquered masses. The first volume of it, *The Financier,* was in fact so American a bolt that it almost lifted him from the literary columns to the financial. And just as he identified himself with his two heroines, Carrie and Jennie, in their need for life and love and ornament, now he writes himself into the character of the financier in his need of conquest.

In Rome, a Mrs. Q. had told him the story of the Borgia family, which seemed to him so important a notch in the measure of possibility that he incorporated it in his travel book in all its extravagance, and naïvely as if it were news.* He liked Mrs. Q. " She was not in the least morbid. The horror and cruelties of lust and ambition held no terrors for her. She liked life as a spectacle." She was of his own kind. Once at a party there was a discussion between Dreiser and the pacifist John Dos Passos, who had spoken of an accident too terrible to look at, he thought. Dreiser couldn't understand it; he could look at anything. Why not? Some time after in the course of talk I submitted the anecdote as instance of both the older and younger realist to the impartial Robert Frost,

* " Once, riding in the subway, Dreiser opened a copy of the Evening World and showed me the line: ' Let us introduce you to the work of Rudyard Kipling.' I scoffed, saying people already knew that work. Dreiser said, ' No, they don't; they have to be introduced to everything.' To believe that, and yet to write novels, requires infinite patience. It also lays the ghost of ' style '; for perhaps one-half of style is repression. The stylist is the man who withholds his pen." *What Manner of Man He Is:* Harris Merton Lyon.

who in chance encounters has seemed almost uniquely a mind exhilarated by evidence. His disposal of it was: " Well, I suppose that when you get so you can look at anything your eyes run the danger of hardening so you don't see things." But do they? Isn't it possible that they might then get strong, not hard. For myself I should think of this quality of Dreiser's as a rare asset for an artist in search of perfection. And if he failed it would not be because of the brain's command to the senses to face experience, but more because of an imperfect set of senses.

In any event Dreiser may well have been glancing back at the Borgias when he wrote the story of the more metallic but not less cruel Yerkes, whom he called Cowperwood. And assuredly he remembered the Romans too, remains of whom in Rome were like —

"the glistening shell of an extinct beetle or the suggestion in rocks of a prehistoric world. . . . Mind was theirs — vast, ardent imagination. . . . They were the great ones —the Romans. We must learn from them."

" Since the making of the Roman Empire the world has held no men so great as the business overlords of America. They were men who thought in terms of a continent."

Except for these analogies to Latins, ancient and modern, there is no exotic ingredient in *The Financier* or in the second volume of the trilogy, *The Titan,* published a year and a half later, May 1914. Nor is there in *The Traveler at Forty,* which appeared in November 1913. Foreign lands excited his imagination, but never influenced his manner which, for all the sophistication that was at length going the rounds of our villages, has remained notoriously Dreiserian.

50

" Whilst others have struggled in vain you have scaled the difficult cliffs."
Masters to Dreiser in 1912

So Dreiser shot his bolt for Harper's in double-quick time. *The Financier* came to 800 pages and yet made a powerful effect. Fifteen years later he rewrote it. In its present form it is as economical as *Sister Carrie,* and a more ambitious though not more tender undertaking. Following on Carrie and Jennie it made him another friend, the poet Edgar Lee Masters. They lasted each other for a number of years. Dreiser regrets his loss, and not more than many of his readers. Where has he gone, this poet? Did the poet in him die and the lawyer with the dead poet's equipment step out of the old skin to write today *Lincoln The Man,* where he indicts Lincoln for not being God. The book might have been called " Case of the States Against Abraham Lincoln." Why this should have happened to a poet belongs not here but toward the end of a baffling book repeatedly attempted and not yet written: " The Rise and Fall of Spiritual America." Dreiser to this day believes in him and perhaps in his country too. His voice values Masters when he speaks of him: " He knows absolute fatality; that life alters and affects man; that man can't alter life. His poems have the deathless ring that there is to great work."

In fact for him Masters was for years the American poet of our day in the sense of the old story of the Western village: " Aint you got no amusements round this town? " — " Why, yes, at six o'clock the whore walks." For the novelist the poet walked and the poet was Masters. As late as 1917 he reviewed in *Life, Art and America,* printed in The Seven Arts, the village temper of the country, nominating Masters as poet. And this at a date when there was beginning, it seemed to others, a galaxy of poets: Robinson, Lindsay, Sandburg, Frost, T. S. Eliot among them.* He admired Sandburg, except that he feared he was a reformer. And today it is Dreiser who is the reformer. Of these other poets he did not catch their " deathless ring." Masters on his side in 1912 had some reservations mingled with reverence. After the first three novels he praised Dreiser for his understanding of American fact, his scepticism, his daring, his rendering of life as if it were a circus parade, both tawdry and enticing. . . . But he said to him and of him that if he found a theme to wholly focus his powers and come forth " fused and molten," then he would add to his work that quality that makes art. The comment diversifies the two men — the emotional Dreiser, who yet wished not to lose the parts in the whole; the finely cynical Masters, who seems sometimes overcome by rhythm and loses the sparkle of various voices in a too insistent blank verse.

But Mencken and Reedy for example were not so exacting as to ask of him to be an epic poet in the final sense. They liked him the way he was. And there were many, many others who were grateful to this writer for encompassing the world they lived in and at the same time taking such direct dives into it. Their world, they knew, hung on the kind of financier portrayed with amazing vitality in these two volumes.

One thing is sure — of his books as works of art both praise and censure are plausible. A favorite query with Dreiser, repeated in his writings, used to be: " Why don't you take hold of life? Why are you content to sip it? Why don't you live to the utmost? " A fair enough question, apt to be resented by the victim. On inquiry he was even willing that living to the utmost should be construed as meaning adornment, travel, possession, adulation,

---

* " To me it is a thing for laughter, if not for tears; one hundred and twenty million Americans . . . one hundred and forty years . . . a rich soil . . . silver and precious and useful metals . . . a land amazing in its mountains, its streams, its valley prospects . . . its tremendous cities and far-flung facilities . . . and yet contemplate it. Artists, poets, thinkers, where are they? . . . Since Whitman, one poet: Edgar Lee Masters. . . ."

grabbed or stolen if need be — in other words tangible high voltage. I remember the question put to me and I tried to answer with a counterquestion: " Why don't you go in for quality? There is more intensity in quality, perhaps more drama even." He seemed to be living under the spell of his own hero of that time, the Titan, nearly a victim of the American delusion, size and numbers. Yet he had, to contradict me, the air of a man imbued precisely with quality; and his answer opened a door to it: " I know — you're right — but the country is big; you can't write about it in a small peckish way; there's not time to polish. Later on I intend to rewrite my books, condense them. Just now I have too much to do, too much to put forth. People need it. They need to know things."

The Financier is the one rewritten book, and yet *The Titan* as if to support his point is the more bewildering canvas. Where the pulse beats there is flesh, and where there is flesh there is quality, whether beautiful or not. Until recently deliberate beauty in a woman was a challenge, almost an impropriety; and in a man forbidden; and native poems and pictures were antique notions. As a nation we have used noise and action, songs and dances, not poems or paintings. We have used motion. If a writer has translated this motion into language, impossible to deny him quality or success, however leisurely his form! In *The Financier* and more so in *The Titan* the pulse beats. With the men we see their pores, moustaches, their hands, stomachs and neckties, their ways of walking and talking and cringing and of being brave, and nearly always their eyes. With the women we get their bloom, or their wrinkles, their fragrance or absence of fragrance, their rosettes and ruffles and petticoats and corsets — it was the day of many clothes. And then we get the cross currents and radio messages set up between them, which, in spite of the often explicit, literal language, make actual worlds in the two books. It must be that structural quantity makes quality in its own right, and that size has its seductions, and that mass of detail, when zealous and integral, creates at moments currents of reality by which one leaps the uncharged spaces, the way an electric car leaps crossings. Perhaps Dreiser is the triumph of subject matter. He wrote about what mattered, letting alone the manner, and what mattered mattered enough to him to create manner.

The story of Cowperwood is near to being the history of Charles T. Yerkes, a traction magnate, operating first in Philadelphia and then in Chicago, New York and London. He is nearer to the temper of Yerkes than Clyde in *An American Tragedy* is to the young man of the murder case from which Dreiser drew the framework of that story. Yerkes began life toward the end of the rule of Andrew Jackson, so distasteful to the grandfather of Henry Adams, when it became the federal policy to confide the property of the people to the care of the States, and the policy of the separate States to confide it to the care of brilliant and more often than not unscrupulous individuals. Yerkes became one of these. Dreiser conceives him in the person of Frank Cowperwood as having taken his cue for behavior from a drama he witnessed at the age of ten. In a fish market window near his home in Philadelphia he had watched a lobster in a tank day by day slowly eating a squid, until it was dead. The theme runs through the two books:

"'That's the way it has to be, I guess. . . . That squid wasn't quick enough,' . . . he figured it out. . . . Things lived on each other — that was it. Lobsters lived on squids. . . . What lived on lobsters? Men of course! . . . And what lived on men? Was it other men? Wild animals lived on men. And there were Indians and cannibals. And some men were killed by storms and accidents. He wasn't so sure about men living on men; but men did kill each other. How about wars and street fights and mobs? He had seen a mob once. It attacked the Public Ledger building as he was coming home from school. . . . It was about the slaves. . . . Sure, men lived on men. Look at the slaves. They were men. . . . Men killing other men — negroes. . . . For days and days Frank thought of this and of the life that he was tossed into. . . ."

"From seeing his father count money, he was sure he would like banking; and Third Street where his father's office was, seemed to him the most fascinating street in the world. . . . This medium of exchange, *gold*, interested him intensely. . . ."

So he described a boy's mind, always an easy task for Dreiser. And he accepted the equation of squid and lobster as the law of life. Surely it was and is prominent in the United States where there has been small time or wisdom or too vast spaces to cultivate the delicate relations between people and people and their things, which in other countries have disguised the crudities of battle. Dreiser was at home in the career of Yerkes. Where writers like Upton Sinclair, Thomas Lawson and Ida Tarbell wanted to scare their squid-like readers into seeing what was being taken away from them day by day by the armed lobsters, he wanted most of all to set it down as the dominant fable of our life, which had for virtues lust and enterprise, and for vices cruelty and greed. He seems to say: "Do what you like about it; my job is to make you feel the drama, and the men and women and children involved in it to their marrows."

Particularly, Yerkes began his career at the moment when street railways came into being in the United States. That might in itself have endeared him to the Hoosier, who far from feeling the discord and shrillness of street cars seems to have loved them about as some poets have loved ships or railroads or airplanes. Sister Carrie loved street cars when she came to Chicago; she loved the tinkle of them. And of Cowperwood's predilection Dreiser makes in his succinct way a prose poem:

> "Chicago was growing fast, and these little horse cars on certain streets were crowded night and morning — fairly bulging with people at the rush hours. If he could only secure an octopus-grip on one or all of them; if he could combine and control them all! What a fortune! That, if nothing else, might salve him for some of his woes — a tremendous fortune — nothing else. He forever busied himself with various aspects of the scene quite as a poet might . . . with rocks and rills. To own these street railways! To own these street railways! So rang the song in his mind."

So this novelist, sensitive but not quite a sensualist, is yet an objectivist. He felt the objective song of American merchants' lives, whether it were cars, cement, gas, plumbing, talcum powder, magazines or deodorants. — That song allowed them by their chaste acquisitive ancestors which has made objects instead of states of mind. And he felt the frequent need of the executive of all races and times to acquire as collector the objects of the one power beyond him — creative art. He knew too the necessity of the conqueror for his many, many vanquished women — a trait of Cowperwood's which most critics call exaggerated. But on the contrary it may be that Dreiser has dealt him a conservative number for a magnate of that huge day and temper. I remember a story told me by a Chicago advertising man some ten years ago, who off duck-shooting with a friend of his, president of a great industry whose goods he advertised, said: " Well, Bill, how many women have you got now? " — " Why, Vick, not so many since the war, rents are too high. I can remember the time when I kept twenty or thirty; I don't suppose I got more than twelve or fifteen now and two of them are pals, they share the same room." Call that an exaggeration, outstripping the Titan's score, but it serves to suggest that force is force in the face or behind the back of every code, gratified by number or by arrangement as the talent runs. There is in fact the whispered legend of one of our powerful financiers, supposed to have found his pleasures with choir singers behind organ pipes — a diversion, whether true or not, far more to his credit, I would think, than the mere bleating of religious emotion without earthly outlet. Yet doubtless there will be those to dispute me.

But what distinguishes Dreiser's hero from the other pioneers is a quality of his own, a daring, a candor, a vanity that defies the accepted code. " In every one of his novels he has tried to break the lockstep of society," one critic says of him. I think rather without trying he has run counter to it. Cowperwood was the same kind of man. He takes in his youth for mistress the high-spirited ostentatious child of a business associate, speculator and city-boss, an Irish Catholic only a life-time from the steerage; and he goes to prison not so much for having speculated with city funds as because this Irishman resenting the use he has made of his daughter withdraws his support in the panic following the Chicago fire. Then, when in later years in Chicago Cowperwood grows into something more complicated and exacting, and she remains the same inexperienced exuberant beauty, he deserts her for a long line of women, who perhaps will each one tell him something new and reward him for his fabulous gift of money-making. It is this boldness with women in company with his boldness in bribing city councils and his boldness in taking luck away from other more cautious, more conventional but quite as unscrupulous leading citizens, that finally defeats him. It defeats him in Chicago just as it would have saved him in Paris, Berlin or St. Petersburg. In Chicago they said, " This man is a monster; in addition to other atrocities he seduces women." In Europe they would have said: " This man is a monster, but perhaps we forgive him; he is so picturesque and women love him."

In Chicago they did not want so extravagant a conqueror. The community accepted his gift of a great observatory with which to study and perhaps exploit other planets than the earth; employed his methods to get rid of him, and dispensed with him as a citizen. He is an electron dropping out of the atomic sphere, Chicago, taking his immoderateness with him, and leaving the place the more careful, stingy, colder town that it cared to be. If Dreiser had continued to live there the same fate would have been in store for him, just as it was to be for the town's most distinguished architect, Frank Lloyd Wright, and as it would be for the town's most creative lawyer, Clarence Darrow — both without extraordinary honor in their own city. Chicago is a market place at the heart of a nation, river-threaded, lake-bound, prairie-winded, where gulls fly and pigeons flutter, generating extravagant dreamers; and then killing them.*

To this extent of daring Cowperwood is identified with Dreiser himself. But there is a lock-step element in the street car magnate's life belonging to the common not the uncommon American which makes native the theme of the novel. Where was it that Cowperwood wanted his money and his wife and his house and art collection to take him? Not into really great pursuits and among great friends, but into exactly that chimera which was the

* Read if you can find them Henry Fuller's finely ironic pictures of his day as evidence, *With the Procession*, *The Cliff Dwellers*, Chicago, 1895 and 1893.

undoing of Jennie Gerhardt — Chicago society. And when that was denied him, into New York society; and when that became impossible, into London society. The theme is the tragic one of emptiness, empty houses, empty prestige. " Residential homes " figure like handsome villains in these two novels, and increasingly in *The Titan*, and figure still, in spite of the hero's acquired riches, from the outside looking in. First the mansion in Chicago was futile, then the palace on Fifth Avenue. The rumor of Aileen, mistress before she was wife, and besides " too rich in her entourage, too showy," added to the rumor of a prison term in Philadelphia, defeated him in Chicago, and then in New York. With Aileen " he knew it was useless to try." The young girl who succeeds her, whom Dreiser himself loves, his one heroine except for his mother, but made out of dreams instead of memories, is described as with a high-bred litheness — " She had the air, the grace, the lineage, the blood — that was why. . . ." And although her Kentucky mother had kept a house of assignation in Louisville, the inference is that in the third volume, never yet published, she would accomplish for him social distinction in London. In the story of the Chicago magnate, this happened in the end. A later mistress, it is said, became a friend of the king and queen of England. That is, mistress she was called; although an old-timer, a wheat speculator, impatient at the refinements of Dreiser's Titan, is quoted as exclaiming: " Hell, she wasn't his mistress; she was his daughter! " After that rude myth by one of the Titan's enemies, I thought how perhaps " the great American novel " could not yet have been written, since the extreme American possibility is scarcely ever rumored. Shelley could write *The Cenci,* Coleridge *Christabel,* Gide *The Counterfeiters,* Delteil *The Five Senses,* and Poe long ago *The House of Usher* and *Ligeia,* to cite at random. But perhaps now the American cult of " being nice " has definitely tongue-tied without their knowing it even the most adventurous of our writers. Too late now to sink shafts as deep as the lowest level of the veins of American possibility? We are brave and bold, but ignorant.

51

" I want to chip off one little piece, if I can, of the leaden weight that keeps men's eyes closed to the truth. And yet I shall be only roundly scored for my pains." DREISER

Always in these books Dreiser was doing his utmost to make live the mingled drama of some national characters — Financier, Politician, Journalist, Merchant, Madam, Mistress, Wife, Leading Citizen, Society Queen, Handsome Office, Palatial Mansion. How well did he succeed? Experts contradict each other. Frederic Chapman, English reader for The John Lane Co. who finally published *The Titan* writes high praise of the book as a powerful document, but criticizes his " knowledge of minutiae, that tell in the matter of truth to period ":

"... So as not to render you uneasy I will say that the trifling anachronisms I detected are concerned only with the clothing of the actors . . . the furnishings of some of their rooms."

James Huneker on the other hand does not detect them:

" I confess *The Financier* which I read in Berlin bowled me over. Where and when did you get all the color, the facts, the old streets of Philadelphia where I was born, where I played in Buttonwood Street as a boy! . . . C. T. Y. I knew well, and his wife (No. 2). I'm curious, I confess, to follow their fortunes."

A member of the Chicago Board of Trade writes him asking if he has not served in a broker's office; his knowledge of finance is so accurate. Masters, the academician, rebukes him for the title, and also for the names of the characters. He notes the deliberate scope of the book, and then again some flaw which he gropes to analyse. Although Cowperwood, he thinks, is more valuable and dramatic than Rockefeller or Morgan, he is equally a demi-gorgon, not a Titan acting against the gods for a racial purpose. With an acute ear for names himself, he wonders why Dreiser does not keep a note-book of real names to resort to. . . . He will do greater work, he tells him. . . .

Dreiser it is said never has kept a notebook, secreting his masses of detail in the cells of his mind. His answer to these critics might be as in an interview about *Jennie Gerhardt:* " My one ambition is to conform to the large truthful lines of life. If I do that, no matter if my characters live in Columbus, Ohio, or not, I will be true everywhere." He is in fact an approximatist, qualifying repeatedly with an " or nearly so." But his approximations give the idea in more ample relation to life as life than do some of the more exact imitations of other Americans.

Take for example the fashionable men and women who finally succeed in ostracizing the Cowperwoods from Chicago. They do not always have just the tone of voice or idiom that belonged to them, but they suggest the singular meagerness of what passed for society in that windy city. As in *Jennie Gerhardt* the superstructure is not completed, but here the drift is uncannily real. As for the low-life characters, if first-hand evidence is of value, I had it at an early age as to two who might have served as models. One August evening in the trout season a pair of Chicago aldermen, the famous Bathhouse John and Hinky Dink, appeared at our camp on Lake Superior. They were going to consult the mayor of Chicago who summered at the snobbish hunting and fishing club beyond, and stopped to ask for the trail. Any strangers so far away from the one wagon road to civilization would have surprised us. But these two were city birds, street birds, an apparition in a primeval forest. They admired the beauty of the place, like Mackenty in *The Titan* when he showed Cowperwood to the door after a half bargain between millionaire and boss : " ' A nice moon, that ! ' he added. A sickle moon was in the sky. ' Good night.' "

Their derby hats, diamond scarf pins, city shoes, " Yes-Mam " and " No-Sir " struck illiterately on the elegance of Norway pines, and afterwards we were told they were " very unscrupulous men "; but we liked them, they were an event. They seemed to belong in the midst of affairs, to tell in a flash more news than some of the members of the mayor's club, who were exactly of that element in Chicago hostile to the unorthodox corruption Dreiser pictures in his epic of Big Business. The mayor himself was accepted there, and yet a little squeamishly; he was not a Republican; he was a Southerner; he was not a snob. Reading *The Titan* today I get the same sudden sense of life I got that evening between Salmon Trout River and Bay — life of raw cities, coarse, inept, dangerous, but without which the West of America was not settled. This phase of the settlement, the much praised Willa Cather consistently ignores or misconstrues, in her nice, heartbreaking, humorless elegies for the old days; and so, I think disqualifies herself as authentic. The less polished Dreiser proceeds to the gist of things — to the red yellow and blue which whirling make gray.

Take again the values he knew how to establish in the slight encounters of Cowperwood with two men who might be thought of as titans rather than demi-gorgons. The first of these takes place in *The Financier* in Philadelphia in his twenties:

> " One day he saw Lincoln — a tall, shambling man, long, bony, gawky . . . as he issued from the doorway of Independence Hall. . . . For days the face of Lincoln haunted him, and very often during the war his mind reverted to that singular figure. It seemed to him unquestionable that fortuitously he had been permitted to look upon one of the world's really great men. War and statesmanship were not for him; but he knew how important those things were — at times."

Perhaps Dreiser meant that vaguely Cowperwood felt the importance of this particular war in relation to his own ambitions. It would be a war which under Republican indulgence would gather back into a centralized power of corporations, though never again into a central federal power, the rights of the people, let out to promiscuous individuals under previous Democratic indulgence.* The

---

* That is, if one shakes together Adams' temperate *Degradation of The Democratic Dogma* and Masters' virulent *Lincoln The Man,* one has a right to imagine some such reciprocal American deal occurring in the

second meeting occurred years later with Altgeld in Chicago, the governor with socialist dreams, who, much as he needed money, refused a bribe of $100,000 to give Cowperwood a free hand in his street car schemes. Dreiser describes Altgeld poignantly; Swanson he calls him:
" primarily soft-hearted, sweet-minded, fiery, a brilliant orator, a dynamic presence. In addition . . . woman-hungry — a phrase which sex-starved intellectuals the world over will understand, to the shame of a lying age, that because of quixotic dogma belies its greatest desire, its greatest sorrow, its greatest joy. . . . In a vague way he sensed the dreams of Cowperwood. The charge of seducing women . . . so shocking to the yoked conventionalists, did not disturb him at all. Back of the onward sweep of the generations he himself sensed the mystic Aphrodite."

[Cowperwood defines the situation] " 'The men, as you must know, who are fighting you are fighting me. I am a scoundrel because I am selfish and ambitious — a materialist. You are not a scoundrel but a dangerous person because you are an idealist.'

[And then Dreiser appraises Altgeld's refusal of the bribe] Life rises to a high plane whenever and wherever in the conflict regarding material possession there enters a conception of the ideal."

Here perhaps is an instance of the value and of the disjunction Masters feels — a teasing statement but made not quite out of elements. The conflict cannot be between the material and the ideal — these are but artificial terms — but must be between the finite and the infinite, the unrelated and the related intellect or vision. Here were meetings and then tremendous separations, between the financier and the dreamer in action, of which this Cowperwood on the one hand and Lincoln and Altgeld are fair symbols. The meetings are rarer now and the separations have so deepened that today we have scarcely an adult statesman to keep house for us, and are further than ever from a department of art or of letters in Washington, which might help to fuse the life of a people by officially acknowledging creative unbiased statement — in other words, Art. Dreiser felt the isolation that existed between these big men, but did not here bridge the chasm in words.

---
course of the nineteenth century; or in fact if one but looks about without reading history.

What if anything hampered him in this epic he had planned? Possibly a shade of idealism in the painting of his hero. Not that there is any glossing over of monstrous deeds. He tells without sparing his hero of the destruction of a building overnight, which stood in the way of the magnate's cable-car ambitions, whose owner would not sell at his price. Also of the snaring of a virtuous mayor with a woman hired to seduce him and turn his love letters over to the Financier. And blaming no one, he tells of the revenge of one of the reputable citizens, whose wife had played with the demi-gorgon, and who raised $300,000 to buy Republican victory to defeat " the monster " in the city council. Mencken pronounces Cowperwood " the best picture of an immoralist in all modern fiction — at least since Thackeray's Harry Lyndon." Reedy writes in The Mirror:

> " Cowperwood is large-looming . . . an artist in evil. In *The Titan* there is something mellower than in any of its predecessors. It is a more urbane, more cultured book. . . . Every page shows the effect . . . of those experiences he told us about in . . . *A Traveler at Forty."*

These two were themselves men of affairs immersed in the American drama, like Dreiser, almost enjoying it. But from across the seas came an outcry of English pain from Ford Madox Hueffer, something of an immoralist himself, and a poet, and collaborator with the great Conrad; too amusing not to include, though by length it makes a slight digression:

> " This is the most revolting book I have ever read, the most horrible, the most demoralizing, the most, perhaps immoral. . . . A book is horrible when it can reveal depths of cynical ill-doing such as the reader had never before conceived to live in human nature. . . . Demoralizing, because the book . . . renders vice so attractive and engrossing that it may well damage forever its readers' sense of proportion. . . .
> " I do not know how many seductions there are in this book. I have counted eleven to the credit of the hero; and I see there are some more seductions toward the end. I have not been able to finish the book, it makes me feel sick. . . .
> " It is indeed characteristic of the topsy-turvy morality of the impossible book that the ends for which the hero

employs his disgusting means are comparatively decent ends . . . to give the public better lighting system, better trams. . . . Perhaps Mr. Dreiser is really an Ironist, since all the comparatively reputable figures . . . are . . . with their obsolete methods . . . upholders of obstructive vested interests . . . forced to employ exactly the same disreputable tactics as the hero . . . to cleanse the city of his evil influence.

". . . All I can say is that if the whole of American life is such a thing as is depicted in *The Titan* I would rather see this country ten times subjected to Prussia than allied for ten minutes with, and victorious by aid of the U. S. But I comfort myself . . . the majority of Americans are quite decent people. Yet somewhere in the interior of that vast continent must be lurking a disease . . . or there never could have appeared on the surface such a running sore as the book called *The Titan*.

"Mr. Dreiser is comparatively illiterate, he is sometimes unable to spell, even in the American fashion . . . [but] I have done him an injustice if I have not given the idea that he does present his narrative with at least the skill and raciness of a reporter. It is a pity that he cannot employ his pen upon relatively decent and heroic subjects — say descriptions of Prussians cutting women's throats. That would leave a comparatively pleasant taste in the mouth, but Heavens! here I am writing in favor of accepted Morality! I never thought to do it. There must be something miraculous about *The Titan*."

The book shocked Mr. Hueffer, now Ford Madox Ford, into forgetting some active epochs of history where lucrative " cynical ill doing " and " attractive and engrossing vice " have equaled anything practised by this Chicago demon. Or he was being an advance English alarmist over the growing menace of the Lost Colonies, and in a British way forgetting that his Empire merely preferred to commit crime in heathen colonies, that they might keep their island home intensively decorous and decorative. But also one feels that, like Masters, he was groping for the reason of aesthetic annoyance with the book.

Is it this? Dreiser's plan is miraculously true and strong — a synecdoche of the American empire in the making. It brought a howl of approval and denunciation in critical reviews, not for or against the defeat of democracy, but for or against Dreiser for uncovering a corner of it. It proved that people could read of the financial parabolas that would result in today's tyranny, without the wish or without the power to fight the progress of them. And the moral of the book has the splendor of honesty; it proposes that honesty is not necessarily the best policy for any one man. It would have been the best policy for Hurstwood in *Sister Carrie*. His theft haunted him to suicide, whereas Cowperwood's crimes carried him through to victories agreeable enough to him. Dreiser sees with a terribly clear eye the inevitable differing paths of different tempers. Carrie triumphed; Jennie kept a brave balance; Aileen went down before thwarted passions, before " separations too hard to bear." All this he knew unswervingly. And yet if the book falls short, so that experts like Masters and Ford ask why, isn't it in the choice of colors with which he paints the hero? The matching of tones is not inevitable. Especially he exalts or illumines in Cowperwood two attributes, love of daring and of beauty, thus obscuring the Titan's callousness. Out of his own love for these traits, he treats him a little the way Marlowe treated Tamburlaine, with awe. Take the attitude of this man to the women who love him. Here, I think, Dreiser, camera-like, has followed native truth, but as if satisfied with it has failed to relate it to the rest of life. How could the conqueror have time for elaborate ecstasies? Another less amorous magnate might steal his cherished deal, should he dally too long lasciviously with a woman as the full moon dallies summer nights above earth. Coldness, if not continence, was a superstition among us; with it men were told they would attain a speed and a skill beyond other nations in business or in sports. Whether truth or not, it has served to hold the winner to a youth of sacrifice to victory and to an old age of atrophied senses, or of unstrung nerves. Dreiser knew his hero — " business first." People of high capacity need many things at once, or one thing in many phases. The more sensitized the artist the more he will try to know one thing in many phases, though it be but common language, paint, stone, wood or clay.

Cowperwood going toward circumferences rather than to centers, and cheating himself, since after all the center is the most exclusive point of the circle, is then given a meaning beyond him. At moments Dreiser nearly confuses him with himself at his best, as if this magnate were a rebel defying the world for an exciting lucid cause, instead of for a mere fortune and entrance into established society. He gives him words he would not have said: " All of us are in the grip of a great creative impulse." Or had he said them, he would not have understood them, since in spite of his collection of jewels, paintings and ladies, he was not curious enough to analyse creation. Creation is that state in life or art, which being original and primitive, new-born, needs few stage properties earned or stolen. Creation is a state of mind or state of energy. To borrow an enticing phrase from physics, the electron jumping to a different orbit, " the atom gives out energy in the form of light."

As if hypnotized by Cowperwood, here he emphasizes certain values at the expense of others, which elsewhere he has been quick to balance. Cowperwood we are told never read; but we are not told that of course he never read because books might bring him face to face with apparitions that would shake his faith in himself. Safer were his cameos and coins and Bouguereaus and Rembrandts, high-priced and silent. None the less here, so far, is the one portrait of an American financier resembling in grandeur a Rembrandt or Titian or Tintoretto. We see him in volume as Chicagoans of that day remember him, a costly enigma and magnet, driving with his red-headed Aileen south on Michigan Avenue toward the palatial home, everyone turning to say: " Look, there is Yerkes," almost no one bowing or waving.

Moreover to be synchronous it is important to say that in the very years of making *The Titan* Dreiser was writing *The Girl in the Coffin, The Blue Sphere, In the Dark;* and would a few years later write *The Hand of the Potter,* where the edge of misery and poverty appears like tattered velvet. Out of this period too come stories of people neither rich nor poor in relation to the theme; *Free, Married, The Lost Phoebe, Chains, Fulfilment* owe their drama not to an extreme of outward circumstance but to inner moods. And, as if this novelist were himself sated with terrifying display, he follows *The Titan* with *The " Genius "* — an heroic project to relate a character, high-powered and sensitive, to the welter of unrelated elements that compose American society. Once to the question: " Did you ever know a self-made Croesus whom you liked as well as anyone," his answer was: " No, I don't think so. I love delicacy too well. The making and holding of great wealth destroys delicacy." And again he said of a short story written at this date: " Of all my stories for me *The Old Neighborhood* comes nearest to art — a thing of mist, which art should be."

We have lived with three religions in our time: the Christian religion going on in churches; the religion of Money going on in banks; the religion of Communism going on in Soviet Council halls. Dreiser, " incurable individualist," he has called himself, repelled in childhood by the Catholic religion, learned to repudiate it and all substitutes for it. Then he imagined he walked alone, and he has more than most people. Yet at some point, perhaps almost unconsciously did he feel too lonely? Or else fighting the enemy, did germs of the enemy enter into him, so that he veered slightly toward the impersonal religion of Money? Today, it is said, repelled by excessive Capitalism, he is veering toward the still more impersonal religion of Communism. If that is true he has ceased for the moment to walk the lonely way of art. When he left *Sister Carrie,* to live at all, he was forced away from an intensely fresh, personal, detached point of view into public issues. The cold fingers of impersonality sometimes operate in the language of later works as they operate in American streets and houses. Then as often he has gone back to an intimacy with himself; tenderly in *Jennie Gerhardt,* thriftily in the rewritten *Financier,* nervously and like fire in *The Hand of the Potter,* terribly in *An American Tragedy.* His later life has been a traveling back and forth between cloisters and forums. The restlessness of this commuting marks his work, without yet defeating him; as it has defeated American society. Some strangeness in him has swung the balance his way.

52

" Art is the stored honey of the human soul, gathered on wings of misery and travail. Shall the dull and the self-seeking and the self-adverting close this store on the groping mind." DREISER

Yet this travel back and forth between market and home was not entirely his choice. He wanted fame, but he wanted it through his works, not through having to fight for them. The same thing may be true of many apparently forensic men; of Mencken and Ezra Pound possibly. The effort to adjust themselves to their environment, Pound to the one he left behind him, resulted in an effort to adjust the environment to them. Or perhaps their case is suggested in a boy's defence of a friend, denied him because he taught him "dirty words," the kind prevailing in Twain's Elizabethan dialogue. The defence was: "I don't think he's really bad; you don't understand him; he's just shy."

Maybe these great rebels have been "just shy," and trying to make themselves at home in a too cold environment. To Dreiser's shyness, if he had it, was added recurring hostility from the outside, and from those of whom he might have expected support, his publishers. More times than any other contemporary, in his thirty years of writing, he is on record as having to turn from creative work to battle with publishers rather than compromise; the last war was as late as 1931 with Hollywood producers. In 1914 at the date of completing *The Titan,* had it not been for obstruction from the outside, he appeared to be on the road to an ease which might have tempered and seasoned him as it has some European giants. He was fast writing about "life as it is," and with success of esteem. *Jennie Gerhardt, The Financier, A Traveler at Forty,* were bringing fame more than notoriety, and were helping to change the minds of editors and reviewers. *The Financier* still caused anger of the old kind: " A work marred by the representation of sexual passion ! " " Such things be . . . their contemplation is unprofitable and unpleasant." But, for example, after the reviews of the travel book, one scarcely ever hears any more of Mrs. Grundy or of " immature readers " as factors in the publishing game. Mrs. Grundy watching over her brood of young people was being relegated to the church magazines; that is, until the male of her, John Sumner and his vice society, came along to revive her fights and make a last stand for polite hypocrisy.

The appearance of *The Titan* released a new outcry against " liaisons " outside of marriage. Axiomatically they were said to be " gross, sordid, ugly, unpleasant "; while those within marriage, one infers, thought of as nearly divested of " sexual passion," were equally refined and spiritual. And reviewers too were still scandalized by the offers of American truth as reading matter. Russian, Swedish, German, French was acceptable; but the truth must not be American. Yet now those most outraged fell under the spell of realism; the book was " masterly, fearless, colossal "; they were left " gasping ": " He never spares the truth, but nevertheless it is a great work," one of them said.

And in other ways fertilization came to Dreiser. Never really without women as *This Madness* and *A Gallery of Women* suggest, now in Chicago hunting the material of *The Titan,* he found a girl to live with for longer, he says, than any other woman between the days of his first wife and his last. She appears in *This Madness* as Sidonie and perhaps in *The Titan* as Stephanie. The child of a Jewish father and New England mother, she had beauty and talent, and was pliant and stimulating. After she was gone " there was no one woman," he says. " There might have been one housekeeper one day and a different one the next. I lived alone, really." Together they made the apartment at 165 West Tenth Street, his address for four or five years. Two long rooms, tall windows from ceiling to floor, finely divided so that they offered the rare light of a century ago; a pair of marble fireplaces where coal burned; a bare grey floor wide-planked, again as of a century ago, and an air of order and space — this house is not forgotten today by those who went there to talk of life and art in America and other countries, and propose schemes, journals, and societies to promote life and art, or to promote themselves or Dreiser, or by those who rang at the door to thank him for *The " Genius "* or it might be for *Plays Natural and Supernatural, A Hoosier Holiday, Free and Other Stories, The Hand of the Potter, Twelve Men, Hey-Rub-A-Dub-Dub* — books belonging to this period. The place was not, I imagine, a temple like Stieglitz' 291 Fifth Avenue. James Oppenheim tells how Dreiser said to him: " Every age has its great man; I am the one of this age." But I think he is rarely as confiding as that. And besides there were too many in those days to dispute him, to make unreserved satellites. Perhaps too he attracted sceptics. But that Tenth Street could be on occasion a lodge for talk is traditional; Dreiser folding and unfolding his handkerchief, and talking when he wanted to luminously without a sign of the diffuseness that readers find in his books. The first picture I ever had of this novelist was from Masters in perhaps 1916, who back from New York described an afternoon there: A bottle of gin between them, snow outside, coals inside, that peculiar light through the Victorian windows, and a world of talk and laughter.

And to this address came like bonuses, enviable letters. It is rare to see so many addressed to one man. They had come before, and would come afterwards when he moved to California, and then back to New York to various addresses, and finally after *An American Tragedy* to the more cathedral Rodin Studios in upper New York. Dreiser is fastidious in his own letters, as he is in some of his poems. Brevity and design mark them. And apparently the magnet of fertile mind operated especially in these years between him and those who wrote to him.

Mencken's envelopes are rarely dated, but they appear to have flowed between 1910 and 1925. Many of them if opened in the morning might have seemed as ethereal as champagne for breakfast or a cocktail before noon, or if they came in the afternoon as agreeable as beer in Munich or Rhine wine on the Rhine between Cologne and Heidelberg. Whether he hopes all Englishmen will roast in hell, or declares he will name his next child Hindenberg, whether boy or girl, or proposes that since suffragettes are enlisting for the war and this will lead to immorality, he and Dreiser should go as midwives, or congratulates Dreiser on his dying words — " Pontius Pilate, I come " — and submits his own last words, too Saxon to pass the censor even today, which Dreiser is to run to the window with before closing his eyes; or begs him to be more diplomatic and not consort with dirty-haired villagers, tin-pot revolutionaries, sophomore advanced thinkers, jitney socialists and other vermin, thus ruining his chances with serious citizens; or tells him the prophecy of the most gifted colored psychic in Maryland that Dreiser will live to a great old age, heart, lungs, kidneys, brain intact, senile changes visible in but one respect; or implores him not to use general delivery, it is a pickpocket's address; or asks why in hell he does not sign his letters, he sells his autographs at 50¢ apiece; or suspects he is a kept man from his stationery; or tells him that every tourist coming back from the Coast has some tale about his Roman levities — " Yesterday I heard that you have gone over to the Theosophists, and are living at Point Loma in a yellow robe, with hasheesh blossoms in your hair . . ."; or asks him to do an article for his new journal, wherein he may call the Methodists by name and call the Baptists the sewer-rats of God; or deplores *The Hand of the Potter* as beyond the pale of production and a poor play at that; or corrects his spelling " the prize is spelled ' Nobel ' not ' Noble ' "; or tells him not to worry over his future, that the ground is solid under him; or gives the news that he heard Billy Sunday the other night, that it was in brief " a convention of masturbators — of such is the kingdom of heaven "; or assures him he will go after his enemies in his next: — " That old bitch is forever at the bat " — " I shall come to the case of the old cow, she is a dirty old slut " — " I will take up the professors as they come along." — " On with the shrapnel, ahead with the machine guns ! " — These letters usually signed " yours in Christ," on occasion " Alloysius Hohenzollern " or " Gustav of Magdala," or " Jesus Baumgartner," are sparkling, wicked, hilarious and serious. Under them runs a current which always is grave and therefore crucial, of two conflicting tempers: Mencken, scholar, wit, protestant, the man of the library in his correct house in Baltimore, of the editorial battle field in New York, of drinking bouts at Luchow's, Knickerbocker, Astor, Algonquin: and Dreiser, the prowler in dark, curious, wilder places, and lighted centers as well; mystic and catholic, boorish and compassionate, approximate and precise by turns. They met at cross roads of realism and enterprise, and kindled bonfires there for fun. In later years perhaps the novelist got tired of having to laugh at himself and the critic of having always to praise another.

Masters' letters in the years 1912 to 1919 were more reverent, often like wine in praise and phrase. It is a loss that, possibly out of a sense of the sacredness of personal relations, he has refused permission to cite from these letters. They possess a devotion to art, and friendship, fragments of which would give solace to lonely readers in a chaotic land. He writes as his friends of those years have heard him speak, exhorting the few heroic spirits to go on even " in the contempt of men," that is of other Americans. Among heroes Dreiser in those days was important to him. He bemoans the country as a dusty chaos of Sunday schools and evangelists. Only great art or great wit can change it, and perhaps not that. As for Chicago, it was a city of despair, as it has been for others too sensitive, too uprooted to endure it without a diminution of creative strength. Some have kept still or even whistled for courage; some like Henry Fuller have spoken in a clear but scarcely audible voice. Others like Masters have cried out in talk and in poems or novels, and then have abandoned their city for other more hopeful lands.

He brightens when he writes that people come around since *Spoon River,* interesting people, but Masters never brightens for long; bores come too and women who want to be refitted. Masters is a poet of rain and fog, dreaming of sun-bright objects across hills. He exhorts Dreiser to keep his blasphemous edge, assuring him he has 'em all beat " and rejoices like a true son of Belial thereat." Of these almost tearful instructions, up to date Dreiser has followed a fragment. In 1931 certainly " in the contempt of men " he will be seen fighting the lowbrow hardboiled decree of Hollywood magnates as to what they cared to make of *An American Tragedy,* his book, not theirs; going on, that is, before the jeers and snickers of the New York movie critics, who appear to champion the Jesuits of Paramount. Or at least they go on record as totally indifferent to an issue concerning them as much as Dreiser — the integrity of American letters.

Then from 1911 until 1920, the year of his death, there are from time to time whimsical serious notes from William Marion Reedy in St. Louis — a flavor to them. They had in common as friends Masters and the young Harris Merton Lyon. *Spoon River Anthology* first appeared in Reedy's Mirror, and was first praised in New York by Dreiser. In 1915 at 165 West Tenth Street Masters read these village epitaphs to a company of literati, New Yorkers who had to credit Chicago with a real poet, indifferent as that city was to the glory of it. Reedy writes of Masters from the heights of near old age:

"I hear from Masters every two or three days and he is still conjugating the verb *amare* with the usual conjunctive calamities that are the accompaniment of such grammatical exercises. It's fine to be beyond Good and Evil. Behold me! I'm 57 and immune to temptation."

"A letter from Masters this morning [he had gone to New York " to participate poetically in the Lowell centenary exercises "]. Little about Lowell, lots about lovely ladies. That man should adopt for his middle name that of the mythical husband of Sappho — Penifer. But this is the voice of envious senectitude."

Then intense letters about Lyon after his death in 1916, with pity for unfulfilment, and praise to Dreiser for trying to collect and get published Lyon's stories and essays. After devoted work on their part it appears the manuscript was snatched back by Lyon's wife, advised not to trust these friends: they might be self-seeking. So the burial perhaps in oblivion of another young American, who came and went too soon, killed by America. Or that is the verdict of those who have read his two books *Graphics* and *Sardonics,* published at Reedy's expense. In fact Reedy appears to have always published in this way; his famous Mirror never soaring into dollars. Here are fragments from different letters:

". . . Back from the wilds of Wisconsin . . . I am in hearty sympathy with you on the proposal to print Lyon's best work. I tried to help him with some of the publishers. . . . I don't blame them much however. I printed 1000 copies of *Graphics* and I think I have sold less than fifty. . . . I think the trouble is with the public and its ten-reel mind."

". . . I was exceedingly fond of that boy and admired his work this side of idolatry — a great man — all too early dead."

". . . Poor Lyon — my God how he burned for fame . . . based on excellence; how he scorned the idea of working for the market. . . . Our last meeting was poisoned by a clash between two women over something the nature of which I was never able to make out. Lyon and his wife decamped from my house — Lyon with his doom on him (as I knew from the doctors). . . . Damn women. . . . But what are we going to do without them?"

". . . It hurt me to read those things — reviving the man — the boy — himself. . . . His very soul bared. . . . And mostly he's in agony. . . . I think there is too much morbidity in the stories. . . ."

". . . I have read *Twelve Men.* . . . Your study of Lyon is wonderful. I was interested also in your study of poor Dick Wood. . . . You know Dick went all to pieces and died as a morphine fiend. . . ."

[and the last letter] "Your phone is a damned delusion. Eleven times I've tried to get you in two weeks. . . . Now I hope you don't think I'm going away without seeing you for I'm not. . . . I'm damned tired, stale, flat and unprofitable. . . . I was thrice at the village in to see my protégé Barney Galant, and had some drinks, but drinks don't help."

Like poems that don't lie these letters follow the arch of lives and fall into sadness with the passing of youth and hope. There is one from Lyon himself, still young but tired, thanking him for trying to get him a publisher:

"It is serious with me. I would write long books if I could [with] the encouragement of a publisher of weight.

It seems to me we are all that way. Balzac, the man of 'incomparable power' would never have kept so assiduously at the grind if his head had not also been filled with the sound of fame ringing in his ears. . . . Some men are blessedly narrow enough to be devoted to their Art; some are silly enough to be able to warm up an affection for Posterity. A common strain in me prevents the possibility of such amours. . . . Not having [a publisher] I sometimes even cease to think at all and drift with the days, letting a pagan materialism suffice me. Even though I itch with longing and disdain, I say, 'After all enough has been written.'

. . . Reedy is sending you at my request his St. Louis Mirror. The Farmhouse series, unsigned, is mine."

Masters and Reedy and this little known young man seem like three of the many advance messengers of the war that wages now between nature and machinery, in which letters are not burned as at Alexandria but are lost in a great oblivion. Impossible for example to get today more than a rumor of works of Lyon,* Reedy is a forgotten Samaritan. Masters is incompletely published and his poems are elegies of such death. The New York Tribune in 1931 speaks of him as " an unknown lawyer from Springfield, Illinois."

Then there were other friends who were gayer. There was George Sterling, the California poet and libertine, who committed suicide in 1927 — a mind enough in the major key, one would think, to be conserved by publishers. He belongs in the end of this book, a friend between 1920 and 1927, but he belongs too in this chapter which is partly designed as a profile of how concentrative American genius can be, and how almost wholly dissipated it has been by its public. As if they were careless children emptying into sand fine pitchers of elixir and then smashing the jugs or deserting them to the weather of beaches or of vacant lots. Sterling was the last and longtime friend of that intolerant wit, Ambrose Bierce, although Bierce cursed him in a letter before he went to be

* It is the same with many others who unlike Lyon achieved fame. Most of the novels of Henry Fuller, for example, are out of print. *Quicksand*, by Hervey White, is out of print, a book which Dreiser puts among the great books of the world. Bierce and Crane are hard to get. — The list of lost artists is long.

lost in Mexico in 1916. Equally it seems his heart included so opposite a soul as Dreiser's, and then as different tempers as Edwin Markham, Robinson Jeffers, Mary Austin, Gertrude Atherton, Witter Bynner, Arthur Ficke, Upton Sinclair, Sinclair Lewis, Mencken and Masters, many of whom would clash if they met in the same room. Sterling apparently went to the last barriers of his nature in pursuit of pleasure and pain, so that wherever the heart beat he was at home. He was an extravagant, and loved Dreiser for extravagant devotion to life. He writes him first in 1920 to Los Angeles, where he lived three years, to invite him to his " cool grey city of love," " not quite the city it was, but the daughter of the vine, though shy, can still be found by the faithful. And there are other daughters." Then follow letters addressing him as Theodore, Beloved Mastodon, Dear Megatherium, Beloved Brontesaurus, Dear Titanosaurus, praising his work, telling of escapades, discussing ultimate answers to chaos; asking and thanking him for a preface to his *Lilith*, and for help to a friend, a young novelist; sending him a ballad, sonnets, satires; in the end thanking him for a gift of money — he lived as he could. Here are extracts:

". . . I've been rereading *The Titan, Sister Carrie,* and *The Hand of The Potter.* . . . How you tower above the snipes and the tirmites. Mencken though he puts up a good fight for you, doesn't give you justice by a long shot. One has to think in centuries to do that." . . .

" I was in the lily pond again, last month, this time with a beautiful blonde. The police arrested us, but fortunately we got our clothes on before they appeared. . . . They took us, at my request, to the old superintendent of the Park, who though in bed, had us released. But it got in the papers. If I'd had a clipping I'd enclose it."

". . . I am eager that *Lilith* should have a good sale, not for any monetary reasons, but to justify faith in it. . . . A foreword from you would ' make ' it and me. . . .
" It takes real nerve to praise a man and then ask a great favor. . . ."

". . . The 'Tragedy' came back safely with your inscription. . . . Heart does not often accompany head to the degree it does with you . . . wish you were with me today by this blue bay.

" I am here with Red Lewis, who like me is in the front

rank of your admirers. But he is upstairs sleeping off last night's jag, and is oblivious to all this pure beauty."

". . . Thanks, a million of them! I knew you'd not fail me. . . .

" As to the philosophy of the poem . . . so keen a mind as yours can discern that Lilith . . . has utterly the better of the argument (. . . the crux of the poem), yet I have put into the mouth of Trancred the best that can be said for the optimist, and many readers will believe that is right. I think that is the better way as denoting the eternal balance between good and evil (pleasure and pain).

". . . Schopenhauer claims that pain is the only reality, and it is indeed the greatest one. Nevertheless, pleasure is more than the mere absence of pain, as witness the violence and individuality of the sex-ecstasy, for instance."

". . . You and Mencken are my sole inducements to a trip to New York. Next year I may make it. . . . Here are fine bright minds in this sex-mad city and I have to waste most of my creative energy on 4th rate short stories under a nom-de-plume. . . ."

" Next year " he was gone by his own hand from sex-mad cities to where " Unheard but of the spiritual ear, — Endures the challenge of the timeless foe — . . . An icy music, mercilessly clear." Two other verses sent Dreiser bridge the country from West to East, or crudely so. One is a jingle; a lumber-jack in the wilderness yearns for civilization, " For a little jazz on the vic," " a jolt of rot-gut rye " and a " whore in her perfumed bed." The other is addressed to a New York critic, modern ten years ago:

"O diligent small Jew! Behold in me
. . . That sluggard once commended to the ant . . .
. . . (Now why the ant? the flea is busier),
Yet marvelling is in me, as I gaze and note
. . . Your lore in magazine and book
Revealing how you love some brother bard
. . . In terms that men are very joyous for.
I, haply sitting on the poor-house porch
Shall see you pass in your swift limousine,
And weeping, cry: O diligent small Jew! "

The reader may object that now I am far afield of my theme, but it is not so. The diligent critic had undoubtedly dismissed Sterling as out of date. Yet these letters show him as timeless in the possession of faith and lust, whereas the selfsame critic, now out-dated, may very possibly have crumbled to pieces out of diplomacy. The moral of it is that fashions like all the devil's decrees are salutary, if revolt is allowed to follow them. If the various fleas and poets of the day had really exchanged goading, the blade of Irony might at length have appeared, and have given edge to the national temper. It was the time for Americans to fuse, and they let the moment pass. Now we must wait again for no one knows how many years for Civilization.

Other personalities appear out of a profusion of letters from vivid men. John Maxwell, dating from the Chicago Globe days writes from time to time salty news; once on receipt of the manuscript of *A Book About Myself:*

"I also took the liberty to cross out about four lines in which I was made to inveigh against the virtue of women and the honor of men. . . . There is no chance to live on earth and express our sentiments publicly. However I have let the sentiment stand that I consider 999 men out of a thousand bastards. I won't renig on that. But a fellow just can't lambast womanhood generally. . . .

"Did you know that the nation is trembling in the throes of a . . . political revolution. . . . It will never win except through bloodshed. What we are hearing now is preliminary tremors of the mighty quake that will end in the destruction of our present government. Yet they are so blind they cannot see. Instead of cooperating, they advise killing and imprisonment, physical torture of one kind or another. But it has always been so."

After the same book came many reminiscences from journalists, rich, failures, venerable and middle-aged. They had known these St. Louis characters, and testified jubilantly to Dreiser's accuracy. One of them tells of a night spent wandering with Reedy about the resorts of St. Louis, when his wife was dying, a Catholic married after divorce; and he was denied their house so that she might receive sacrament and enter heaven. "The things Reedy said to me that night I shall never forget," ran the letter. These men contradict critics who have called Dreiser authentic as novelist but loose as biographer. Their anecdotes are sometimes epitaphs, so many of these figures dying violent, dissolute or strange deaths. They are letters that have, as in some of Masters' poems, that almost toneless monotone and twang of Western voices, trained to be afraid of intimate statement, and lowering the voice for scandal, even in letters. The voices take you to sentiment and jokes and sudden cackle on village porches summer nights, to leaves of trumpet vines and wild grape vines, to big yards and Main Streets back West, even where the writers have graduated to cities.

Thomas B. Mosher, the first American publisher of physically aesthetic books, usually small reprints of the classics, is one of these and comes as an unexpected find in Dreiser files. In a letter to Reedy his voice is mellow and rustic and breaks the monotone. He speaks of a Mirror review of *The Financier:*

" It is certainly, Bill, beyond me to express the admiration I feel for a cuss like yourself who can take up his pen and sling liquid lightning. . . . This you have done, my son, and . . . I have only to say you struck it to the heart. I greatly admired Clayhanger and yet Arnold Bennett is not in it with Theodore Dreiser. Old man your head for once is bigger than your heart and it would be hard to chase that fat fantastic heart of yours into all the holes and corners it has probably crept since the days when you were a newspaper boy and I was a damned poor clerk in St. Louis in '79."

Then there are just as many letters with a literary tone of voice; naturally cultured among the older men; fashionably rough-neck among the younger. Among them are Alexander Harvey, George P. Jenks, W. E. Williams of Kansas City, W. H. Wright (S. S. VanDine), Charles Yost, Thomas Boyd of St. Paul, Charles Fort, Max Eastman, Edward Smith, John Barry, Fremont Older out in San Francisco, Sherwood Anderson, Frank Harris, John Powys, Ben Hecht, Jim Tully, Burton Rascoe, Matthew Josephson, David Karsner, Dudley Nichols, Sol P. Carson and Claude Bowers who writes:

" Have just read your opinion of the intelligentsia . . . of our delectable city in the World. I have long known there was something miserably wrong with our Best Minds for the most part. . . . You have hit the nail on the head. They are men in petticoats."

" Spinsters in trousers " might have driven the nail out of sight. But the intellectuals of this correspondence are not in this class. In fact a marvelous vigor operates in these letters back and forth between Dreiser and their writers — some of these men so grateful, they insist, for his books and for his " blasphemous," fearless integrity. It gives them courage to go on. Perhaps only Ben Hecht writes with tongue slightly in cheek, a little patronizing, more inquisitive than sincere — a harbinger of today's attitude toward seriousness. Dreiser on his side appears in this correspondence as one repeatedly solicited to find an editorial job or to find a publisher or to write a preface or to inscribe a book for friend or stranger. Almost always a later letter discloses that he has done his utmost; or sometimes it is he who offers help on his own initiative. Sherwood Anderson writes him in 1916:

" Some one once told me of the difficulty you have had with publishers so perhaps you will sympathize with me . . . I want you to read one of my novels. . . .

" I have written four long novels and none of them have been published . . . I am nearly forty years of age. . . ."

". . . I must personally thank you for your . . . article in Seven Arts Magazine. It sets forth as nothing I have ever read . . . the complete and terrible fact of the wall in the shadow of which American artists must work.

" To any of us here in America the one really hopeful note of our times is your own stout figure pounding at the wall.

" Our hats off to you, captain."

And Charles Fort repays Dreiser's find of a publisher for him with fantastic letters out of pools of friendship, and the invention of a " heathen cocktail " which he names after Dreiser. To some laymen he appears to make fiction out of scientific lore and rumor, and appears to believe in a land above the earth, complementary to it, from which rain frogs, blood, meteors and other phenomena, and occasionally ambassadors in the likeness of men. Perhaps Dreiser is related to him on the side that seeks to surround the network of facts with explicit mysteries. Though " realist " he has paid homage to a number of miraculous doctrines — Christian Science, mental telepathy, spiritualism. Have they been the more plausible to this child from " credulous " Indiana because of that background of Pagan-Catholic ghouls, saints and devils? Or has it been quite simply his wish to propose imaginatively that " anything may be true," — a proposal, isn't it, that Arthur Eddington, the physicist, makes mathematically. . . . And then from that premise does he sometimes favor, again like Eddington, unproved sequences . . . ? The cocktail is made after this recipe:

" You take a glass of beer and put a live goldfish in it — instead of a cherry or olive or such things that occur to a commonplace mind.

" You gulp.

" The sensation of enclosing a live organism is delightfully revolting. I think it's immoral. I have named it the Dreiser cocktail."

53

"The pains lie among the pleasures like sand in rice, not only bad in themselves but spoiling the good." HERMAN MELVILLE

These letters tell of time crowded but unhurried, of moments of fulfilment. Then in most cases the liaison ends, not always by death; often by that " changefulness " which, he says, " is mine and life's," and we get imitations of the final change death. Today on his sixtieth birthday an interviewer quotes him in words that chill the blood, perhaps to shock her and yet palpably his words: " I have never wanted friends, and have never been in a position where I didn't have to fence myself in." One wonders from signs like this if his " changefulness " is not in part another word for fear of criticism. Fact is, the years have cut him off from some of these finest intimacies. Is that why he disdains them now? Mencken explains it casually: " Oh well, New York is a washer-out of friendships." And it used to be repeated, " He stands weather-beaten and lonely . . ."; yet then and always as these letters show, and friends and ex-friends bear witness, he was living many lives and nearly as many deaths, their number dependent on changefulness — a chain-stitch life of people. The fire and ashes of them appear in his pages.

In five years, 1914 to 1919 Dreiser published eight books * all of them luminous, that is, giving forth light, if read faithfully; each of them deeply concerned with why and how we live. And less concerned with how to say it. In the same years, however " weather-beaten and

* *The Titan*, 1914; *The " Genius,"* 1915; *Plays of The Natural And The Supernatural*, 1916; *A Hoosier Holiday*, 1916; *Free And Other Stories*, 1918; *The Hand Of The Potter*, 1919; *Twelve Men*, 1919; *Hey Rub-A-Dub-Dub*, 1919.

lonely," requests came to him for articles from people as various as Ray Long of The Cosmopolitan, Max Eastman of the New Masses, David Karsner of The Call, and on special cross-roads James Oppenheim and Waldo Frank of Seven Arts, Frank Harris owner of Pearson's, and on a main cross-road Mencken and Nathan of The Smart Set and The American Mercury. He is in these years a terrific lesson in energy; a nucleus for people so foreign one to the other that it is fabulous to believe they all wanted him. He responded with story or article, sometimes to be turned down even by solicitors, who had their public to think of. But nothing deterred him. A wraith of a story, *The Lost Phoebe*,* was sent out a dozen times through two agents from 1912 to 1915 before finally The Century accepted it, and later Famous Short Stories reprinted it. Its first agent wrote that in his opinion it was useless to send it to The Saturday Evening Post — the mere sketch of an insane tottering old man, who can't believe his wife is dead; and he wanders calling her until he dies. The Post, Mr. Reynolds reminds him, and it could not have been news, " prefers stories of youth and happiness or of action." But Dreiser insists that the Pollyanna temple shall have its chance of refusal, which it takes. In 1918 however this same journal prints *Free*,* more gloomy and harsher than *The Lost Phoebe*. William Griffiths of The National Sunday Magazine would like " mighty well " to have something from Dreiser, but if it is " sad " he doubts that he wants it; he would like one of his " strong stories " like the one about a railroad section-boss he had seen in McClure's. Colliers begs him to put " plot " and " emotional interest " into his work. Douglas Z. Doty of Century, accepting *The Lost Phoebe*, warns him they can't publish it at once on account of war news being " rather grim "; their " only chance for lightness is in the fiction." So the spectres of the Howells days, Sweetness and Gladness join now with " Pep " and continue to pronounce their rancid curse upon our letters. In 1916 however the Cosmopolitan pays $600 for *Married* * — a brief contrast of city and village, and of how life is cruel, turned to light in two people's hearts. In 1918

* *Free And Other Stories.*

they print *The Second Choice* * as desolating as Tchekov at his greyest. Sewell Haggard accepts an article for Hearst's for $500. The Sunday New York Tribune prints a story called *Love* which loses the editor his job. So, patiently Dreiser places his wares for money or for next to nothing, $30 once from The New Republic for a story. He submits short plays, but editors high-brow and low-brow feel that " dramatic material is not available for magazine use," or that the plays are too " psychologic " to be dramatic.

He had to count on the lively editors of Smart Set and the Little Review to see these plays in print and on a future life to see most of them on the stage.† Mencken and Nathan regret repeatedly they can't pay him more; they are involved in a battle themselves to " put some genuine intelligence into that decrepit and maudlin sheet." They submit to months without salary in the cause of national exhilaration, and finally give up in favor of a fresh start, their Mercury. The Smart Set remains for all their effort " as righteous as a decrepit and converted Madame," Mencken writes. Yet not before they have published a number of novelties including the first stories of James Joyce to be printed in America.

So it went, this battle for lively letters; a formidable lesson in endurance, for which men appear too tired to-day or spineless. In addition, with Dreiser sales were crucial; he lived by what he wrote, counting nickels, riding in subways and street-cars; even the 5th Avenue bus was a luxury. Today he praises hardship, a spur to good work, he says. But sometimes perhaps the repeated melancholy of it dulls the sharpest " blasphemous edge." His record is the more grilling when one considers the handicap of at least three major battles with his publishers in these few years, in one of which Mencken was a devoted ally.

The first engagement came in the winter of 1915. Harper's had accepted and printed *The Titan*. It was all

---

* *Free And Other Stories.*

† In 1917 *The Girl In The Coffin* was skilfully produced by the Washington Square Players and in 1921 *The Hand Of The Potter* was execrably played for only two weeks by the Provincetown Players. Otherwise Dreiser's plays have never reached the commercial footlights.

but bound. Then out of a cloudless sky, the Doubleday incident repeated itself. Over the telephone the book was withdrawn, and with no new reason given; " a bit too strong " was all they could say — Messrs Duneka, Hitchcock and Leigh, now dead. The remaining editors of that day, Mr. Wells and Mr. Hoyns, can remember nothing of the affair. Mr. Hoyns, when asked, agrees that it was curious for a firm to go so far and then retract; he can remember no other incident of the kind in his connection with Harper's. Mr. Thomas Wells thinks it was due to the typesetters, one of whom, he remembers, came to Mr. Duneka's desk next to his, with some of the proof sheets, and the advice not to publish *The Titan*. His colleagues in the printing room had all agreed that the book was obscene and objectionable. Apparently then some $2,000 (or at least that is what Dreiser says he eventually had to give them for the plates) was jeopardized to save the delicate feelings of the typesetters. Rumor however had it differently at the time. It was hinted that a would-be ambassador to England blocked the way — the very Colonel Harvey who back in 1910 " did not want to meet " the author of *Jennie Gerhardt*. The last mistress of the great Yerkes, now fashionable in London, or at least with king and queen, could, it seemed, be more valuable to the Colonel than a great novel could be to his publishing house. Others said that a Chicago newspaper might sue for a libelous rendering of one of its founders. So two years' work fell like a card house. Nothing to do but to send the book elsewhere. Mitchell Kennerly likewise would not touch it. It seemed that he too wished to stand in well with the favorite of the traction magnate, who, it was thought, resembled the young and beguiling Berenice, last in the list of the Titan's loves. A legend had it that Dreiser himself was infatuated with this princess of American subversive royalty. This he disclaims: " I admired her, she had that mysterious trait — style. If she gave a dinner or a luncheon it was staged like a play, but there was no chance to know her; she was too much the diplomat and wrapped herself in importance. She received from a green onyx couch covered with furs and brocades."

Letters and telegrams fly between Dreiser and friends of his on the one hand and the publishers on the other, most of them interested but scared. The " lovable " B. W. Dodge tries to help him, with the suggestion of Dodd, Mead & Co., but takes it back:

". . . if . . . too strong for Harper's it would surely be too rich for D. M. and Co. . . . The entire family are very pious Presby's. There is not a black sheep in the entire flock which is a large one. The only book they ever published which shaded the Ten Commandments was " Pam " . . . and they have regretted it ever since.

Also, Dodge writes, he " is strictly sober " now and would like the novelist to go back into the publishing business with him. Dreiser does this with the loan of some money. Not many years after Dodge died, owing him some thousands of dollars dating back to the *Sister Carrie* returns, the loss of which he says he never regretted, so much he loved him. D. Z. Doty of The Century, publisher of *A Traveler at Forty,* is sorry that his house is afraid of *The Titan.* Mr. Charles Scribner writes squeamishly from the Century Club he is certain of refusing the book before reading it, but that no doubt it will make a financial success and there are " publishers who would jump at the chance." Doran decides after a careful reading he " would not publish Dreiser if he were the last author on earth." Mencken writes:

"An eternal pox upon the Harpers. And Doran be damned for his flight. God knows this country needs that weekly, once planned. . . .

" It is high time you stopped listening to the vapid criticisms of publishing donkeys. Such vermin over-estimate their own sagacity and what is more their own importance. Imagine Kennerly objecting to a book of yours. . . ."

Finally at Lengel's instigation John Lane and Co. show a spark of interest. Their American editor however, J. Jefferson Jones, was about to turn the book down, when again an Englishman as with *Sister Carrie* came to the rescue. Lane's English advisor, Frederic Chapman, also translator of Anatole France, happened on the scene. He made this report:

" I have not the slightest doubt that as far as John Lane Co. is concerned this is the most important chance that has come its way since the establishment of the New York business, and while I should not anticipate in England anything like the sales which may be counted on in America, the book is certain to rouse a good deal of discussion and to be treated with unqualified respect by the more serious reviewers.

"The ostensible causes upon which Harper's have withdrawn the book are quite negligible. . . . Mr. Dreiser records his hero's fluttering from one flame to another with entire passivity. He hardly commends and certainly never condemns, but he has handled his episodes in so masterly a fashion that I do not think there is the least chance of the prurient public getting flustered. A ready retort to anybody . . . would be to refer them to Mr. Galsworthy's . . . Dark Flower . . . which is infinitely more immoral (supposing immorality to exist in either) . . ."

So now all is well; even the English publication of *The Titan* went through, to the regret of Mr. Mitchell Kennerly, two of whose letters to Alexander Harvey are almost proof of the rumor that he was the poison in Dreiser's candy, and all for fear of treason to majesty. The novel, he thought, should never have been published in America and could not possibly be published in England without incurring legal liability. He had written John Lane to that effect. He presumed he would not wish to bring the book out on account of "his friendship of many years' standing with Miss Grigsby." That publisher must have looked on style and story as separate issues. *The Titan* appeared in England, apparently without detriment to himself or his friend, the American heiress.

Yet it looks as if quite surely "High Society" had the importance which Dreiser, for one, never afraid of ridicule, has had the intellect to give it. And in the drama of our letters the socially elect and the socially aspiring appear to have played the part of Villain not of Friend to Art.

54

> "*Whatever his faults of composition or construction, and there are not so many as his friends endeavor to make out, he has magnificently booted the reading public, the morally subsidized critics and the very publishers in the coarsest regions of their bodies — their souls. And for this . . . I acclaim him as the only real, uncontaminated genius of these States and pray to God that my friend Sherwood Anderson will hurry up and get published so that there will be two of them.*"
> The Scavenger, Little Review, October, 1916

Now Dreiser again unconsciously was setting the stage for a second and more spectacular engagement. This time it would be a storm center about which would flare for a while the forces of Methodism and Conservatism, and the scattered amateurs of free speech; an incongruous clash of people never meant to meet even in battle, the kind of grim play that our democracy is addicted to. On the plateau of achievement to which the largeness of *The Titan* had taken him, he completed another tome of life, *The "Genius,"* and made a contract for publication with Lane in July 1914 — the book was published in September 1915. He has said, perhaps it is his favorite work. By implication, not by dogma, *The "Genius"* indicts American society for the destruction of treasure it ought to prize, just as his *Tragedy* accuses it for the failure of a common man to be a healthy animal.

The hero, Eugene Witla, a painter, stands for all those he had known and heard of, possessed by beauty, who were constantly dying in suicide or drink or insanity or worldly success, defeated by a raw industrial disorder. He had four men in mind when he wrote it, his young predecessor of the Delineator; the erotic illustrator, Everett Shinn; himself, especially as to outward circumstance; and a fourth unnamed. The composite stood in his mind for the artists who could not propose asceticism like Emerson, Thoreau, Sandburg or Frost; who had to surround themselves with the luxuries, and yet had to be haunted by that small silver clarion voice calling to unexplored mysteries. It would not let them rest or be complacent. The voice for which men immolate themselves in isolated workrooms in agony of birth. For Dreiser tolerant and hopeful, these men were not infrequent, and if they had any of the sheen of genius at all they were sacred. People complaining that his hero from Alexandria, Illinois, is not the real article malign the portrait. Illinois could give birth to genius; though it might repudiate it; Dreiser knew this. Quite clearly he has endowed him with that something of Endymion, devastating to women, envied by other men, a prowess, a " deathful glee," which does not always lead to mastery in art. Dreiser has made him lovingly, the kind of hero he himself used to wish he could be among the village girls and boys back in Indiana:

"Why, I have been . . . a lord
Of flowers, garlands, love-knots, silly posies,
Groves, meadows, melodies, and arbour-roses . . ."

So endowed out of a kinder childhood than his own, Dreiser exposes him step by step to the very life he himself had been through, exchanging writing for painting. Out of it grows a different ending. His hero's gifted sensuality finally exiles him from the American market, whereas a greater ruggedness and enforced austerity has kept Dreiser there, too big for it and yet within it.

Conversely to the Titan, the nature of the Genius is true, and not the masterpieces attributed to him. No use to deny that here the book leans on a mistaken premise. The hero, both voluptuary and " great painter," acclaimed in Paris as Dreiser had been in London, was impossible to the United States. He could not have happened here in that day or yet today. One way or another provincialism follows us, try as we do to escape in airplanes and through dollars. Winslow Homer and Albert Ryder could paint, but they were stoics, willing to live apart, unknown certainly to France; Whistler emaciated his exacting art by taking it to Europe, and it would have died had he stayed at home. Nor has there been a painter of self-tutored power equal to Dreiser's own or to Masters' or Frank Norris'. Being a country blind to color how could we be a country of painters? Pascin knew it when he said " It takes twice as much genius to paint in America as it does in France and no one has that much." Dreiser's innocence of this, and of the art of painting, discolors the truth of his hero.

No use either to deny Dreiserian lapses into language too sweet or banal, giving delight to detractors. Nevertheless *The " Genius "* is greater than its faults — a new undertaking not to be scorned by true snobs. As he wrote it, Masters' words might have sounded for him, " to be fused and molten," and his own words, " to have a canvas as big as the back of a church." It is bigger than that, appearing out of a tumult of life, and a convulsive knowledge of death. The wistful green village like Warsaw; youth in fabulous Chicago; Bohemia in amateur New York; the dreamy midwest farmland of the fiancée too binding to forget; robust drive of day-laborers, sweat and salt; rich varnished magazine world to which the Genius is diverted; native excursion into Christian Science; and then the solitudes of the heart or resonance or conflict of two hearts together — all is made as if experienced.

In the erotic theme of village and farmland, and in the last act, describing a circle of birth, surgery and death, the phrasing is that of a master. Especially the climax in a New York hospital reads like more than a play; it reads like an opera whose finale orchestrally binds the themes of the book. You feel the earth revolving in its haze of mimetic cries, quick acts and gestures of human beings — here of surgeons, nurses, a new child, and the bond broken between two people who had tried life together and failed. Magnificence brings to mind the Homeric hymn where birth and the turn of the generations is chanted. Mencken's claim is supported here — " Dreiser derives from the Greeks." Style is maintained as in the decline of Hurstwood in *Sister Carrie,* and in the drowning and death-house scenes of the *Tragedy* — evidence that Dreiser might always have disciplined words to obey his will had he not been distracted by other pastimes. In 1915 and again when the book reappeared in 1923 he was strangely censured for this feat of language; childbirth, a Caesarian operation, were " impossible subject matter." Even admirers merely tolerated it for the skill of it. Yet the next decade of critics, fashions changing, would tumble into praise of the same theme more selfishly treated in Hemingway's *Farewell to Arms.*

The influence of this ending alone should have given Dreiser a passport to victory, " fused and molten," but Masters, that severest critic, could not quite confer it. He says to him intimately in letters, and more elaborately in a review in the Chicago Evening Post that he is greater than the book:

> " [Dreiser] understands what a man almost a genius must contend with in this disorderly land of rhetorical freedom and societal tyranny and banality. . . . Over the book one can hear sometimes Gargantuan laughter; at other times a trembling sensitiveness seems to vibrate through the pages. . . . He seems to me our greatest novelist now writing. . . . Dreiser has recorded the definite figure of a man moving through an America that required strength of the first order to overcome, if any strength could do that. . . . He can be glad . . . that he revolutionized American fiction. It can never return to the old standards of reticence about life. But he has not reached the climax whither his genius inevitably tends. That climax must come . . . that book, when it shall be written will be . . . more quintessential than this one."

Reedy, who confessed he once turned down a story of Lyon's because a hat-pin was specified as an instrument of abortion, did not like *The " Genius,"* " the multiplication of amours." And even Mencken was unexpectedly prudish. His review of *The " Genius "* is called *A Literary Behemoth.* He was glad of its Greek quality, but found lapses of taste, not always lingual either, but as to topic — one where, as he phrases it, " the young man runs his hand up under the girl's skirts — unnecessary!" in his opinion. As written, the episode, surely not unknown to erotic traffic, is lascivious and grave; part of "a transport of agony and delight" broken by the girl's fears. With it is told the grief of conflict between puritan and pagan, a theme of the book; and the hero asks Dreiser's choral question: "What is life? . . . What is the human body? What produces passion? Here we are surging with a fever of longing and then we burn out and die." Another time, succumbing to him, the girl makes the ancient threat of death or marriage:

> "He thought of her with her beautiful body, her mass of soft hair all tarnished in death. . . .
> 'You wouldn't do that?' he asked.
> 'Yes, I would,' she said sadly. . . . 'You know that little lake, I'd drown myself! . . .'
> ". . . Thus he stood by the bank of this still lake marvelling at the subtleties of reflected radiance, twining and intertwining it all with love, death, failure, fame. . . . It was romantic to think that in such a lake, if he were unkind, Angela would be found. By such a darkness as was now descending would all her bright dreams be submerged. . . . It would be as beautiful as romance. . . . He stared at the fading surface . . . silver, lavender, leaden gray. Overhead a vivid star already was shining. How would it be with her if she were really below those still waters? How would it be with him? It would be too desperate, too regretful. No, he must marry her. It was in this mood that he returned to the city, the ache of life in his heart."

For libertines like Mencken, like Reedy, to turn prude; not to take glee and grief together as Dreiser knew how to weave them, must have bewildered him. Perhaps in part it accounts for his habit of repetition and emphasis. He had to tell people until they understood, in what language he could find and in euphuisms like *bosom* and *quivering limbs* if necessary. In 1915 American prose held no precedent for erotic event. When approached it was by way of asterisks or snickers. Mencken, however, was soon to waive prejudice and give months of time to the defense of *The "Genius."*

There were others under the complete spell of the book. The poet and aesthete, Arthur Ficke, overseas now — the war is on for Americans — far from his dis-

tinguished collection of Japanese prints picked up *The
" Genius "* and wrote a poem to Dreiser:

    " Tonight I am alone,
. . . A long way from that Chinese restaurant,
. . . I have just turned the last page
. . . Of a book of yours —
. . . Now there are passing before me
    Interminable figures in tangled procession —
    Proud or cringing, starved with desire, or icy,
    Hastening toward a dream of triumph; fleeing
      from a dream of doom, —
. . . Through a chaotic and meaningless anarchy,
    Under heavy clouds of terrific gloom
    Or through ravishing flashes of knife-edged
      sunlight —
. . . Their heads haloed with immortal illusion, —
    The terrible and beautiful, cruel and wonder-
      laden illusion of life."

Jim Tully, ex-pugilist, wrote him: " There are two men I have always wanted to meet, Thomas Hardy and Theodore Dreiser . . . it is a vast piece [*The " Genius "*] — and as long as you can turn out a book like that — you can tell old lady Frank Harris to go to hell. . . . Just think if I get a book over it will be the first one by an ex-pugilist . . ." Frank Harris, admiring Dreiser, had felt " forced to admit " that *Sister Carrie* was his best book. The critics and the public were to blame as well as the writer, but " no explanation," he decreed, " can justify such a fact." He accused the " German paste " in him for blindness to " beauty of words." In the same article Harris gave himself away preferring the softer and prejudiced David Graham Phillips. Phillips' " Susan nodded delightedly " and " sneered he at Wright," as synonyms for " she said " and " he said " are insensibilities typical of Phillips to which I for one prefer Dreiser's " he looked into her eyes, the same were filled with tears." Why not admit that as a people we are not " language-minded," except in jokes?

    F. Scott Fitzgerald at the end of the decade freshly delivered from Princeton and into his own creation, the Jazz Age, was another to pay tribute. Especially *The " Genius "* got him. Perhaps he found himself there. Though a more frivolous and more moral version of that hero, he too, judging from his stories, conceived of life as impossible without the luxuries, and has not succumbed to their market price for the moment without authentic work to his name. Sometimes lyrical to the point of strangeness, a kind of youthful, syncopated, crystal-gazing! One evening he made a pilgrimage to Tenth Street. He arrived presenting a bottle of champagne, which Dreiser put in the ice box. A circle of owl-like faces were drinking near beer. Very little was said. It seemed impossible to talk. So ended his gallant effort to do what with the exception of Howells and the Concord School, no one has done in these States — talk and bridge a generation. "Americans are infinitely repellent particles." The Gaelic Ernest Boyd in a portrait of Fitzgerald describes the same visit between "the master and his youngest disciple" with foreign glee over our disconnected history and scattered genius, all for lack of medium of exchange. The picture, he says, is "testimony to the survival in Scott Fitzgerald of respect for honorable achievement, under difficulties certainly unknown to him or his contemporaries." * Perhaps not entirely unknown; yet his friends for a fact had already gone over to Proust, Gertrude Stein and James Joyce, who did not particularly want them.

John Cowper Powys and Randolph Bourne were other important actors in Dreiser's behalf at this time. Powys, novelist and poet, came to the United States early in the decade of *The " Genius,"* and became for some years an evangelist of culture, bearing rumor of art to the villages. He was loved by many women's clubs for his Greek head and fire of mind, and lived through it to achieve less promiscuous days. To him goes the distinction as foreigner of having preached our living writers to us — among them Dreiser and Masters, hot from the iron. Between him and Dreiser exists a friendship violated by neither: " A man derived out of Emily Brontë, Hardy and Dostoevsky," Dreiser says in his most caressing voice, " lack-

* *Portraits: Real and Imaginary*, 1924. "Being Memories and Impressions of Friends and Contemporaries; with Appreciations of Divers Singularities and Characteristics of Certain Phases of Life and Letters Among North Americans as Seen, Heard and Divined by Ernest Boyd."

ing Hardy's terrible fatality, but possessed like all of them by a sense of inanity and cruelty. He really believes in devilishness. I can't see it that way. Most people are too busy to be possessed by devils. Take a butcher cutting meat all day or a factory hand or clerk, they haven't the time. . . . Powys is amorphous, wonderful, I count on him."

For Englishmen more than for most Americans Dreiser has had an aesthetic appeal. Powys knows him that way. He first heard of him some fifteen years ago on a train coming out of Toledo; the Toledo Blade opened at a double page interview called, perhaps, " Apostle Of Chaos." The headline caught him, and when he read, " I have no hope, yet I do not despair, life drifts," he thought can there be such an American? He first met him at Maurice Browne's Little Theater in Chicago. Afterwards he knew him well in New York: " I always had the impression of someone hard and firm, aristocratic hands, Nordic, athletic, countrified. He wore tweeds and had the European fashion of carrying a stick . . ." To Powys " there are two kinds of force, one from the sun, the other from the cold, beyond the stars' rays. A man touched by force of cold can draw on it at will as through a long thin pipe. Dreiser is such a man; endowed with a planetary consciousness; possessed of brains that create an order." Once on a walk in California he told Powys that his critics wanted to make him into a materialist: " I am not one, I have never taken life at its face value." — " He is superstitious like an old Roman, believes in signs, and that a certain type of person seen at a certain time will bring good luck or bad. . . . At one time when I was an invalid of all the people who came to see me Dreiser was as considerate as a woman; he alone went off promptly at ten o'clock. . . . He lives in no middle distance between himself and others and when there is not serious exchange, attempts approach through sportive badinage difficult to answer verbally. . . . He has no cold malice, is non-human, and morbidly sensitive." So this friend described him.

In 1914, the year before the publication of *The " Genius,"* Margaret Anderson's left-wing Little Review had been born in accordance with the vigorous enterprise of these days both for the exotic and the native. She was a young woman according to her memoirs who liked chocolates and disliked reality, that of sex included * — " My greatest enemy is reality . . . I have fought it successfully for thirty years . . . I have always held myself aloof from natural laws." In which of course she was a native, also in a genius for selling. For thirty years she sold Art not as a merchandise but as a luxury, and with high spirits made the most seriously lively journal yet published in these States. Before she fled reality and took her journal off to flirt with Europe, and in American fashion marry manners which had little to do with American matters, the Little Review was perhaps the only conveyance remarkable for native prose and poetry we have had, that is, of any duration. In November 1915 she published an article by Powys who was traveling in the opposite direction, away from Europe and toward America — a review of *The " Genius."* For him Dreiser bridged the gulf between the old countries and this new one. Over his bridge where sex and tragedy finally walked, might now come other American prophets of reality, and a language might be established that would purge us of provincialism. The Little Review followed this with *The Dionysian Dreiser,* the outburst of one of those engaging youths of this period who thought the wilderness was this time just about to bloom with life and genius, calling himself Scavenger:

"Really, you of the firm-fireside-faith, what is there to be done? Here is the Dionysian dastard who dares proclaim that life is a decent, orderly routine and that life is also a wild, warm passionate thing; that it is also a flame in which there is only one color, the red, golden color of youth.

And the answer is — howl. A howl will go up I swear it. It will start from the critics.

I can almost read their forthcoming reviews as I close my eyes.

* " Dick was one of those civilized men to be found exclusively in America it seems, who are more interested in an idea than in a woman."
" . . . Bauer being enormously interested in Duncan's dancing as art, I being totally uninterested in it as sex."

From *My Thirty Years War*
by Margaret Anderson.

'A sensually depraved and degenerate type.
'Striking at the bed rock of public solidarity, of home happiness, of everything decent and worth while. . . .'
Howl, you who have stultified your artists and buried them under the gingerbread morality of your own monotonous lives. Dreiser is the one novelist being published in America today who doesn't listen to you, who describes you at your various bests, who wrings the pathos and joys out of your little worlds; who paints in with the brush of a universal art what you and I are doing in Alexandria and Chicago and New York and all the milk-station stops between. . . ."

And Randolph Bourne in older prose salutes Dreiser as an equal of European novelists in an article for the New Republic called *Desire as Hero;* as the opposite of " Booth Tarkington who makes business the master motive of life to which religion and sex are incidental ":

"Of course no great Continental novelist ever believed this, Rolland or Dostoevsky or Tolstoi or Frenssen or Nexo. The major motives of these continentals is almost always the inexorable desire of life . . . a desire which consists of walking in the mud with the face toward the stars. . . . No matter how badly Mr. Dreiser does his work, he would be significant as the American novelist who has most felt this subterranean current of life . . . our only novelist who has tried to plumb far below. . . .

His hero is really not Sister Carrie or the Titan or the Genius, but that desire within us that pounds in manifold guise against the walls of experience."

Here was an American critic, it was said, who should not have died. The War killed him. For such a critic to publish and live in New York in war time was out of the question. He appeared to his friends to burn with that impartial mind sometimes called Greek, to which democracies used to dedicate themselves when they were born. Mind, creative not destructive, living in the moment, seduced more by the future than by the past, but scarcely more. Whitman dreamed of it for his new clean United States with his one forgetfulness that grass grows best out of mould.

In the midst of this decade in 1916 on the eve of our entry into the Great War, a number of fairly young optimists, James Oppenheim, Louis Untermeyer, Van Wyck Brooks, Paul Rosenfeld, Waldo Frank, founded a magazine called The Seven Arts to meet the renaissance they conceived to be " bursting in the sky over the heads of an amazed people." Dreiser, though " lumbering," Sandburg, Masters, Frost, Mencken, Amy Lowell were like " rockets from unconnected quarters." " The Seven Arts would be a channel for the flow of these new tendencies." " We were wild enough," Oppenheim says, " to believe that while Europe was cutting its own throat the artists and critics could dominate America." Randolph Bourne joining with them, though certain that the war would put a stop to this brief bright awakening, fought for it to the last moment. Especially he fought the intellectuals who in sentimental numbers (among them his own teacher, John Dewey, and Van Wyck Brooks too), were going over into the war hysteria, and enlisting what wits they had on the side of this " fashionable war." Mind should not be drafted like this without his caustic dissent.

In the meantime, in a year and a half The Seven Arts published besides these first rockets, newer writers, Sherwood Anderson, Bodenheim, Padraic Colum, Dos Passos, Jack Reed, Van Loon, John Dewey, Carl Van Vechten, Eugene O'Neill, Spingarn, and " stacks of others " including " all the poets from Frost to Sandburg." Then Bourne's articles about the war killed The Seven Arts. In 1917 endowment was withdrawn. With no place to publish, the blow killed him. " Had he lived," his friends say, " the Twenties might have been more sparkling than they were." Bourne was " deformed, humped-back, a longish medieval face, sewed-up mouth, and ear awry, but his speech held you spell-bound and you looked into eyes as young as a spring dawn," so Oppenheim described him; and also a visit to him after he had died: " I lifted the sheet from his face. He seemed to mean all that had been stopped." Dreiser, as deeply moved, speaks of him as " a beautiful monstrosity, the one gem-like critical mind of that day." Perhaps they exaggerated and idealized him as critic, feeling the crying need of a critic, where all that was alive was reeling and shifting. But if not, it is a strange symbol of these States, that when the mind arrived it was lodged in a warped and twisted body, and that they killed it as quick as they could.

Here exactly is the moment, 1916 to 1917, the hour of this fruition and this death, when, with the stage set as described, the principal battle of Dreiser's story was waged over freedom of letters. Who gained and who lost seems yet to be hanging in the balance. "The howl" over The "Genius," prophesied by the young enthusiast of The Little Review, broke loose. Since its publication in 1915 along with the acclaim had sounded little shrill shrieks, venomous enough, from posthumous Mrs. Grundys. One of them signing herself N. P. D., literary taster for the New York Globe and Commercial Advertiser, had always shivered at Dreiser as at a snake or a bedbug. Now she despised him more than ever. He was a "pro-German," a friend of Mencken, of Hun extraction and from low steerage people at that. Against The "Genius," whose hero she confuses with Cowperwood of The Titan, she launched her prettiest sarcasm. First quoting the letter of a correspondent which she said "should dispose of Dreiser for all time as without humor, without pity, and without the least love of art or nature," then she lightly amused herself:

> "The 'Genius' is probably Mr. Dreiser's most subjective work and it is the ugliest. What interest it has is pathological. One may be sorry for a man who sees nothing in life but girls, an unending procession of girls, hardly more to be differentiated than the Pink Leg and Blue Leg of the chorus. . . . When Zola (Mr. William Lyon Phelps points out) saw a dunghill he saw nothing else. . . . Rostand looking at the same unlovely object, beheld the vision of Chantecler. But Dreiser would never see Chantecler; only the dung and the hens. . . . We understand that the Tauchnitz publications are about to be resumed. . . . We hope that The 'Genius' will appear in a German translation. That's how kindly we feel toward the Germans."

This lady in the same column discloses with her scorn of legs a love of anthologies, Home Book of Verse, Treasury of Irish Verse; a tenderness for humorists, Stephen Leacock, "our own Dooley and George Ade"; and for romanticists, E. Temple Thurston and Lord Dunsany. She betrays a fear of Jews and their miraculous Art Theatre — Pinsky's The Treasure is facetiously disparaged; and a passion for Women's Suffrage. When

Dreiser had previously complained of her, Mencken had tried to soothe him: " Who in hell is N. P. D., some lousy old maid? No one reads the Globe anyway." Instinctively the realist divined that these very no-ones who read the Globe were among those who would support legislation for war, prohibition and censorship; in fact that by force of their respectable numbers they were the acquiescent chorus that would make possible our gloomy plutocracy. And Mencken himself was this time aroused:

"The secret of the Globe braying lies in the last paragraph: the grand crime in these days is to bear a German name. Who is this N. P. D? I have a little list. There must never be any compromise [with] the common run of 'good, right-thinking Americans' . . . we must stand against them forever, and do what damage we can to them and their tin pot democracy. . . . I am waiting patiently for her to write a book. The Lord God Jehovah, soon or late, always delivers them into my hands."

From Chicago Mrs. Elia Peattie, literary editor of the Chicago Tribune, also an advocate of votes for women, makes a more passionate onslaught, dated December 4, 1915. Perhaps there was danger in giving American women the vote who had had from their men so little else. Mrs. Peattie was vehement:

" John Cowper Powys refers to *The 'Genius'* as 'the American prose epic ' . . . I will never admit such a thing until I am ready to see the American flag trailing in the dust dark with the stains of my sons . . . and the Germans completing their world rule by placing their governor general in the White House at Washington. . . . An epic as I understand it is a narrative of elevated characters describing the exploits of heroes. . . . If this is an epic it is the epic of a human Tom-cat. It is a back fence narrative. . . . I repudiate it as the American prose epic. . . ."

This she does in the name of Ibsen, Whitman and Lincoln, who knew " love and temptation " too, but who like her had never had such low feline thoughts as Theodore Dreiser. Mencken was jubilant:

"This Peattie stuff is a scream. The fair wench is a novelist herself sweetly praised by Hildegarde Hawthorne. By all means let me have this masterpiece of the ovarian school when the time comes to write the review of reviews."

And now an eminent college professor joined the ladies against the Tomcat. College professors, as Mencken has scrupulously computed in his *Book of Prefaces,* 1917, had always expressed their disapproval of serious contemporary native genius by ignoring it in favor of minor celebrities. The 1892 edition of Richardson's *American Literature* disposed of Mark Twain . . . " with less than four lines," ranking him " below Irving, Holmes, Lowell . . . below Artemus Ward, Josh Billings, and Petroleum Nasby." By the year 1910 Professor William Lyon Phelps could chide Richardson for this; and then in 1916 in his *Advance of the English Novel* could dismiss Dreiser completely by not a single mention of him.* And this was true, according to Mencken's vigorous statistics, of the 'other " heavyweights of the craft, the new Dunciad," he labels them — the Pancoasts, Hallecks, Babbitts, Brownells, Pattees. In their tomes and treatises on modern American writers of that day he has discovered praise of O. Henry, Sydnor Harrison, Owen Wister, Hopkinson Smith, R. H. Davis, R. W. Chambers, but never a word for or against the author of *Sister Carrie, Jennie Gerhardt, The Financier, The Titan,* and *The " Genius."*

The jocular N. P. D. apparently owed her witticism destroying Zola and Dreiser to Professor Phelps, but for the most part he kept still about this Hoosier cock and tomcat. And it is certain he never advised him as reading matter for his young charges at Yale. It took a professor from Dreiser's own land, the more zealous Middle West, to celebrate him by actively denouncing him. Out in the golden fields of Illinois Professor Stuart P. Sherman held the chair of English in the State university. There he devoted his life to cultivating the nerves of the sons of farmers and mechanics. Also from the midst of that vast culture of rye, corn and wheat he was able to sell now and again his wisdom to friends and editors back East. He was with other professors a missionary trying to perpetuate the Colonial tradition, in his case to the far reaches of the plough and the McCormick reaper. Together these scholars held the trenches against the new America. In the Nation of December 2, 1915, Professor Sherman launched his offensive at what he con-

* *A Book of Prefaces,* pp. 131 to 134.

ceived to be the enemy of the moment, the tomcat author of *The " Genius."* He was too wary to admit him among the "realists," knowing that what with Balzac, Hardy, Flaubert, and the lately translated Russians, as well as the popular Bennett and Wells, the term had taken a favorable meaning. Instead he coined for him a new epithet, "naturalist," and hoped he had packed its meaning with verbal poison. Dreiser's crime lay in treating men and women as if they were animals. To many of the poets and priests of history this would have been to flatter them, but to a temper like that of Sherman it was an irreverent sphere from which to draw analogies. Condensed, the indictment runs like this:

"In his books the male of the species is characterized by cupidity, pugnacity and a Simian inclination for the other sex; the female is a soft, vain, pleasure-seeking creature devoted to personal adornment and quite helplessly susceptible to the flattery of the male. . . . His people have cat-like eyes, feline grace, sinuous strides, eyes and jaws which vary from those of the tiger, lynx and bear to the tolerant mastiff and the surly bull dog. . . . In his *Financier* two lovers run together like leopards. . . . Raising human stock in America evidently includes for Dreiser feeding and clothing but not the most elementary moral ideas of conduct. Routine is dull, moralists are asses, respectability is unctuous, teachers are owl-like conventionalists, faithful parents lead an apple pie order of existence. . . . We turn with relief from *The 'Genius'* to the scandals in the news sheets."

So this professor perversely paraphrased Dreiser and strengthened the Dreiserian myth, so welcome to his students, the new generation. Therein a man given over to difficult achievement, and darkly wondering what is right, what wrong, was construed as a wicked sensualist, leading women and children astray. The myth grew, and perhaps drove the real Dreiser in an effort to be understood into exploring regions as dreary and forbidding as the mind of the Jewish moron in *The Hand of The Potter,* and the mind of Clyde Griffiths in *An American Tragedy.* Against the ignorance of a typical scholar like Sherman, who had nicely digested Emerson's serene philosophy, perhaps Dreiser began to feel that he had been born to fight, almost alone and single handed. Darkness contradicting light, evil contradicting good — was it his mission to fertilize American minds with the luxury of these contrasts? At length he may have thought so, and let the enemy in him crystallize.

The professor as if to prophesy battle and revolution ended his Nation article with a threat: " This theory of animal behaviour cannot be an adequate basis on which to study human nature. . . . And when one half of the world attempts to assert such a theory, the other half rises in battle."

And so in the course of time " the other half " did. The article pays Dreiser the curious compliment of being a whole "half." No other rebel or scientist, not Zola or Rodin or Anatole France, not H. G. Wells or Pavlow, not even Whitman is lined up with the offending Hoosier. In July, 1916, *The " Genius "* came to the notice of a Society belonging to Sherman's " half of the world," the New York Society for the Suppression of Vice, which at length begins to be remembered as a quaint antique. And yet American " vice " today takes its color from the suppression of yesterday, and is accordingly simple.

55

"... *What I hate*
Is that crude Demos which shouts down
the minds,
Outvotes them, takes those silly lies that
move
The populace and makes them into laws,
And makes a village of a great Re-
public." EDGAR LEE MASTERS

"*No ship of all that under sail or steam*
Has gathered people to us more and
more
But Pilgrim-manned the Mayflower in a
dream
Has been their anxious convoy in to
shore." ROBERT FROST

It was a fanatic from the backwoods of Connecticut, Anthony Comstock, who invented this fine society which, aiming to suppress vice, succeeded rather in suppressing wit, wisdom and beauty. He inaugurated it in the autumn of 1873 in the rooms of the Young Men's Christian Association, with the help of Morris K. Jessup, William E. Dodge, J. Pierpont Morgan, Robert R. McBurney and other eminent citizens in whom sense of poetry and satire must have run low. Exclusive Circles again were dictators in matters which they did not prize. The tragedy of American Art has always so consistent a plot that it falls naturally into one's hands. These rich men like Comstock were rooted spiritually if not actually in the hardships of our Puritan past; and on the crest of Northern fortunes made secure by the Civil War, they were launching the pious merchant plutocracy supreme a generation later.

There are critics today tired of blaming the Mayflower Puritans for our puritanism. They like to find a less hackneyed cause. Is it that they dislike to admit that victory for Cromwell's Dissenters has run to its dreariest measure in our States, although at the same time to glittering heights? Some of them blame machinery and they may be right. Morris L. Ernst and William Seagle in their study, *Obscenity and the Censor* * accuse democracy for thwarting sex and therefore art:

> "If the age of faith adopted the index of heresy, the age of Divine Right, the index of treason, it was inevitable for the age of democracy to adopt the index of sex. . . . It is one of the penalties of civilization."

This might be all very well, and we could settle down to the alternative, sexlessness or tyranny, perhaps choosing tyranny, if it were not for the precedent of the French Republic, where pleasures of sex and art appear to have survived not only democracy but machinery. Mr. Ernst and Mr. Seagle however may be among those who dispute the axiom that France is civilized. They go to great pains to ferret out examples of suppression in France, and of course in England, as absurd as any we have committed — curious as incident, misleading as evidence. Even England, its cradle, has survived censorship intellectually. The truth appears to be that censoring societies in these older countries have ruled the minds of their members but have not colored the life of a whole nation as with us. Compare our letters and images with theirs, compare the faces in our streets and subways, stores and homes, with the faces in theirs, and a vast difference invades the senses, for which a prohibition of reality would be enough to account. Or for those who can't trust their own senses, the story was expertly compressed in 1917 into one chapter, ready to swallow, *Puritanism, a Literary Force* by H. L. Mencken. He tells there how after the Civil War it became fashionable to be a millionaire, and the millionaires were expediently churchmen. Therefore it became fashionable to be pious. The Puritan doctrine armed with money grew militant and aggressive. And, he might have added, it tinged even the temper of the

* *To the Pure . . . A Study of Obscenity and the Censor.*

Catholic Church in America. St. Paul, inventor of chastity, could finally see his strictest dreams come true. Go from St. Paul to Calvin and Cromwell, from them to Emerson and Longfellow, from them to Rockefeller, Edison and Ford, and you will tumble into a typical American home of the early 20th century not quite extinct today.

To protect this cherished institution from turbulent changing America, Anthony Comstock conceived laws and corporations. Perhaps as a young man among the birches and maple trees of Connecticut, intoxicating himself each Sunday with ecstasy of virtue in the cool white meeting house he was a rustic poet like Bunyan, evolving a vision of purity. For this one can understand him. Who has not had moods imagining a world without vice or misery? Perhaps tortured by rumor of the great cities he had said, " I, single handed, by the grace of God, shall go up and eradicate sin from the market places." It may have been with him at the start that same expensive Christian dream conceived for charity and health, ending in cruelty and disease. He was a rustic with simple faith perhaps; although Mencken who has studied him does not think so. But for worldlings like Jessup, Dodge, and Morgan, especially Morgan with his art collection and library, to endorse him, and for no one of their world to oppose them or to laugh at them, places American society of the Seventies almost outside of history and untouched by it. Long before this elsewhere occasional aristocrats and originals, that is, those without fear, had begun to tire of Christian idealism, and had developed a protective irony against it. And now it was the very age of scepticism and adventure. To a friend who had shuddered at an Egyptian image, Baudelaire had said: " Best to beware when you call that god ugly, perhaps he is the true God." In America a genius, Whitman, was passionately proposing the mysteries of reality. But the lords of American finance as a body apparently still preferred the ignorant Comstock, and his musty parlors of Christian endeavor. In any event they joined with him to fight the reaffirmation of nature.

First of all they had to create legal precedent, not to be found in the original Constitution, celebrated for proposing free speech and religious tolerance. In 1842 however a Federal statute had been passed to exclude the importation of obscenity, giving custom officers the right to confiscate at the port "indecent and obscene prints, paintings, lithographs, engravings and transparencies." Under the heading of prints fell some of the more salacious classics, so that for example it is likely that Emerson had the privilege to be exposed to a less fecund past than say Jefferson or Benjamin Franklin. But until 1868 no one had felt the need of a statute to curb native indecency. People were too pure to require it. If ever heresy was committed the inherited English Common Law was enough to take care of that. But now in 1868 the Connecticut Yankee Comstock took it upon himself to propose and put through a New York state law, entitled " An Act for the Suppression of the Trade in, and Circulation of Obscene Literature, Illustrations, Advertisements " and so forth. American children, he found, were growing up again, out of the dirt of their own soil this time, and must be restrained once again from growing up.

Five years passed in prayer and lobbying, and Comstock saw his further scheme of a society to enforce this law come true, and himself secretary. It was incorporated under a special act of the legislature of New York — the Empire State — with the right of search, seizure and arrest. In the same year, 1873, this untiring crusader with his churchly friends put through the first Federal statute to hamper native imagination and intellect. Now all " obscene, lewd, lascivious, disgusting, filthy, indecent matter " was to be barred from the mails. And now the couriers whom " neither snow nor rain nor heat nor gloom of night " can stay in " their appointed rounds " could be stayed by vice commissioners from carrying readable reading matter to Americans. Soon after this the Western Society for the Suppression of Vice was born in Cincinnati, and the Watch and Ward Society in Boston. Almost coincident with these, other extra official bodies grew in power licensed by the Government to do their work for them — the Y.M.C.A., the Order of Gideon, the Christian Endeavor, the Anti-Saloon League, the Purity League, with back of them quite certainly the magnates of gas, railroads, steel, copper, gold. And the fun began for the reformers, favored by an incipient Oligarchy which would in the end banish Democracy, like a worn-out wife, to a comfortable Home in Washington.

So now the germ was fertilized by which Indecency grew with weeds and skyscrapers to such rank proportions as the tabloids, and movies, and speakeasies, and other rackets of today. This happened in the decade of Whitman's full fame and in the years that gave birth to Crane, Norris, Dreiser, Masters, Sandburg, Anderson and Mencken, as if cure should follow cause in a not yet ended circle of cause and cure, cure and cause. These new men grew up with the birth and growth of militant Puritan reform in America, invented to thwart them as best it could.

At first the temper of the day was with the reformers — day of the old Concord school and the young Howells; and there was not much native cleansing to do. When once trivial commercial pornography had been stemmed, though certainly not choked, the crusaders turned their attention to expurgating importations, ancient and modern — Rabelais, Casanova, Boccaccio, Shakespeare, Swift, Voltaire, Rousseau, Balzac, Zola, Daudet, Hardy and even Du Maurier. *Jude the Obscure* was banned, *Trilby* attacked. A frenzy of purging came over the country. Librarians, district attorneys and ministers turned censor. A minister in Boston undertook to issue a pure version of the Bible. Heretofore seriously daring books used to die of neglect; now they were made notorious. This happened to *Leaves of Grass* twenty-six years after it was first published, and brought it new fame, but also shelved it among forbidden volumes in places of learning. At length in the Nineties as polite a story as Frederic's *The Damnation of Theron Ware* was banned and Garland's virtuous *Rose of Dutcher's Coolly* was threatened. Any native writer concerned with real experience was suspect. Recently D. H. Lawrence's *The Rainbow* had been banned. The work of scientists was prohibited — *The Sexual Question,* Forel, and *Psycopathia Sexualis,* Krafft-Ebing. Comstock grew strong and smug. He boasted that his percentage of convictions in forty years ran to 98.5; and that he had destroyed "enough books, stereotype plates, photographic negatives, and photographs to fill sixteen cars, fifteen loaded with ten tons each, and the other nearly full." * But the names of these many criminals and their works were always withheld from a free people. Write today to his successor, John S. Sumner, for statistics and his reply is: " . . . we know of no prepared list of suppressed books in this country. There are obvious reasons why such a list should not be published." Comstock's printed slogan, preserved by Mencken was: " MORALS, Not Art or Literature." And he might have added not honesty, or laughter either.

In their fifty years these societies enacted many unconscious farces dear now to satirists: Benjamin Franklin, father of the Post Office and the Saturday Evening Post, was barred from the mails when it came to his *Advice to Young Men on the Proper Choosing of a Mistress.*† To this moment it is difficult to find it in libraries or bookstores; young men have had to get on without it. In 1912 the report of the Chicago Vice Commission was prohibited the mails. In 1923 President Warren G. Harding accepted the honorary chairmanship of the Founder's Committee of the New York Society; and in 1927, to protect their dead chairman, Mr. Sumner with six policemen had to invade a printing plant and carry off the plates and sheets of what was said to be the story of an illicit love of Gamaliel and the natural daughter thereof.§ These reformers never allowed themselves to laugh; and their opponents got to laughing too easily. The jokes became simple and in terms of one syllable — *prude,* or at most of two — *prison.* The huge crime of the reformers was in excluding people from human experience; the more baffling crime was in barring them from subtleties. What chance to refine tone or gesture of speech and image, when by dull moralists intellect is driven to consider merely subject matter, the facts of living, which should be basic to art? What chance for impeccable manner out of a

* Puritanism — *A Literary Force.*
† *To the Pure* by Ernst and Seagle.
§ The book is called *The President's Daughter.* The incident is recorded in *To the Pure.*

moral background which murdered mystery quite as a radio announcer can murder silence?

In 1915 Anthony Comstock died, rich, ridiculed and respected, leaving an organization so efficient as to carry on without his initial fervor, as long as the millionaires would pay the salaries of its officers. He died in the year of *The "Genius"* appearance. Eleven months passed and the message of that book with its beauties and imperfections had gone to thousands of people. " In July 1916," as Mr. F. L. Rowe, secretary of the Cincinnati society, told it at the time, " Rev. John Herget of the Ninth Street Baptist Church became acquainted with the book, when he was called to a telephone by an unidentified person who complained. Immediately," Mr. Rowe assured his interviewer from the Cincinnati Inquirer, " we procured a copy of the present issue, and find that it is filled with obscenity and blasphemy. We have succeeded in having it removed from practically every book store in the city." But this was not enough. Ecstatic over new-found treasure the Society appealed to the Post Office Department in Washington, which took no action because the complaint " had not been presented in the proper form."

Sumner, however, was not squeamish about " form " and leaped to the challenge with the advantage of living near the very source of the evil, the John Lane Company. His appetite was further whetted by the receipt in his mail of pages furiously torn from a copy of *The "Genius"* belonging to the New York Public Library. Naming " 75 lewd and 17 profane passages," Sumner confronted the publisher and ordered them deleted or the book withdrawn and the plates destroyed. Lane's American representative, Mr. J. Jefferson Jones, withdrew the book, awaiting " further action " on someone's part. But he took the precaution to ask Dreiser's permission before destroying the plates. Dreiser got possession of them and stored them in a warehouse in New Jersey. As formidable as that did Sumner and his public seem to Mr. Jones, who yet with English support in the case of *The Titan* had dared where Harper's feared to tread. Frederic Chapman, who had constituted the support, was no longer Lane's literary advisor in London. Soon after he died.

On August 20th, 1916 the New York Tribune featured Sumner and Dreiser on the same page with headlines of the Great War:

"Allies Strike 155 Mile Line in Balkans — Drive to Win Back Serbia Closes Ring of Gunfire — Enemy Routed in Macedonia — Offensive on Fourth Front Opens Wedge Along Salonica Railroad — Vice Society Works Out New Method of Censoring Literature — Plan Tried Out on Dreiser's '*Genius:*'

"The essential feature of the new method is to get rid of objectionable publications without giving authors and publishers the benefit of free advertising, such as followed Comstock's attack on the picture 'September Morn' and the novel 'Hagar Revelly.'"

The "Genius" was the first powerful American novel threatened by the vice crusaders. Garland, Harold Frederic, David Phillips, Upton Sinclair had less cavernous visions and a less unswerving hold on them. They had not the austere talent to secrete and display worlds of life in three dimensions as Dreiser could. So in attacking him these moralists were attacking the very volume of newness which threatened them, in the hope of purging it of all but commercial and industrial currents. Perhaps for this or because a ferment was at work in the country on the verge of war and yet so newly awakened to a sense of itself, *The "Genius"* case became a rallying point for rebels. The wine of consciousness was in the air out of a double crisis — birth and death, the agony of final arrival and the despair of sudden going. A few men and women like some of those back of the Seven Arts, the Little Review, the Poetry Magazine, and others in scattered positions wanted to hold on to what had finally been won by scientists and poets and critics for native intellect. By virtue of being American some of them still dreamed with Jefferson and Whitman that a new society would emerge into history with a freedom of its own, a progression in the spirit, like that of Athens or of France or of England. Coincident with this moment in any event, if not out of it, came a fruition of impulses which had been trying to survive since the difficult days of Melville, Poe, Thoreau, and Whitman.

In this year 1916 and in the next years Dreiser grew

to full strength as an opposing force. And as different and startling crusaders as Mencken, Frank Harris and Ezra Pound came to the defence of *The " Genius,"* or rather to the attack of censorship. Not one of the three was much interested, as it happened, in the work itself, but they were passionately aggressive against that too " crude demos " which was making United Villages out of the only land of their birth. And then there were others, Harvey O'Higgins, Felix Shay, Alexander Harvey, George Keating, Elias Rosenthal, Joseph Auerbach, Sherwood Anderson, Randolph Bourne, who admired *The " Genius "* as well. The case brought many names associated with quite different phases of thought into relation with one another, and all into relation with the single name of Dreiser. It seemed as if the country might conclude a moment of fusion. Some of these men valued precisely Dreiser; the balance of power was with him whatever his sins. Others like Mencken and Harris valued Dreiser but deplored *The " Genius,"* a decline from literary grace. Still others like Ezra Pound, already in England teaching Yeats to be modern and himself to be ancient, had not much use for author or book. Dreiser was not brief enough or fused enough to please them. He was too American. Yet they must all have felt " a formidable integrity " * at issue, or it is not likely they would have made this incident of censorship into a nucleus around which to fight from freedom of art.

* Sallie Kussel, who typed most of *An American Tragedy* said of Dreiser: " I shall never forget his formidable integrity."

56

" MORALS — not Art or Literature."
Anthony Comstock

" The dirtiest book of all is the expurgated book."
Walt Whitman

" A man mounts toward the height of Olympus . . . he is already half transported to the sky; but a wretched jailor's hand drags him back into the gutter. If you hold converse with the Muse they take you for a debaucher of girls. And they will make you stand, my friend, at the bar with thieves. . . . Earth has its boundaries but human stupidity is limitless."
Flaubert to De Maupassant

The counter move on the part of the John Lane Company was to ask the support of the Authors' League of America, of which Dreiser was not a member.* On the 24th of August they called a special meeting of their Executive Committee. The sense of it was that *The " Genius "* was " not lewd, licentious or obscene " and that the Vice Society may, if not checked, " prevent the sale of many classics and of much of the serious work which is now being offered," and that " the League take such action as may be possible to prevent the suppression of the work complained of." The resolution concluded with the typed signatures of the Executive Committee, George Barr Baker, Rex Beach, Thompson Buchanan, Ellis Parker Butler, George Creel, Arthur I. Keller, Leroy Scott, Louis Joseph Vance, Kate Jordan, Helen S. Woodruff. But of these the names of Butler, Baker, Keller,

---

* According to Dreiser he was invited to join the Authors' League two or three years after its start. But when he asked them what they did " for the average author, they took umbrage "; and he never joined.

Scott, Jordan and Woodruff were absent from the formal protest drawn up some days later, and finally distributed under the auspices of the League. As one goes over the files of this curious battle it becomes clear that the Authors as a body found " action " impossible. Too many of their members recoiled from Dreiser, the naturalist, the pro-German, the crude craftsman. And " sex " and " the dark side of things " were too " unpleasant." Yet they allowed the protest to go, framed by the bolder members:

"We, the undersigned, American writers, observe with deep regret the efforts now being made to destroy the work of Theodore Dreiser. Some of us may differ from Mr. Dreiser in our aims and methods, and some of us may be out of sympathy with his point of view, but we believe that an attack by irresponsible and arbitrary persons upon the writings of an author of such manifest sincerity and such high accomplishments must inevitably do great damage to the freedom of letters in the United States, and bring down upon the American people the ridicule and contempt of other nations. The method of the attack, with its attempt to ferret out blasphemy and indecency where they are not, and to condemn a serious artist under a law aimed at common rogues is unjust and absurd. We join in this public protest against the proceeding in the belief that the art of letters, as carried on by men of serious purpose and with the co-operation of reputable publishers, should be free from interference by persons who, by their own statement, judge all books by narrow and impossible standards; and we advocate such amendments of the existing laws as will prevent such persecutions in future."

The Secretary of the League, Eric Schuler, contributed the further service of a talk in October with Mr. Sutherland of the Post Office Department in Washington, who thought that in all probability the Department would " take no action in the matter of *The ' Genius.'* " A later letter from U. S. Attorney H. Snowden Marshall to Dreiser's lawyer, on November 2, 1916 confirmed him " that it was not a case in which prosecution was warranted." At this point the Authors' fervor for freedom of American letters appears to have waned. Also The John Lane Company, who at first talked of bringing the matter into the courts at their expense, were afraid to fight for Dreiser. Mr. Jones generously advised him " to let his attorney, Mr. Stanchfield, loosen the dogs of war on Sumner and his crowd at once." Mencken thinks that the publishers lacked the money, and were failing in New York; but Dreiser must have had less money than they. Now once more it was up to him to wrench from conservatives the right to tell about life as he saw it, and survive the telling in the United States. The Comstocks had already cut off his income from *The " Genius,"* $2,400 in less than a year, and could impose a fine or prison sentence, or both, if upheld by the courts. In the event of this they planned the suppression of all of his books. Some years later he is quoted in an interview as having " fought the '*Genius*' battle single-handed." Perhaps at the time he felt isolated enough, and as the years passed looked back on the persecution as that of many against one. But the records disclose that he had in energy and money the support of a few devoted allies, and offers from others. It may be they quarreled among themselves and with Dreiser as to the best method to defeat the Comstocks, so that he felt the loneliness of opposition, never acceptable to genius. In any event he fought with a vigor which had grown out of sleek alluvial valleys and Catholic and Mennonite discipline. His first exclamation to reporters was in their own " that's-telling-'em " language: " If my name were Dreiserevsky and I said I came from Moscow I'd have no trouble. But I come from Indiana — so goodnight!" But he did not go to sleep. For two years he gave out interviews which went into news columns as if ideas were events. To the New York Sun he said:

> " I look on this interference with myself or any other serious writer as an outrage and I fear for the ultimate intelligence of America. A band of wasp-like censors has appeared and is attempting to put the quietus on our literature, which is at least showing signs of breaking the bonds of puritanism, under which it has so long struggled in vain. Poe, Hawthorne, Whitman and Thoreau have in turn been the butt and gibe of unintelligent persons, until by now we are well-nigh the laughing stock of the world. When will we lay aside the swaddling clothes forced on us by . . . antiquated moralists and their uneducated followers? . . ."

And to the New York Tribune:

> " To me the issue is a contest that goes to the very roots of thought in this country. Are we going to succumb to

Puritan thought, or is it possible for the United States to accept a world standard of thinking? . . . We are always talking about the great American novel. How, I want to ask intelligent men, are we going to produce that? By adopting the standard of criticism which has permitted the publication of Flaubert, Balzac, and others in France; Tolstoi in Russia; Moore and Bennett and others in England, Strindberg and Ibsen in Sweden and Norway? Or are we going to let Major Funkhauser, who obtained the withdrawal of *Anthony and Cleopatra* in Chicago . . . and Sumner to read and decide how far our minds shall go?

" Is this a free country? Is an artist to be allowed to interpret life as he sees it, or is he to conform to a carconductor standard of literature? There is something sickly about the whole mental attitude of this country. . . ."

To the Chicago Herald-Examiner:

" No mythical Heaven about which no one knows anything . . . is going to serve any longer. Man should unite and make war on the other forces of nature that now oppress him, reorganize his religious conceptions, as well as the theories of the state under which he lives, until he has brought all of them into tune with his own great needs."

To the Brooklyn Eagle:

" It is dreadful to think of shackles being forged which are going to hold the mind . . . in a vise-like grip of timidity utterly precluding initiative. There's little enough courage as it is. . . . I have my following, and that is all anyone could expect . . . all anyone could possibly want. It would be absurd to desire unanimous approval. It isn't necessary. But . . . if something doesn't happen to break down the . . . hide-bound tradition, which is the enemy of the race, man will go to seed."

He asked the public to remember " the incident of Gorki's reception, to whom even Mark Twain had been afraid to extend the hand of welcome. And Gorki, the head of an important paper in Russia was using his power to spread his distrust of America." A few weeks before he had seen in a newspaper " a rabid attack on Edgar Allan Poe, which summed him up as a failure, Poe the most precious heritage of the land! A failure! "

His friends fought with him for his and their " great needs." A defence committee was formed with a secretary, Harold Hersey, who set to work to send the League's protest to authors all over the country for their signatures. Among them Mencken gives to Harvey O'Higgins the chief credit for this work. But according to the documents Mencken himself appears to have labored for signatures until they reached the number of 478. " Perhaps," he said, " it was as much my secretary in Baltimore as anyone else; she worked untiringly for all of two months. . . ." As for himself, he added, the affair engaged him because it gave him a chance to canvass the intelligence of the country. Especially he delighted in following up refusals or failures to answer with a personal letter. Sometimes in the case of an important signature he wrote and replied three or four times. The files show on Mencken's side a devotion to making history and keeping its records. He is a creative statistician. When I interviewed him fifteen years after these events he volunteered to send me, a stranger to him, all of the papers, protest, lists of names, clippings and letters, a heavy package. They might provide my book, he thought, with an amusing paragraph or two about this phase of Dreiser's career. They could do more than that; they could make a novel of ideas, a kaleidoscope of the American point of view in 1916. Mencken himself once promised his public to write this novel,* but may have wearied of the issue. When I returned the material to his office he pronounced its epitaph, as if the cause of wit had been foredoomed to failure: " Well, this will go back into my files now, where it will gather dust, I suppose until my death, and then be sold at auction, knocked down for thirty cents — article 517. . . . And that's what will happen to Dreiser some day, too. And to you as well," he added, as if the idea delighted him. A dreary verdict! I could not resist anticipating a livelier death — That something of our past might remain, if only a theorem, surviving annihilation, to amuse or challenge or give background to the future!

In the first autumn of *The " Genius "* battle Mencken was hopeful. He was like a hunter bagging his game at

---

* *Prefaces: Theodore Dreiser*, page 143: " Among my literary lumber is all the correspondence relating to this protest, and some day I mean to publish it that posterity may not lose the joy of an extremely diverting episode."

each new important signature or absurd refusal. Unlike Dreiser he could enjoy the affair as a sport, a contest. He exhorted in warlike vocatives, " On with the machine guns! Forward the Zeppelins! I am planning a general offensive. . . . I am full of hope that shrapnel will play a part." And yet it was his policy to try and convert Puritans. Constantly he coached the novelist not to alienate them. In one letter he scolds him for flirting with " tenth-rate geniuses "; in another he warns him that the best way to get signatures is to " besiege the leading authors of the country: by leading authors of course I mean those best known to the public. The signature of such an old ass as Brander Matthews would be worth a great deal." Hersey writes Mencken that he is much disturbed by Dreiser's excursion into the " red ink crowd." * Specifically that seemed to refer to a visit on Mitchell Kennerly's advice to the office of John Quinn, who, it was known, had a collection of modern paintings, sculptures and writings, still thought of in America as " crazy, insane, lunatic." † John B. Stanchfield, an admirer of Dreiser, and a collector of exciting classics, rather than moderns, had been chosen by right-wing friends as the safer legal advice. Dreiser, who antagonized easily but seldom harbored resentment, perhaps never, apparently could value the advice of one like Kennerley who had attempted to block him. In his impartial way he computed that loyalty did not necessarily mean judgment. On the same afternoon he paid a visit to both lawyers to see which one he liked best. Mr. Hersey was in despair, but as it turned out Stanchfield was more suited to Dreiser's taste. John Quinn belonged among Americans who were already *émigrés* to older lands. It may be that the author of *The " Genius "* felt the cleavage — a not unfriendly but critical sophistication. Mr. Stanchfield offered to defend him at his own expense, just as John Quinn a few years later did in the case of Joyce's *Ulysses* for the Little Review.

None the less it was Dreiser's bolder method to mus-

* " Red ink " denoted red wine of Italian restaurants, where the intelligentsia liked to go to escape from Home.
† Matisse, Picasso, Derain, Brancusi, Duchamps, James Joyce.

357

ter all the rebels, exotic, disreputable, dangerous, obscure or snobbish, in the manner of Paul Revere on his midnight ride; to make a new start for adult America. One cannot compute which was the wiser instinct, his or Mencken's. The nature of their separate ways indicates a society too backward to embark on complicated journeys. A Brooklyn newspaper covering the event vindicates Mencken:

> "The protest contained some well-known names. . . . But on this same list is that of Rose Pastor Stokes, recently sentenced to ten years in a Federal prison, and Max Eastman who has figured in the courts quite frequently." *

On the other hand Mencken did not make converts of many of the "old asses." Such dignitaries as Brander Matthews, Shakespeare authority, Nicholas Murray Butler, president of Columbia, William Lyon Phelps and Bliss Perry, Yale and Harvard professors, William Dean Howells, Hamlin Garland, Agnes Repplier, Arthur Pier of Youth's Companion, Paul Elmer More would not fall into his trap. They evaded the issue by pleading ignorance of Dreiser's work; or else they wished the cause of freedom had a better case; or like Garland, Matthews, and Perry they chose to "suspect that the movement was being pushed by his publishers for advertising purposes" — "a piece of very shrewd advertising," according to Hamlin Garland. Howells wrote to Francis Hackett:

> "I have no doubt that half literature, prose and poetry, could as reasonably be suppressed as Mr. Dreiser's book. . . ."

Yet not having read it, this venerable dean of letters preferred to imperil half of literature than take a chance. He felt quite secure about his own half.

There were other incurables more honest and confiding. Writers like Ellis Parker Butler, Louis Pendleton, Mark Sullivan, Thomas A. Jenkins, Clara Louise Burnham, seemed to turn hysterical at the first hint of sex or tragedy. An occasional one of them would sign out of respect for Mencken. He was a scholar; it is the habit of prudes to go for sensation to remote cultures. Here

* Both for so-called political offences.

are some of their responses to the merciless sleuth of Baltimore:

". . . Some books can be so rotten that they should be destroyed. . . . Private censorship is the best way. . . . Things are not necessarily truthful because they stink, or strong because they smell. . . . A man is not more manly for going about without pants or underwear."

". . . I don't know what's the matter with me — perhaps I am just hopelessly middle-class or middle-aged before my time, but 'the frank discussion of sex' in fiction has always given me the feeling of distinct nausea. . . . There are a few honest men like Dreiser . . . but also . . . there are many of the Cosmopolitan school — nasty little fellows who are willing to do a little tickling in this line for the cash. . . . I am going to sign the protest not enthusiastically, but because I have just as much contempt for the paid smut-hounds as I have for the dishonest smut purveyors. . . ."

". . . Is it merely putting his books in library 'locked cases'? If that is all, I don't think it calls for a protest, as it is well to keep such literature from very young persons of both sexes. . . . I am now reading *The 'Genius'* . . . taken from a locked case in the Philadelphia library. His insight into beauty in all nature appeals to me, but his sexual stuff is not very convincing and leaves me cold."

"This author should be hanged for his breaches of good taste . . . if not for writing . . . the most pernicious book. I'm no prude. I have read Zola and much of Balzac . . . Tom Jones . . . Boccaccio . . . even parts of Rabelais . . . Burton's *Arabian Nights*. The classics named do not offend . . . partly because oceans and ages roll between, but . . . Dreiser knows no restraint. What other writer living or dead would have staged a childbirth scene and given details of the horrible Caesarian operation? . . . I am opposed to the fettering of genius, but . . . Mr. Dreiser delves in the revolting and the filthy. . . . I have no desire to protest against an effort to check the flow of literary ditchwater."

These comments accorded with Comstock and Sumner. Felix Shay, editor of The Fra, East Aurora, New York, a disciple of Elbert Hubbard, baited Sumner by letter, and got the same kind of answer from headquarters:

"This is a matter of almost ancient history. We received serious complaints against the book . . . and it was very apparent that its circulation was a violation of the law.

... You say, 'I think you make a serious error in annoying a man of unquestionable character and accomplishment.' ... What possible difference can this make? The law makes no distinction as to social, literary or other standing of the offender; nor is any consideration given as to the intent of the author. ... What the law seeks to prevent is the harmful effect produced on the immature mind by a certain class of book. ... I think it is well understood in the book trade that any publisher who makes a practice of putting objectionable literature on the market soon goes out of business. ... We are looking at this particular book from the standpoint of its harmful effect on female readers of immature mind, and by this we do not necessarily mean youthful readers."

From this rigid, unrelenting stand, jump ahead a dozen years and contemplate the riches acquired by the very kind of publisher there referred to, and you will tremble for the tranquillity of Mr. Sumner's latter years. I asked Mencken to describe Sumner. " A Sunday-school scholar," he said, " A feeble fellow compared to Comstock or Chase of the Boston Watch & Ward Society. Chase was a bombastic Methodist teacher, sadistic." Back in the days of tyrannical " purity " Shay having hooked his Sumner, played him for all he was worth, perhaps more; and prophesied the change about to take place in the temper of American public and publishers:

"There *is* a difference in men. ... There is a difference in the intent of men sufficient to change the entire application of your laws. Whether his '*Genius*' is one of the great novels ... neither you nor I are qualified to judge. But both of us should have the good taste to leave it to fame or to oblivion.

" If you are sincere, and I wish to think you are, I warn you beware a misuse of power! Beware of false zeal! ... To tear down a man and build up a theory! Beware in your attempt to protect 'the immature female mind — not necessarily youthful' from the 'harmful effect' of this book. Offhand it seems to me gentlemen of your persuasion more than Dreiser, have insisted that female minds not necessarily youthful remain immature!

" Why not open the windows of their minds in the blessed sunshine of knowledge. ... Give the immature female mind a chance to grow through exercise!

". . . Come Sumner, we don't want to drown the intellect, stop the tongue in a pail of sanctimonious whitewash, do we?

"... Last night I read Genesis, Chap. XVI, verses 2 to 5.... Why don't you suppress the Bible if only your 'law' is supreme? I ask sincerely ... and anticipate a logical action. No, not really a logical action! I don't want you to suppress the Bible."

One point in Sumner's letter not challenged by Shay, especially shocks the innocent democratic mind: Sumner's word was law; the question was "ancient history" before it was tried.

Beside the moralists of the old school another class of writers was loath to sign. They were talented craftsmen, some of them at the start, who had found their best work too costly. Now they were filling orders for romance, acceptable to the magazines, and were jealous of Dreiser. They knew how to write and how to invent; why should "a mere plagiarist from life" get more fame than they? And they were uneasy that out of his momentum might come a change of fashion in fiction to displace them. A letter to Mencken from Henry Sydnor Harrison, author of *Queed* and *V. V.'s Eyes* slyly reflects their fear of encroaching realism. Mencken, he says, has "set his foundations to rocking in a review of a book of his own"; yet he is unwilling to sign:

"... I cannot say whether *The 'Genius'* is decent or indecent until I have read it ... something I am unable or unwilling to do. But I can say there is such a thing as indecency in art, and ... Sumner was exactly right when he said that authors as a class were no better judges of indecency ... than any other class....

"I can't see the necessity of this protest ... the American philistine is precisely the person, I supposed, that Mr. Dreiser holds in particular contempt.... It is hardly conceivable ... that the most resolute of our naturalists should turn now to care for the approbation of these persons with the sale that it carries. As an offset to the annoyance of persecution ... he has the memory of the distinguished example of Flaubert ... and he possesses a standing as an artist hardly matched by any other living American writer.

"You see I am saying that it seems to me Mr. Dreiser has fared very well."

To this snobbery which invited Dreiser to starve on the memory of Flaubert, Mencken, sensing jealousy, replied that though his own point of view was "almost unbrokenly literal," he admired Harrison as the best of our craftsmen, and begged again for his name:

"I leave it to your own blushful remorse. . . . Imagine Brahms refusing to hear 'Die Walküre'! . . . As for your second objection it pains me even more. Who is better fitted to judge novels . . . men of letters, or a small clique of filthy minded Puritans? Have you ever read Comstock's pamphlets, — the Bible of the smut-hounds? Read it and weep! . . .

"Third, what you forget is that the Comstocks are trying to pillory Dreiser before the world as a merchant of mere pornography, a low and lewd fellow . . . and to send him to a Federal prison for five years. . . . Is this the sort of thing that should go unchallenged in a free Republic?

"Personally I don't care for *The 'Genius.'* But I know that Dreiser is a serious artist. . . . If we put his failure to meet our personal notions . . . above the principle that every artist should be free, then we plainly hand over letters to a crowd of snooping and abominable Methodists, and say goodby to all we have struggled for. . . .

"The one aim of the protest is to enter a caveat against such . . . intolerable proceedings, and to give public notice that the authors of the United States . . . are united against the common enemy as the authors of France were in the Zola case."

Flaubert, Mencken might have added, was acquitted before the tribunal of Paris of the charge against *Madame Bovary*. But for all his righteous eloquence this critic did not make a convert of his craftsman, nor unite the authors of America. Harrison, whose implicative style sometimes recalled George Meredith, wrote back that "critics and artists should live, not like brokers in unity, but aloof and apart." In this he had his way. Isolations continued to prevent exchange of ideas among them. They continued to seek relations with ideals; the conformists with decorum and prosperity, the radicals with license and martyrdom. Out of the cleavages grew snobs in both camps. By the one kind Dreiser was firmly put down as "a lewd and low fellow"; Sumner was upheld. By the other, as the years went on, and lewdness and lowness became fashionable, he was condemned anew as old-fashioned and serious. Out of the upheaval one common thing continued to triumph, brought over on the *Mayflower* — intellectual frivolity.

Whether practised by moralists or immoralists we do not yet escape from it.

In the autumn of 1916, the very month of the *Genius* controversy, I first met Dreiser — not in the least uncouth, on the contrary, distinguished by eyes and mouth that related him to Yeats and Henry James, not long before on exhibition in the United States. Visionary and workman in him had recreated loose Indiana features. He spoke of his battle with the Vice Society but not at length, or as if it much concerned him. He agreed that common controversy was the death of art, the murder of mystery. But how anyway was there to be art when there were no vital women as women, except those of the streets or music halls, and they unconsciously so? American colleges were neutralizing women. Men too, I said. No, he thought there was more appetite left in men. Look at our cities, power plants and railroads, the work of wonderful imaginations. But what intellectual women of passion did we have? — Mary Garden and Emma Goldman, that was all. Jane Addams was as sad as a whipped animal. Isadora Duncan? Perhaps. Where had I been educated? Bryn Mawr? He had just written an article, *Life and Art in America,* where he had asked his readers to name one woman of any distinction or achievement out of the twenty-five years of that institution. Perhaps he would amend it.* So we talked. . . .

But if in what was called society one ventured to speak of Dreiser as a figure important to New York, it was soon to find that his name if recognized at all was dismissed with a shudder. As in earlier days he was improper. I remember once an author who after the subject had been changed murmured, " Do you know what woman Dreiser's living with now? " Upon my ignorance as to that, the first and last spark of interest in " America's foremost novelist " died.

* This he did not do: " There is not a chemist, a physiologist, a botanist, a biologist, an historian, a philosopher, an artist of any kind or repute among them. They are curators, directors, keepers. They are not individuals in the true sense of the word. They are not free. . . ." *Hey-Rub-A-Dub-Dub,* pages 260–261.

Now the story flows out of these narrow corridors of conventional thought. Born within or escaped to the greater world beyond correctness, there existed an enterprising minority. Their responses, to Hersey and Mencken in *The " Genius "* case, follow along the gullies of change. They fall like rain on the arid soil of conventional opinion. They make rifts in the clouds; they have about them the stir and breath and lights of dramatic America, as of theatre signs reflected on wet pavements or of stars in city puddles blown toward unknown goals:

" I take great pleasure in signing . . . when any American writer succeeds in getting anything except Sunday school optimism past our first two trenches — the magazine editors and the book publishers — he should not be forced to endure any additional trials of censorship. . . ." Robert Wason, Norwalk, Connecticut.

" Ye Gods! Are we reverting to the Stone Age? Like to sign it a dozen times." Frederick Isham, Detroit.

" Anything I can do submerge the prurient puritanism of the Comstock castrati will be done with all the energy I possess." William Lee Havery.

" I hope that what you say, that the case is already won, is true, and that I will have an opportunity in a very short time to rejoice with you." E. W. Howe, Potato Hill Farm, Atchison, Kansas.

". . . I am very glad to add my name to the names of those who are fighting the powers of narrow-minded darkness." Amelie Troubetzkoy.

" For Dreiser personally I have a strong feeling of affection, . . . for he is one of the few men who tried once upon a time to do me a distinct service. . . . Had I listened to Dreiser, perhaps I would now be dead, but I would not have suffered the pangs of such slavery as is now imposed on me.

" He is not a craftsman, or I am — well, write me down as an ass.

" But to the point, if you are serious in that lowly I affix the signature that has sent many a good man to the chingow, I do hereby do it. . . . I have less use for moralists than I have for Dreiser. . . ." Leo Crane, Moqui Indian Agency, Keams Canyon, Ariz.

" I . . . should have regretted not being able to throw what weight I have in the scale of Liberty and Freedom for the arts to develop themselves as they think fit. Nothing could be more pernicious to the future of literature in America than to have it in the hands of a few bigoted and fanatic people. . . . No country can hope to develop itself unless its authors are permitted to educate it. . . ." Amy Lowell, Dublin, N. H.

"Willingly I sign the protest. Let 'em look to the sex-rot of the movie." Opie Read, Chicago.

". . . You'll be shocked by my colossal ignorance. You see I am only a Bostonian . . . all the same I am curious to know what more appalling enormity poor Mr. Dreiser has perpetrated than the rest!

[In answer to Mencken's reply to this]: "I suspect that Mr. Dreiser's work belongs wholly or in part to the order of fiction I should never glance at. . . . Yet I do not believe in any personal literary censorship . . . and we are all in this world to help, not to hinder one another. . . . I am signing the petition." Lilian Whiting, Boston, Massachusetts.

". . . Shades of John Milton! What are we coming to in this country! Not long since I used the awful words 'eunuch' and 'seminal' in some verses, and they were returned to me with a shocked and grieved letter by one of our leading editors. . . . A trivial instance, but, I fear, typical. . . ." Lee Wilson Dodd, New Haven, Conn.

"Let me thank you for calling my attention to the Dreiser protest. . . . Curiously enough, I lunched with Wells and Bennett in London last summer, and they spoke of it with great feeling." Isaac F. Marcosson, New York.

"Thank you for the opportunity to sign. . . . It is, as you say, a matter which should appeal vitally to all American writers; both in justice to Mr. Dreiser and in the name of saneness and honesty in all literary art." Mary MacLane, Butte, Montana.

". . . We must unite, all of us, to do away with this hideous . . . early Victorian provincialism which has been brought to light by Dreiser — to the intense astonishment of the world of letters. . . ." Cosmo Hamilton, New York.

". . . As a man he is impossible, but as an artist he is entitled to every pound of energy and every dollar we can spare to protect his work. . . . I confess it with shame, I am so buried in the movie business trying to earn a huge salary . . . that I did not know, until I picked up Pearsons last week. . . . Count on me in every way, financial and otherwise." Forrest Halsey, Fredericksburg, Virginia.

"If I can be of any assistance, financially or morally, in having the law amended, please call on me." George T. Keating, New York.

Then there were four replies from Frank Harris, Ezra Pound, Sherwood Anderson and Robert Frost, the first three from the social point of view; Frost's from an inner mind which refused to be delayed by public thought, and yet was more related than the others to Dreiser's conviction: "Life is not reasonable — reason has but little influence over us compared to chance."

Harris wrote to Hersey:

"I have signed your protest and I have withdrawn from the Author's League of America because they have not taken energetic action in the Dreiser matter, which I desired and expected. I think any decent Author's League would have got up a defense fund to stand the cost of the whole case for Mr. Dreiser. It is a disgraceful prosecution, lower even than would be tolerated in England. . . . I refused to join the Author's League in England because I regarded myself as an American. I joined the League here because I thought it would make itself felt, but such an opportunity having passed unnoticed I withdraw my name. . . . To any movement by authors to defend Dreiser I will cheerfully contribute."

And Ezra Pound wrote to Hersey from London:

"I hasten to return signed Dreiser's protest. Will have it printed in *The Egoist* as soon as possible. Am glad the Author's League has been at last aroused to do something. Can you inform me if it has ever before attempted to *do* anything for the freedom of American letters? Or whether it has not until the present date been typically 'American' after the fashion of . . . the general religious dinginess of American 'associations'? Is there really an Author's League? And what is the Academy of Arts and Letters? And are there two men in the country, or are they all Comstock's dogs and pot lickers?"

And the romantic Anderson to Mencken, from Taylor Critchfield & Co., an advertising agency in Chicago, in a frenzy of reason:

"I am with you in believing that the preservation of Dreiser's right to print books and sell them is the most important matter that has ever come up in America. Jesus Mariar, the question of whether America goes to war or not is secondary. Will you accept my thanks for the big part you are taking in fighting this morality monster. If Dreiser wins it will give us all more breathing space."

And the fastidious Frost in New Hampshire, whose poems had not been published until 1914, and then first in England, wrote to Mencken:

"With all my heart — on general principles — though I don't know much about Dreiser's books beyond that they are honest, and though I don't care a hang for 'the ridicule and contempt of other nations' . . . I had not heard that the Comstockians were after Dreiser. . . . These fools should consider where H. G. Wells has come safely out in his latest by being left entirely alone to think things out for himself. The way our wildest attempts to think free always end in the same conclusion is the saddest proof that no other conclusions are possible."

Seven august Englishmen cabled their joint signatures to the protest, and there was great rejoicing at their voluntary support: Arnold Bennett, W. L. George, William J. Locke, E. Temple Thurston, Hugh Walpole, H. G. Wells and Lewis Wilkinson. Signatures and promises came and went like sparks. But "these fools" did not "consider." The John Lane Company never got back its courage to sell *The "Genius."* And yet it happened that these "wild attempts to think free" did not end in quite the "same conclusions." They went into the making of another formula, maybe as sorry as the old one, but not as rigid. By its nature Puritans were soon to admit that the last word was no longer theirs. There were other words to come.

Frank Harris in Pearson's, Ezra Pound in The Egoist, Mencken in The Smart Set and the newspapers, Alexander Harvey, editor of Current Opinion, and Dreiser in numerous interviews and articles fought for the issue violently. Randolph Bourne and Mencken made analyses of his work such as could not have been elicited by "lewd and profane writing." * And although he did not become innocent in the eyes of the courts or of respectable people, he became a kind of dark pool or cavern that stood to many others for mystery and reality — an element of wonder. All of those who could not dare but wished they might, found solace in Dreiser. And those born to dare found precedent in him. He became a source of thought and of action.

In the fusion of the moment on January 5, 1917 "at

* Bourne: *The Art of Theodore Dreiser.* The Dial, June 1917. Mencken: *The Dreiser Bugaboo,* The Seven Arts, 1917.

the home of Mr. Frank Harris, 3 Washington Square, Mr. Theodore Dreiser, Mr. Harold Hersey, Mr. Frank Harris, Mr. Karl Karsten, Mr. Theodore Schroeder," according to the minutes of the meeting, "met to discuss the foundation of an author's aid society." It should operate to counteract the Societies for the Suppression of Vice, and be potent where the Authors' League was inert. Dreiser suggested " propaganda to develop more wholesome public opinion," and " an attack upon the censor for the protection of books perhaps once in five years." Harris proposed "lobbying in the Legislature to shift the burden of censorship from private societies to the Attorney General, and then only after expert advice; the discovery and exposure to ridicule of the people who supported the Comstocks; and the issue of a periodical." The lawyer, Schroeder, an authority on laws pertaining to obscenity * proposed an attack " on Comstock and his successors for alleged violation of trust funds." They decided to hold a founders' dinner. Frank Harris agreed to arrange it and to invite among others:

"Otto Kahn, Samuel Untermyer, Ida Tarbell, Edgar Lee Masters, Percy Stickney Grant, John Dewey, Jacques Loeb, Marcella Sembrich, Mary Garden, Senator Borah, Princess Troubetzkoy, Francis Hackett, Felix Warburg, Frederick MacMonnies, John Quinn, William Marion Reedy, Mrs. Harry Payne Whitney, Stephen S. Wise, D. W. Griffiths, Carrie Chapman Catt, Gertrude Atherton, Finley Peter Dunne, Arthur B. Davies, Gutzon Borglum, Frank A. Vanderlip, Arthur Brisbane, Elizabeth Marbury, and perhaps Booth Tarkington, B. W. Huebsch, Amos Pinchot, Max Eastman, William Randolph Hearst and Mitchell Kennerly."

A shining project! And who knows, history might have been made if these financiers, opera singers, suffragettes, movie magnates, ministers, statesmen, fashionable women, politicians, scientists, educators, painters, publicists, poets and novelists had dined together in the name of art. It was before Prohibition. But study the various biographies of these celebrities and you will see that the solar planets could sooner have met in one room. Tough as they were, Dreiser, Harris and Schroeder appear to

* Author of *Obscene Literature and Constitutional Law.*

have believed in miracles. There was never another meeting toward an author's aid society " to aid indigent authors of approved merit and their dependants as well as to defend ably and freely censored authors in need. . . ." Capital was not ready yet to shift its support from morals to art. Is it seriously ready today? Is there yet a department of art and letters in Washington or in any State capital in pursuit of the aims proposed at this meeting of optimists? In the sense of private enterprise the Guggenheim scholarship foundation at length acknowledges native artists and scientists; but have helped them to leave the country, not to stay in it.

In March 1917, through the firm of Stanchfield & Levy, Dreiser brought suit against his publishers for failure to fulfil their contract with him. A "friendly suit," they agreed — the court was to decide. In May 1918 the case was argued before the Appellate Division of the Supreme Court. Joseph S. Auerbach in his brief for Dreiser made a distinguished summary of the novel,* save for throwing its emphasis, as I suppose lawyers must, in the direction of accepted morality: The hero, he told the court, a painter in a country which had no use for art, forced to marry a girl he was tired of, sought to deepen life and marriage with " sexual excesses." These led to the defeat of his painting and to excursions elsewhere, both financial and amorous. And these in turn led to financial ruin after fabulous success in the advertising game. The moral to be drawn was as clear as water; the five judges must see it: go the narrow road, disobey your senses, and you will be rich and successful. That the book discloses the cruel reaches of such a code over natures alien to it, that the hero's environment as well as his own "excesses" combined against him — this, Auerbach was careful not to say. He proved beyond a reasonable doubt that *The "Genius"* was a moral work of genius. With this he submitted that according to precedent serious contemporary art should be immune to censorship, or else the works of Chaucer, Shakespeare, Laurence Sterne, the playwrights

* J. S. Auerbach, "Authorship and Liberty," North American Review, June 1918.

of the Restoration, and many parts of Old Testament Scripture would be imperiled. As examples of books less reticent than Dreiser's novel, and acquitted by the courts, he offered *The Triumph of Death* by D'Annunzio, the works of Voltaire, Flaubert's *Madame Bovary,* Moore's *Memoirs of My Dead Life,* and he lightened his argument with the opinions of New York judges Seabury, Hiscock, Cullen, Werner and O'Brien: " It is no part of the duty of courts to exercise a censorship over literary productions," Judge Seabury had ruled. " To condemn a standard work because of a few of its episodes, would compel the exclusion from circulation of a very large proportion of the works of the most famous writers of the English language," Judge O'Brien had once said. ". . . There is no . . . precise test by which to determine what constitutes decency or indecency either of words or acts. . . . The question . . . must . . . be tested by the prevailing common judgment and moral sense of the community . . ." was the opinion of Judge Hiscock, in sustaining the dismissal of an indictment for indecent speech at a public meeting.

The five judges, Clark, Laughlin, Smith, Page and Shearn, presiding at the trial, despite the 478 signatures of protesting American writers and of seven English writers, perhaps felt that the prevailing moral sense of the community was against *The " Genius."* Or they were persuaded by the argument of the defendant's attorney, John J. Kirby. He asserted first that " good intent . . . did not enter as a factor in the defense of cases brought under Section 1141 of the penal law of the state of New York." Second, that even if " good intent were a factor," there was nothing in this case " to indicate that any intent existed in the mind of the author or in the plan of the publisher other than to reap financial benefit from . . . this book." It had been agreed between author and publisher that the loss to Dreiser, if the contract were not carried out, would be not less than $50,000. But since continued publication constituted a violation of the penal law, the publisher was guilty of no breach of contract; and the plaintiff was not entitled to damages or " to any other relief whatever." Thus the friendly Kirby. He had proved that the book was " obscene, lewd, lascivious, indecent, filthy, or disgusting," because, although the hero suffered punishment for his immoralities, the women, including his wife, whom he had seduced before marriage, " had these experiences without apparent harm to themselves or their position in society." Mr. Sumner had said as much at the outset: " The book is demoralizing because its women characters apparently suffer no harm in their social standing."

In the week preceding the decision the Brooklyn Daily Eagle condensed the issue into an appropriate headline: " Five Judges Will Decide if *The 'Genius'* is Genius, Tommyrot, or Plain Filth." And other papers over the country had a sly laugh at the "highbrows" so that all good citizens could titter with them. The five judges possibly influenced by journalistic mockery sided with the plain people: They found themselves without jurisdiction of the action. Immature minds were thus protected from further corruption. American writers had legal warning that their characters could " sin " unpunished only at the risk of search, seizure and arrest of their books.

It was open to Dreiser to appeal the decision. But without money from his most sensational book there was not the means. Those who had vowed support out of the lapse of time lost interest. Stanchfield died. It seemed less futile to turn from legal action to his own profession, writing. He published among other books *Hey-Rub-A-Dub-Dub, A Book of the Mystery and Wonder and Terror of Life,* an answer and a challenge in terms of his philosophy to the moralists who had not left him alone to think things out for himself. For five years *The " Genius "* rested in the dark of the warehouse across the Hudson. Again, as eighteen years before with *Sister Carrie,* Dreiser waited.

57

"*Art walks into Nature the source, and comes out with Form the aim — of every thing.*"

"*What really is caviar, nightingale tongues, de foie gras, cheese — if not cruelty, indecency and relish?*"

"*Snow flakes fall voluptuously. High-noon sea and leaves, shells and insects, rapture ended, turn obscene; afternoon is censor. A moon, a fruit, a joke, a drunkard, a lily and an orchid might be lewd. Filth a luxury to fertilize a fern.*"

"*Art, an acrobat, a juggler, balances far out where others are afraid to go.*"

DOROTHY DUDLEY

So with these thousands of words over *The "Genius,"* all the great abstractions had been popularly invoked in newspapers, meetings and journals. Out of the welter it is clear that in one sense the American spirit was united. At this date except for a few originals, conservatives and radicals used the same tone of voice. Even the originals suffered at moments from righteousness. Both Comstocks and Intellectuals were zealots in the face of an exaggerated condition.

For human beings in America, Sex, it is clear, had been crystallized into one of two fictions. Sex had become a vague abstraction, a hidden necessity by which children slipped invisibly into the world. Or Sex had become an exalted luxury, a forbidden drug, beyond the hopes of a race who believed they were foredoomed to prose. Put down the cash, buy a woman — by a curious impersonal name men called the purchase. Or save your dollars, marry the nearest approach to the girl of magazine romance; and spend a life wondering why she gave you nothing, nothing at all promised in the unexpurgated Arabian Nights. Sue for breach of promise. Such was the fate of conquerors.

None the less we had come over on the Mayflower proclaiming independence, for ourselves. We had cheated the Redskins, burned the witches, got rid of French and Spaniards, cast off the English, freed the slaves, and would enter the World War, singing the battle cry of freedom. As Christ died to make men holy, we lived and died to make men free. The song caught the throat in a sob. Immigrants the earth over heard the song and joined us. We had behind us no organic 13th Century art and order to offer them; no radiant renaissance bearing a foliated 18th Century to proceed from — to romanticism, to realism, and then to modernism. But we had for background and future our own invention, Freedom, distant god of a people who got up in the morning to work, and went to bed early to get up still earlier in the morning to work — for liberty. It was our pursuit of happiness. Science, machinery and money were bringing us victory.

Now by this second decade of the new century, the snake, Time, not measured by clocks so much as by change, had really and truly shifted its position in the grass. Hygiene, plumbing, the telephone, electric lights, steel construction, automobiles, electric power, phonographs and movies had come to stay. They were classic achievements to make men free and happy, north, south, east and west. To an orchestra of steam shovels, piledrivers and riveters, to banners of smoke and confetti of advertising, a nation proclaimed jubilees and festivals. And yet freedom evaded us. We were rich in things, suddenly poor in spirit, so the critics said. Mind and imagination were imprisoned. The radicals protested now with fervor equal to that of the Puritans this hoax of wealth which the pioneers had foisted on them in the name of liberty. Of such were the defenders of Dreiser, impressive, righteous, and sometimes rigid like his enemies.

These critics of art did not say " ' Bawdy, indecorous, licentious, gay, ribald, equivocal, obscene! ' — you accuse us and we are; just as we are ' orderly, delicate, painstaking, compassionate and undefiled,' we who venerate life and seek to celebrate it." They made no defence of pornography in the sense that on one side of art is always a church, on the other side a bordel, and that art is the proposal of daring in a problem of balance. A crisis had been evoked and had to be evaded, for lack of critical intellect experienced enough to design it. It was a moment arising out of the times and dealing with them, and yet as unrelated and unimplicated as an alien child with its parents. If there was a challenge out of Dreiser and now out of Masters, and a year or so later from Sandburg, Carlos Williams, Sherwood Anderson, it was for the critics to say to the churchmen: " We repudiate your Anglo-Saxon code. We are mixed from all the races of the earth, and claim a mingled standard of whim and conduct." Or else to say to the conservatives: " We accept your hypocrisy because we have to. This ghost of yours who crossed on the Mayflower and goes back on the Mauretania continues to rule our great melting pot, with its law of separations and right of property. But since happily you permit the lowbrows, the rotarians and their girls, their lewdness of shows and newspapers and nation-wide conventions, we shall take our pleasures too in the pursuit of understanding, and read what we like, write what we like, say what we like." But the editors and critics made together no such bold stand. In this day they were like the timid children of explorers, admiring their fathers, Whitman, Dreiser, or Masters, say, but afraid of their mothers, Mrs. Clemens, Mrs. Doubleday, Miss N. P. D., Mrs. Peattie.

In the case of Dreiser his supporters either disciplined him or sanctified him. Floyd Dell complained because neither Titan nor Genius was a political rebel leading the nation out of capitalism to freedom. Burton Rascoe a few years later made Dreiser into a respectable saint and his detractors like Professor Sherman into liars. Mr. Rascoe sees no " sex thrills, no pornography, no immoralism, no destruction of standards . . . in the general tone of Mr. Dreiser's work. . . . Contrary to the current opinion Mr. Dreiser does not undermine moral foundations." In fact except for the passages which he quotes from his books he makes him out a very dull prophet. This was a portrait published in 1925, but it is typical of the righteousness of the intelligentsia of 1916 to 1918, that moment of popular controversy between radical and conservative elements. Somehow the radicals missed their chance and went over to the moralists. They liked to say that Art was serious and free, and therefore virtuous. Dreiser, they thought, was an emancipator and therefore harmless. With serious artists and uncompromising art journals we should be emancipated. Even they went so far as to invite Sumner and his cohorts to attack, censor and ban the music shows, the dance halls, the movies and the tabloids. His legitimate field, they said. And yet wasn't it the field out of which expression was growing? Happily such censorship was impossible; popular art paid too well. Or else we might never have had Bert Williams, Ed Wynn, Marilyn Miller, Frank Tinney, Joe Cook, Al Jolson, the Marx Brothers, Charlie Chaplin, Ring Lardner, Anita Loos, and a hundred others, often not in the least Puritan and sometimes lascivious lewd or obscene, intricate and subtle. At least *they* remained unmolested to exhilarate the Land of the Free; and to be the darlings of a later set of cognoscenti, who, piously too, felt they must have their folk lore. But that is the epilogue to this story.

Out of such a carnal, ribald, vulgar and limber background Dreiser had come. He tells it himself in *A Hoosier Holiday*, in *A Book About Myself*, in *Dawn*, in each book he writes. He was one of the immoral, indecorous, conquering Americans, allowed to live when they dealt in the medium of money, but apt to be censored when they worked with words. " It is you who have put aside Puritanism and gone straight to the heart of life," one disciple wrote. But this was an inverted compliment. He had not gone to, he had come from the heart of life, which has always put aside Puritanism and every other inconvenient code. " You are the one man in the country whose productions can hold a man's attention. Our literature until you arrived was made up of books by females, for females, the females having in some cases . . . the external aspects of masculinity," wrote another victim to our segregations. To him evidently men and nature were worthy, women and pederasts negligible. Yet his hero had written five novels, and several plays recreating the fierce chasms men and women were trying to cross to find each other again after Christianity and after Puritanism. Still another moralist wrote a poem elevating Dreiser to a lofty mountain; Sumner had followed. The writer had given " a great round laugh " at which the reformer had fallen off the mountain to ignoble lowlands. Yet this German-Slav's distinction was not one of exalted isolation but of mingling with crowds low and high, of tunneling and excavating through muck, dirt and rock, in search of " the mystery and terror and wonder of life."

Five years later when *The " Genius "* appeared again, the Jewish publisher took the precaution to introduce it with a preface from so earnest a radical it is a pity to betray him. It is done only in fastidious pursuit of my plot. He said that it was not the kind of " an immoral book that appealed to the baser passions." It was a book for " safe and sane readers." It was a work of art. A work of art " appealed to the aesthetic feeling." This feeling was to be gained " from reading a great book, from hearing great music, viewing great paintings, going into a great cathedral, or looking at Niagara Falls, or the Grand Canyon of the Colorado." Almost pointedly great women or small ones were left out of the category. I know little about Niagara Falls, but it is certain that the Grand Canyon of the Colorado appeals, if at all, to the baser passions, and anyone viewing for long this masterpiece of an arch-fiend might become dangerous and insane.

In that stupendous chasm, obscene perpendicular granites contradict and deride the precise order of soaring, fluted mountains — colossal pomp and mockery, proposing death to human beings. Nothing crosses the vermilion, purple, saffron miles on miles of formal battlements and uncouth obelisks, unless a crow or raven. Nothing lives there unless unseen and unknown presences. Even tourists have been known to perish in this mineral despotism. If typhoons, paranoics, massacres, volcanoes in their mobile violences appeal to the aesthetic feeling, then the Canyon makes that appeal in its monstrous indifference. If what is at once terrifying, salacious, decorative, implacable, appeals, then invoke this king of chasms.

In as far as American civilization, forgetting New England hills and streams, has run parallel to that far-flung precipitous scenery which, after the long slopes from the Atlantic, after the Prairies, after the Rockies, drops more abruptly to the Pacific — to this extent Dreiser's novels, in the sense of being American digits, do bear analogy to the Grand Canyon and the Yellowstone Geysers, the Great Divide, Death Valley and the Badlands. The Indians of the Southwest had propitiated with ceremonial this extravagance in which they found themselves. Their way was to celebrate the color and order with impeccable song, dance and image. Ours was not to propitiate but to conquer, to outrival the magnitude and cruelty. Dreiser's characters, for example, are men and women forced out upon perilous voyages, some of them so spirited or resilient they cannot quite perish in a wilderness; many of them not strong enough to live there except in masses.

In a new transitional migratory age Dreiser's problem as an artist was as different from that of Pueblo Indians as festivals are from storms. After centuries of migration from Asia perhaps to South America and back to New Mexico and Arizona, the Redskins had established an order by which to live, large enough, they thought, to conciliate the elements, narrow enough to take care of their needs. The new American on the other hand was recording life in the process of violent changes. While the artist dreamed and planned, the newspapers and the advertising men at an unscrupulous rate of speed ran off with his inventions, and made the language and made the décor of a people. Dreiser worked so fast he hoped to get ahead of them, and in the hurry he lost some of the plans he was capable of. None the less spontaneously he initiated one phase essential to art, by which his calculations resembled Indian ceremonial more than our own up to that date. He invoked profaneness to correct exaltation. He was one of the first to do this.

In the Pueblo corn ceremonials the Koshari are clowns performing against the rhythm, as if to say the other side of grief is gaiety, the other side of refinement is vulgarity.

At variance with the music, with obscene joke and gesture, they ridicule the other dancers, who impervious to the clowns step ecstatically to the chant and drums, throb of the earth, pulse of time. Nothing grows, the Indians say, without mockery. The Koshari, privileged in the tribe, provide the scandal without which art becomes tame; the others the solemnity, without which it is trivial. In their understanding elements are mingled not separate. With them it is impossible to unravel the lewd from the chaste, the noble from the ignoble. Their dances are not safe or perilous, they are critical; not mad or sane; they are balanced.

It was like this with Dreiser as near as he could come to it. His enemies were proposing safety, his friends freedom. With what ceremony he had at his command he was proposing, like primitive races and like the great individuals of all time, the forces of nature together, as often scandalous and tyrannical as they were orderly or exalted. Life, human or inhuman, was seductive, revolting, dirty, clean, lyrical, discordant, delicious and desolate by moods, years and moments, no matter what the epoch. Art was accordingly dangerous. But in an era of transition with no one phase subordinated to another, except all to the element of change, danger above everything rode the air. He supposed he was in the vanguard of this giant migration from old times to new. So friends and enemies seemed to think. He had not yet become old fashioned. Yet he had not, like many moderns, forgotten the uprooted souls struggling in the rear to carry the burden of tradition along with them over ruts and cracks. He was one of the few modern Americans who valued venerable culture; " Life is to be learned as much from books and art as from life itself, almost more so in my opinion," he wrote in 1916.

By this token he could understand reformers like Comstock and Sumner, professors like Sherman and Phelps. They were right, *The " Genius "* might easily lead people to fornication, adultery, failure, despair; and *The Titan* to greed, enterprise, robbery, murder and conquest; and so might the European classics and moderns which these church people had censored. They were trying to save old American customs from the new wilderness; he was hoping somehow to save more primitive elaborate cultures than those dreamed of in New England philosophy. That was the one difference. Except that it might very well be that everything would get junked in the wilderness, and while the moralists would accordingly lament, whatever happened, it was his one certain code to be prepared for change.*

For a time, however, it looked perhaps as if Methodists and Presbyterians would get junked first. In 1919 *Jurgen,* a book more salacious than *The " Genius,"* recalling the realism of 13th Century Provence, the work of an amateur libertine at that,† was banned; but reinstated in less than two years and at the expense of publisher and censors. This was an advance over Dreiser's experience. He had been one of those to prepare the way. In 1917 Gauthier's *Mademoiselle de Maupin* had been attacked by Sumner, and at once acquitted — by theme and style so insidiously erotic that a child, reading it in Chicago or New York, might defy father mother and democracy to attempt as elegant and luxurious a solution in the United States. In every way an inexpedient book, corrupting accepted morals, causing nostalgia for days never known in America and long since gone from France. Yet, though repeatedly attacked by the censors, *Mademoiselle de Maupin* was always upheld by the courts. Clearly the vice societies were losing ground. It was the same with books of science which like works of art led to experiment in sex rather than to prohibition. They were attacked as often, but less often convicted. Sumner and his friends were beginning to be behind the times. Every value was in a state of flux, changing into undefined values. Dreiser was ahead of the times, or preferably outside of them like all lovers of beauty. Most of his friends were at least abreast of the times. Together they had helped to bring about this change of sentiment. Yet really he himself had not asked for change, as much as for the right to record customs and changes and their interrelations. He was an American interested in balance.

Nor did he, like his admirers, claim for his books ex-

* *Hey Rub-A-Dub-Dub: Change.*
† James Branch Cabell, wistful scholarly Virginian.

emption from censorship on the ground that they were great achievements. Among the timorous fictions of the day they were as bold and faithful as he could make them; how near to art he could not say. Except he was certain that beauty had never been timid, and that no one had reached it without honesty. Nor did he have contempt for all puritans. They might be important actors in the drama at hand, who suffered and inflicted suffering. He had suffered with them when he created the fathers of Jennie and of Aileen, and his own father for example. Often they meant more to him than some of the radicals who might be merely colorless spectators or weak actors.

He told me once of two unintentional converts of his, and he was not especially proud of them. One was an editor he had known, who hated his novels — " uncouth, vulgar, impossible! " One day he became insane. A mutual friend went to visit him where he lived in the country. There he was sitting on his front porch, believing himself to be the " Genius," Eugene Witla, and boasting of his amorous exploits. In the telling, Dreiser let his carefully pleated handkerchief unfold without emphasis, and laughed a little. A grim joke, but there it was! And then there was the professor out in Illinois, Sherman, who somehow regretted his scholarly life, and resigning from the cornfields, had come East to find reality before it was too late. *Spoon River Anthology,* Sandburg's poems, *An American Tragedy,* all the moderns he had abused, had jarred him out of sleep. And he had done " the naturalist " a wrong, he wrote in the New York Tribune. A novelist who could drown his heroine in a lonely lake and send his pitiful hero to the chair for their sins, was a great and good philosopher after all. His own life had been spent in futile security, it seemed to him. Not many years later by some caprice of nature, Sherman's own end came by drowning in a lake. . . . And yet Dreiser wanted to be neither reformer nor rebel. On the arc of a flood of change he was only trying to tell about human beings, and relate their hidden passions to the old and new values which preyed on them. If on such an expedition of understanding some of those who chose to join fell by the way, it was by malice of nature, not by his choice.

58

" To the artist there is never anything ugly in nature. . . . A big gross woman might be ugly, but tell her once that her son has died and you will see how beautiful she is. It is the same with character. There are no vices, there are only phases. . . . If a man sets himself to the making of bad sculpture, that is evil. . . . Art is only the truth, but the truth is scattered. One must have the gift of scenting it. . . . One arrives at that through taste."
Rodin to a critic

" Life is not reasonable, it is dramatic. . . . The beggar sitting by the roadside is dramatic. . . . It is thrilling to see the way he ekes out a living. Besides being dramatic life is beautiful. . . . The beggar just mentioned is beautiful. His dirt and his rags, his bandaged feet and his sores are all beautiful to me. They may not be pleasant but they are artistic. . . .

" When it comes to immorality in books the so-called ' best seller ' type of fiction is vicious in the extreme. . . ."
Dreiser to a reporter

Two men in our time have been possessed by an engrossing passion for observing, that is, a prodigious appetite, Rodin and Dreiser, Parisian and Hoosier. And of course there have been others in accordance with the greedy character of the epoch now closed. Both these men, as it happened, so far apart, were hated for this appetite. Rodin living in a country whose villages, cathedrals, farms, women and meals have been designed by Taste felt the force of program. The man washed out of ancient river deposits known to us as the valleys of the Wabash, Ohio, Missouri, Tippecanoe, to float as best he could on the haphazard streams of our big cities, felt the force of Accident. Rodin had the greater talent for his craft, or more leisure or more background in which to learn it. Both of them desired and found extreme intimacy and variety in women, and were called immoral. And both thought of themselves primarily as workmen, not as innovators, and of Nature as their one teacher. Both were labeled in their day pioneer, realist, revolutionist, and neither of them cared to be labeled or to found schools or movements — nor did they care to be disputed. They felt authentic.

In the years following the *Genius* controversy, titles did not interest Dreiser. He laughed at being called a modern, a saviour to put us on the map, to save us from provincialism: " I am not an instrument, that is only silly, I am a symptom of change." Instinctively he wanted to be judged outside of time and place, of a new century and a new country. The success of acclaim was not strange to him, but more like refound parents who gave him at length a house and security. He joined no societies and did not change his way of life. On the contrary, in the same apartment on Tenth Street he appears to have gone back in these years to the directness of youth. He began to write poems that recall the boy that used to rock by the south window of the house in Sullivan, his dog in his arms, dreaming of alliance with clouds, lizards, fish and wings: " My early poems were no good, but I struck a measure just before the Great War, and wrote five poems printed in *Moods*. I did them out of a mystic despair," he said. Then the other poems came along in the next few years.*

He wanted the strength of dreams for his books. He wanted to count as a primal force, feeling in himself an ancestry back of tribes, back of mammals, back of cells, back of suns, leading yet no one knew where, or leading nowhere unless into an unofficial intimacy with life. His novels unfolding in Chicago, New York, Missouri, In-

* *Moods, Cadenced And Declaimed*, June 1926.

diana, Tennessee, Wisconsin and tourist Europe, should for all their detail, or really because of it, lead from leaf to branch, branch to trunk and trunk to root. What, after all, did Carrie's need of food and lights, jackets, lace ties and little shoes have to do with time or place? And what did Jennie's need of love and loving have to do with them? Or Cowperwood's need of conquest, verve and beauty? Was a Corsican, were the Borgias not precedent for like passions? Had Roman, Macedonian, Persian, Egyptian, Peruvian not been possessed like Cowperwood by the necessity of magnificence? His " Genius " Eugene Witla, was he so different from genius of other nations, always endowed beyond the understanding of orderly obedient men and women? It was not the man, it was his story which Dreiser had designed to differ sharply. His talents came to grief sooner in the United States, or rather were diverted from art to finance, in which field alone Americans were allowed to break rules and make new ones. That was the one difference he could see. For him it spelled failure if the crux of his meaning was lost to readers in the detail of the vast chaotic settings to which his characters belonged — the only settings he was sure of, the only characters he knew well.

In these years, 1910 to 1920, this writer, often called the world's worst great writer, was ambitious and humble about words and their magic. As he wrote he knew very well he " would like to go back and polish and condense." Yet always as in St. Louis over his first poem, he was " eager to be on with his meaning which had to do with this tangle of life." Both Mencken and Masters wrote him that they need not remind him of his fault of prolixity; he was aware of it himself and would correct it in time. This was true, he was so anxious to conquer it that he went to school for style with friends he trusted. Mencken read *The Financier, The Titan, A Hoosier Holiday* in manuscript, and suggested cuts and contractions. He wrote him once in these days, " I have read about 75,000 words of *A Hoosier Holiday* and I am proceeding forward steadily at twenty-five miles an hour . . . the best writing you have ever done. A genuine feeling for style is in it. But I am constantly outraged by banalities due to wordiness, and it seems to me they should come out."

The novelist did not resent this criticism, even felt that he deserved it. But when Mencken ridiculed him publicly for lack of style, then apparently he protested. The critic replied suavely, rather mockingly: " Many of those articles in the Smart Set were forgeries. English spies wrote them. Nothing issuing from my actual hand has ever failed to make three things plain: that you have an adept and lascivious style, that you are a baptized man and that you are the handsomest man in the Republic."

He turned then to Floyd Dell and asked him to read and edit *The " Genius "* for him. Dreiser thinks now that he accepted the cuts to the extent of about 35,000 words, but Mr. Dell believes that for the most part Dreiser did the work himself. At least he said: " I remember going to see him one day and there he was at his desk erasing my blue pencilling." Another friend, he tells it himself, strengthened passages by deleting repetitions and connectives, without changing a word. " I need an editor, I know it, but one who will understand my intention and change nothing from a sense of propriety," I have heard him say. Mencken, he thought, sometimes confused the issue with diplomacy: " Some of your discussions of women in the college chapter [*Hoosier Holiday*] seem to me to be very unwise. Also the D. A. W. episode had better be changed. He is now a highly respectable Baltimorean. . . . The slightest suspicion that he ever engaged in so carnal an enterprise . . . would cause his expulsion from the Unitarian Church and probably would lose him his home."

He had then a veneration for style, condensation he called it, and used to be humble over his weakness for explicit repeated detail. He amazed me once in these years by an invitation to condense the writing of *Twelve Men*. I was young and a snob about manner, and imagined that a writer even in America would want to decide upon each comma and semicolon; and that quality transcended quantity, and that haste was vulgar. I asked him why not? Again he said in effect that mere quality was lost in the United States, there was no audience for it; it was of course the aim of art, but left to itself in our country it could only end in anaemia. American writers still had too much to do in putting out genuine material. If the plans were true and the work had movement that was all that could be expected of them in this early moment of our civilization.

It seemed to me he had not the least egotism about his writings. He appeared to look upon them much like an architect or a mural painter of old times designing for the sake of the city, who left detail to apprentices; that is if any one would acknowledge him as master by consenting to be apprenticed. He seemed not to be quite sure that they would. He admitted that he asked of them a wisdom of detail in relation to his plan he himself pretended not to have mastered. Yes, he knew that a paradox was involved here, but what of it? Yet I imagine that perhaps no one ever refused to help him if they could. He had an importance of being, not to be withstood.

Afraid to tamper with another's record of himself, I did very cautiously cut from six of the portraits in *Twelve Men* what seemed to be gratuitous phrases and connectives, and excessive repetitions of the same words. And too, I think I allowed myself the frivolous delight of deleting *sex-life, love-life, enthuse, colorful, to sense, to glimpse,* feeling a little guilty for fear that then Dreiser would not be Dreiser. And I may have divided into their parts some of his suspended sentences wound up like tops, if I thought that finally they would not spin. Always he agreed gratefully to the changes, but in the midst of the work he made an excuse of my slowness and finished the revision himself. It was better so. Dreiser lives and has his being in a tangle of qualitative phrases and parentheses, which perhaps an intimate, but no outsider, could change for the better. They are introduced or excused by *to the contrary notwithstanding, which latter, which same, and the like, I could not help but think, at the same time, in other words* — a quantity of clichés apparently agreeable to him. It is his nature to offer *other* words, a clustered choice of them for any one link in his thought, and to subordinate these to a larger cluster of choices. And it is his nature to use the careless diction of his own people,

Americans. In that way, he seems to say, they will understand me and my idiom will be telltale and pantomimic.

Ford Madox Ford tells of lunching with him not long ago. Always the talk turned on style. He was amazed at Dreiser's knowledge of the theory of style. He seemed to have read every authority (perhaps like a novice who studies methods and positions of loving). "Why then," Ford asked him, "when you know so much, do you use a phrase like 'He looked into her eyes, the same were suffused with tears'?" The answer was immediate: "I live in a country of business men, my characters are colored by business, love or hatred of it. I imagine by using that language I get nearer to them." This may be true, but almost I believe that Dreiser like all spontaneous workmen invented first and excused afterwards. Over and over he recalls the douanier Henri Rousseau. Wishing for the salons, studying the ways of the salon, aiming beyond the provinces, he had nevertheless to use the manner at hand, the manner of his own villages; and yet made thereby universal images.

Walt Whitman has the name of deliberate intention, but perhaps he too created first and analysed afterwards. Fact has it that he wrote but one book of poems, and spent years making them more deliberate. Consider the long lists, the alternatives and co-ordinates in Whitman. They bring to mind the leisurely lists occurring with Dreiser, and occurring in American talk. We step lively, but we take our time talking, if we talk at all; some Americans have never finished a sentence. Also consider the inevitable participial dependent clauses, loose, rangy, haphazard, and at the same time expressive like American workmen and mechanics, like our cities and villages, used both by Whitman and Dreiser. Graphically they proclaim the uncertain conditional planes on which we shift from phase to phase, as if living with us were a suspension without roots or foundation, a world in the air, one thing today, another tomorrow.

There however the likeness ends. Whitman is a poet of "must" and "must not," declaring health. People must not ask to know or be sophisticated, but like animals in the forest, like fish in the sea, like birds along rivers, they must try to find their human balance again. Dreiser is a writer pursued by fatality and doom, in the sense that men have made cities, hierarchies, perfumes, music, perversions and refinements beyond their mastery. Simplicity and nature seduced Whitman. Complication and artifice concern Dreiser. Yet if he could not relate these through language to the unknown forces out of which they spring, he would rather not have written.

His need of language was imperative. He worked prodigiously for mastery. Out of this intensity came his novels with moments of precision and passages of approximation. At the same time practice produced, as if easily, short stories, plays, poems and essays, many of them possessing a virtue for which he is too little known — economy of form. They have the shove and push, grief and success of America in them. They mingle the jokes of day laborers building railroads, the terror of workmen digging a tunnel when barriers give way and the river rushes back on them; the curses of reporters who have lost to more brutal reporters; the glee of politicians and magnates when the weak are framed and they shoot into power; the voices of trainmen in moments of accident; the drop of a murderer behind box cars and over a dark river pier, the police upon him; and the muffled voices of human hearts asking for the death of one, the presence of another; the sharp cry of futility when the death comes. The obsession of one for money, of another for excitement, of another for love or beauty, of another merely not to die; and above all the scarcely ever concordant aims and whims of human beings — these preside like apparitions in his short stories and plays.

Under them run primordial passions, struck to flame by the fact of sex, the wish for power, the desire to live; and frustration or fulfilment is always at the expense of one or another. *The Second Choice, St. Colomba and the River, Chains, Typhoon,* nearly all of the stories ring the bell of fate. Stitching back and forth with the aid of his many connectives, always to the amusement and horror of critics — yet they write their logic the way the stock ticker prints the rise and fall of prices, or the electric pencil in railway stations tells the arrival of trains. No other letter file of Dreiser's contains so many testimonials from strangers, because he has guessed their secrets, as the responses to his two volumes of short stories. "How could you have guessed?" they keep saying. Many so-called stylists have not written with hands so supple and alive to mystery. A man's style is a man's self. Style is direction.

Tonally the plays go beyond the stories. They have the truth of distinct language dictated by the characters, and no less of form. *The Girl in the Coffin, The Blue Sphere, In the Dark, Laughing Gas, Old Ragpicker,* * *The Dream,*† are exclamation points or question marks. The one long play, *The Hand of the Potter,* is a deep perforation from life. The plays multiply skilfully the ghosts and voices of the past and the subconscious, in whose intangible atmosphere any one wave of events gathers and breaks.

It is the size of the longer books, and the lack of time in America to encompass it, that has given Dreiser the title of "the worst great writer in the world," "crude," "clumsy." A selection could be made which would give him the opposite name. To those who say, "what does it matter?" these plays answer: "To see crisis, to verbalize essence, matters." They turn everyday life into mimic events. Death, love, jealousy, murder, deformity, accident, dreams, destitution — these commonplaces, over which we stretch the tight smooth skin of convention, here spring to view like inner organs after the surgeon's incision.

* *Plays of the Natural and the Supernatural,* February 1916.
† *Hey Rub-A-Dub-Dub,* December 1919.

59

*". . . . . I'll have grounds
More relative than this: the play's the
thing,
Wherein I'll catch the conscience of a
king."* SHAKESPEARE

Had Dreiser's plays been produced on the American stage, had he turned his strength from books to the theatre, I think he would have impelled a progression in our drama, which in turn would have helped intensify our direction as a people. Kings and subjects who never read or never exchange their views about books, sometimes find themselves in the same theatre, and for a minute united by the same message.

The Girl in the Coffin, as produced by the Washington Square Players in 1917, went for verity of tissue beyond the plays of Eugene O'Neill. For all his facility and effort our national dramatist remains, like the hotel in a Western town: " It ain't the best, it's the only one." Dreiser's play, merely an atom of drama, was American fibre in speech and action. O'Neill's plays, especially the late ones, are his fears and fantasies speaking to people of like fears and fantasies about the life they have to lead. They have not the power to recreate American flesh and blood the way that Tchekov could Russian, or Synge Irish, or the actor Grasso could Sicilian, or the actress Sadda Yacco once could Japanese. This transmission of our own life through speech and gesture is a miracle that rarely happens over our footlights. We have received real records of nearly every other people on earth, and but few of our own.

The Hand of the Potter was played with no great skill by the Provincetown Theatre and for only three weeks in 1921, two years after it was published. Even so, like the shorter play, this tragedy transmitted a quality so rare with us as to be shocking — the sense of life conceived in cubic volume. I remember the middle act of *The Love Nest* by Ring Lardner as giving also the acute shock of life; the first and third acts having been tacked to the drama by others to make a Broadway evening. *The Moon is a Gong* by John Dos Passos; *The Racket* by a Chicago writer; and to some extent *The Great Gatsby* from Scott Fitzgerald's novel — from these plays too came the direct sense of American reality. They were plays, not recipes for plays, not confections like *The Front Page, Broadway,* and Kearney's dramatization of *An American Tragedy.** They were plays, not personal vagaries like nearly everything from O'Neill and his followers.

Though few may agree with me I have a suspicion that if our theatre had acknowledged and presented first rate talent like Dreiser's, Frost's, Ring Lardner's, and probably Masters', who have all been ambitious to use the medium of the stage, our culture would have gained in body and precision. Or, rather, had we not been the kind of people who for example prefer drugstore and speakeasy drinks to real wine and liquor, such writers might have become stage favorites.

As it is even in love and money-making, we are expected to use our faculties to evade the issue; we call money-making " service " to others. We call women prostitutes, débutantes, secretaries or wives. Finally we may become the most synthetic and successful liars of history. Our lies may achieve such virtuosity as to invent truth. Chaplin's films, some of the best music shows, the Marx Brothers today, suggest what truth of manner may after a while come out of American indirectness when handled by artists.

There are other brilliant examples. A devoted artist, Edward Steichen photographer, and an American philosopher John B. Watson, who has influenced popular knowledge more than any other since William James, have gone over to the vast hyperbole, Advertising, quite like Dreiser's " Genius." Steichen justifies his desertion by an analogy between our business world and other great

---

* Kearney's own play *A Man's Man* belonged more truly to the first class of plays, those that transmitted the current of reality.

periods of commercial art, Athenian, Gothic, Venetian.* Watson's change of front supports one of his own premises: Knowledge is action out of response to stimuli; a man who cannot respond properly is a failure; the proper response to American stimuli is to make money; he, Watson, will not be a failure; so he acts to sell Pond's facial creams and becomes vice-president of one of the greatest advertising companies in the world. " In a store, and doing well." . . .

But why is it that whereas in truth Phidias, Praxiteles, Michelangelo and Titian worked for the big business men of their time, neither Matisse nor Picasso nor Steichen's own preceptor, Stieglitz, nor Einstein nor Pavlow have permitted their art or science to be harnessed to commerce or to communism? They remain, to borrow Watson's term apparently " unconditioned " by expedience. If we knew why they have preferred this to popular success, some modern sophisms might be dissolved.

Dreiser is one of the few Americans who has preferred disgrace to success, although capable of both. Repeatedly he has made " improper responses to stimuli." In the realm of intelligence he is an American high-water mark, not British, not exotic, and yet achieving waves that fall beyond. *The Hand of the Potter* is one of the waves. The theme and substance is native, but the fact of its declaration is still as foreign to us as it was once for Whitman to say, " I sing the body electric "; or as it is for Whitman today to say, " To the States or any one of them, or any city of the States — resist much, obey little." This tragedy discloses secrets never elsewhere spoken of with us, in dispassionate detail and with passionate relation of detail to whole. The play has two superficial flaws. The occasional Irish characters speak with a brogue inaccurately recorded; a good actor could have changed this. And in the last act for a few pages discussion outbalances action. For the Provincetown Players Dreiser cut and condensed this discourse. The second edition of the play is thus revised. Had he turned into a playwright he might have come to sacrifice leisure altogether to form.

Otherwise *The Hand of the Potter* in contradiction to

* *Steichen: The Photographer* by Carl Sandburg.

his other big works gives the excitement of tone as dictated by detail, exactly in the sense that the tonal message of trees at a distance is concerned with each leaf and pine needle. The play was written in the fall of 1916 directly after the attack on *The " Genius."* It seems to say: if you object to the havoc of sex and the sordidness of business and the subterfuge of Christian Science and the fatality of childbirth, all of which goes on around you in your own class as well as in every other, I will give you something more terrible, more basic, more inexorable to contemplate. He selects for the stage as the mainspring of the action that same force most feared in America, sex, but this time acting through the soul of a pervert, and therefore uncontrollable. He is the son of an East Side Jewish family, the father a peddler of thread and needles; and he has been two years in prison for assault on a child, and is out on parole. Thus the tragedy originates on what would be conventionally thought of as the lowest plane of life; and from that shocking premise branches into drama.

The action takes place on the road between the old and new worlds. The parents and the lame sister speak the rich mournful memory of Odessa. The younger boy and the other daughters, one a manicure, the other married to a smart Jew on the way possibly to Park Avenue grandeur, are already new Americans, cheerful, strident and practical. On the one side is the family under their hot tin roof; on the other side, the neighbors, passers-by, workmen and shop keepers, Irish, German, Jewish — the European world, hot with conflicting languages and customs. On a July Saturday afternoon, when the rest of the family are gone to the park or on joy rides, the encounter with rape and murder of the crazed youth and the little girl with pink face and red braids from an Irish family in a tenement below, joins violently for a moment these two elements — the family and the streets outside. Together now they in turn are poured, like a sudden flood from pipes bursting, into the bigger New York world of courts and newspapers, into official violence and indifference. The private paths of human minds, the public thoroughfares of a big city are crossed here in accuracy of drama. A clock ticking noisily when other sounds cease, the mother's box of rags, a yellow oilcloth on the family table with which the young man wraps the child's body, a vacant lot outside seem like other characters in the first two acts, as do the city newspapers in the fourth act. When hunted into a hall bedroom the murderer with what mind is left him decides to lie down and die by gas, the newspapers swarm around him, speaking of him and to him of his crime, crying extras in the street below " All about Isadore Berchansky!" and on edges torn from newspapers he scribbles last notes to his family and the world, which pieced together make poetic sense of insane discord — a requiem of the acts before and the last scene to come.

" ' I'm guilty and insane caused by the beautiful make-ups of girls that has set me very passionate. Don't cry. . . .
' I want to say if I don't die this way I'll take my medicine just the same. Fields, carriages, four trees.
'. . . Poor mom! You think I'm innocent, even yet, don't you? Mothers is wonders! Great! I am too, only I ain't made right. . . . It don't do things right always. Can you blame a man when he ain't right?' "

The play enters into the very nerve cells of a criminal, an imperfect organism; yet a kind of symbol of many of us, and of what happens to people suppressed by tin roofs and churches — a revelation as intimate as with Hurstwood in *Sister Carrie,* as with Clyde Griffiths in *An American Tragedy.* After death the gates of intimacy are down. Reporters, police, the landlord enter in: " Ach, my house! My gas! "

Here Dreiser has been severely criticized. While the reporters wait for the police inspector and the father to arrive, they ask each other what should be done about such pitiful mishaps as the dead murderer under the sheet before them. One of them speaking as if he might be the Hoosier of twenty years before on the night service of the World, advocates the study by state officials of Havelock Ellis, Freud and Krafft-Ebing. Critics said that reporters were not learned enough to invoke such authorities, or to give a damn; and that the discourse was too long. It is true that length here originally broke the suspense. But that American reporters who have had as fare for years the unpopular vitals of our life, while they served the roasts to the public, disguised in stereotyped sauces, would be incapable of scientific thought, given such a half hour of grim leisure, is to underrate them. The critics forgot that Poe, Ambrose Bierce, Stephen Crane, O. Henry, Sandburg, Dreiser have all of them been reporters doing police court service. In fact if we have ever had popular ballad makers and philosophers, they have been the newspaper men. It is part of Dreiser's logic that he gives them in this tragedy the rôle of the detached chorus discussing the ways of the gods and of fate.

The choral debate yields to the entrance of the police inspector and later of the father, to identify the body. He speaks " heavily and sadly," and the landlord in shrill retort. They make the final discord on which the tragedy ends:

"'Yes, dat's my son. Dat's my boy. . . . Gas? Vell, it's better den de oder. . . . Dat he should end so! It is strange. Four years ago ve lived next door.'

'So he vuz your son, vuz he? Such a scoundrel! He owes for t'ree veeks rent, yet. And he should come by my house! . . . I should lose two t'ousand dollars [the reward]. If I know, he vouldn't 'a' been here long. I t'ought he acted strange.'

'I vill pay! I vill pay! — only not today, please. I heven't so much.'

'An' you! Vy shouldn't you bring up your children right? If you should bring him up right — if you should keep him off de streets, den he vouldn't do such a ting!'

'My friend, hev' you children?'

'Yes!'

'Den you should know. Vy pull at de walls of my house? Dey are already down!'"

So the play ends in a sorrowful mean give-and-take of words between the two eternal factors of life, tenant and landlord. This time both Jews, both poor, both fathers of families, that so-boasted unit in the Land of the Free. And the quarrel is over a room too miserable for anyone, even a crazy pervert to die in. . . . Everything is told just as it happened, not exaggerated or underrated.

Yet the play was derided and cursed by some of Dreiser's own friends. They had begged him all these years to be economical with language, " fused and molten." At length he was. And now they complained more than ever. He could not be negligible and yet he could not please, it seemed. . . . It was not until he had written *An American Tragedy* nine years later, 840 pages to these 209, dealing with a like theme, that " America's foremost novelist " was honored as such. Strange that one must say a thing over and over and at such great length before finally it engages. I asked Dreiser once soon after the publication of the play, why he did not write again as close to his subject as in *The Hand of the Potter.* His answer was: " No one can touch always the exposed nerve of life. It would kill him or people would kill him for it." He waited some years before he went as close to heart beats and nerve reactions again. Then for a brief moment he was at length acclaimed as heroic.

In 1916 he took his play to Arthur Hopkins, a courageous producer in New York. In December of that year Mr. Hopkins accepted it and gave him an advance of one thousand dollars. In April 1917 he abandoned the project and the advance to the author: " It is the best American play that has been submitted to me, and I would eagerly have produced it had not Dreiser imposed on me so many bulls, caveats, and salvos," he was quoted as saying. The bulls, caveats, and salvos, according to their author, were merely his refusal to change the play in order to lessen the horror. According to Nathan a fashionable theatre critic of that day: " That Dreiser wrote *The Hand of the Potter* with a Rolls-Royce in view seems to me as certain as that he writes novels with nothing in view but the novels." Mencken begged him frantically to destroy the play, burn it or put it behind the clock and forget it:

" I say the subject is forbidden on the stage . . . banned by that convention on which the whole of civilized order depends. . . . If the thing were possible I'd advocate absolutely unlimited freedom in speech. I think the world would be better off . . . if the stage could be used to set up a more human attitude towards sexual perverts . . . if novels could describe the precise process of reproduction from the first hand shake to lactation, and so show the young what a bore it is. But these things are forbidden. . . . The play is a piece of pish — clumsy, banal, unnatural, almost idiotic. Its publication would lose you the respect of all intelligent persons, and make every man who labored on the protest look like an ass."

For some years the two men continued to be intimates, but it may be that here was the first serious wedge to separate them. For one thing the critic now placed himself on record as bored by the processes of nature, always enthralling to Dreiser. Not nature but argument and document amused Mencken, and they must not be too identical with reality. Then they became poetry, and poetry shocked him. Moreover he truly believed that this play was treacherous to the cause they had fought for side by side, the freedom of letters. The moralists, would be right this time; it was "plain dirt."

Three years later another disagreement widened the distance between them. Dreiser was living in California; Mencken wrote him generously that he would "go to the mat with Sumner," and persuade him to compromise so that *The " Genius "* could be reissued. Or else possibly he rather hoped to see it abridged; often he had urged him " to cut a lot of stuff " in the novel which seemed to him over erotic. The meeting and the compromise were accomplished, Mencken thought rather to the advantage of *The " Genius."* Dreiser's refusal of the compromise seems easy to understand. The passages which the editor was willing to sacrifice, I should think, were among the most engaging and important in the novel. But what went hard on friendship was that this book was finally reissued without *any* cuts in July 1923, and without a word of explanation or of thanks to Mencken — an unfairness, a lack of manners, he could not help thinking, both to him and Sumner.

Mencken is a man of code and etiquette. He believes in fair rules and then in keeping them. Dreiser says of himself, as if pleased with the idea, " Sometimes I think I am a wild animal." And of Mencken, " All you have to say to him is the one word, 'mysticism,' he leaps up in the air." A few years more and a few more disagreements and the stimulant of banter and advice and schemes between these two undoubtedly ceased. Perhaps each regrets at moments the loss of the other. When I asked Mencken the cause of the estrangement one of his answers was: " Well, we have different customers now." Then he added, " Besides, what fun is it to defend a man who no longer needs defence ? . . ."

But to return to *The Hand of the Potter* its author would need defense for a long time yet. Denounced by " his most faithful critical mount," and the play reviewed as an interesting but venal enterprise by Nathan, it was, one would know, ill-fated from the first. Mencken had insisted that " no intelligent publisher," let alone theatrical manager, would touch it. And Dreiser himself began to wonder. Since *The " Genius "* John Lane had brought out two more of his books, the short plays and *A Hoosier Holiday*, February and October 1916, neither one of them storm-centers, but both increasing his fame. Now in the face of Mencken's entreaties to burn it, he offered Lane *The Hand of the Potter*. They refused it pointblank, and were no longer fighting Sumner in his behalf, in fact " had never spent a cent on that fight." He had no other big work to offer them. It came over him of a sudden, he says, that in spite of his reputation, really he had no publisher. Living as he was on advances, he was perilously near to destitution once again. Moreover his German descent was against him at this time, also his name as a libertine in this most moral moment of our history. It was just before the disillusioned young men came back from France, those who did, to make jazz and whoopee, and jeer at pretentiousness and hypocrisy.

What to do? Dreiser was at a loss. Then one day in May 1917 he saw advertised in a catalogue that *Sister Carrie* was to be published by Liveright & Seltzer — the first he had heard of it. Previously out of friendship he had given permission to Frank Shay, owner of a Greenwich Village bookstore, to make one special edition of *Sister Carrie,* no more. Otherwise the book still belonged to Harper's. Immediately he says he telephoned to Horace Liveright, then an unknown beginner, who came to Tenth Street to explain. His story was that Shay, who had gone into the army, had sold him *Sister Carrie.* " On whose authority? " Dreiser asked. Liveright did not know, but made a sweeping offer. If he would let him go ahead he would publish every Dreiser book he could get hold of, past, present and future. He and his partner, he said, were moderns as against timid conservative publishers, and were out to go the limit and see the fun. " Did they have enough money? " They could get it, Liveright was sure. The act of advertising *Sister Carrie* had been not too fastidious. On the other hand Dreiser had instinctive faith in enterprise and youth. Here was a young man who insisted that he would publish him no matter what the censor did and said. The luxury of this idea appealed to one who had been bandied about for seventeen years from publisher to publisher. A contract was made whereby Liveright and Seltzer should acquire his books as fast as they could.

The first manuscript he gave them was his own favorite, *The Hand of the Potter*. They read it. As Dreiser remembers it, Liveright telephoned: " I'm advised it's too strong. Why not wait and give us something else first? Seltzer says it's too strong." The answer to this was: " No, I'm through with publishers who quibble with my stuff. Send back everything," and he hung up. Within a half hour Liveright was back on the telephone announcing their decision to publish the play. At last, at the age of forty-six this fighter against odds had earned the power to dictate. From then until 1931 when Hollywood pirates got the best of him, he has had liberty almost to present " life as he sees it."

The first new book however to be issued by the new firm was *Free and Other Stories* in August 1918. Publication of the play was delayed by the Coburns, who in the same month had accepted it for production. In December they lost courage and abandoned the scheme, like Hopkins giving and forfeiting an advance. At length in April 1919 *The Hand of the Potter* appeared in book form; and in the same month *Twelve Men,* which book of portraits went a long way to regain for its author the confidence of Mencken and other friends. They are keen and tender biographs. Many faces and hands, voices, shoulders and mouths are in them. But they do not make the acute victory over tone volume and intensity made by the unpopular *Hand of the Potter.*

60

" Deep below deep lie the mysteries, and theories flourish like weeds in a garden — or let us call them flowers, for at times they are so artistic. Arts spring out of the mysteries, but the arts . . . grow stale if left to themselves. . . . Life will have none of anything forever. . . . We build up rules wherewith life is to be governed, and behold! — some fine day the character of life itself changes and our rules are worthless."

" But speaking for a nation that wishes to stand forth . . . among those that lead, must not thought — intelligent, artistic, accurate vision — be among its primary characteristics? . . . Then why are we so bent . . . upon more money, and when not that, upon idealistically misinterpreting life. [Our] few genuine thinkers thus far are taboo: Poe, Whitman, Twain. Only in one field, finance — not in war, politics, the arts and sheer intellect — do our essential individuals compare favorably with those of other lands. . . . And is it not possible . . . that . . . where the power to think is lacking failure follows?" DREISER: *Hey Rub-a-Dub-Dub*

In the alliance with Liveright once again Dreiser made part of an historical moment. And at this time he had not had to force it altogether; he had been invited to join. When he wrote *Sister Carrie* he had raped an unwilling moment; publication was a tour de force. When unwittingly he had enlisted English understanding

399

which permitted the appearance of *The Titan,* it was taking advantage of another phase of our history. It was the day when England still counted with us, and when due to Whitman, Poe, Norris, Crane, Dreiser and Frost we were beginning to count with England. Now when it looked as if he might have to lose out again, a new element had begun to make its appearance, which would as much as Dreiser himself change the tenor of American thought. It was the advent of Jewish intelligence, about to seize new moral and aesthetic values, and turn the moderns from martyrs into money-makers.

Under their direction not only intellect for its own sake and art for its own sake, but also " books that tend to corrupt morals " for their own sake, would begin to pay. Prosperity was at hand. A kind of crude artistic licentiousness soon would blaze, extrinsic to great art, but perhaps a prerequisite with us before we could grow up and be mature. A more subtle complicated state of license would have been proof that already we were grown up. The contract between Dreiser and Liveright in May 1917, between Middle West and Near East, was an unconscious symptom of rough change.

The battle with publishers was finally won, so much so that except for Boston the battle with the public was also won. And Boston indeed had come hardly to count, so wholesale its disapproval of the melting pot, and so cruel and thoughtless its disapproval of the new country, the enormous child, to which New England had once contributed not birth but anyway conception. The Boston book massacre of 1927 by which *An American Tragedy* was banned along with nearly every other readable book in the world, curiously enough happened to be the year of the execution of Sacco and Vanzetti.* In that black year, Boston the cradle of the nation, utterly disowning its own progeny, though perhaps with some reason, was discredited and had to take a sorry back seat, very far back. Parents have never been eminent in the United States.

* In the suppression of *An American Tragedy,* the Protestant vice society had the support of a Catholic judge and jury, who banned the novel, according to Arthur Garfield Hays, chiefly because of a passing reference to birth control.

These parents did not want to be. They kept saying to themselves, " Why couldn't it remain like in the old days of Emerson and Lowell? "

The new trustees of the Melting Pot, self-made like everything truly American, with their genius for presentation were finally putting the country on the map. St. Paul had had to wait for his dreary dream of chastity and hypocrisy to be fulfilled in North America. Likewise the ancient Jews wandering for centuries had to wait for their promised revenge to come true in the same United States, who had most disdained them together with other foreigners, Indian, French, Spanish and Negro.

Revenge for what? Possibly for having been the one race of Earth seeking at once poignant emotional and intellectual unity — that is, the one race untouched by cynicism. In other words the most ambitious of the sons of men. Wasn't it probably for this difficult program that they were originally punished by surrounding tribes and by their own pragmatic prophets? Early in their history they had of their own accord reached an impasse. They had invented a God who commanded of them a contradiction in behavior: " He that is wounded in the stones or who hath his privy member cut off shall not enter into the congregation of the Lord." Yet ignoring the hardship which might thereby be inflicted on those qualified to enter into his congregation, the Lord synchronously decreed: " Thou shalt not commit adultery." Also in taboo of art and celebration which follow out of sexual passion, " The Lord spake . . . lest ye corrupt yourselves and make you a graven image . . . or when thou seest the sun and the moon and the stars . . . shouldst be driven to worship them."

Such a worship of knowledge coincident with such a prohibition of living undoubtedly reduced them to a state of neurasthenia, so that they succumbed to other less highly sensitized peoples. And as it was prophesied they were scattered among the nations, and entered the house of bondmen; though not before " one of their boys," as they like to call him, had been first executed and then deified by the Romans, the last conquerors of their land before the day of their dispersal. And then it came to pass in the course of two thousand years that they found their way to America, taking always the statutes and commandments of the Lord along with them, keeping them all the days of their lives, teaching them diligently unto their children. And their children became bond salesmen, so that the word of God was fulfilled: " They became blessed above all people " with money. And they did begin to conquer some of their enemies who had been mightier than they, as God little by little delivered them up unto them.*

Coincidently these wanderers achieved a second revenge, this time against their own Deity — a revenge for that day thousands of years ago when in Mohab he spoiled their fun; broke in on their dance and song, and forbade them to worship the calf of gold, made for them by their artist Aaron, out of the earrings and ornaments of their wives. A number of them began again the worship of gold with song and dance, usually Negro, in open defiance of the covenant with their God. And they coined some of the gold out of the wisdom of whatever artists and scientists they could find around them — out of that sacred abstract flame for which once they built the tabernacle; that word of God, that inspiration which more than any other people they had been trained to worship. Their intellect condensed through passion, their avid wish to hold concourse with Deity in rich clothes worthy of Him, to wring from Him his last secret, their sheer curiosity coupled with the need of revenge for centuries of persecution — this combined Jewish element finally arrived to take over Yankee Anglo-Saxon America, that country most hostile to them.

Dreiser lent himself to this Oriental holiday. So, for example, did Frost and Sandburg when the critic Louis Untermeyer appointed himself advertising agent for all the new poets. It was really the most irresistible thing that had yet happened in America, the control by

---

* " And the Lord thy God will put out these nations before thee by little and little: thou mayest not consume them at once, lest the beasts of the field increase upon thee. But the Lord thy God shall deliver them unto thee, and shall destroy them with a mighty destruction, until they be destroyed." *Deuteronomy.*

Jewish intellect of Gentile invention all out of the great melting pot. And yet what was wrong with it? Was it too late perhaps for the two elements to know how to mingle? Or were the first years of mingling inevitably naïve? The alliance was in the case of Dreiser naïve. He had too much plain Indiana sense and dreaminess, too earthen a temper to know how to join with these Eastern cerebral voluptuaries. He did not fit quite with the champagne by cases, Shebas from the Follies, and shimmying from Harlem, with which the new-style publisher liked to overwhelm such favorite authors as Dreiser, Anderson, and Bertrand Russell, say, by way of bonus. And yet of course it was " hopeful," Dreiser thought, to see a kind of liberty and color and luxury invading the Home of the Brave. Hadn't he hoped for it all these years?

Once walking through a park, he had deplored to his companion the fact of a policeman who was separating two lovers, and his friend had laughed: " I suppose to you the policeman is the criminal? You would like to see public pavilions in parks for love-making? " — " Certainly, why not? " was his answer. " That's what this city needs! " At that date he was sure of it. Yet a number of years later in 1930 he was not so sure. He said sadly: " If I have had any influence it seems to me it has been merely to turn people upside down." — " What in childbirth is called the breech-presentation? " — " Yes, that's about all . . . when what I wanted was to see mind and body united again! " — " I know — an equal development of intellect and senses? " — " Why not? Nothing counts without mind and taste." — " But mind and taste come only with background. Americans are a people detached in a foreground. You can't blame them if they are merely tumbled upside down." — " No, you can't blame them. We might start a club to cultivate background."

In this talk I remember Dreiser as with eyes looking backward through generations and forward, shaping images of people brilliantly engaged, despite the wreckage and seaweed around American moorings. He looked the intention of his books — that they should be potent and inclusive, even if they could not be hopeful.

In 1917, 1918, 1919, when the summary of his philosophy, *Hey-Rub-A-Dub-Dub,* was published, he availed himself little of the new society which the editors and producers, his publisher among them, were forming in New York, and which promised to be a triumph of what the excluded could do when once they had collected themselves to exclude. Who were his hosts after all? Procurers not creators! And he more than they had consumed energy and time to dig canals from life itself into publishers' offices, through which now other streams from kindred geniuses were more easily released into print. Creation at last filled the air contagiously. He felt that, whether they acknowledged him or not, he belonged if anywhere among the craftsmen of no matter what race; not among the editors and propagandists.

Impatiently as Dreiser talked with others in this day he pleated and repleated his handkerchief — that singular habit of his. What else was there to do with people who reckoned by clocks and bank accounts? Sometimes he flung the handkerchief out like a challenge in case anyone would like to reckon by intensity. What other gesture was there to make among companions who were either poor in emotion or poor in intellect? When would there ever be in the United States a merger of the two, which alone produced great art in individuals or in races? In a lonely way he was certain of the need and the lack of this merger. His intention had not in the least changed since the days of *Sister Carrie* — " Art was life seen through a temperament." But one had to be by temperament at once realist and mystic to see life the way it was.

Even his great friend Mencken, he was beginning to feel, perhaps unfairly, was " interested only in the visible face of life," not at all " in the invisible mechanism with which science is always concerned." Yet judged by his writings this critic was devoting himself to the pursuit of technique, by which intangible route alone one can proceed surely to frontiers. But he approached technique more diffidently than the novelist, in fact meticulously step by step along paths of language trod by others. And sometimes he got detained by the others. Dreiser on the other hand took tremendous strides by way of underbrush and swamps and over deserts and precipices, any plunging way he could find to arrive at the barriers of the unknown.

His book of philosophy with the plaintive title was a paraphrase of his intellectual journey up to this time. Though Mencken had begged him to write it, now that it was completed he let him down: " It is not so much unintelligible as unintelligent," that is, " uneducated . . . I don't think you argue well." Dreiser's answer was that he didn't care. He was sure he had " blazed a chemical trail " in the book, and someone would come along who would get it and " make it very clear." The essays, he said, contained " the sub-stone of a new philosophy, on which could be reared a sounder approach to life than is now voiced." The soundness of the approach, the book implied, was in direct ratio to the attitude of uncertainty, of vagueness really, with which a philosopher was willing to go, seeking his way into the mysteries. A voice in the play *Laughing Gas* expresses the floating pier on which the positives and negatives of his philosophy rest:

> " No high, no low! No low, no high! Time without measure, measure without time. A rising, a sinking! An endless rising, an endless sinking. . . ."
> " Behind, before, beneath, above, presence without reality, reality without presence. . . ."
> " A rising, a sinking! An endless rising! An endless sinking! Outward without inward! Inward without outward! "

As for certainties he was certain only of his desire to present enigmas, and given health he would find all of them worth the effort. Two interviews to newspapers, one in 1911, the other in 1921, show how consistent and flexible his attitude was in these ten years. In 1911 before sailing for Europe he confided to a reporter:

> " I can see no intelligent sequence of cause and effect in life. . . . No, I don't feel any less happy on account of that. . . . Life interests me intensely for that very reason. . . . It is more thrilling than the most gorgeous spectacle that man ever planned. . . . Besides being dramatic, it is beautiful, and I believe that beauty is eternal. . . . That would be the reason for life, if there were any. . . .
> " No, I don't think there is such a thing as progress in the sense that we use the word. It is merely a change. Who can say that it is better to worship the home as we do today than it was in the old times to worship a bull or a spider?

... Who can say that the teachings of Jesus Christ have really held for two thousand years? Certainly it isn't true today that one should turn the other cheek."

And in 1921, in the high tide of "realism," as if to repudiate his title of pioneer realist, another interview seems to say, "I refuse to be named or labeled. Expect anything from me except lack of instinct":

"Today in America the realistic novel is at its climacteric . . . 'Main Street,' 'Zell,' 'Moon Calf' . . . 'Erik Dorn,' 'Brass,' 'The Narrow House' and others. . . . We are growing a crop of rugged, hard-hitting, outspoken novelists and this is not a matter to be deplored. . . . But . . .

"What we miss in American fiction is power of imagination. . . . Perhaps it is not out of place to speak of this at the time of the centenary of . . . Dante. If there are all the chain cigar stores, chain drug stores, haberdasheries, movie theatres, and big hotels in Manhattan to describe, here are also Hell, Heaven and Purgatory of the soul, which Dante would have found. It is that he would have gone beyond mere realistic description and shown us the half-monstrous proportions of our city like a giant sphinx with wings. The power of such imagination would lift a modern book into glorious fantasy.

". . . The mechanical miracle around us . . . keen works of science and philosophy . . . it would seem that men should be stimulated as never before. Yet . . . vigor our novelists possess, but little exaltation. . . . They are content to examine the inside of a boarding house or chronicle the mere number of windows in the colossal stone and steel shells of our buildings. They stick close to the curbstone. They rarely climb any such heights as Dante climbed to look out over the tremendous waste of lives. . . . The true epic of a modern city has never been written. It is no longer a theme for poetry. It demands an epic treatment in prose. . . .

"The modern city is as mystical a thing . . . as a paradiso. It is so crowded with grotesque, ironic, evilly fantastic things. . . . Nothing is too terrible, absurd or sublime to happen here and now. The palette is prepared with every conceivable color for a master painter."

So Dreiser gave to the newspapers his own plans in the name of the great Florentine. He had tried but apparently he had not realized them yet. There must have been moments in *The Titan, The "Genius," The Hand of the Potter*, where his intention was clear? But perhaps not.

Anyway it was proved that the play was *not* the thing. He had done his utmost to make a potent play. " First and last " he had wanted to do that. And yet apparently it scarcely counted in current calculations. It was the same with his essays. Daring as they were, they went almost unchallenged. Younger Americans took the trail he had blazed, but as yet they have not made it clearer. In fact so far they have let windfalls block the way.

At length however he had a publisher who promised to let him live and write as he saw fit. And it must be said for Liveright of the copper mask that as nearly as he knew how he kept that clause of the contract. By this time it was an almost unpopular thing to do; since in spite of achievement for others as well as himself, America's " outstanding " novelist was beginning to be demoded. There were new writers, whose freedom he had partly made possible, who for some years were dressing in more alluring clothes than he. Indeed they were more fashionable. They were moderns in manner. Yet Liveright with Hebraic instinct for the inner flame of the temple, in other words for the truth or the search for truth, believed in his Hoosier. In the end he was repaid in fame and gold; and could afford to be as rude as he liked, and have offices fitted with a near Gothic-Jacobean music room.

In 1919 the Hoosier took himself off to California far from his favorite city, New York. There for three years he lived — a kind of vacation. Yet there too he completed his second volume of autobiography, *Newspaper Days*.* And under the title *The Color of a Great City* he collected his sketches of that earlier New York which was already changing into a new premise from which to compute reality. And always he played with the idea of the new Inferno, which was to make a " mystical drama " out of modern life as dictated by the city, and which would perhaps place him among the poets. The tenacious Mencken wrote him repeatedly:

"Why don't you come back? Younger men have taken your place. You are being forgotten. What in hell are you doing in Los Angeles? The town must be unspeakable, a

* Called *A Book About Myself* and published in November 1922.

huge den of Baptists. . . . Every tourist coming back from the Coast has some tale about your Roman levities. Yesterday I heard that you had gone over to the Theosophists, and are living at Point Loma in a yellow robe, with hasheesh blossoms in your hair. . . ."

As part of the luxury of this period he planted a garden, made vegetables grow the way they used to in Sullivan. And he initiated what seems to have been the most coherent of his many relations with women since his first marriage. She was a young and beautiful Hollywood novice, who, it is said, abandoned her career as a screen actress in favor of Dreiser. At last his wishes had come almost true. He had a liberal publisher, enough money to live on and write, and would have more when *The " Genius "* was republished in July 1923 and sold at once 50,000 copies. And now he had the American, perhaps universal necessity, " the beauty of youth " without which " life was a joke . . . yes, the beauty of eighteen [or not far from it]. It was the standard, and the history of the world proved it." This he had written for his " Genius " to say as if the words were his own, and he has written it in autobiography. He had this now without complications; with no pledge, as with his first wife, that she must be all he would ever have. There were other relations that still concerned him; there might be new adventures. He has recorded himself as exercising the right of these. It was a part of his code as conqueror and logician. Why other men did not make it part of theirs he had often wondered. On these terms life was luxurious in Los Angeles. He would not have come East again, he thinks, except that he was forgetting to work and he had work to do. Perhaps too he was homesick for the more nervous air of New York, nearer to Europe and to old cultures which he valued as shamelessly as he did youth and beauty.

Dreiser has said that he pondered over the tragedy of Americans from 1918 to 1923. One climax of tragedy was murder. Franklin Booth the illustrator, whose guest he had been on his Hoosier holiday, remembers a conversation one night in New York, back in 1907, one of those impersonal exchanges that happen only between intimates, and in the detached clarity of night. They had both wondered if murder was not the most dramatic act a man could commit. Dreiser said that to be entirely experienced perhaps a man would have had to commit murder. But lacking that, a novelist to realize the gamut of life would have to be brave enough to imagine himself in the clothes and skin of a murderer. He was incompetent yet to write such a book, but some time vicariously he would get there. . . .

The Hand of the Potter was the first fugue on this theme. The play scarcely reached an audience, but always the theme engrossed him. He would pose the problem in a different more exhaustive form. He would take a man nearer to normal, supposedly responsible for his actions, and show how he too could get caught, and precisely how in accordance with the aimless inchoate American world, or rather where the one social aim was exteriority — money, fun and show. A letter dated July 1916 from a writer on the New York World to Jack Pratt, lawyer or librarian, reveals Dreiser as always busy with the problem:

"Just a line to introduce America's greatest novelist — Theodore Dreiser — who would like to read the Orket clippings — Will you fix it for him and oblige. . . ."

The book like all his books must be drawn from reality — a weakness according to his detractors (who like to say that he is only a reporter, a plagiarist from life). His answer might have been that by that last token so then was Homer, so was Balzac, so is André Gide a plagiarist from life. But Dreiser has never taken the trouble to answer for himself unless directly challenged by the law. He read and discarded, he says, five American tragedies, before he came on an actuality whose circumstances provided him with the frame he wanted. And then he varied the tangle of events slightly, in order, so he told me, to pose a criminal problem which no one could answer. In such a way his masterpiece, as it is called, grew through years in his changing mind. An interviewer quotes him as saying:

"I never make notes. I carry my plots around with me year after year before setting pen to paper. By the time I am ready to write I see the book as plainly as if it were a tree rising up before my eyes. Root, trunk, branches, twigs, so to speak, are all there; it is only the leaves that require to be sketched in."

In 1922 he came back from California to work at sketching in the leaves. By November 1925 the leafage of *An American Tragedy* was completed, and a cycle turned for Dreiser.

61

"*Pigeons on the grass alas.*
Pigeons on the grass alas.
Short longer longer shorter yellow grass
Pigeons large pigeons on the shorter
   longer yellow grass alas pigeons on the
   grass
If they were not pigeons what were they.
If they were not pigeons on the grass alas
   what were they." GERTRUDE STEIN

This plaintive and precise succession of words, meaning I know not what in relation to its context, describes to my liking these ten to fifteen years of awakened consciousness at which the United States had arrived. And William James has somewhere analysed such a period — the throb and defeat:

"Sporadic great men come everywhere. But for a community to get vibrating through and through with intensely active life, many geniuses coming together and in rapid succession are required. This is why great epochs are so rare — why the sudden bloom of a Greece, an early Rome, a Renaissance, is such a mystery. Then the mass of a nation grows incandescent, and may continue to glow long after the originators . . . have passed away. We often hear surprise expressed that in these high tides . . . not only the people should be filled with stronger life, but that individual geniuses should seem to be so extraordinarily abundant. This mystery is just about as deep as . . . why great rivers flow by great towns. It is true that great public fermentations awaken and adopt many geniuses, who in more torpid times would have had no chance to work. But over and above this there must be an exceptional concourse of genius about a time, to make the fermentation begin at all. The unlikeliness of the concourse is far greater than the unlikeliness of any particular genius. . . . Why, the very laws of physics are conditional, and deal with *ifs.* The physicist does not say the water will boil anyhow; he only says the water will boil if a fire be kindled under it."

Of course there was the water, there was the fire; there were many geniuses and some steam and a brief boiling point. But how much incandescence, that is the question? There was the grass, longer, shorter, grass; there were the pigeons, large enough, but how much concourse?

After Dreiser's *Titan,* of books of genius easily remembered *Spoon River Anthology* came first, published in book form in 1915, composed between 1909 and 1914,* and first printed in Reedy's Mirror and Poetry. This pigeon came from the iambic, dactylic, trochaic, anapaestic, but chiefly iambic Masters, the lawyer in Chicago with village birth and city hopes and universal brain. He could say in lightest talk to Edward Sheldon, a romantic dramatist of that day, at a luncheon from whose table Masters had removed the arrangement of Venetian glass flowers — they were in his way: " Poetry? You think of it as romantic? A lyric has to be authentic as a drop of dew."

And he wrote lyrics authentic in the sense of dew, together with poems authentic like a drought. But in this period of reaction from romance his bleak *Anthology* so gratified his readers that afterwards few would notice any other book he published. In the years to come perhaps they will discover his *Toward the Gulf, The Great Valley, Domesday Book*. They will find in them the same authentic brain of the *Anthology,* but creation more elaborate, more provocative, and perhaps not quite so free. Radical Americans almost always end by going back to Europe. Masters went back through rhetoric and prosody, unwilling to survive in the cadences and idiom of his own land which were too brutal or too leisurely. He went back into British metrical conventions, the way a lady from Kalamazoo would buy a seignorial castle on the summit of a Maritime Alp. Among them he lived estranged.

Yet in 1915 what confidence Americans had in Edgar Lee Masters, with intellect equal to Dreiser's and a greater verbal wisdom! His brief conclusive epitaphs

---

* As Masters tells it in his dedication of *Toward The Gulf* to William Marion Reedy.

spoke to them of life and death truly American, not British, not metropolitan. They voiced the forgotten talk of a whole segment of the country, from which the rest of it could be reconstructed — of poor relatives, of disreputable people, of nonentities unknown to High Society. And they spoke their irony from the heart, not in thin staccato of *Main Street.*

Some years before the *Anthology* was published or heard of, Dreiser first met Masters, a lawyer in Clarence Darrow's office. And he told the young newspapermen, who hung by eyelashes to culture at Maurice Browne's Little Theatre, that here was an American poet; they must watch for him. They laughed at Dreiser, a mere stupid genius they said, but two years later marveled at his foresight. These two, novelist and poet, thus flagged each other in the new American dawn, both desiring civilization; and then in later years abandoned hope of it for their country in their time; and in time the poet abandoned the novelist.

Out of Illinois too in this day came Nicholas Vachel Lindsay, revivalist poet, the nearest to evangelism that letters have come. Poetry, A Magazine of Verse was sponsor for him; the assistant editor, Alice Corbin, had found him. *General Booth Enters Heaven, The Congo, The Chinese Nightingale* took Americans white, black, yellow, reformed hoboes, Negroes, laundrymen back to where they thought they came from — Heaven, Africa, Nanking. Lindsay's father had been a missionary in China. He himself believed in opposites, lewdness and chastity, god and devil, flesh and spirit. His poems filled with precepts were sure of himself, sure of America, sure of his home-town, Springfield, Illinois. He had a gift direct from William Blake.

In 1913 William Butler Yeats praised him at a banquet in Chicago designed to celebrate Miss Monroe's new magazine and to honor the Irish poet. He said that given this poet, the only modern he had read, there must be others. He was right, there were. First after Yeats had spoken, Edgar Lee Masters read a poem *Silence,* that thing more praised than song by most Americans, perhaps because we have more noise than song. Then

Lindsay, who had the charm of preferring song to silence, rose and, eyes and forehead rolling, read for the first time his *Congo*, tobogganing up and down, back and forth over the cadences of the poem. Yeats, who had just been preaching native art to the banqueters, was yet horrified by the oratory of this missionary voice — voice akin to William J. Bryan's, an American free-silver voice capable of drums, lutes, calliopes, a band of instruments. " Can't someone tell him that a poem is a matter of art, not of self-abuse ? " Mr. Yeats murmured to himself. But the Illinois dancing poet did not care, did not notice. The praise or censure of a master meant nothing to him.

A banquet however was a banquet, and this banquet, Lindsay told the wife of the toastmaster, who had tried the best he could to combine culture and creation in the hog butchers' city, had been a gala evening: " I've had a real good time " were his words in the down-state lingo he affected. And he added, " Now I'm not one to be carnally minded — I wouldn't want you to think so, ma'am, but you've got some pretty fine looking young women at this barbecue, dressed up in what looks to me like genuine Parisian rags. I wouldn't care if I met two or three of them again." A dinner party followed. I appeared to figure in the number, but soon to fall from favor. Sitting next to the new poet I felicitated him on praise from Yeats. His reply was meant to annihilate:

" Well, lady, where have you been ? It looks like you've led a pretty sheltered life. . . . Now I want to tell you something. I don't care what an Irishman or an Englishman or a Chinese or an Australian has to say about me."
— " What do you care about then ? " I hazarded, and found out — " I care what the people of Springfield, Illinois have to say about my poems, and that's about all." I asked out of mere bravado if the people of Springfield, Illinois were not sheltered too, but in reality I was frightened. I knew then at that party following the Poetry banquet that the old world was over ; a spirit back of nations had cut the rope that tethered us. The new world was on its way, and the people would not care for Nicholas Vachel Lindsay for very long or for any other poet or

artist at all. His own indifference was a prophecy of the flood of forgetfulness soon to come.

He went however on his way " exchanging rhymes for bread " south, east, north, and west. Sometimes people gave him bread and listened to the rhymes, especially in Chicago, New York and London. But in Kansas, Missouri and Tennessee, he tells it himself, sometimes they gave him the bread at once so they would not have to listen to his often impeccable ballads and lyrics. Yet before the waters closed over on this period, the militant localism which Lindsay preached and sang bore fruit in the United States. He was one of the sporadic geniuses. His poems were pigeons out of which came other lonely pigeons to adorn the blue green yellow grass. . . . Eighteen years later a chance remark of his betrayed that he too must have been more cynic than optimist. It was not many weeks before his death that he happened to say: " I have been the world over looking for another such audience as I found in Chicago in 1913. I have not found it." It must have been that the people of Springfield, Illinois had disappointed him after all, and that he longed for the shelter of experienced judgment. He like the rest of us apparently felt the stir of creation in that day and, though loath to admit it, knew finally that it had come out of America by way of Europe — both immigrant and patrician Europe.

And that was not all — the banquet in honor of Yeats was again a forecast of books to come. A newspaper man, Carl Sandburg, born of Swedish parents in Galesburg, Illinois, spoke for the first time to a poetry audience. He said these words, phrased like a song:

" I am riding on a limited express, one of the crack trains of the nation.
Hurtling aross the prairie into blue haze and dark air go fifteen all steel coaches holding a thousand people.
(All the coaches shall be scrap and rust and all the men and women laughing in the diners and sleepers shall pass to ashes.)
I ask a man in the diner where he is going and he answers: ' Omaha.' "

After the last three syllables O-ma-ha, which sounded and isolated the value of an American name for almost

415

the first time in a line of poetry, there was a murmur and a sigh in the hall. Yeats could not complain of oratory. Here was another deliberate poet, knowing that "the muses love violence" and love delicacy too. And certain that a poem comes to the poet from everyday speech and action.

For him how different the source from that of the Irish poet! For him it would be Milwaukee, Chicago, Cicero home of gangsters and machine-guns, Maywood or Elmhurst where he lived, or any station between, from which poems would come to him "asking to be written." It would be the office of the Chicago Daily News or Wabash Avenue and State Street scene of race riots, or the Stock Yards or the rolling mills at Gary and South Chicago; or the frog-puddles along railroads in April, or the utter fire of rye and wheat fields west of Maywood — it would be wherever he went that "deliberate speech" would come to him and give him "letters telegrams and radios." They were messages that chose to ignore "what love is, what beauty is, what truth is, what art is," or to dismiss them as worn-out words. Decoded, these messages speak the song of blood and muscles, glands and bones, in animals, laborers and strugglers, akin to the song in stars, sea and mountains. They tell how when men get very rich or want to get very rich, they pay the price of having lost that song. They speak of travelers and natives met by the way, but they speak elliptically and in the chosen free verse of their special free forms.

While Whitman chanted monumentally intending to inspire; while Dreiser wrote humbly and hugely wishing always to elucidate; and Masters wrote tearfully and bitterly to lament; and Lindsay sang lustfully to uplift; Sandburg picked his way elegantly, an aristocrat of our slang and idiom. Like the others he went directly into nature and came out with as much love; and with a more precise ear for poetic form as related to promiscuous America than anyone before or perhaps since. Lindsay borrowed older cadences with which to celebrate his country. Sandburg was the first intentional poet to set America to its own music, the way that the anonymous songs of mountaineers, prisoners, Darkies, ranchmen, railroad hands had unintentionally set the country to music. Such a kinship he felt with American folk song that in 1927 he published a volume assembling every example of this art; and he has been inspiration for others to do this. Such a kinship he felt that he has feared to go in thought too far beyond the psyche of these native singers. He has preferred to tell them that much is better lost in silence, sleep, solitude and mist, than to force issues too painful for them to face.

Three years after the prophetic banquet his *Chicago Poems* appeared, and then in successive years *Cornhuskers, Smoke and Steel, Slabs of the Sunburnt West, Rootabaga Stories, Rootabaga Pigeons, Lincoln The Prairie Years, Good Morning America!* He translated America into speech selected from it, but chosen with more preciousness than is yet native to us. Like Dreiser he was both native and stranger.

And both were pioneers. That is, they were instruments or symptoms of change; the one whereby American thought became freer, the other whereby American language and gestures became more flexible. Dreiser forced terrific issues which, fought for, yielded more confidence in sex, in art, and in science destructive to old dogmas. Mencken had preached the American language, others before had used it. Sandburg made it resonant, the speech of the learned and unlearned, of outcasts and working men inclusive. Dreiser had the virtue of not changing the subject, Sandburg of not changing the diction or the décor for the sake of propriety.

These two strong natives, both passionate over their new country, belonged to a wedge of change that was of itself yielding a new style of thought, a new style of society. Some of their own desires could be more effective in an epoch when fortunes were changing hands over night, or were paper-born out of inflated moments. There had to be a break-down of old class barriers. With that had to come the downfall of Colonial morality and of the King's English and the courtiers' clothes. For a few years High Society became almost unfashionable, not destroyed as in Russia, but neglected. The new plutocracy today established speaks American and has a new set of morals or no morals at all.

Suppose that in these years of flux originators like Dreiser and Sandburg and the few others who heightened the chance of a creative society, had all of them exchanged ideas. Wouldn't American letters have better fulfilled the hopes of each of them? But " the unlikeliness of the concourse is greater than the unlikeliness of any particular genius." Of the others the one equal in vigor to these two was the Californian, Robert Frost. Dreiser, Sandburg and Frost were three of the elements essential to a great fermentation in this time. But they never made a triangle, never made a constellation. Probably they had friends in common who sometimes spoke of one to the other, but without arousing curiosity, or barely so. They remained like separate sources from whom many younger writers separately depend. They remain the three creators with one thing in common — strength to survive, though by a narrow margin, a country and a period hostile to art and friendly to extrinsic creation.

Once I had in my house a yellow Chinese chow and a black Persian cat, both pedigreed. One day in the spring the cat went out into the shrubs of the backyard and brought back a transient thrush. The pacific chow, whose hope it was always to find a bird in that Chicago yard, rushed to the Persian to felicitate her, one might think, to be repulsed by an arch of back, a hissing and snarling through jaw and whiskers, a superb protection of her game, terrifying to mere human beings. Dreiser's admiration of Sandburg's accomplished poems, met by the poet's disdain of the " varietist's clumsy efforts," has reminded me of that encounter between friendly dog and proud cat.

In 1914 Masters showed Sandburg's poems to his friend the novelist in New York. True to his veneration for art Dreiser tried to sell them to his own publisher. Although the poems found a publisher through other friends, they continued to have his support. He recommended them to Mencken and to all other unconventional editors of his acquaintance. He said explicitly they were wonderful. In return he got no thanks from their author who had vowed hatred against everything explicit, *The*

Titan for one; and especially perhaps against explicit statement as to sexual and religious discords in American life. He was inclined to say that such statement was "gratuitous, cocksure, garrulous." . . . "Art was implicit":

"Poetry is the tracing of the trajectories of a finite sound to the infinite points of its echoes.
"Poetry is the capture of a picture, a song, or a flair, in a deliberate prism of words."

Subtle definitions for fastidious ears and eyes! Yet on the other side of this poet was the important unimported cat, Frost, with a meaner verbal creed; almost ungracious if taken narrowly in relation to each word:

"Sometimes I have my doubts of words altogether, and I ask myself what is the place of them? They are worse than nothing unless they do something, unless they amount to deeds, as in ultimatums or battle-cries. They must be flat and final, like the show-down in poker, from which there is no appeal."

If Frost did not arch, he has been known to stretch slightly at what he seemed to think was vocal ornateness in the Manchurian Sandburg, who undoubtedly ages ago derived from the wealthier East through Mongol and Finn on the way to Sweden and Illinois. The Chicago poet and the New Hampshire poet have met, it is said, and are friends. But American letters show no record of their crossing each other's intellectual path; no record of their having sifted out together their relations to the craft of poetry, of having agreed or disagreed. In fact there is no record, unless Sandburg's later poems by their greater subtlety and restraint indicate an effect on him of that most exacting critic, Robert Frost. In the early days of their renown it was said by eavesdroppers that, except for the lyrics which Frost admired, and maybe envied for a sensuousness he lacked, to him Sandburg was often farfetched; just as to Sandburg, it is rumored, Dreiser is nearly always rambling.

In fact, each in his way felt indifferent to the other. The author of *Smoke and Steel* disdained "the artifice" of rhyme and regular metre in Frost's poems. He heard them always as extrinsic to poetic meaning, and therefore not of the first elegance. Each poem should be like a new shape out of wild wood or driftwood. And Dreiser had his scorns too. He grew to think of Sandburg as a reformer, and of both these poets as " probably afraid of sex," or why didn't they come out in the open and speak of it? Of marriage, birth, death, sleep, work and crime, of trees, birds, flowers and stones, they spoke plainly enough, but when it came to the exciting fact of sex, he complained, they invented codes and puzzles to hide it in. What was wrong with it? Didn't it have its place too in " this rigmarole called life " ?

Here then were the three tough creative spirits of the new country producing at the same moment. Masters made a fourth for a time. Like Dreiser he thought of personal relations as essential, and at first they paid each other tributes of acknowledgment. But for the most part the four scarcely took note of one another. Each was too busy with his own work, and besides who cared? If ever they had had it out together as to literature in journals or saloons or parlors, distinctions might have resulted to tighten American thought. The more reticent Sandburg and Frost might have said that in their opinion poetry could name by name only things that people spoke of naturally. For unspoken facts and emotions, dictionary words and borrowed words were clumsy. Symbols, even asterisks were better. Or they might have said: Sex is a mystery; each line a poem writes has in it the tones and overtones of that mystery. Dreiser could have answered back: But death and birth are mysterious too, and you speak of them without disguise? And they might have conceded to him his daring as to theme, their own as to manner. But nothing like this took place. Much as Dreiser set store by exchange among equals, perhaps these others thought he was an inferior. He was too " metropolitan " Sandburg used to say. And Frost always kept away from strangers; they had to come to him.

Unconscious of each other they had moments of essential agreement. Frost's definition of poetry has a dependant clause: " All poetry is a reproduction of the tones of actual speech." *Sister Carrie* and *An American Tragedy* agree to this basically if not always in detail. *Chicago Poems* and *Good Morning America* agree to this aesthetically and often impeccably. Yet Frost, if he were candid, and he might be, would have a right to say that among American high-brows he has the record for cracking clay pipes and clay ducks in the shooting gallery of the tones of actual speech. An expert like Ring Lardner has not beaten him at that game. On the other hand which extends far into wilderness, Frost has not, like Dreiser or Sandburg, attempted to recreate the speech of the whole melting pot, in a kind of superb compassion for the newcomers to the Home of the Brave.

Frost, returning from California at the age of ten to his grandfather's home in Massachusetts, has lived almost always since in that State or in New Hampshire or Vermont. Being a poet he had need of a language and chose New England speech. None of his verse is influenced by the voices of Sussex, England, where he went in 1912 to sell his poems, scorned at home. In three years he came back with enough fame to get an American publisher, and just enough money to buy a farm in New Hampshire, and to publish three more books of verse. So the legend goes. Nor are his poems affected by the voices of Michigan students, to whose university he went in later years to advise young Western poets. He had chosen as the honey-comb in which to secrete his moods New England idiom, without ever patronizing it.

Surely it had its faults of cadence — a mean cadence: It is a speech spoken flatly and finally, not in the nose as out West, but in the front of the mouth as if it were dangerous to go back into the throat in the direction of visceral and then genital emotions and acts. Frost accepted it, not especially because he liked it, but because he lived within range of its statement of life. It was as good for his purpose as another speech, since as long as there was life there were tones of voice, and in that case could be poetry, given poets to make it. Besides, New England speech had its compensations. It was thin but delicate, sounding most of the letters. And the voices understated rather than overstated — a virtue for Frost whose verse is an unlabelled challenge to American advertisers, the verbal teachers of the greater part of the nation. In contrast his poems identify themselves to a far decimal point with knowledge, the way the last cricket sings sharply of the summer when the others have gone.

Dreiser's books use figures of speech, most often similes; and are sometimes identical with nature or else tell about nature. Sandburg's poems and stories sometimes use and sometimes are figures of speech, mostly metaphors. They create equations in the algebra of life, or they are letters to people sorrowful or joyful over bad or good fortune. Frost's poems are figures of speech, synecdoches he calls them: " a synecdoche is a figure of speech whereby a part is made to stand for the whole." Probably every visionary who writes would say he was a synecdochist, but each one would differently define the specifications.

Frost might say: For a passage of words to describe the whole of which a single birch leaf is a part the words have to be aware of the shape, the veins, the color, the weight and position in space, according to the moment of the season of the birch leaf. Then the words convey the relation, dramatic or lyrical, of leaf to tree, tree to forest, forest to region, region to the universe. . . . Sandburg might say: There are likenesses and differences between osage leaves in Illinois, palm leaves in India, cactus leaves in Arizona which a poet apprehends. In thinking of a single leaf he creates a symbol, an image, a flash of words to convey the leaves of many trees, and of life analogous to trees, or by differences opposed to trees, from which initial symbol secrets of life and death will invade you, provided you have ears to hear, eyes to see. . . . Dreiser says to himself and others: Shucks, no one leaf is enough to even suggest the multiplicity of nature, shrouded in a mist no one has penetrated. For me I must make leaves, leaves, leaves. The more I make, no matter how imperfectly in a harried lifetime, the more multiple facts there will be from which others may try to guess the evasive riddle.

Being of similar strength they were not so different in scope. The universe was not too big for them. They have a flair for the infinite. Compare three statements from the three:

Dreiser, when asked in 1929 what people he liked to talk to in New York, answered: "The scientists dealing with reality and mystery. Front line trench of an army facing wild nature. On the firing line where I want to be." Then a year later: "I am through with scientists. They don't see mysticism."

Frost when confronted in conversation with new marvels of science, less gullible than Dreiser, said: "Isn't science just an extended metaphor; its aim to describe the unknown in terms of the known? Isn't it a kind of poetry, to be treated as plausible material, not as cold facts?" When reminded of Einstein's theory of relativity he is quoted as saying: "Wonderful, yes, wonderful but no better as a metaphor than you or I might make for ourselves before five o'clock." *

Sandburg too might make such metaphors before morning. Here may be one of them:
"History is a living horse laughing at a wooden horse.
History is a wind blowing where it listeth.
History is a box of tricks with a lost key.
History is a labyrinth of doors with sliding panels, a book of ciphers with the code in a cave of the Sargossa Sea."

Three views of knowledge possessing similar gravity and an immense difference of manner. No one would have expected or wanted these writers to go arm in arm. But it is surprising that they have never even challenged each other. It must have been that so vast and scattered is the United States, so brutal the gaps between races and classes, and then between individuals of any one class, that men with original work to do felt the futility and even the danger of personal relations.

Then minds with less to create or lose read them and ran and interpreted them. In this way American thought was placed on a plane suitable to universal upper mediocrity. Thereby for example Europeans scarcely know that we have had original vintages of more body to give them than the second drawings from the mash, like Sinclair Lewis, Ezra Pound, or Ernest Hemingway. The last two are from both native and exotic fermentation. They are tourists, Hemingway a gifted youth, writing to the folks back home in words of one syllable easy for them to understand. Such men have come to be a sudden unexplained background for new America.

* Reported by Genevieve Taggard.

Is this owing to a complex in the more adult American minds, without whom these adolescents would not have existed — the unwillingness to analyse or explain? Whatever the reason, criticism after Poe and the Concord school went out of fashion, and has been handled by inferiors. Walt Whitman led the fashion against critical distinctions, for all his talk of growth and savor:

" To elaborate is no avail, learn'd and unlearn'd feel that it is so."
" Encompass worlds but never try to encompass me.
I charge you forever reject those who would expound me."

Undeniably he spoke here in keeping with a pioneer sentiment that action was better than thought; and that the act of a critic was not action. Nor did it help matters when the behaviorist Watson came along proving that what had been named thought was merely action. This discovery served all the more to exalt action. There is the fable of the general at headquarters who wrote to the officer at the front, " Here are the specifications for the bridge "; and the answer: " Thanks, the bridge is already constructed." A story that pleases every hundred-percent American! . . . " Don't criticize your country," a well-known New York painter said to me, " Leave it alone, do your own work." — " But," I asked, " what if my work is that of a critic? "

Americans abominate criticism, as much as a room without a bath. Poe was the one high-geared critic of the past, the one ancestral precedent for any stray moderns still believing that analysis is a civilizing force. Whitman contradicted him. In the next generation Ambrose Bierce, by temper a live critic, cherished such a hatred for his country that he used his talent to destroy American writers. Once however someone brought him Crane's *Red Badge of Courage,* thinking that surely Bierce, a veteran in war and letters, would demolish the book: " This young man," Bierce said, " has the power to feel. . . . He knows nothing of war but he is drenched in blood. . . . Most beginners . . . spatter themselves merely with ink." * Of *A Farewell to Arms* I think of Bierce as saying: " Here is a writer who knows something

* *Bitter Bierce:* Hartley Grattan.

of war, but the typewriter separates him from bloodshed." *Three Soldiers* and *The Enormous Room* seem to care less for chic and more for grief.

Of course always the country contained critics in spite of themselves. No great work is ever done without the grace of judgment watching over it like a holy ghost. By this token Melville, Thoreau, Whitman and Mark Twain, contemporary with Bierce, were critics. From Mark Twain finally came an anonymous work and a posthumous work, fearfully critical — *What is Man?* and *The Mysterious Stranger,* though they analysed society more than art. A generation later, overlapping the life of Bierce, Edwin Arlington Robinson burned with selective fire, turned in toward his own poems, as if he were a good Christian and preferred not to suffer hell-fire. Over his work he maintained a close discipline, not even released, it is said, in talk.

Always interested in experts and heroes I have sometimes asked what Robinson talks about when he talks. I have not heard from anyone that he talks outside of his poems. He is enveloped in the legend of a recluse. Once, it is said, he lived with another poet, but got tired of him and left. Years later he rang the doorbell; his friend answered the ring and asked, "What do you want?" — "I thought," said Robinson, " that I wanted to come back, but now that I see you again I don't believe I do." No chance of concourse from this poet! Yet he is one of the few Americans to explore human minds more than external events. In his poems he uses for themes the tangle of thoughts of the heart. His themes issue from Americans with enough leisure to think at all; and the tangle of psychic events takes place in the dead wood and underbrush and new growth in which unwittingly his characters have come to live. Robinson, the hermit thrush of cerebral thickets and swamps!

Suppose however that our history had been slightly different. It might have been a shade different with fewer English and Germans, more French, Spanish and Indians surviving. Every *if* is a big *if*. Imagine just enough difference so that these mineral "moderns" of fifteen years ago had felt a native relation one to the other, and to writers producing before them and around them. If they had felt the background of Bierce, Mark Twain, Henry James, and Robinson (who though younger was yet related to the past in point of view), they would then have made a figure denoting creation; the parts held together as much by repulsion as by attraction, the way of all units in conjunction. To such a constellation might have been joined Masters and Lindsay, and then Sherwood Anderson, Carlos Williams, the unknown Carnevali. Out of such a figure, changing from year to year, dropping one unit attracting another, out of the antagonisms and agreements of such brains, if even for brief moments they had crossed to agree or disagree, civilization in the United States might recently have had more iron of thought, and more specifically the steel needle of direction. I use these names of writers as not the most widely known, but as those most tinctured with the salts and phosphates of life, as those nearest in speech to the earth.

To imagine such concourse in the United States is so unreal as to be laughable. Yet a human geometry like this has happened in the creative epochs of other countries. Take France in the time just preceding the War: the critic Apollinaire is said to have brought men of different ages and of different styles and races into relation; as different as Cocteau, Picasso, Satie, and Brancusi. And this period hung upon a previous period, through recognition expressing differences — Zola, Anatole France, Rodin, Toulouse-Lautrec, Renoir, Degas, Cézanne, none of them unacknowledged by the other. Back of this was the epoch of Baudelaire. . . . Or take a vast country like Russia. Consider what intimate relations and savage contradictions would come to play their part, if one should evoke the story of Dostoevsky. In the recent United States one does not find evidence of such complicated engagements.

I have not heard that those most actuated by faith in art ever met except in twos, scarcely ever in threes, never in fours. " Americans are infinitely repellent particles." Dreiser and Masters for a time, Masters and Sandburg for a while, Lindsay and Sandburg for a minute, Frost and Sandburg for a walk or two in the country, Williams and Sandburg for a second, and the two of them together with Anderson taking note of Carnevali until he left the scene for Italy! Few others knew or cared; yet, since Poe, Carnevali was the first intimation of a critic in America who did not separate poetry and criticism:

"Art theories are ages old . . . the only newness that can be brought into such topics may be the weight of a personally suffered tragedy, or a golden gift of song, torn out of a man's own heart, his heart of today, of today's sorrow and today's laughter. . . . Only a very personal emotion validates and differentiates a man's art theories. Then . . . it matters little that similar things have been said by someone else before; then indeed one may rejoice that they have been said by someone else; then one no longer strives for originality, but for a communion . . . for the frenzy of the extreme loneliness of being together with the great. . . . Such loneliness is perhaps what is meant by originality. . . . Only eyes of fire may look at the sun. . . ."

Belief in such timeless communion was not shared by his colder friends, Waldo Frank, Kreymborg, Bodenheim, or even Carlos Williams, who especially was seeking a new fresh language and technique by which to save America.

There remained only the democratic Sherwood Anderson with a sense of communion. His Latin blood — Italian, he thinks — mingled with Northern, appeared to value human beings, as if they might be friends and would like to know each other. He too was after the "Splendid Commonplace" proclaimed by Carnevali, but without the ardor and the hurry. He was an American with more patience. He could stand delays. In fact he derived from other natives, Dreiser, Sandburg, and Gertrude Stein, as well as from Freud and, one would think, Tchekov. Keeping always his own voice, a new voice, as derivatives do in civilized countries, he felt for a time a kind of debt to those to whom he bore this relation. In 1923 one of his finest books, *Horses and Men*, is dedicated to "Theodore Dreiser in whose presence I have sometimes had the same refreshed feeling as when in the presence of a thoroughbred horse." And this book of an Ohioan who had known race horses, Ohioans, Chicagoans and many people, makes reference to Masters, Sandburg and

Mencken. A foreigner reading the stories might think that already thought and imagination as well as oil were going the rounds of the United States. The foreword called *Dreiser* belongs in this history.

Edgar Lee Masters had paid as great a tribute before in a poem published in *The Great Valley*, 1916:

. . .
      "One eye set higher than the other,
      Mouth cut like a scallop in a pie,
      Aslant showing powerful teeth.
      Swaying above the heads of others.
      Jubilant with fixed eyes scarcely sparkling.
. . . Moving about rhythmically, exploding in laughter.
      And the eyes burn like a flame at the end of a funnel.
      Or else a gargoyle of bronze
. . . Turning suddenly to life
      Full of questions, objections,
      Distinctions, instances.
      Contemptuous, ironical, remote,
      Cloudy, irreverent, ferocious,
      Fearless, grim, compassionate, yet hateful,
      Old, yet young, wise but virginal.
      To whom every thing is new and strange;
      Whence he stares and wonders,
      Laughs, mocks, curses.
      Disordered, yet with a passion for order
      and classification — hence the habitual
. . . Folding into squares of a handkerchief.
      Or else a well cultivated and fruitful valley,
. . . But behind it unexplored fastnesses,
. . . Gorges, precipices, and heights
      Stirring up terrible shapes of prey
      That slink about in the blackness.
. . . The silence of it is terrifying
. . . The look of his eyes makes tubes of the air
. . . He needs nothing of you and wants nothing.
      Self-mastered, but beyond friendship,
      You could not hurt him.
      If he would allow himself to have a friend
      He could part from that friend forever
      And in a moment be lost in wonder
      Staring at a carved rooster on a doorstep,
      Or at an Italian woman
      Giving suck to a child
. . . On a seat in Washington Square.
      Soul enwrapped demi-urge
      Walking the earth,
      Stalking Life!

A year or so before on the threshold of modern times, Harris Merton Lyon made an equally violent tribute, authentic by its wording:

"In many ways . . . the one man writing in this country today . . . worth the lot of them. . . . The Tarkingtons, Beaches, Londons and the rest may play their little light-hearted game and fare on into the dusk. . . . They are for the most part dead before they die, and so no mystery. But here is a fellow who now shows as if he may never die at all. . . . This man is mysterious. . . .

"A huge rootabaga; a colossal, pith-stricken radish. In this body dwells this amazingly fascinating mind. . . . He sits articulating with a drone . . . folding a pocket handkerchief eternally into a strip, folding the strip, accordionwise.

"For such a writer we may well concoct a paradox: everything is really so unimportant that it might well be treated as important. . . . Every hour in a day is so important to every character that [he] must feel like a clock with a conscience.

"Yet patience alone does not explain him. . . . What does this recluse keep from us, behind those lolling, uninitiated eyes? . . .

"That he keeps poetry is one thing sure. . . . To a man who, in the backward-running holes of his mind, keeps caves for poetry any inappropriateness of genius is credible. . . .

"He was the first man who taught me to think. He would . . . make some comment . . . so clear and arresting that I used to gasp. But . . . there was no sustained flow. . . . From him too I learned that there are always two, and possibly three or a dozen sides to everything. This is enough to make anybody tongue-tied. . . .

"Dreiser is important. There is no American writing today the condition of whose health, vigor and spirits is more important. . . ."

Here is the kind of statement presupposing a premise from which life may become "intensely active." The premise is a simple one, very shocking to Americans: The arts are important. Ten years later Sherwood Anderson's foreword to his *Horses and Men* gave the same kind of importance to the same man in relation to the arts and in their same shocking relation to life — retrospective now as to Dreiser and roseate concerning the American future.

"Theodore Dreiser is old. . . . I do not know how many years he has lived, perhaps forty, perhaps fifty, but he is very old. Something grey and bleak and hurtful, that has been in the world perhaps forever, is personified in him.

"When Dreiser is gone men shall write books . . . and in the books . . . there will be so many of the qualities Dreiser lacks . . . a sense of humor. . . . More than that . . . grace, lightness of touch, a dream of beauty breaking through the husks.

". . . That is a part of the wonder and beauty of Dreiser, the things that others shall have because of him. . . .

"Heavy, heavy, the feet of Theodore. How easy to pick some of his books to pieces, to laugh at him for so much of his heavy prose.

"The feet of Theodore are making a path, the heavy brutal feet. They are tramping through the wilderness of lies. . . . Presently the path will be a street, with great arches overhead and delicately carved spires piercing the sky. Along the street will run children shouting, "Look at me. See what I and my fellows of the new day have done" —forgetting the heavy feet of Dreiser.

". . . the prose writers in America will have much to do that he has never done. Their road is long but, because of him, those who follow will never have to face the road through the wilderness of Puritan denial, the road that Dreiser had to face alone."

62

Interval of departures more than arrivals

It looks now as if "those who followed" have merely a desert to face made out of their parents' inexperience and out of their own indifference — that Wasteland which the first of them, T. S. Eliot, lifted into a sound film. "Those who followed," were no longer denied; but as much because they found themselves without desire as that the way was free. Or they only followed with the faint desire of being snobs, of getting to Europe and into "New Composition, World Lore Totality, Magic Synthesism." * Or else the desire was to get religion and join with Soviet Russia in a world revolution, an equally cabalistic motive. The desire today is to join, not to be free. Those who followed were like children whose parents were too busy fighting for liberty to teach them what to do with it. Or they were like the family who saved for years and bought a piano, but forgot they had not learned to play. Take the Puritanic lid off the kettle of American Desire, easily removable now, and you will find that ambrosia for the moment boiled away. The fire is out.

Appetite is gone. Nothing new to eat, nothing fit to drink. They drink whatever is brought to them from over their frontiers. A nation drinks without appetite to cook a meal. They smoke cigarettes made out of listlessness and indifference. They should care! Is that why in time we might cease to be a world power? "Where the power to think is lacking . . . ?" And the power to love . . . ?

What Sherwood Anderson prophesied in 1923 came partly true. The younger men of any creative spirit who

* Bywords of the journal *transition* published in Paris from 1927 to 1930.

followed, not beneath his arches and delicate spires, but beneath innumerable sky-scrapers and elevated tracks, hurrying in and out of taxis, subways, publishers' and speak-easies, did forget the heavy feet of Dreiser; forgot the catlike step of Sandburg and Frost as well, forgot Lindsay, Masters, Robinson, forgot their past (although some of them still imitated these writers). They remembered only Anderson. Enough to laugh at him. His books like Dreiser's are easy to laugh at, though not for carelessness of diction. But while Dreiser is ruthless, unsparing, formidable, Anderson is so tender, so sorry for everyone of his countrymen warped by repression, that sometimes his words seem to keep a nursing home for nervous cases. It is easy to laugh at his records of insanity and death, especially for those who have gone far from it into World Lore Totality, Magic Synthesism, Montparnasse and other cures. None the less the commitments and the funerals go on, Sherwood Anderson the last near relative to mourn.

It is often said that Dreiser as much as anyone blocked intellectual exchange in the years of its promise. His victorious battles had defeated him. He had become the veteran general not the equal he could have been. I have heard, for example, that he resented Anderson's tribute. To be called old, very old, heavy and humorless displeased him. He could laugh and did, and he was not so old or clumsy either. He would show them . . . and did with *An American Tragedy* coming two years after Anderson's epitaph. Yet consciously as much as anyone he had hoped and worked for tone and flavor as essential to America. In 1919 after The Seven Arts was killed by the War he started to create a similar magazine, but found that no one wanted it as coming from him. The Little Review, Contact, Others, and still others were under way in a new direction, seeking an exotic sophistication. For the rest Mencken was already planning his Mercury, about as much as unsociable natives would be able to swallow. There would be plenty of kidding and snickering in it; it would be manly.

Failing that project Dreiser tried again in the same year, 1919, to inaugurate a society endowed to help those too daring or too subtle to arrive through regular channels. He wanted, he said, to make it less possible for genius to be lost or prostituted in the United States. He thought of a long list of artists he had known through the years back of him, too sensitive to stand up against commercialism. The uncommercial Reedy's Mirror in St. Louis was apparently the one vehicle he could find to advertise his scheme, and only two writers, one unknown, responded publicly. He gave up " concourse " for a time and went to California. Ten years later I asked him what had become of this society: " Nothing," he said. " We had a meeting. But no one seemed to care what happened to the other fellow. Each one was out for himself."

America's foremost novelist for a time after the War was strangely lacking in prestige. Or was it magnetism? Had a life of neglect, of attacks and reprisals destroyed the original talent he had for mingling with others? In truth he had long had a name for boorishness, although he prized above everything, outside of his right to live and create, the hope of a social fabric, backed by learning and imagination — what he called " artistic vision." To this end he would talk to anyone, known or unknown, who professed an interest in expression, whether reporters, editors, beginners or arrivists, if they wanted to talk. He gave in these years many interviews, made many articles, wrote a number of prefaces for books he liked. He was near to becoming a publicist, not so much for money or publicity, I think, as out of hunger for society. A book of his prefaces would show him as a critic who has made subtle and vigorous distinctions, hastily written but the outcome of difficult contemplation.

No, it was not merely bad manners that destroyed prestige for this giant. It was a question of changing fashions. The mere fact of poets bent on the just word as well as the just theme convinced the new Americans that a fused native art was at hand, as bold as Dreiser's and more choice in manner. First Frost, then Masters, then Sandburg, then Anderson and Eliot in turn seemed to shine for sophisticated eyes. Now Dos Passos, Jack Lawson, E. E. Cummings, Hemingway were swinging into view, and probably others.* As each light was turned on, the one before was dimmed a little more. By the year 1923 all the earlier lights were nearly extinguished. Disgraceful to speak of them! They were dark; save for the constant glow of Frost's poems like particles of radium easily lost but potent, the unacknowledged mazda lamp of Carlos Williams, and the night-light of Sherwood Anderson. Those who followed were ashamed of those who had led the way. Did the leaders care, as they went out of momentary fashion — Masters with his rhythmic sensitive *Domesday Book,* Sandburg not long after his great work *Lincoln, the Prairie Years?* The Spoon River anthologist, who kept count more than the others, must have cared and dwelt in bitterness, which culminated in *Lincoln the Man.* Was it a revenge against Sandburg's greater love of Lincoln and wider popularity?

Did Dreiser the initial voice know or care? Difficult to guess. Outside of his books he is a man of secrets, and in native fashion rarely personal. Asked once what he thought of his apostle Anderson, who had somewhat taken his place as pioneer, his answer may have been a kind of reprisal, or else was it truly critical? " I admire him," he said, " but there's one thing I don't get about him. He harps too much on one subject." — " Sex, you mean? " — " No, that would be impossible. He glorifies day laborers and mechanics to the exclusion of all other classes. I can't see it that way. There must be something to the intellect, to the upper classes. If not, we're done for."

What made these quick changes of fashion? Stars extinguished almost before they had been signalled in American skies? Quite true that in France in these years Anatole France and Rodin were dethroned the minute they died, but not before they had led long lives correcting the ages before them, clearing the way less for children than for great-grandchildren. Moreover in their day and in epochs before them, going back to the time of Voltaire and Diderot, such leaders knew each other as individuals, not as movements or schools. Personal distinction ruled. Whereas in the United States there was not save by moments any faith at all in the leaders of this period.

* Let the reader supply the others' names.

It was, I think, because when the road was finally cleared for younger people to think for themselves, they were faced with a contradiction made poignant to them by recent letters. The tragic isolation of Americans and their living language shaped now out of their own soil were two phases of the country difficult for them to reconcile. It was something to cry over — the prodigal beauties discovered by the new poets, and always wasted and lost through the return to American dogma, banks, offices, and Christian Endeavor. In the meantime some of them had through world's fairs and then through the War, the greatest world's fair of all, crossed the ocean to Europe, the Near East, Russia, the Orient. They could not ever again go the impervious way of American pioneers. They were young and impatient. They asked themselves what was it that separated their country from other countries? Unconsciously they knew it was lack of manner. We had no wisdom of manner. This must be corrected at once from the outside, if necessary. The new generation involuntarily became snobs in pursuit of fashion. It was then that Manner or Style was set up as a god to worship, just as theme or statement ten years before had been the refreshing distant goal, not yet fully realized. To this new end a number of writers seemed to pledge themselves, Bodenheim, Kreymborg, Marianne Moore. . . . It must have been however that William Carlos Williams, the one vital creative brain among them, was their chief stimulus. To their crusade he contributed his lingual metaphysics.

As much as Dreiser he lamented the absence of women in the United States, and more than that novelist the vacuum between men and women; since Dreiser had managed to cross over and explore and exult. Williams' poems rarely exult. He is partly Spanish, partly Virginian, partly Puritan, or why has he protested so much? Or why been so wistful, as if at odds with himself? Or why pinned such faith to doctrine? He practises medicine in Rutherford, New Jersey, apparently against his wishes. Asked by the Little Review to answer their dying questionnaire in 1929 as to his likes and dislikes, he writes: " I'd like to be able to give up the practice of medicine and write all day and all night." In an article published in This Quarter

1925 his fears for America equal Dreiser's and Masters', and go beyond them in swifter hatred and scorn:

"We believe that life in America is compact of violence and the shock of immediacy. This is not so. Were it so, there would be a corresponding beauty of the spirit — to bear it witness; a great flowering, simple and ungovernable as the configuration of the rose — that should stand with the gifts of the spirit of other times and other nations as a standard to humanity. There is none. . . .

"Here through terror, there is no direct touch; all is cold, little and discreet: — save just under the hide.

"'Don't let's have any poor,' is our slogan. . . . Cults are built to abolish them, as if they were cockroaches, and not human beings who may not want what we have in such abundance. . . . Let everybody be rich and so *equal*. But what a farce! What a tragedy! It rests upon false values and the fear to discover them. Do not serve another for you might have to touch him and he might be a Jew or a Nigger.

"Machines were not so much to save time as to save dignity that fears the animate touch. . . .

"We fear simplicity as the plague. Never to allow touch. What are we but poor doomed carcasses, anyone of us? Why then all this fury, this multiplicity we push between ourselves and our desires. . . .

"It is the women above all — there never have been women, save pioneer Katies; not one in flower save some moonflower Poe may have seen. . . . Emily Dickinson starving of passion in her father's garden, is the very nearest we have ever been — starving.

"Never a woman: never a poet. That's an axiom. Never a poet saw sun here . . .

"We have no feeling for the tragic" [just what Henry Adams knew and Frost and Dreiser]. " Let the sucker who fails get his. What's tragic in that? It's funny. . . . He didn't make good that's all. . . ."

The cry of all the rebels since Herman Melville who have tried to write in and about America. In this sense he belongs among them; he has their mineral quality.

But what after all is Carlos Williams' solution? In one of these years between 1915 and 1921 he published a journal called CONTACT. Was it like the old-time Rotarian — " Mr. Sims, Mr. Jones, touch flesh " ? No, it was not a fleshly way out. He pointed to another road: We have gone so far away from elements through clichés and public language, we shall never get back unless we are willing to search for ourselves, however ugly we are, and for our immediate equivalents in words, however surprising they are. He was an apostle of the stark, immediate word. He preached immediacy as a cure for American delay. In the name of contact he broke with everyone found guilty of a cliché, except Ezra Pound, in whom he chose to ignore years of exhorting freshness in stale language. Williams' idea was to revive and reform language and then morals would take care of themselves, and come up-to-date.

What happened? In a land of advertising this advertisement to end advertising could not sell. To ask people to use a naked live language, free of euphemism, free of optimism, was to indict the texture of American society. A publisher advertising such a pure scheme would have no selling talk at all, no ready stereotypes. What to do, publish with Les Imagistes under Pound and Amy Lowell, until that journal became stale? With Others, until that became affected? With The Dial through Marianne Moore, until it died? Make a journal of his own with his friend McAlmon, until there was no money to make it? Publish in the Little Review? But the girls had gone to Europe. Go to Europe, that was the thing to do for publication. "The struggle to get the principle of modern writing accepted in America is too difficult, especially when the tools are only a spoon handle," Williams wrote to a wondering admirer.

Off to Europe they must go, all the purists in the wake of this poet and the few who shared his belief. Off to Europe, to Broom, to This Quarter, to Transition, to McAlmon's Contact Editions. There was an exodus in the name of modern writing. There at least the devotees would be in touch with moderns, with the founders, James Joyce and Gertrude Stein, who had little in common, with Ezra Pound, the propounder. And all around them would be the modern French, oblivious of them. But no matter!

They went, and have finished by making a very exclusive order of mystics with pass-words, codes and signs, a certain etiquette in writing, an academic correctness. They have become a school, careful of their verbal manners in print. Williams himself remained in America one of the solitary peaks, one of the exclamation points denoting separation. If he is not so high or wide as the others it may be because he has had to write immediate poems and prose between office hours; and like Dreiser has spent much of his time fighting for a native speech. Only unlike Dreiser he was too proud to make a contact, except with emigrants to Europe.

It was a curious departure — this return of young Americans to the old country. They have accomplished a group, but has the group accomplished fusion? Are they "vibrating through and through with intensely active life?" Or were they so bent on the wrappings of their art, as first inspired by Matisse, Picasso, Brancusi, Joyce and Gertrude Stein, that they came to forget the contents. Like children with Christmas presents do they still hold on to the bright wrappings — new and newer esoteric papers, mottoes and strings? Today one gets the uneasy feeling that the presents have some of them slipped out of the covers and disappeared. In the revolution of the written word could it be that exteriority, the old American vice, has come to the top of the wheel again? Between theories and technique have these younger writers like their Victorian ancestors forgotten what they want to say? An outcome, never proposed by the mordant Carlos Williams, hunting herbs, roots, tinctures, and hot-house flowers!

On a New York afternoon in May, ten years ago, I happened to invite a situation which caught the crossing of these two periods. Something which had seemed new-born, strong and eager and not completely grown was passing. Another cleavage was on its way, a break from individual thought, a return to group thought. The scene was a still older Victorian room on Twelfth Street, high cornices, marble mantels; tea, cocktails and jokes; plane trees through the backyard windows — a twilight propitious to a frivolous meeting of libertines. They included Dreiser and a formation of newer writers. Several of them Communists, one or two of them aesthetes, none of them "bourgeois," most of them novelists, nostalgic for Europe, protesting the superiority of America. Like the moralists of the Nineties they did not want to meet

the youthful, boisterous Dreiser. They shied away from
him; he was literary, they said; at the moment laughing
immoderately at a quaint story told by Carl Van Vechten.
They had no glimmer of curiosity to bestow on the epochal Dreiser. Curiosity was indelicate.

If however Sandburg ever came to town they would
not mind meeting him — he was old-fashioned now, subjective, but he knew moulders, type-setters, dishwashers,
he knew the working men of America. A flood of sympathy had just spread from Russia to New York and had
become confused with art. Frost? No. He knew nothing
about Freud or sex or communism. Psycho-analysis had
likewise spread to New York and been confused with art.
Robinson? He was a back-number belonging to a bourgeois society. Carlos Williams? Perhaps — he believed in
sex, in contact, in modern technique. Did he believe in
communism? They were not sure, but he believed in James
Joyce. What of Sherwood Anderson? He was all right,
but why pursue the subject? Chiefly they hated to meet
celebrities; they liked ordinary people"!

It seemed to me that these talented young men were as
loose as that in their talk. No thread to the screw. They
were like boys out on a raft on the Atlantic vaguely pad-
dling toward Europe. Not very old myself, yet I felt the
futility of effort in the United States as if it were a drug
whose fumes invaded the room, the city, the country. It
was effort without complication or contrast. Numerical!
Inorganic! Moreover if in 1923 these not-ordinary beginners disdained to meet extraordinary predecessors, that
in itself divorced them from their immediate past. The
heroes of that date were excused. The period of the unknown hero was begun.

63

" I am an enormous commonplace rolling over your delicate miniatures, I'm an enormous lady with large feet, such large feet that she can't help but step over your little flowers. I am the same enormous lady crying as sincerely as she can over the beautiful flowers that her feet destroyed."
CARNEVALI

" To be shut off from beauty entirely is what makes us suffer most poignantly. Even a scrubwoman finds beauty in the pot of geraniums on the fire escape. This alone will penetrate her dreams as nothing else she meets all day."
DREISER

Had the oldest actor in this American renaissance of letters ever dramatized himself, he might like the youngest one have done it in the name of " the shattered enormous truth of which sophistication is only the chips." But without theatrical ease, such as belonged to Whitman, Sandburg and Lindsay, Dreiser was too American to dramatize himself. He was audience as much as actor. Carnevali, young by years, old by race, came from a country where sophistication and vanity were in the air. Everyone, obscure or important, was capable of drama in his peninsula. He was an immigrant at sixteen looking for a new wilderness of people to whom he might be prophet and poet, in the company he hoped of a few others to be discovered on the way, who would be his friends. It would make an adventurous voyage from periphery to center.

Dreiser, on the contrary, at the age of sixteen had come from the center of American village life, and had fought his way gradually to the periphery in search of electric individuals, men and women to make the years important to him. He found a few, but not enough. In the last of his novels I imagine him as deliberately going back into the depths of the Commonplace. He would discover if he could the whole substructure of ordinary American life, which above ground could be beautiful, and dramatic, but was for such far distances humdrum and banal. He would find the wide dark pools of tragedy in which the foundations stood.

Unlike the young writers, he wanted as much as ever to meet extraordinary people, if there were any. But, it seemed to him, for the most part Americans were remarkable only in one sense — the power to make money. The pioneers like Yerkes had come and gone; had flung their railroads and lighting systems, their bridges and skyscrapers into air, across deserts — an old story. Time was when he had celebrated their creative use in history. The rulers were different now. They were bankers conserving in terms of dollars the dreams of pioneers, or they were speculators imitating them; shooting higher and higher buildings, multiplying the machinery of motion pictures, deluging the market with cars, chewing-gum, toothpaste, radios, victrolas, cigarettes, not for use or for art, but for more and more easy money. Greed, not adventure, controlled the country. Dreiser, on the watch for drama, saw it now in the masses preyed upon by capital. Obscure individuals were in turn the strugglers and dreamers, just as before the financiers had been fighters and dreamers. The tremendous Commonplace so betrayed by money had become heroic to this novelist. He could see the hungry story in individual eyes, in restless shoulders and hands and legs that would not be still. He could see it in any subway, any street; and could hear it in the voices. After years of contemplation, in three years' time he wrote their story, 840 pages — *An American Tragedy*, standing really for rich as well as for poor.

Sister Carrie, The Hand of the Potter, and this great structure appear to me the most intense and intimate of Dreiser's list of powerful works. The three share to a high degree that particular style, that personal distillation, by which one has to call a work of art perfect, since one is without the wish or the skill to improve it. This last novel concerned with basic America however shifting and uncertain, is yet not a repudiation of art. It is made for the sake of absolute verities. By structure, by balance, by intensity it will stand with great documents of other modern nations, which cause in a few readers the desire for revolution; but in most, cause only nostalgia for reality.

In the very days in Los Angeles when Dreiser was first shaping his *Tragedy,* to reporters who interviewed him, to whom habitually he talked freely as if to intimates, he was always proclaiming his one aim, Art:

"I want to be back where there is struggle . . . I like to wander around the quarters of New York where the toilers are. . . . That's health. I don't care about idlers or tourists, or the humdrum, or artistic pretenders that flock out here, or the rich who tell you — and that is all they have to tell — how they did it. They would have interested me when they were struggling. . . .

"There is no art in Los Angeles and Hollywood. And never will be. . . .

"We are not an artistic nation. All we care about is to be rich and powerful. . . . The one aim of existence is the ease of life. . . .

"There is no place for the artist. Mention anyone from Sappho to Shakespeare. . . . They would have a lovely scramble to get a meal ticket. . . .

"It is wrong and it can't be righted. When you know that the unalterableness isn't going to cause you any tears. I don't worry about it. One could lose his mind if he took it to heart.

"I don't care a damn about the masses. It is the individual that concerns me."

When he got back to New York the trip across country had not cut the connection of his thoughts. He said to another reporter and friend, David Karsener, in answer to an editorial question:

"The task of leading minds in this crisis is to stop aimless population . . . and to organize mankind so that the intelligent shall survive."

So after all he did worry. What individuals there might be among the masses haunted him. He must have been sometimes near to losing his mind not over himself now but over his country. Eagerly he watched every sign of " letters of a liberal and artistic character," toward which he said " the same slick Americans who can build a moving-picture concern, a great popular magazine, a bank, a real estate concern, are as dull as oxen." He found hope in the very young who did not want to meet so "literary and old-fashioned a leader." Asked by a reporter in 1923 what he thought of contemporary writing, what he thought of Willa Cather, for example, he conveyed in a flash what he thought:

"Enormously clever. . . . Material, which done in another way would be significant. As it stands it is . . . full of things intended to comfort the average American. James Branch Cabell? His method, his style is fascinating to me. Mencken? I think he's a great force. For what God only knows. A force to cause people to revalue what values they happen to be conscious of. . . . Sherwood Anderson? Essentially a great poet. He would like to be a novelist; he will never escape being a poet. . . .

"One thing astonishes me . . . the score of little publications like Broom and The Double Dealer . . . in almost every town, Indianapolis, Milwaukee, New Orleans . . . always written by a group, not just by one man. . . . Way back from 1894 to 1897 there was just such a burst of publications, only they were individual efforts . . . Elbert Hubbard, Vance Thompson, William Marion Reedy. It seems to me that this present burst is more sincere . . . and more determined. . . . If even a percentage of these people find themselves in the next fifteen years we can look forward to a literature. . . .

"I think the movement is too forced, too radical and too obvious an attempt to be different, but that radicalism will freshen the traditional methods of writing. It might even develop a new form of writing, just as free verse is . . . the one thing that this generation has given to literature. . . .

"Perhaps it is a manifestation of a new spirit arising in America."

Two years later, to a reporter again, he says pondering over new writers: " Literally thousands of people have an amazing desire to write realistic books. The odd thing is that most of them want to indict life, not picture it in its ordinary beauty. . . . What is lacking in the experience of these young writers to make them think there is no beauty?" So we see Dreiser already isolated from the new intelligentsia, though some of them were near to his own age. Of course he had satellites, mostly from the newspaper world, from which he has never estranged himself. The rest were sceptical. For one thing, here was a man who could see beauty in the midst of stupidity and monotony. Such a stubborn appetite tried the patience of the moderns.

Ezra Pound, their European trustee, never in twenty years returning but always corresponding with his country from London, Paris, and Rapello, said of Dreiser in an interview: " If he is so eager for expression, for culture in America, why has he never given a cent to an uncommercial journal? " — " How do you know he hasn't? " I said. — " Well, never a penny to any known to me! " — " You mean your Exile, or This Quarter or Transition? But would the editors have accepted any of his writings? " — " Probably not. Why should they? " was Mr. Pound's honest enough reply, by which he answered his own query.

Dreiser in truth was cut off from those who followed him, those for whom he had blazed a trail into publishers' offices. He spoke of them as hopeful strangers. He himself was one of the three or four Americans able to live in the United States and turn it into words, without the stimulus of indicting it, without the cocktail of sophistication. To do this he divorced himself from everything fashionable, even from his own friend, Mencken. He was like a man who had taken the United States for wife. However much he fought with her and hated her, he felt forced to be true. Again he was like a man who had taken as mistress a stranger to his country, Art, Creation. He would not abandon her either.

As I see it *An American Tragedy* is the mournful changeful building he made for himself to live in among his own people. The various walls of this book separated him sufficiently from the streets of America to give him peace, and yet connected him enough to give him excitement as none of his previous books had succeeded in doing.

Other epic novels, being those of Melville or James, or else of Europeans, are different. *The Idiot, The Brothers Karamazoff* lead from mansions in stately parks, or from apartments on sophisticated streets, to forests, to deserts, to mountains, and then to precipices of the mind, where the characters we have come intimately to know topple and are lost. *La Peau de Chagrin* is a brilliant wilderness in the midst of civilization, which was Paris. *Madame Bovary* is a small town whose lime tree shaded avenues lead to the country and to the unknown; the design of a landscape gardener turned undertaker. *Moby Dick,* back in the Fifties, is an inhuman world shifting from deep oceans to the decks and holds of ships, whose human beings have deserted mankind, finding nothing on earth to arrest them. Dreiser's novels, *An American Tragedy* in particular, are structures each composed of a number of structures, now poor, now rich, now private, now public, doors leading to doors through the corridors of his close imagination. When you enter, you enter interiors never quite personal, since the country aims to be impersonal. Except that you enter solitary rooms and closets of the hero's mind, where his secrets speak, as if Dreiser wrote from within that mind.

Reading this book, I think of the incessant construction in America during my lifetime, the insane wish to destroy wilderness; the constant chorus of saw and hammer, and in the cities of pile-driver, cement-mixer, riveter, and of machinery to create machinery. Such tools have made the wooden shanties, the drug stores, the grand hotels, the whore-houses, the freight cars, the exclusive clubs, the factories, the wealthy residences, the pleasant homes, the boarding-house, the churches and church parlors, the amusement park, the summer homes, the summer hotel, the farm-houses. They have made the camps, the sidewalks, street cars, railroads, depots and jails; the court houses, the prisons and death cells, the politicians' offices, the haberdasheries and laundries, the automobile roads, and the older lumber roads, the governor's mansion — which altogether spell America and which figure in the drama of this book. How encompass it in less than 800 pages? Here Dreiser has practised economy.

Or rather only a novelist, a man of creative imagination, who comes once in ages, could make the likeness of so vast a nation, sounding the casual trivial voices and the momentous trivial voices with whom the story is concerned, in that space of pages. By selecting a single atom, Clyde Griffiths, and going with him, not detached but always surrounded by young and old, from the age of twelve to the age of twenty-three, the extent of his life, Dreiser has synechdochized America. " How are we to write the Russian novel in America — As long as life goes so unterribly ? " Frost asks. We are not, is Dreiser's answer in this book, unless we take it between twelve and twenty-three years or thereabouts, the span of life for genuine natives; and then take it unprotected by privileges of money. Up to a certain age such embryos follow the path of the oldest highways. And then curiously they are forced to lose their way. The way is lost in guilt and fears for failure to keep the impossible contract of American society. The tragedy is a young and humble one; since desires are sterilized at an early age throughout the nation. Except possibly among the very poor who sometimes escape to Gangland, or perhaps for the inordinately rich, who, it is said, escape to Speed. Yet is not speed a form of sterilization?

With such a child from a street one evening in Kansas City Dreiser goes through the door of an old time mission house where the boy's parents save the souls they have corralled with prayers and hymns. The boy and his sisters and brother perhaps are innocent and powerful, since who knows what may come of children. Only, Dreiser makes it certain, the blight of a fusty religion is already on them. Unkindly germs are in the faltering air. This is the beginning. The end is that the boy, Clyde Griffiths. well-made as to body, alluring enough as to soul, slips through the last door, death, strapped to the electric chair.

Between the doors of the mission house in Kansas City and the death room in Sing Sing what trivial front doors and momentous back doors and secret front doors are imagined by this mystical realist, once upon a time born in Terre Haute, Indiana! Through the brightly-lighted revolving door of a great hotel, the boy escapes from his religious parents to the bell-hops' bench. Therein were doors and doors. Go in at one or another with the baggage of a guest from Europe, the Orient, New York, Honolulu, and a bell-boy learned about life, grandeur, sex.

Then out of the back door of hours-off what picnics of bell-boys with their girls, what joy rides in borrowed cars!

At length one night in the hurry to get back, the killing of a child on the outskirts of the city, the wrecking of the stolen car! Then the getaway of the still innocent but implicated hero of the Commonplace, by the back door of freight cars. In at the employees' door of the Union League Club in Chicago — a respectable oasis of wealth dating back to the time of Jennie Gerhardt's carriage manufacturer, to the day of the Titan, Yerkes, who was never quite welcome there. A transient millionaire uncle proves that melodrama is occasionally realism. He is a white-collar manufacturer of Lycurgus, or Syracuse, New York. Like a chip on far-off rivulets the son of his disowned brother is carried down stream into markets nearer the sea.

In Lycurgus two doors confront him, one into the collar factory, the other into his uncle's residence on the main boulevard of the city. Of joys within the house the Kansas nephew gets a brief view. The aunt and cousins ignore him. In the factory, where he is foreman over twenty-five women who stamp the size and trade mark of collars, a rule forbids him to be seen outside with any of these girls. One of them a farmer's daughter is so alluring he commits this business crime.

Not to lose him she lets him in at the door of her room. Here Dreiser more lyrically than before leaves the hustling world and enters with two lovers into their isolation — as ecstatic in upper New York state as elsewhere in history. Here circles and ovals of lakes and poetry begin to interrupt the rectangles of buildings and prose. The foreman and the girl had first met by chance, one Sunday afternoon, on a lake where " from certain marshy spots, to be reached by venturing out a score of feet or more, it was possible to reach and take white lilies with their delicate yellow hearts."

An American Tragedy is a geometry of conflicting circles, ovals and rectangles, expanded into figures of three dimensions, crossed and re-crossed by the wiry paths of delicious desires and grievous decisions. The book possesses that cubic volume which modern European art has insisted on, and has achieved in the case of a few great artists. Each character, and there is a stream, a host of characters, is made with his or her difference of being; and made in the round or angularly, according to age and charm. Years are the deciding factor in the American Commonplace. So veritable is the result that one can walk around and among all these men and women and children in the air of the United States.

Finally and by chance the hero goes in at the doors of the rich houses — those hierarchies so longed for. He is taken up by a fashionable beauty in the same set with his cousins, and through his talent for romance becomes her favorite. What more natural then than for him to wish to forget the factory girl who could never take him to a plane above his beginning. Suppose she has conceived a child, and by him. Why should that destroy his whole chance of success according to his popular theory as to what life should be?

Doors of drug stores, doors of doctors' offices, with the hopes of contraceptive means! Nothing to be done! In an insane frenzy for dreams to come true and not be thwarted by mere circumstances, slowly, hypnotically he half plans her death, suggested by a double drowning he has read about in the newspapers. With a promise of marriage to " see her through " he takes her from her father's dilapidated farm to a lake again, eerie and wild in the Adirondacks, loses courage to drown her, but when in a quarrel the boat capsizes, he lacks courage or will to reverse the reflex of his schemes utterly enough to save her. Here Dreiser, called lumbering, follows like a flexible wire the baffling tangle of thought-prints of the mind.

To the society girl's summer camp, darting with canoes, riding horses, speed boats, dancing, tennis, and all the costumes that go with these, the pallid young man makes his escape for what he hopes will be his reward. But never after the drowning able to decide whether swimming away meant that he was a murderer, and shaken by the fear of pursuit, there was no reward. Afterwards forced away through the back door of the camp by the revolvers of sheriff and district attorney he enters the door of fame and the county jail. Then there were successively the doors of court houses — the trial in the Adirondacks, the appeal in New York. And the doors through which his attorneys, hired by his uncle's millions, will climb to importance as criminal lawyers; and by which sheriff and district attorney reach high political prestige in the county of Big Bittern Lake. Beyond that all the little farm houses pour out their citizens to exhort judge and jury to drive the murderer to his death.

Now the door of the mission house removed to Denver is flung wide open by newspapers. Out of it his mother walks, determined to prove his innocence. She goes even to the governor of New York imploring pardon. Obscure Evangelism meets high officialdom in vain. She sends a minister of the faith to lead her son through the last door to Christ. Convinced at length of his own guilt, since he swam away, he makes his final effort to count in a letter to young men urging them to follow the narrow way, his mother's way, through Jesus to Heaven.

The waters close over. The newspaper magnates, the lawyers and politicians, are the richer for this tragedy. The country is the poorer in spirit, whose code has made life impossible for two young people. If for them, for how many others! Impossible to read the book without tears! In one passage Dreiser describes the temperament of this boy as " fluid and unstable as water." Yet he seems to readers not more unstable than any other element acutely sensitive to the vivid world outside. He seems not more unstable than Romeo or Hamlet, merely less distinguished, less developed. The conclusion is that human beings endowed with full senses are as fluid and unstable as water. Sometimes, dammed up, they acquire the force of torrents. They become instruments of drama and destruction.

Here then is *An American Tragedy* — the apex of the experience meeting between Dreiser and his country. What did it do for America, what did it do for Dreiser? As for the public the book went into seven printings between December 1925 and December 1926, and then on through other years. Thousands of people read it; debutantes and news-stand dealers — I have seen them. Yet just for sensation they did not have to read the book. They had always the tabloids, which every day superficially, but more and more, copied Dreiser's method of presenting crime; just as blurbs and advertisements imitated Sandburg's and Anderson's ways of presenting pleasures. Great Americans are often accused of journalism in their art. I think it is the other way around. The journalists and copy writers have imitated the poets, being themselves would-be artists. Wasn't Dreiser in newspaper days exhorted to study Zola, Loti, Kipling? And then there were men like Eugene Field, George Ade, O. Henry, Ring Lardner. Hard to know which they were, poets or journalists. But one thing is sure, they left their mark on American journalism more than they were branded by it.

The populace did not have to read this tragedy for mere excitement. Dreiser himself was amazed at the sales and the réclame. He had built the work to please himself, and as he says in a letter to a friend had begun it with " the damnedest qualms and struggles ":

"I have written and written — and at last I hope, if I don't change it again, gotten a fair start. . . . When I set out to write a novel I worry so over the sure even progress of it. What I ought to have is someone who could decide for me when I have the right start, when I am going ahead, or one who would take all the phases I pen down and piece them together into the true story as I see it. That is eventually what I do for myself. But oh, the struggles and the flounderings!"

Two and a half solitary years more of these, and the work pleased him — he called it complete. But why should it please anyone else, save for a few adherents? It was more drab, more grim, more tragic, more salacious in material than *The " Genius," The Titan, The Financier, Jennie* or *Carrie*. If those novels were questionable, this one surely would be hateful to Americans. It was long and uncompromising!

Yet *An American Tragedy* sold and sold. Almost as much as an electric refrigerator, or a radio set. It was deluged with praise by both simple and sophisticated critics; by the very young who used to think that Dreiser was old-fashioned; by his old enemy, Professor Stuart Sherman, who enlisted the interest of churches and colleges and good people in behalf of the " naturalist." In some universities the novel became part of required reading. Why? Its author, an authority on his country, himself did not know. He thought perhaps that the book was popular, "not because it is a tragedy, but because it is American":

"The type of life that produced it has not changed. For years I have been arrested in stories and plays by the poor young man who marries the rich man's daughter. I have had many letters from people who wrote: 'Clyde Griffiths might have been me.'"

For myself I think the interest cut deeper than that. The year was turning into 1926. There had been fifteen years of superfine and less fine intellects saying to America, the child of the melting pot: " Look at yourself. See how beautiful and promising you are," or: " See how ugly and adolescent you are." The United States, the most spiritually ambitious nation of earth in modern times, but busy with this invention or that, this improvement or that, finally acquired enough curiosity between "business deals" to look at itself, as portrayed by the high-brow. Already they had looked at negatives within the covers of *Main Street* by Sinclair Lewis, Red Lewis — with that nickname he might be a football player. But he wasn't. They found out that all he had to say to virile America was what their mothers and sisters had been exhorting for years: " Get culture, get culture, we're ridiculous without it." The masculine, sometimes weary, answer had been: " Okay, go and get culture! Here's a letter of credit and a ticket to Europe. Bring it back if you can."

Or some night when they couldn't sleep at some goddamn house party they might have picked up the plaintive poems of Edna Millay: " Sure they were beautiful, as good as Keats or Shelley or maybe Shakespeare or Marlowe, remembered from college days. Good old college days!" What were the women nagging them about anyway? We had culture . . . we had this dame who could write poems as good as anyone, and "sleep with them" probably, if they wanted her. Yet after all there were plenty of girls who would do that — next week in fact, when the wife was in Europe and the kiddies! Or instead of an Edgar Wallace, they might pick up a Joseph Hergesheimer, maybe a Jew but a good fellow, and to their consternation, by gosh, he seemed to think their wives were attractive. Even those over forty, even those over fifty. Really, the man knew no age limit. Hell, it wasn't the wife, come to think of it, this kike fell for. It was that French perfume, those clothes which *he* had paid for, bought last year in Paris. . . . Heigho, the money went out as fast as it came in. . . . Just the same better give the little woman a look. . . . Anyhow she was refined. Yet how did he know? Hergesheimer made a man think.

But now on the guest room table another book. God help us, wouldn't Americans ever stop printing books no one had time to read? *An American Tragedy!* by a fellow who wrote about Yerkes. He knew a thing or two about finance anyway. . . . Christ, it was long. . . . But the boy in it was pretty well done . . . exactly like himself thirty years ago, only he went to the chair. Why? It didn't seem quite right, a nice enough boy just about like himself twenty years ago. What seemed to be the matter? He got into trouble with one girl beneath him socially, and wanted to marry another above him. Both beauties! He himself had done nothing like that. Never in his life! Not so weak, or else could it be that he was not so strong? . . . Long ago there had been a girl he wanted, beneath him. He dreamed of her still sometimes. He had run away from her: there would have been hell to pay. He would have lost his friends, his job. And didn't he use to dream too about millionaires' daughters? But he knew enough to marry a nice girl from his own set, not very exciting . . . but there had been banquets and conventions; he had had his fun. And now that he and the Missus both had money they went where the liked; they met millionaires' wives by the dozen, too old of course to have a good time with. But it wouldn't be long before they got into that class themselves, if the boom lasted, and it would. . . . On the whole a pretty fair book this *American Tragedy!* The same cities, the same hotels, the same people he came in contact with daily. Everything the same except for the lake and the electric chair! Pretty tough on the girl even if she did go wrong, and on the young fellow too. A hell of a note! A god-damned country! Well, he himself would change all that after he had made a couple of million.

It is for this that I imagine Dreiser's tragedy made a mad success. It was like your own fortune told by a wizard, your own photograph taken by a master camera. And the overtones produced were irresistible to serious Americans. The author was not a reformer, but the book made them wish for the world to be different. The book was not ironic, and yet the effect of it stabbed them with that indescribable torment called the irony of fate. After years of evasion finally Americans wanted to look at themselves.

64

"A work of art reuniting the qualities of freshness and of emphasis risks being too round, and rolling at all speed toward the black hole of the great public."
JEAN COCTEAU: *Le Mystère Laïc*

An *American Tragedy* rolled into the maw of the public. For some days readers congratulated themselves on this work of genius, which made them important even if it seemed to prove them part of a great catastrophe. What on the other hand did " the Mount Everest of American fiction " do for Dreiser? He became with incredible swiftness " the outstanding literary figure of America." Since the Colonial days of Emerson, and then Howells, we had always wanted a " national man of letters " but had been unable to find one suited to our needs. Mark Twain was " outstanding," but as a clown, not a sage. Dreiser came back from Florida where he had gone to rest after the labors of his book, to find himself wrapped in editorial superlatives. This ogre, vulgarian, behemoth, lobscause, pachyderm, violator of American womanhood, slaughterer of the King's English, dangerous citizen, hated genius, found himself " great " like Edison, Rockefeller or Ford. His publishers saw to it that now he should be dressed from head to foot in illustrious adjectives. Reviews of his book were broadcast over the country in that synthetic voice of the radio announcer, abasing himself before some miracle of pancake flour, bedtime story or washing machine. Royalties came in as never before. The book was made into a play by Patrick Kearney, to be produced by Liveright. It was a chain on which were strung like beads the more salacious and terrifying episodes, and it kept none of the architecture of the original. Yet Dreiser, now a little way down the public throat, after thirty years of struggle to be read at all, to live at all, in this moment of success was too tired or too dizzy to protest. Presented to packed houses, while he was in Europe, the play brought in more royalties and more prestige. Although retaining some of the iron of the novel, it counted as Dreiser's initial and unintentional sacrifice in exchange for the "public pourboire." He was being turned as if blindfolded from a great writer into a public character.

There is no blame attached to Dreiser or the public. It was not his fault or theirs that he went now among prosperous inferiors, rather than among his own kind. There was no society of equals to engage him, and he craved society — a sign of being civilized! The men of like voltage were the solitary peaks of the last chapter of these computations. Puritanism in truth had been defeated, but the reward of victory was promiscuousness, not distinction! There was but rarely as on Dreiser's part, a desire for distinction; and probably for the simple reason that most people were too humble to wish for the moon. For one thing the women who came out of the melting pot — and on women, too, civilization depends — were as incapable of projecting any far-reaching complications as those before them. There *were* no women, except always for the wives and business agents, stage favorites and Harlem yellows, as yet insoluble elements. Dreiser himself knew it, and yet reached for the moon.

He knew too that already he had lost friends most eager for civilization, for whom in other days his Tenth Street apartment had made a meeting place. Yet he could not believe this crazy truth of his country — that it was too numerical for personal relations. He rented a large apartment on Fifty-seventh Street, somewhat Jacobean according to the naïve taste of New York architects and decorators, yet beautiful with a big window framing theatre signs and skyscrapers in snow, rain or blue night sky. There surely he could realize his lifelong dream — an intellectual artistic society in his own city. For five winters on many Thursday nights there poured into this studio intelligent and expensive New York; novelists, poets, singers, dancers, scientists, actresses, editors, critics, publishers, and a painter or two; once Nigerian dancers bearing with them a mask of their crocodile god.

But it seemed that the procurers of the arts dominated his room with their tactile eyes and hands and inhuman silences, exactly as they dominated New York City. If one looked hard there might be a poet from the Argentine or Mexico or a turbaned friend of Ghandi, or a scientist from the Rockefeller Institute, or one or two old friends of Dreiser's, genuine and native. But they were lost among the owl-like dealers who silently drank and petted, coming up to breathe now and then in moments of literary politics. The difficulty was that this cherished scheme lacked any kind of medium of exchange. Not even that violent current of excitement between men and women when the work of day is over could unite them. Scarcely a look passed between one and another save that of New York hatred and distrust. The engineer of these parties was wonderfully alive and real among his guests with an air of earthly experience; as if some day with enough rehearsals these figures would perform together as he had seen it done years before in London drawing rooms and again recently in Europe. He seemed to be saying to himself: You can't get all these interesting people together for an evening without some kind of a plot evolving from it. He did not yet know how mentally aseptic and timid the intelligentsia of New York could be.

Also in January 1926 a meeting took place which engulfed him further in publicity. Since their advent he had had his eye on the movies, and yet had been afraid of their happy endings and their ignorant liberties with authors. Now Liveright told him that Famous Players was after his *Tragedy*, just as it stood. By this his publisher, according to a contract dating from 1923, would get 10% of the transaction. The idea was exciting to both of them. Yet on the same day when he signed away the theatrical rights to his novel, Liveright had corrected this news: after all Lasky was not interested until the play had been produced; and his offer would not be more than $35,000, if that much. In that hour Dreiser's instinct for business, so remarkable in Delineator days, which for fifteen years he had neglected in order to write about life as it is, came to the front. He negotiated a clause in his contract by which the publisher should get nothing at all in the event of his selling the movie rights for $30,000 or more, before the play was produced. Then they ambled out together to lunch at the Ritz with Mr. Lasky and Mr. Wanger. How much did Dreiser intend to ask? Liveright inquired on the way — $100,000 — He would never get it! — Perhaps not, but that or nothing! Well, whatever he got over $60,000 would he give it to Liveright, since he had opened negotiations with the movie kings? Certainly not? But would he take care of him in spite of the new clause? Yes, he'd take care of him.

According to Dreiser the lunch at the Ritz was not smooth. After the *hors d'oeuvres* Lasky said: "Liveright tells me you'll sell for $35,000." If that was the idea, the author replied, the party was agreeable but in no sense a business affair. "How much then?" — "$100,000." — At this point Liveright left the room so that the others might talk "unconstrainedly."

When he came back the deal had gone through: "Then," he said, "I get everything over $60,000?" — "No," said the novelist, "you get your 10%." — "I knew you'd throw me — you said you'd take care of me," he remembers Liveright's anguished words. — "I said I'd take care of you up to our original agreement, and I don't even have to do that." — "You're a liar!" was what he heard from his liberal publisher. And then it was that Dreiser fulfilled one of those legends that have grown up about him. He threw his cup of coffee, some say hot, and some say cold, in his benefactor's face. That is the story according to Dreiser and according to Liveright in his own repentant letters to his star author. Such was high finance in literary circles in the United States. The sequel to it is the still more terrible rumor that Liveright in revenge shot Dreiser's cow in the country place he had bought in Mt. Kisco. . . . But Dreiser says no, he has never at any time owned a cow.

There were, however, intrinsic rewards out of *An American Tragedy*. There were reviews and letters from extraordinary men and women; prisoners, business magnates, crusaders and artists. Of these he resented Stuart Sherman's praise which made him into a moralist. But two notices especially must have pleased him, one from Clarence Darrow, another from H. G. Wells. Darrow, ten years older, had a philosophy not identical to Dreiser's, but parallel! He had always said: No one is guilty, unless the hypocrite, and I doubt if he is guilty. Dreiser had always said: Everyone is important and even beautiful unless it be the hypocrite, and sometimes, curiously he appears to be the most important of all. So these two men threw pebbles into the wide American sea which made ripples. It is silently believed that we have gotten rid of their influence and gone back to older ethics, but I doubt it. It is more likely that their national visions will come to life in younger genius, just as the visions of Lovejoy and John Brown were finally lyricised by Lincoln.

Wells, visiting America in 1926, selected Dreiser for praise the way that Heinemann and Bennett had done twenty years before. He wrote a review of *An American Tragedy* less poetic than Darrow's, and yet the certificate of one giant to another:

> " Dreiser is in the extreme sense of the word a genius. He seems to work by some rare and inexplicable impulse enormously. . . . His *American Tragedy* is, I agree with Bennett, one of the very greatest novels of this century. It is a far more than life-size rendering of a poor little representative corner of American existence, lighted up by a flash of miserable tragedy . . . but I would disagree with Bennett's condemnation of its style. It is raw, full of barbaric locutions, but it never fatigues . . . it gets the large, harsh superficial truth that it has to tell with a force that no grammatical precision and no correctitude could attain. . . ."

Here the great Englishman himself forgot precision. How can truth be large, harsh and superficial? Isn't it agreed that truth is the most delicate, profound and evasive of all abstractions? Of course in a mere newspaper article it is only fair to interpret Wells as meaning that, after his trip across the American continent, our life appeared to him large, harsh and superficial, exactly as in

Dreiser's *Tragedy*. His review betrays also a racial difference between the two men. I imagine that to Dreiser "one little corner" of existence is not necessarily "poorer" than another, when lighted by tragedy or emotion. Yet beyond these British words Wells proves himself here a great spirit, one who understands foreign values better than most natives, better than most English intellectuals choose to do. A letter of his to Dreiser in 1929, championing the importance of the individual, contradicts some of his own books which propose "group consciousness." He writes in answer to a question of Dreiser's:

> "To hell with editors! . . . I don't know whether your phrase is true . . . or actionable. But I'm whole-heartedly for your resolve to say what you damn please about it!
> "You are a great man, Dreiser, and I send you a twenty-one gun salute, my homage, and all the best wishes in the world."

In the second year of Dreiser's splendor the Soviet Government, in the same sense agreeably inconsistent, acknowledged him. They invited him to come to Russia and see for himself if theirs was not the one right way to conduct society. Here is something which few governments, certainly not the United States in recent years, ever ask of any intellect, known as such. Especially, American intellectuals and governors do not meet. Formerly gentlemen were used abroad and business men at home to take the place of brains in government positions. Recently business men only need apply.

Dreiser in Russia was both repelled and attracted; delighted to find a country whose newspapers were free of scandals about sex and money; desolate to be told that Tchekhov, Shakespeare's tragedies and his own *Hand of the Potter* could not be played in Moscow. The proletarians, they explained, would be over-sensitized by such portrayal of reality. The senses for a time had to be atrophied. How else to make a Communist government? That sounded to Dreiser tragically like home. He did not know what to think. He sent back his articles as he wrote them to the North American Newspaper Alliance, like any other reporter. He was fascinated by this crossing of most ancient and most modern thought and custom. But on his return, March 1928, he hesitated to make a book about Soviet Russia. Why should he? It was too soon; it was an experiment; and what could he know in eleven weeks? His articles in the World and other newspapers were merely letters; a book would be pretentious. Yet somehow in October 1928, between publishers and publicity his papers did appear in book form, called by the hackneyed title of *Dreiser Looks At Russia,* an outsider's title.

In due time it was discovered that passages in this book were identical with parts of another book about Russia by Mrs. Sinclair Lewis (Dorothy Thompson). Her cries of plagiarism made headlines. She filed a complaint with Dreiser's lawyers asking that the book be withdrawn. They replied they were ready at any time for her to bring suit. The novelist himself made no explanation to friends or reporters except to deny plagiarism. Cryptically he said that gallantry forbade explanation; he thought it was a case of persecution. It was a rule of his never to explain except in court. He said they had met in the same hotel in Moscow and in lazy journalist fashion had exchanged and used common sources of material. Miss Thompson to avoid publicity, she said, never actually brought suit. The passages remain identical; the matter remains as much a mystery to her, she insists, as to the public. It is curious, however, to discover among files that one of Dreiser's articles sent in February to the syndicate while he was still in Europe, published in March on his immediate return, contains one of the offending passages, published likewise by Miss Thompson a few weeks before in the New York Evening Post. One wonders exactly how Dreiser had access to that newspaper while still travelling in Europe?

Here was the first break imputed to Dreiser after he had become " foremost and outstanding." There would be more to follow. The newspapers, which could sometimes tolerate him as a martyr, began to hate him as a conqueror, especially with his fortune out of the movies, for which apparently he had not sold his integrity. Other eminent writers joined in this wave of jealousy. Critics and columnists combed his books for specimens of plagiarism. They found three. The drummer in *Sister Carrie* had been suggested by one of George Ade's *Fables in Slang*. Certainly, Dreiser admitted it. George Ade told the papers he was flattered:

> "While some of us have been building chicken coops, or possibly bungalows, Mr. Dreiser has been erecting skyscrapers."

Then they found a "lively parallel" between a poem in *Moods* and the description of a woman in *Winesburg, Ohio* by Sherwood Anderson. Again Dreiser did not explain, but Anderson telegraphed from his farm in Virginia:

> "Mr. Dreiser is not the kind of man who needs to take lines from me or anyone else. It is one of those accidents that occur. The thought expressed, I am sure, has come to a great many men. If Mr. Dreiser has expressed it beautifully it is enough."

These last two transgressions appear to me natural for two reasons. First, Dreiser's originality is not that of language, but of structure; of emphasis and relations, not between words but between events, both psychic and external events. Second, perhaps no novelist has ever had a more prodigious memory than this American. Ask him the names and dates of hotels and towns where he has stayed, and of people he has met up with in fifty years; his answers are immediate and have the ring of precision. His books contain the exact names of things belonging to an endless variety of life; and always, he says, he remembers without the aid of note books. Such a warehouse of words and phrases and rhythmic images cannot always know if the source is his or another's; and will be too hypnotized by the work of the moment to care.

But the enemies of this great somnambulist among words, who wakes up at the right moments to bring them into action, into an engagement with life, were not through yet. They looked again and found the final proof of his duplicity in *An American Tragedy*. They accused him of piecing his novel together from excerpts of the court records of the tragedy that happened in 1906 in

Herkimer County, New York, and from the accounts of this story as reported in the New York World.

This on the face of it was absurd. It was like saying that Rodin's Age of Bronze was a cast from a living model. Or that Shakespeare's plays were plagiarisms from older Italian stories, or that Gide's or Proust's novels contained men and women who have actually lived. It was accusing Dreiser of the inaccusable; unless to write about life as it is constitutes a crime. In such an event only a fantasy like *Alice in Wonderland* or the myth of the Trinity could be a work of art, and these might be plagiarisms from the dreams of children who have really lived.

Dreiser according to custom never protested or explained. Yet insidiously this rumor began to destroy the bloom of his last big work. It was the fashion to say, even among intellectuals: " Mere journalism! Any star reporter could have done a better job; he would have made it briefer." In 1928 Morris Ernst and William Seagle printed in their study *Obscenity and the Censor,* often quoted as authority, the following libelous information, which Mr. Ernst admitted referred to Theodore Dreiser:

" The Elizabethan tragedies based upon contemporary murders set a fashion which has been continued to our day. Only nowadays the reports of the press need no rewriting. . . . A great American novelist . . . took the newspaper account of an actual sexual crime as the basis of his tragedy. The reviewers praised particularly the remarkable realism of a series of letters in the novel . . . supposed to have passed between the lover and his mistress. The truth was that the letters had not only been copied almost verbatim from the newspaper columns but had been made up by the reporter to tide over the public craving for news in the dull days when nothing happened on the assignment."

Interviewing Mr. Ernst I was told that he could not remember where he had heard this story. It might have been Franklin Adams, it might have been Joe Anthony; he thought it was the latter. Mr. Anthony however disclaimed knowledge of the incident and of the reporter, except that it was one of those rumors floating about town, emanating he supposed from the Algonquin or the

Coffee House. He thought it was a mere yarn of what might have happened or might happen to any writer. Dreiser himself said that it was sheer fiction; the book was *his, quite his,* but what difference! If *An American Tragedy* survived him and became a remembered book, then such stories would fade from memory. If not, again what difference! But since I was attempting not merely a biography, but the analysis of the relation of a remarkable figure to his country and his time, the value of the rumor interested me. Within it, at least, there seemed to grin that flippancy toward all serious artistic work, which is singularly typical of American history. In pursuit of accuracy I read the court records of the People of New York State *vs.* Chester Gillette, and also the briefer, less absorbing sob-stories in the New York World of the year of that trial. In both newspaper and court records the love letters were identical, except as abridged by newspaper delicacy. The letters had *not* been invented by the World reporter.

Dreiser on the other hand had copied nothing " verbatim " from either newspapers or courts into this book. In fact to have done so would only have impeded the progress of his drama. A perusal of these three chronicles concerning what Mr. Wells calls " one poor little corner of American life," proves once for all how differently court stenographers, newspaper reporters, and creative minds work — that is, when working as such. A court stenographer, a newspaper reporter outside of hours might yet be a great artist. But while on the job the stenographer has got to be a formal droning musician at best, about like a bee; in fact abrupt, trivial, eloquent, endless as nature through a dictaphone. A newspaper man has got to be as coherent, optimistic, evasive, inventive as the politician who dictates the policy of his paper. The poet or novelist has no obligations; except that the tradition of art demands a personal selection of material toward a more terrific understanding of reality.

The letters between Dreiser's characters, Roberta Alden and Clyde Griffiths, do borrow phrases from the letters of Grace Brown to Chester Gillette, buried now in dusty files or perhaps in the hearts of a sister or brother still living. There are phrases like: " I have cried my eyes out — it never rains but it pours — please write me even though you don't want to — I'm so blue, I need somebody to talk to and I can't tell anybody — If you don't come I don't know what I shall do — I wish I could die — I have been bidding goodbye to some places today — I feel as though I were never going to see my home again — And Mamma . . . I love her so. Sometimes I think if I could tell her but I can't. She has had enough trouble. . . ." The phrases that many girls in despair and solitude must still use to distant, unprotecting lovers! The phrases of so many popular songs! But the drift and the weight of Dreiser's letters are as different from the court records as the tempers of his American boy and girl are different from those of the actual tragedy in Herkimer County in 1906. The difference lies in the intention and deliberation of the book as contrasted with the haphazard incident of everyday life. Sometimes the biographies of great people read like works of art, though Lytton Strachey persuades that even the great in crucial moments fail of what they hoped to be. But *An American Tragedy* is drama selected out of the commonplace. There is no better proof of Dreiser's mastery of speech than to compare the inchoate photographic court records and the newspaper romancing of this tragedy with his novel; all three of which are concerned with the same framework of circumstances — that is, up to the event of the drowning. Within this frame Dreiser enlarges his characters so that they become universal. Especially the drowned girl and electrocuted boy for Dreiser's purposes are less scatterbrain, less trivial than those revealed by courts and newspapers. The young man he has created could not flippantly " get rid " of his girl, as if life were nothing. They are more like Dreiser himself, more eager, determined lovers of life. The court records of this case are like an endless ménu card or the time-table of a vast railroad. Different authors going to them could come away with different meals or different journeys according to their various palates or tickets. One can imagine O. Henry or Ring Lardner, had they ever been courageous enough to engage with tragedy, coming away with stories nearer to what happened in Herkimer County. Their genius in fact *is* American surfaces! As for the newspapers, artists have sacrificed themselves to their columns, but these columns have not the structure of art.

65

" Each spirit acclaimed as powerful begins by the fault that makes him known. In exchange for the public pourboire he gives up enough of his time to make him perceptible — dissipated energy in order to transmit himself and to prepare gratification among strangers. I have dreamed that the strongest people, the wisest inventors, the most exact connoisseurs of thought, would be misers, men who die without confession."

PAUL VALERY: *Monsieur Teste*

The reels turned over and over. Within them Dreiser published *Moods Cadenced and Declaimed*, 1926; *Chains*, a book of short stories, 1927; his book about Russia, 1928; *A Gallery of Women*, 1929; *Dawn*, an autobiography of early youth, 1931. Most of these had been written through the years before, many of them already printed in magazines. They belong to his intellectual life of the period preceding *An American Tragedy*. Many of the poems and stories represent him at his best, having his own economy of direction, his thrust, his intimacy with his project. But *A Gallery of Women* as a whole is more remote. The details and episodes are inviting but colder. They have not that intense desire for verbal creation which marks most of Dreiser's previous work. One would have expected the maker of *Sister Carrie, The Titan*, the *Tragedy*, to have keyed these enterprising stories into a closer relation with himself, before they went into book form. What else in truth heightens style but a concise intimacy between speaker and speech?

A Gallery of Women tells about fifteen women worth

noticing, but does not contain that many live figures. Ida Hauchawout, Olive Brand, Ellen Adams Wrynn are immediate living creatures, but not all the others. Ellen Adams was a painter who went to France in the early days of Matisse and Picasso. It was she apparently who, on his first trip to Europe in 1912 not only cured the Hoosier of Bouguereau but unintentionally, it seems, made him discover his own relation to other moderns, whether writers or painters — a relation still ignored by critics:

" After a while I asked myself: What about these things? Are they not somewhat in step with what I actually see here and there in life? Not all is as Ingres would do it, say, or Vermeer. There are strange, trying, gloomy, rancid effects on every hand . . . what is it that I am personally trying to do? A smooth countess with a white book in a long green lap? A lady absorbed by a Persian bowl filled with orchids? Not at all! By degrees I came to see that however offensive, (like war, say,) here was something new, vigorous, tonic. . . . These things, I said, are destined to blow the breath of life into older forms. They will have a great effect."

Over this painter, when I asked about her, Dreiser revealed something of himself: " She was one of those women where I lost out. She didn't want me, that is, not until years later, and then I wouldn't have her." — " Why not; was she old and unattractive? " — " No, she was just the same. But it's a rule with me not to moon around over anyone. Besides I don't want a woman who has known a lot of men. I felt the same way about Olive Brand." — " Isn't that unreasonable, considering your own code," surprise forced me to ask — " I suppose so. I know it's illogical, but it's a rule with me. Without it I should have been destroyed long ago by this or that woman " — " It must be an easy rule for you or you would have often broken it? " — " No, it hasn't always been so easy." — " Have you yourself ever been possessed, annihilated, like your own ' Genius ' by the girl who ruined his career? " I asked, expecting not to be answered. — " Yes, four times," was Dreiser's quick reply. — " How long did it take you to get over it? A year or two each time? " — " I have never gotten over it, not in any of those cases. I still feel the scars. There is a certain discoloration, don't you know, after being knocked out by a woman. . . . Perhaps to be happily in love is even more unfortunate; it makes you ignorant. In failure there is always understanding. . . . But that particular kind of failure is one of the deadliest things that can happen to a man. . . . Once it just about swallowed me up, devitalized me. I made it a rule then to break at once before I was done for! A clean break! How could I have done any work otherwise?"

This, it appeared to me, though said to a mere biographer, to be written down if I wanted to, was more like the Dreiser of other days, so close to life that he could touch it. To this conversation he added: " Love requires as well as emotion a mental flare — at least for me, just as it does in art. There has to be some beauty of the mind, some personal appeal; otherwise I care almost nothing for it. It is in fact repellent. Beauty is not enough; there has to be the gift of passion which in some sense is related to wit. . . . I remember a young girl in Pittsburgh when I was a reporter and starved for friends, as beautiful as any Greek figure. She lived near me in a cabin up in the hills . . . the daughter of working people, not conventional; she seemed to like me. But she didn't know what it was about. To take hold of her was no more than to take hold of this glass. . . . I moved away."

It was the same with books: " Most people can't write; they lack the magnetism that draws readers. Christ Almighty, it's insane, the number of useless novels written today. Mary Squeaks from Indiana finds life difficult and that's supposed to make a novel. Or all this talk about style, what does it amount to? Just so much straw! There must be something wrong with the publishers' minds to put these books on the market, and with the readers' minds to stand for them." Yet when asked, he has never dared to refuse to read a book or get some competent judge to read it for him, for fear that genius might get lost in the shuffle.

So Dreiser in talk still returns into his strong clear mind, but in action lately goes out into the market place. Even lets his publisher surround his books with an atmosphere belying them, as he did with *A Gallery of Women*. During the winter of 1929 an almost nauseating blow to the eye was the Liveright delivery car on which were papered fifteen Miss Americas, supposedly the novelist's favorites, and above, an ecstatic appeal to read Theodore Dreiser who " bares the heart and mind of womanhood "! One was a morphine addict, another a maundering fortune teller, another a blowsy Irish cleaning woman, another a stark Missouri farm woman. But Liveright represented them all as bonbons! Nor was there a hint of passages as delicate as this:

> " It was the thing that was never flatly characterized by either of us, yet was always present, as real as any floor or door; in short the absolute thing out of which floors and doors are made and from which primarily they take their rise. And it was the jeopardy of this relationship which was now causing us this thought and worry."

Success was making Dreiser the victim of modern advertising, instead of the novelist of human relationships. He was in the market place now, almost the property of others. After years of working at a desk to create worlds of people, or prowling the streets to find them, perhaps it was a relief to become part of the actual world; if always he might be a useful part. For one thing he wanted to import the official Ballet and Pantomime of the Soviet Government to the United States — an old and new form of art, he believed, which would renew the life of our opera and theatre; bring the two most modern peoples into relation, exchanging their specialties, art and industry. He organized the project on a grand scale as if to unite art, money and fashion — his lifelong belief in a fused society. Among other potentates he solicited Henry Ford in a letter synthesizing the relation of Ford to Russia, and of Russia to art. But he was soon to know that this financier was not Cowperwood, craving aesthetic and social victories. Nor did it evidently interest Ford to be told by Dreiser that he, Henry Ford, was enormously in the minds of the poorest Russians: that his name like Lenin was part of their religion. The River Rouge king did not answer his letter. I doubt whether he or Edison or Harvey Firestone had ever read *The Titan* or the *Tragedy*, or heard of any American writer of importance younger than Mark Twain.

Whether brilliant or not, this project failing, Dreiser was persuaded to organize the Film Art Guild, whose black glass and steel circular theatre on Eighth Street in New York had been especially constructed to give pictures as modern as in Berlin or Moscow. It would rival commercial Hollywood with silent movies. Much of the propaganda for this theatre Dreiser wrote. He shared the modern dream that the movie camera would become an instrument of the imagination in the United States; that the silver sheet would say what could not be said otherwise and create a new form of art; just as before the theatre and then the novel had come into being to make life more vivid. All these public works were turned toward what he hoped would be the refinement of America; none of them purely selfish any more than his books. The film project failed, probably for lack of genius in that medium. I do not know then how many outside enterprises seduced this writer; all his life caught half-way between what was intimate and what was extensive. I feel certain that his exit into the world was not one of mere self-importance, like that of the great French romanticist, as according to Cocteau: " Victor Hugo was a madman who believed he was Victor Hugo." Dreiser did not perfectly believe in his divinity. He had hoped for it certainly, but had never been allowed the assurance of it. Just recently an eminent wag, Chesterton, had reviled him in print, in revenge, it might be, for the Hoosier's hatred of the Catholic Church:

> "Exponent of a philosophy not bright enough to be called a nightmare . . . without wit, without will, without laughter or uplifting of the heart; too old to die; too deaf to leave off talking; too blind to stop, too stupid to start afresh, too dead to be killed, and incapable of being damned, since in all its weary centuries it has never reached the age of reason."

Ring Lardner, asked by a producer to serve with Dreiser and Robert Frost as one of three founders of an American theatre for only American plays, refused on the ground that Dreiser was both ridiculous and immoral.

Frost on the other hand appeared to be seriously amused by the scheme, and would give his name and a play, if he could finish it without being hurried, on one condition: The policy of the theatre must be " daring." The plan remained only a plan.

There were plenty of others to whom Dreiser was ludicrous, nearly any sophisticated New Yorker, especially one with a humorous column to conduct, loved to say so. After these many years of ridicule the novelist had learned to laugh at himself or else take small notice of his deriders. Sometimes he excused them: " Well, they are jealous of me, or they can't stand my morals. What difference, I have my following." Or again he might say: " In a measure they are right; I am vulgar and uncouth." It was not, then, for the fanfare due a great man that he neglected creative work and became a publicist. It was, I think, in search of space and action, even of understanding.

In May 1930 he went on a vacation. He was tired, he said, of the trespasses on his time; of his apartment and his Thursday nights. . . . Money was nothing, vitality everything. Taste was all that counted. He would as soon go back to a hall bedroom, give up his quarters on Fifty-seventh Street. They oppressed him. . . . During this vacation, traveling west to San Francisco by El Paso and Santa Fe, north to Seattle, and back to New York by way of Dakota, this man, who over and over had written that he was never certain of anything, took sides. And the sides he took were those of the now dwindling army out to fight Capitalism. As he traveled he became delirious over the physical beauty of the United States, and after thirty years of suspicion, increasingly sure of its ruin at the hands of the great corporations and the ignorant moralists. This double hypocrisy was more than the country could stand. He said this to any reporter who would listen:

" Modern business has made American citizens into nothing but trudging asses. There is no great contemporary literature. If there is to be any in the future it will have to take the form of satire or expressions of despair. . . . Big business movements are making it impossible for men to express themselves as individuals. Because they cannot hope to succeed in small enterprises they have lost their initiative and their power to think.

"There is hardly any such thing as an individual left in America. Just name a single great writer. Supposing there were one, what chance would he have of becoming popular? . . .

"And why do we have all this legislation of morals, all this snooping? Movies, radios and newspapers contribute their share of setting millions of plastic minds in a mold which produces the same sort of figurative marbles running down a trough — until they fall off. . . .

"All that financiers think about is money. They get so much they don't know what to do with it. . . .

"The government has ceased to function . . . the corporations are the government. . . .

"The difference between the four Wall Street banking houses that run this country and the Soviet Central Control Committee is the difference between Tweedledum and Tweedledee. The breakdown of individual enterprise is pointing the way to communism, no matter what we call it."

With such denunciations and many of them Dreiser made newspapers ring for the two or three months during his survey of the country, and after his return. His words screamed sometimes the way that Debs and Haywood must have wanted to yell, had they thought it wise or possible; and the way Upton Sinclair would have done, had God given him so reckless a voice. But no one was afraid of Dreiser. He was only our national man of letters.

Why was it that he allowed himself this blowout? He who continually had said: "I want only to write about life as it is; it is not the place of an artist to judge or to fight, except for the right to publish unabridged, undeleted." Did he become in this fashion forensic because it was easier to be a public character than to concentrate on a great project — his *Bulwark,* a novel, partially written, for example, or the last volume of his *Trilogy of Desire* concerning the Financier after he had taken his millions from New York to Europe? Or was it sheerly in accordance with the sudden conviction, after thirty years of optimism, that there were no readers in the United States? How could there be readers where there were almost no individuals, none with "the initiative or the power to think?" From *Sister Carrie* to *An American Tragedy,* through books of short stories, poems, philosophy, portraits, plays and novels, had he not described substantially the same thing — tragic America; yet with its compensations, bright hopes, great moments for individual actors, as became an artist occupied with the particular as opposed to the general? Had anyone effectively noticed these creations, or those of other authentic minds in his lifetime? Wasn't the country less civilized today than ever before? What was there now to do but generalize, to go to war, which is a form of generalization?

Two episodes belonging to this date support such a theory as to why he should turn publicist. In the summer and fall of 1930 the boy who was born in Terre Haute, and had gone to school in Warsaw, then on to Chicago with various mean jobs to keep him going, with a year of college in Bloomington — this boy, now acclaimed a great writer, completed the first volume of his autobiography. It was a review of the country and of himself in these early days. He made the book out of a number of previous efforts to think back, and he honestly saw to it that now he should reap the reward of years of battle with censors. The account is full and unashamed as to his family and bringing up; and gives in detail his initial knowledge of the act of sex, and other experiences of the kind in these years. It contains a structural account of his mother, the one heroic woman of Dreiser's larger novels; and it contains events delightful as to the manner of telling them. But, and there is a *but,* the record as a whole lacks complexion. Almost the book lacks skin to hold the separate items and organs together. One keeps thinking: here is an enormous tract to the cultivation of which a writer, freed from the pressure of making a living, should have devoted further months. He let it go too soon to that realm of publicity where authors abandon their works. Why? Was he so much interested in his tragic country, which he thought he could help to save, that he had no time to complete his book? Or was it merely that style such as he could achieve did not seem to matter any more?

In the great cataclysm which was taking place after many migrations from the old to the new, from this land to that, from Christianity to Science, did readers today care only for one aspect of a book, that it should release secrets, especially those of sex, and those against inept religion? There seemed to be truth in the last premise. A New York writer, known as a connoisseur of art for art's sake, spoke of Dreiser's *Dawn* as his greatest work. " But," I objected, " manner is so neglected there that for once the meaning really suffers." — " Oh, I don't know," was the aesthete's delicate rejoinder, " the man can't write anyway, but he found adequate words to tell about several engagements of his from the age of fourteen to twenty-one — every variation, every afterthought of girl and boy — his most important book by all means! " What really did drama, what did style mean to this reader who was yet by name more than most experienced in matters of art: yet less than most, apparently, in matters of sex!

Again in the fall of 1931 a talking film was finally made from *An American Tragedy,* produced by Paramount under the direction of the imported Von Sternberg, through the scenario of a friend of Dreiser's, Samuel Hoffenstein. The picture lied so patently as to the meaning of the novel, was certainly no more profound than any other " murder film," that Dreiser after futile protests in Hollywood appealed to the courts to prevent its release. What was the answer of the lawyer for Paramount, and of a judge of the Supreme Court of New York State? The lawyer smirkingly argued that the book was just a lot of crap, taken from court records; the novelist had written it to get himself on the front page. The judge in his final decision seemed to accept this opinion and further ruled against the author, since Paramount pitifully had spent so many thousands of dollars on its production. Arthur Garfield Hays, attorney for Dreiser, pointedly wondered in court why Paramount had not gone direct to the records of the " The State *vs.* Gillette," rather than pay a large sum for the rights of the novel. But no one, least of all the newspapers, wondered with him. More than usual they laughed at their foremost novelist. What was he kicking about now? Didn't he have the dough? Paramount was paramount. Authors dead and living had no rights against their millions. . . . I read the story in the papers without much wonder that Dreiser had deferred writing as an art and was out to fight the great corporations of America, so hostile to civilization — that is, to civilization as it has ever been known or described before.

The journey, then, for an outsider, from the obscure beginning in Terre Haute to this stage of triumph in New York reveals heroism, substance, gaiety and power as belonging to the United States. But no use to deny that along with these assets the journey symbolizes the tragedy of America; in truth explains the reasons why Americans leave home. It suggests to those who worship intimacy, which is art or love, that there are two paths, one into isolation and neglect; the other into publicity. Take the first and a genius is victim to loneliness; take the second and he is victim to that very condition he most abhors — impersonality.

Hot summer of 1931 in New York: one's thoughts had to wander from the flatness of the bodies on benches in Washington Square, Bryant Park, Central Park, to the sharpness of towers of lighted skyscrapers the length of Manhattan, spilling over into Brooklyn. There was no other path for thoughts to take. One wondered as to the world of people between these extremes. Were they sensitized, were they rotarian, were they gangsters? What were they? Surely they were impotent or they would never allow this contrast between lighted skyscrapers, reaching to eighty stories, and bags of bodies like dead men without song or laughter on the benches of city parks — without jobs and without women as well. Times were hard, the crash was brutal; but not too hard or too brutal for officials to observe American segregation, American chasms. For the matter of that the buildings seemed septic too. Each indecent tower, indecent because excessive, seemed lighted with the unfulfilled desires of some magnate, maybe Jew, maybe German, Syrian or Yankee, who, having in his lifetime in spite of millions been definitely excluded from the socially-elect of his home town, out West, down South, up State, had built his bungalow on the roof of his business building. There, by God, he could be king, he could exclude whom he pleased. So I used to imagine in the summer of 1931 the life of terraced towers and of lowly bodies on park benches.

Certainly it seemed to me that we knew nothing of ourselves unless by words, voices, gestures; and these were lost in the explosion of traffic. We knew nothing of actual life from earth to stars, from gutter to skyscraper. It might even be that the gutters went up some nights in the elevator to the drunken, lonely isolation of the twentieth story or more. I wished for writers to give us the voices and gestures of the country. Where had they gone? To their retreats in the country, to the sand dunes of Michigan, the hills of New Hampshire, a village in Rhode Island or Virginia, and always Paris or St. Tropez?

To make matters worse I knew that if one entered the great market place from New Jersey or Long Island, day or night, mammoth painted or electric signs proved that the American language had gone over from implication into declaration and command:

> Take the Golden Trail Tour; Richfield Oil! Get a Home in Rego Park! Eat More Vitamines: Sunkist Oranges! Shift for Freedom: Royal Typewriter! Use Paragon Paints for Economy! Buy Wrigley's Juicy Fruit! Buy Chrysler Eights with Dual High Gears! Mother Says Use Quaker Oats.

Why should eyes used to words performing like these read any others, unless the super-narratives of crime in fiction or tabloids? Entering the Subway, headlines told you that " Baby Bandits *Must* Go To Chair," or that " 24 Miners in Harlan County Face Chair for Crime They Claim They Did Not Commit! " or that Gangsters two hours before had shot down innocent bystanders, including Children, in Booze War.

With the Land of the Free thus printed on my mind one afternoon I had a final call from Theodore Dreiser as to my account of this experience meeting between him and his country, to which he had once agreed to lend himself. His first question was like that of a ship-news reporter to one returned from Europe: " Well, what do you really think of this city now that you are back? " — " For me, I think of it as sinister, but since everyone else seems to think of it as brilliant and beautiful, I don't suppose I count." To my surprise the man who had written volumes over the seduction New York had for him, who had boasted he could look at anything, and always proposed the acceptance of change as the one sure virtue, said quite simply: " I think it is sinister too. More than that I think it's ugly. I'm through with it. I'm going to give up my apartment and leave it. . . . I used to love to walk these streets, but now they are too miserable. They are meaningless. I can't bear the brick or the cement or the color or lack of color that goes to make up the city. New York is a handsome woman with a cruel mouth. The people are like sawdust; there can be only impact from the outside, none from them toward anyone else."

Here finally seemed to be the divorce between these two, Dreiser and his city, which was a symbol of the country. Amazed, I said, " But is it so much worse than it used to be in the Nineties? What about your own character Hurstwood carried down stream to suicide on a wave of greed and misery? " — " Yes, it's much worse today, and I ought to know. Then, I was one of the starving myself, and yet I felt something adventurous and exciting about New York, about the whole country; if not for me then for others luckier than me. There was a hope for individuals. Today I have plenty to live on, and I see no hope anywhere. For one thing in the Nineties, and really up to a few years ago, there were great personalities in New York. Mark Twain meant something to this city. There were young men like Norris, Crane, O. Henry. There was a promise of competition, of wit and understanding. And for that matter we have had a few years of it. Today I don't see it, unless it is in the youngsters who want to change the whole face of the country and follow Russia." — " What good would that do? " I asked. — " It would make a change at any rate, like a change of woman for a man, or lover for a woman." — " A change of government would be nothing without a change of heart, a change of mind, and you if anyone must know it." — Yes, he supposed he knew it. Then he added: " I would do anything if the moment came and asked for it, an important moment, one that asked for sacrifice." — " I thought every moment was an important moment? " — " For what? " — " For expression, of course! In your case, for the books that only you could make. I think we need intellect more than Communism in the United States. I think we need to become sensitive, critical, in the sense of the word crisis. Critical judgment is rooted in the senses, isn't it? " Dreiser's answer was: " I can't see it that way. It has gone so far that there can be no change except a violent one from the outside. People have forgotten how to read. Besides how can a man write or read with thousands of people starving both mentally and physically? "

Unanswerable question for an outsider! Yet some day it may be that what with war and starvation and readjustments, possibly communism, Americans will again escape the miserable extremes of poverty and wealth. New America, finally born, may become an organized society. Dreiser in the meantime might retire from investigations of, and framings by, the " Interests " and might turn again to the even more difficult task of describing the inner circles of human lives. If he does, it is my belief that he will not fall short of the far limits of thought he reached in the years before. He might in fact, having, pioneer-like, prepared the way, broken barriers and made roads, become an indisputable libertine, savage, aristocrat, artist.

INCONCLUSIVELY

The strongest desire known to human life is to continue living. The next strongest is to use the instrument by which life is generated for its own rewards, not for the sake of generation. The third potent desire is to excel and be acknowledged. In Western countries the first of these has become an abstract virtue. Suicide is looked down on as a feeble way out. The third likewise has been placed among the virtues, provided always that one man's excellence does not interfere with that of another endowed with greater strength. Then the dogged pursuit of fame becomes a crime or at least a nuisance. The motive second in degree of force arising out of sex, has mysteriously turned through Christian centuries into a hated, secret vice, and nowhere more so than in liberal America. The very words to describe it, whether popular or technical, used to be forbidden in print and are as yet awkward. Spoken words as common as daylight — fine crisp words among them — are just beginning to be printed and then out of bravado by impatient or discourteous writers. And the technical terms for these pleasures and instruments are equally out of place in art. Those who seriously have tried to give back to the English language rightful speech fall sometimes into diffidence. D. H. Lawrence has resorted to the third person *he,* and Ernest Hemingway to the neuter *it,* to avoid two simple terms. In truth IT is the American equivalent for all that is seductive in man or woman. The French use plenty of other words to describe what to us is indescribable. Their Catholicism has not subdued them and shamed them, as the Church has done to people more Northern in their wit. The French continue to be a nation with a frontage on the Mediterranean. They keep facets which correspond with facets of ancient races.

This journey from 1870 to 1930 is lined with evidence that we are in the extreme a people afraid of the two elements of being, male and female. And any other record could return the same evidence. Our literature is cramped with this fear. Walt Whitman is dyed with the fear of this fear. Mark Twain is permeated with the forced approval of this fear. This fascinating enigma, fear of sex, has brought about among Americans fear of mystery of every kind, and therefore fear of union; has brought about our now accepted separations. Henry James in an early novel lets one of his characters define the fear of mystery:

"I like the beginning — I delight in the approach of it — I revel in the prospect. . . . But now the thing has come I don't revel. To be fascinated is to be mystified. Damn it, I like my liberty — I like my judgment."

The historian, Henry Adams, wrote in 1905:

"Without understanding movement of sex history seemed to him [Adams] mere pedantry."

"Neither of them [St. Gaudens or Matthew Arnold] felt goddesses as power. . . . They felt railway train as power; yet . . . they complained . . . all the steam in the world could not, like the Virgin, build Chartres."

"Adams began to ponder, asking himself whether he knew of any American authors who had insisted on the power of sex, as every classic had done; but he could think only of Walt Whitman. . . ."

When sometimes a writer, harnessed though he was to American prose, let his five senses take him back to primal experience it might be that initial strength leaped free in him. Out of words came shapes that symbolized the meaning of building and door, of lock and key, of explorer and wilderness, of horse train ship airplane and the destination in space — the meaning of man and woman. Then this occasional poet frightened nearly every one. Poe was such a poet, and it is said was "thrown out of the houses of gentlewomen for making obscene advances." * He was the image of a stranger in his own country.

Take on the other hand a native lingual genius, O. Henry. Consider what he says of himself:

"If I could have a thousand years — just one little thousand years — more of life, I might in that time draw near enough to true Romance to touch the hem of her robe."

* Krutch: *Edgar Allan Poe.*

And then to belie his own ambition:

"I have been called the American Maupassant. Well, I never wrote a filthy word in my life, and don't like to be compared to a filthy writer."

What then was all his brilliant American idiom worth if he thought the hem of true Romance was eternally clean; if to him no "filthy" word ever came up from "men on ships, waste places, forest, road, garret, and cellar"? Or Eugene O'Neill — what of the philosophy of his famous play, *Strange Interlude,* whose heroine says, as if he approved of her:

"Let you and me forget the whole degrading episode, regard it as an interlude . . . in which our souls have been scraped clean of impure flesh and made worthy to bleach in peace."

The more modern Dos Passos in a late novel says of two lovers, "There was something tight and electric and *uncomfortable* in the way their thighs ground against each other as they walked." The italics are mine to denote surprise.

It is a prime refreshment in the works of Theodore Dreiser that he is free of the mysterious sense of degradation, of filth and discomfort into which most Americans and many Europeans have translated one of the three elements of desire. Life then in his books is free to assert its own volume, where the huge desire to live, the wild desire to love, the insane desire to excel, variously mingled, produce various action. And they disclose the special chasms that have come about because in some hidden way we have sacrificed the second to the first and third of these angles. But without dogma: "They can't put me down as a liberal or free thinker," he insists. "I don't know, I wouldn't say I knew. I know nothing."

Perhaps it required an America to make souls as untrammeled by custom as this. The same trait of mind once sparked American financiers, inventors and politicians, and made our restless informality, and the bywords, "Let's go," "Push on." Before we forget them, if their boldness were to take root and branch in the field of the intellect, projects more exciting than mechanical playthings might come to life here. Dreiser's story gives and takes away this hope. There are chapters that hint at a reason for the long distrust of sex and slow dying of the senses. And between the lines one wonders, may not nerves and muscles follow this death? Is it Nature on its way to destroy human nature — a revenge on Thought, and that last child of thought, Machinery?

Dreiser by moments denies and affirms the chance of this, according to opposite moods out of his doctrine of acceptance of change. When thereby fortified he projects a brave concept of life, which once in talk he described: " Men and women get to living as if in a cave like criminals, outcasts, mad people. A crust has formed about them. Then waters well up, the crust gives way, the cave is gone. You see them alive again in a new medium. I believe life holds such revaluations, a breaking down, a welling up of strange waters."

When disheartened by sordidness of change, he retracts, and leans like a native toward confusing what is American or modern with universal values. In his *Credo* denying all belief, published in the Forum 1930, he describes New York today as if it stood for all cities and all time:

> " For here we have what? Bricks, stone, glass, wood, plaster, paints of the surrounding buildings. . . . But representing what? "

In older cities often representing beauty, balance, understanding — his own concern. It is certain that neither he nor any modern of the machine age has yet forced the issue here involved — the new victory of ignorant material over the ancient skilful investment of material with spirit. The newest of modern problems, it is but dimly recognized as a terrifying phase of history. Or it is recognized to be ignored.*

But of issues known to him he has evaded none, and of limits accepted none; which adventure places him outside of criticism for his forms of speech. A mimic may imitate another who has that something called style, and critics will say, " Superb writing." A pioneer or an original is committed to his own style with exactly his faults and

---

* A matter even of persecution, as in the case of Georges Duhamel following his analysis of American civilization.

exactly his virtues. Dreiser's fault is a careless over-burdened ear: his virtue a careful triumphant brain or imagination. There is in him a gross precision; foreign matter surrounds it. There is in Poe, for one, a fine precision. Dreiser has pith, Poe is pith. Many writers acclaimed as stylists have not center and are not centers. They have color, shape, line, but not that force.

American speech, when engaged with song or talk of railroad men, teamsters, taxi-drivers, base-ball players, salesmen, chorus girls, bartenders, song writers and racketeers, is alive and sufficient. But here is a writer who has sought to describe analyses, formulas, infinite relations, in brief the drama of civilization. Without the ear to contrive loans, he has had to use for these intricacies American as he knows it — a medley of English archaisms, technical terms, newspaper clichés and slang. The country, an expanse with small philosophic or critical intercourse, has yet to perfect a language for philosophers and critics. Our wisdom will not be native until it finds native expression.

With our vagrant speech as guide he has looked back into a remote past, days of dinosaurs, glaciers, savages, through the centuries of pagans, mystics and puritans, and forward to modern days of physicists and metaphysicists; out of which have come the man and the brain, the woman and the child of human history. Facts and fabrications, those that came his way, he has handled and rehandled hoping to discover which were which. For solace he has been ruled by a compassion that might help to make fertile some of the chasms between our peaks and precipices. A number of years ago I remember saying to Dreiser: " I imagine tragic art would not have been except for maladies like indigestion and unrequited love? " His reply was unforgettable: " How can you say that? Neither one nor the other has anything to do with tragedy. Grief comes from separations too hard to bear."

Edgar Allan Poe, Edgar Lee Masters, Theodore Dreiser are the three Americans who to me have made most unbearable the sense of separations dividing Americans one from the other. Equally Poe, Masters and Dreiser, Whitman, Frost, Mark Twain and Sandburg are

Americans who have given me the opposite sense, that by only a narrow margin these separations have occurred. That by the lifting of a hand all might be different.

Old surfaces have cracked, floods enveloped bewildered nations. In the United States we are at sea on our own new strange ocean. There are those who think that a second revaluation has recently occurred — a return to the safer past, except that the leaders will battle as never before for the separation of body and mind, as against the spirit. But it is difficult to believe that this reaction will have its way at once. It is unnatural that creative minds, such as have lately appeared in the one realm of American writing, should be lost before their word has had time to mature. Their enterprise has been too real and too verdant to run out so soon.

History deposes that roots are not in vain.

SOURCES

Fact and Document, origin of which is not each time cited in the body of the book, derived from talks with Dreiser and with people who have known him, or who have been concerned with the same literary drama. Or they derived from his files, which through his generosity were open to me, dating from 1900 to 1931, containing reviews, interviews and letters. Beside these *A Hoosier Holiday* and *Dawn* furnished sources for the years 1871 to about 1890; *Newspaper Days,* formerly called *A Book About Myself, Twelve Men* and *A Gallery of Women* for the Nineties; the last two books and *A Traveler at Forty* for later years. All other sources are acknowledged in text or footnote.

To every one who gave me time in pursuit of this story I am deeply grateful; and perhaps especially to those who shared my belief that the salvage of yesterday is essential to the flowering of tomorrow.

D. D.

Paris, 1932